Soviet Ground Forces

About the Book and Authors

No book on the Soviet ground forces has been published in any language, including Russian, for many years. This study is the first comprehensive treatment of this central element in the modern Soviet military structure. The dramatically improved Soviet ground forces are the most powerful and dynamic military arm in the world. Highly flexible and easily deployable, they are considered a strategic force in and of themselves.

The book begins with a full-scale historical analysis of the evolution of the forces from World War II to the present. John Erickson, eminent historian of the Soviet military, uses his network of personal contacts within the Soviet military command to present an inside view of the changes in the army and its probable future course.

Colonel William Schneider, a former U.S. Army attaché in Moscow, also draws on personal observations and a lifetime of study of Soviet military institutions to describe how the Soviets train for war and how their ground forces would actually fight a war. He contrasts the Soviet method of abstract and objective normative standards for judging military performance with more subjective U.S. criteria, which are based primarily on operational testing.

Since the air component is an integrated element of ground forces operations and a major factor in modernization policies, it receives special treatment. Dr. Lynn Hansen, who has lengthy first-hand experience with Soviet air force troops, analyzes the use of air power in conjunction with land strength. He discusses current techniques, available technology, and the expected evolution of the force through the end of the century.

With their Warsaw Pact allies, Soviet forces are generally considered to be superior to NATO forces in numbers and roughly equal in quality. This equation is further weighted toward the Soviets by their capabilities for rapid reinforcement and the relative lack of political constraints upon the Soviet defense budget. This powerful and destabilizing influence is examined in detail by these three uniquely qualified specialists. Their book provides essential background information for an assessment of Soviet political behavior and explores the heart of Soviet conventional military strength, capabilities, and intentions.

John Erickson, an eminent authority on Soviet military history, is director of defense studies at the University of Edinburgh. **Dr. Lynn Hansen** is on leave of absence from Texas A&M University as deputy head of the American delegation at the Stockholm Conference on Confidence and Security Building Measures and Disarmament in Europe. **Col. William Schneider** (ret.) was liaison officer to the Commander-in-Chief, Group of Soviet Forces, Germany, and army attaché in Moscow. He is now an assistant vice president of the BDM Corporation managing USSR-related studies.

Published in cooperation with
the BDM Corporation,
McLean, Virginia

Soviet Ground Forces

An Operational Assessment

John Erickson, Lynn Hansen,
and William Schneider

Westview Press • Boulder, Colorado

Croom Helm • London and Sydney

UA
772
.E69
1986

All rights reserved. No part of this publication may be reproduced or transmitted in any form or by any means, electronic or mechanical, including photocopy, recording, or any information storage and retrieval system, without permission in writing from Westview Press.

Copyright © 1986 by Westview Press, Inc.

Published in 1986 in the United States of America by Westview Press, Inc.; Frederick A. Praeger, Publisher; 5500 Central Avenue, Boulder, Colorado 80301

Published in 1986 in Great Britain by Croom Helm Ltd., Provident House, Burrell Row, Beckenham, Kent BR3 1AT

Library of Congress Cataloging-in-Publication Data
Erickson, John.
  Soviet ground forces.
  Includes index.
  1. Soviet Union. Sukhoputnye voiska. 2. Soviet Union.
Voenno-vozdushaia sily. I. Hansen, Lynn M.
II. Schneider, William, 1925-   . III. Title.
UA772.E69 1986   355'.00947   86-5583
ISBN 0-89158-796-9

British Library Cataloguing in Publication Data
Erickson, John.
  Soviet ground forces: an operational assessment.
  1. Soviet Union—Armed forces.
I. Title. II. Hansen, Lynn. III. Schneider, William.
355'00947   VA770
ISBN 0-7099-0972-1

Composition for this book was provided by the authors.
This book was produced without formal editing by the publishers.

Printed and bound in the United States of America

∞ The paper used in this publication meets the requirements of the American National Standard for Permanence of Paper for Printed Library Materials Z39.48-1984.

6 5 4 3 2 1

Contents

List of Figures	xi
Foreword	xv

CHAPTER 1
INTRODUCTION TO THE SOVIET GROUND FORCES:
AN OPERATIONAL ASSESSMENT ... 1

CHAPTER 2
THE EVOLUTION OF THE
SOVIET GROUND FORCES, 1941-1985 ... 9

The Great Patriotic War	9
The Red Army Rebuilds	14
The Beginnings of Combined Arms	16
Command and Control	19
Ground Forces Structures and Soviet Military Posture	20
Ever Increasing Tempo - The Breakthrough	24
Post-Stalin Period	26
The Advent of Nuclear Weapons	26
The Fluid Battlefield	27
The Brezhnev Era	30
The Resurrection of Massed Armor and Artillery	31
Sustainability-Viability-*Zhivuchest'*	35
Force Levels and Force Structures: Deployment and Organization	36
Alliance Cohesion and Military Integration: The Warsaw Pact	43

CHAPTER 3
SOVIET OPERATIONAL PROCEDURES 51
Doctrine 51
Principles of Soviet Military Art—Doctrine 52
Summary of Principles 55
Offensive Operational Procedures 56
Methods of Initiating the Attack 61
The March to Contact 62
The Meeting Engagement 70
Initiation and Conduct of the Meeting Engagement 75
Attack of a Defending Enemy 80
Breakthrough 83
Conduct of the Attack 93
Offensive Tank Operations 97
Tactical Breakthrough 98
Pursuit 99
Defensive Operations 103
Conduct of the Deliberate Defense 106
Support of the Defense 108
Withdrawal 110
Operations in "Special Conditions" 111
Mountain Operations (Not Counterinsurgency) 111
Operations in Extreme Cold 113
Operations in the Desert 114
Combat in Urban Areas, Forest, and at Night 115
Assault River Crossings 119
Airborne and Air-Landed Operations 120
"Special Operations"—Conclusions 121
Logistics Requirements 121
Organization for Battlefield Supply 125
Recovery and Maintenance 127
Medical Support Operations 128
Personnel Replacements 129
Command, Control, and Communications C^3 129
Communications 134

CHAPTER 4
NORMS 141
   Place of Norms in Soviet Life 141
   Norms in Military Practice 142
   Calculations Using Norms........................... 143
   Tactical Calculations: Organizing the Battle 146
   Norms Used in the Soviet Army Today 152
   Echelonment Norms 161
   Frontages and Zones of Advance - Attack 164
   Air Defense Norms 166
   Norms for the Defense 167
   Firing Norms for Artillery.......................... 169
   Artillery Fire Planning 169
   Supply Norms 175
   The Key - the Second Echelon...................... 176

CHAPTER 5
THE AIR COMPONENT 181
   Direct Support of the Ground Forces................ 181
   Reconnaissance 183
   Command and Control 184
   Air Accompaniment 186
   Close Air Support 188
   Employment Principles 190
   Air-to-Ground Operations.......................... 191
   Helicopter Reconnaissance 193
   Airborne Command Posts 194
   Helicopter Landings 195
   Air Supremacy.................................... 198
   Tactical Air Supremacy............................ 199
   Operational Air Supremacy 199
   Strategic Air Supremacy........................... 200
   Independent Air Operations 201
   Into the 1990s 205

CHAPTER 6
ASSESSMENT OF THE SOVIET GROUND FORCES 209
    Toward 2000 217

GLOSSARY 221
A FEW WORDS ABOUT SOURCES 245
SELECTED BIBLIOGRAPHY 249
INDEX 259

Figures

1.1	Type Motorized Rifle Division (MRD)	4
1.2	Type Tank Division (TKD)	5
2.1	Soviet Tank/SP Artillery Production: 1941-1945 (to June)	10
2.2	Loss Analysis/Tank Army Operations	11
2.3	Rifle Division Establishment (Manpower)	12
2.4	Distribution/Characteristics of Tank Army Losses (Offensive Operations)	13
2.5	Tank Army and Corps Establishments	14
2.6	Soviet Strength: January - June 1944	17
2.7	Combined-Arms Armies: 1941-1945	18
2.8	Mechanized Corps: Establishments 1942-1945	19
2.9	Rifle Division (11,013) Postwar 1948-1950	23
2.10	Organizational Change: The Motorized-Rifle Regiment as an Example (1967-77) General Evolution of the MR Regiment (1967-1977)	32
2.11	Motor Rifle Division 1967	33
2.12	Tank Division 1967	34
2.13	Soviet Forces in East Germany	38
2.14	Distribution of Soviet Forces in Europe (1985): 1st and 2nd Echelons	39
3.1	Types of Successive Operations	57

3.2	The Categorization of Depths and Delimiting of Objectives.	58
3.3	Depths and Objectives	59
3.4	Type (Army) Deployment for Offensive Operation	60
3.5	Type Front Deployment for Offensive Operation	62
3.6	Advantages and Disadvantages of Types of Attack	63
3.7	Tactical March of Motorized Rifle Division	65
3.8	Deployment for Attack from the March	68
3.9	Various Formation Arrangements	69
3.10	Meeting Engagement Circumstances	71
3.11	Spectrum of Attack Tactics	82
3.12	Introduction of the 2nd Echelon into Combat	85
3.13	Typical Combat Organization Motorized-Rifle and Tank Regiments	88
3.14	Type Division Deployment for Attack of a Defending Enemy.	96
3.15	Assault Formation of MR Battalion in City Attack	117
3.16	Ground Forces National Level Logistical Organization	123
3.17	Supply Installations	126
3.18	Medical Evacuation and Treatment	130
3.19	Reinforced Tank Battalion Nets	137
4.1	Basic Formula and Blank for Calculations of Norms	144
4.2	Nomogram for the Calculation of Required Quantity of Antitank Means.	145
4.3	Eight Steps in the Development of a Soviet Critical Path Chart to Determine the Earliest Time an Attack Could Be Made (Figures 4.3a and 4.3b)	147

4.3a	A Soviet Critical Path Chart (Steps 1-4)	148
4.3b	A Calculation of the Earliest Time That an Attack Could Be Launched	149
4.4	Type Army Deployment for Offensive Operation	154
4.5	Echelons and Objectives: Times of Commitment and Attainment	155
4.6	Normal Intervals and Variants	156
4.7	Motorized Rifle Regiment Marching as Part of a Division Main Force (a Variant)	158
4.8	Meeting Engagement Lead Regiment with Division Follow-On	159
4.9	Company Attack Formations (Mounted)	160
4.10	Space Norms for a Regiment Engaging the Enemy in "Average Terrain"	161
4.11	Echelonment Within First Echelon Regiments	162
4.12	Tactical Force Ratio Norms, Main Axis of Attack	163
4.13	Zones of Advance and Attack Frontages	164
4.14	Normal Deployment of Division Elements for an Attack . . .	166
4.15	Air Defense Coverage	168
4.16	Coverage in Hectares, Based on Type of Target and Length of Assault	170
4.17	Ammunition Expenditure Rates, Rounds Per Hectare Per Minute, and Coverage in Hectares for *PSO* (Successive Fire Concentrations)	170
4.18	Norms for Expenditure of Artillery and Mortar Rounds for Destruction of Fixed, Unobserved Targets	171
4.19	Average Times for Changing Artillery Positions	172
4.20	Assigned Lengths of Sectors	174

4.21	Tactical Deployment Norms	174
4.22	Contingency Commitment: 2nd Echelon Forces May Be Committed Earlier Than Planned If Necessary to Assist in Attaining the Element's Immediate Objective	177
4.23	Assignment of Objectives	178
4.24	Pursuit - 1st Echelon Division (Not to Scale)	179
4.25	Hasty Assault River Crossing – Tactical Variants	180
5.1	*VNOS* as Command Relay-Constructed According to Information Contained in Ye V. Koyander, *Ya - Rubin, Prikazyvayu* (Moscow: *Voyenizdat*, 1978)	185

Foreword

The <u>Soviet Ground Forces, An Operational Assessment</u> is an appraisal of the capabilities of the Soviet army as they exist in late 1985. For the past two and a half decades, the Soviet forces have shaped my life and occupied my thoughts during most of my working days. This can also be said of the three authors, whom I have also known for many years. During those years, the Soviet forces have been in a constant state of change, either deteriorating as in the Khrushchev years or improving as in the last twenty or more years. This book does not attempt to count tanks or planes or guns on any given day but rather examines the methods by which the Soviet forces conduct operations and the standards they set for themselves. While I do not mean to imply that these assessments are timeless, force levels change slowly and some aspects of the Soviet forces change hardly at all. The Soviet military *mirovozrenie* or world outlook has shaped every facet of their activities for decades.

In recent years there have been controversies about deep thrusts, daring raids, second echelons, operational maneuver groups, and other forms of offensive maneuver. It is my belief, based on extensive records and contact with Soviet officers, that these are all reflections of a mindset that is at least as old as the Soviet Union itself and will probably be as enduring. Decisive offensive action is the hallmark of Soviet military doctrine past and present. Soviet strategy, operational art, and tactics support this doctrine.

The 1980s are but another chapter in the evolution of Soviet Ground Forces' tactics and operational art. The Operational Maneuver Group (OMG) is but another evolutionary development in long-held operational (Army and Front/Army group) and tactical (corps/division and lower level) concepts developed in the late 1920s and early 1930s by Tukhachevsky, Triandafillov, Kalinovskiy, Isserson, and others and publicly outlined initially in a <u>Red Star</u> article in 1932.[1] The ability to execute the "deep tactics" (*glubokiy boy*) and the "deep operation" (*glubokaya operatsiya*) has increased over the years as weapons, equipment, and training have progressed.

A former captain in the Czarist army, by the name of Varfolomeyev, and later a Soviet Army and Front Chief of Staff during the Civil War, became Deputy Head of Strategic Studies at the Frunze Military Academy. Varfolomeyev was the author of the books entitled, <u>Shock Army Offensive Operations</u>, <u>The Modern Art Of Operations</u>, and <u>The Academic Approach To Strategy</u>. In November 1932 he wrote an extensive article in <u>Red Star</u> entitled, "The Deep Operation." According to Varfolomeyev's article, the principal task in the organization of an offensive on an operational scale

(Army/Front) was to rapidly overcome enemy resistance throughout the depth of the operational (Army/army group) defense by simultaneous attack throughout the entire depth. The operational defense was considered to include the reserves of the high command deployed in the rear and oriented toward potential maneuvers.

To overcome the depth of a modern defense force, the Frunze Military Academy theoreticians specified that the attackers should be echeloned in depth, as only a deep formation would support a deep attack developing into a Deep Operation.

The Deep Operation, conducted on a basis of simultaneous action against the entire depth of the enemy defense, had as its mode of operation that of "mechanized units, close fire support, light and medium aviation, and automobile/transport --in length... an average of 100 km from the line of departure."

In the Deep Operation, there were two major problems or phases to solve: (1) an attack to break through the tactical defense, deep attack (*glubokiy boy*); and, (2) attack in the enemy rear with the object of breaking the enemy's operational defense, exploiting the tactical breakthrough into the rear, and developing the tactical success into an operational Deep Operation. Varfolomeyev warned that only after breaking through the front is there a possibility of launching follow-on forces through the breach being formed into the rear of the operational defense.

Organizationally there were two echelons: (1) The breakthrough echelon of a rifle corps (comprised of rifle divisions) with heavy tank/artillery/aviation reinforcement; and, (2) An echelon for exploiting the breakthrough, composed of motorized/mechanized units, cavalry, aviation, chemical, engineer, and communications/control means. This was based on a mechanized corps composed of tank and motor-mechanized brigades.

In the 1932 article, Varfolomeyev called for the practical solution of a series of important problems such as optimum organization of the breakthrough frontal attack (with formation, size and concept of forces, relation of objectives, and supply). This was somewhat similar to the concept of British General J.F.C. Fuller who, in May 1918, advocated a new employment of tanks in offensive operations, with the simultaneous defeat of the entire depth of enemy defenses, based on a breakthrough of fast-moving tanks to hit division, corps, and army headquarters, railroad junctions, and assembly areas. To do this by the spring of 1919, some 30,000 tanks and 10,000 supply trucks were to be ready (but the war ended in November 1918).

In July 1933 in <u>Mechanization and Motorization</u>, N. Ernest, a Soviet military theoretician, wrote that "to develop a deep operational breakthrough, a tactical breakthrough is first accomplished by advancing infantry to the rear of the fortified tactical defense (3 to 4 km) and then utilizing mechanized units to convert tactical success into a deep operational breakthrough." He further specified that "mechanized units should only be committed after the breakthrough is made" and that "modern tanks, with aviation, long range artillery, and motorized and cavalry forces provide the opportunity to execute the [deep] offensive operation, converting tactical success into operational."

This was further codified in the 1936 Soviet Field Service Regulations (FSR) which in Paragraph 102 stated, "modern means of suppression in the Front with the tanks, artillery, aviation, and mechanized assault employed on a large scale, provide the possibility to organize simultaneously the attack of the enemy throughout the entire depth of his combat formation with the aim of his isolation, complete encirclement, and annihilation." The use of airborne troops also was added as an integral element of the Deep Operation, having been demonstrated in one spectacularly successful field exercise.

Many of the officers (and most of the higher ranking commanders) who had practiced the Deep Operation in large-scale pre-war maneuvers at Kiev in 1935 and Belorussia in 1936 were victims of the purges that began in 1937. Stalin also radically changed the organization of the Red Army as a result of some faulty conclusions regarding tanks and aviation drawn from experience in the Spanish Civil War (1936-1937). However, Georgiy Zhukov, a former cavalryman retrained as an armor commander, remembered, and demonstrated the worth of the Deep Operation against the Japanese in 1939 at Khalkhin-Gol in Mongolia. That victory also encouraged Stalin to revert to the tank-heavy organizations that had originally proved the worth of the Deep Operation on the plains of Russia. The organizational reconversion was underway when the Germans attacked in 1941.

Seventeen months later at Stalingrad the Russians revived the Deep Operation with a vengeance. The mechanized corps had been expanded into tank corps/mechanized corps and tank armies. There were some draft changes to the regulation (FSR-1936) on the Deep Operation, but the theory was nearly intact. Its execution stopped the Germans in their tracks and turned the war around. Subsequent Deep Operations out of the Kursk Bulge across the Ukraine, across Bulgaria, through Rumania and Hungary, and on to Berlin proved the efficiency of the theory, which was in many ways similar to the German Blitzkrieg and the idea of Fuller which had inspired both the Germans and the Soviets.

It is interesting that the 1936 Field Service Regulations, which outlined the concepts of the Deep Operation, was not officially replaced until the appearance of the 1949 FSR.

In the post-war era, the third edition of the Great Soviet Encyclopedia described the Deep Operation as "the breakthrough of the front of the enemy's defense by a simultaneous attack to its fullest actual depth and the immediate introduction of an echelon of mobile troops to turn the tactical breakthrough into an operational success."

In 1976, Army General Nikolai Ogarkov, soon to be Chief of Staff of the Armed Forces, wrote in the Soviet Military Encyclopedia that in the post-war period the basic principles of the Deep Operation continued to develop on a higher technological basis with the creation of new military equipment and "weapons of mass destruction." He pointed out in his article on the Deep Operation that the armed forces were equipped simultaneously with nuclear weapons and the latest conventional weapons and that all units from division to front level were motorized and mechanized, increasing their mobility, firepower, and shock action capability. This, he maintained, significantly increased the possibility of simultaneous cooperative organized action throughout the enemy rear, the high speed breakthrough of his defenses, and the rapid development of success. According to Ogarkov, "the general principles of the theory have not lost their significance at the present time."

Later in 1982, then Chief of the General Staff Marshal of the Soviet Union Ogarkov, in his monograph, <u>Always in Readiness to Defend the Homeland</u>, wrote of the value of electronics, automated troop control, helicopters, rockets and missiles, an ever increasing air role, the need for airborne forces, motorized armor protection for infantry troops, and unspecified changes in organizational structure. The result of this "ensures the conduct of operations and combat with a rapid rate of advance and rapid deep exploitation," i.e., an updated and evolutionary concept of the Deep Operation on a larger scale. In fact, Ogarkov pointed out that the principal operation is no longer at Front level but at a theater strategic, *Teatr Voyennikh Deistviy* (*TVD*), level where two or more frontal operations could be conducted in succession "even without pauses."[2]

In a September 1984 <u>Red Star</u> article, Major General Vorobyov, one of the long recognized principal spokesmen for Soviet tactical and operational concepts, pointed out that "under present conditions it is possible to simultaneously influence by firepower practically the entire depth of the enemy's military formation."

Yes, in the mid-1980s the evolutionary Deep Operation is alive and well. The OMG role at operational level, resulting in what Ogarkov termed "changes in organizational structure," is but one of the recent improvements. Nuclear firepower, an expandable airborne capability which includes air assault, air mobile, special purpose forces (as well as the basic airborne units that played a significant role in the original Deep Operation), and the technological capabilities for automated troop control systems do not invalidate but only invigorate the long-standing concepts, theories, and practices of the Deep Operation.

In this book you will encounter a number of different organizations and concepts that support the offensive *mirovozrenie*: advance detachments, mobile groups, operational maneuver groups, and so on. The Soviets are a land power and think in terms of land warfare and armies. Their aviation forces and airborne forces may wear an air force uniform and think in terms of air superiority, but they, too, support the offensive *mirovozrenie* of the Deep Operation.

Colonel Frederick C. Turner
(USA Ret.)

NOTES

1. Mikhail N. Tukhachevsky, 1893-1937, MSU, Deputy Peoples Commissar for Military & Naval Affairs, Deputy Minister of Defense; Vladimir K. Triandafillov, 1894-1931, Deputy Chief of Staff Red Army, Corps Commander; K. B. Kalinovskiy, Inspector of Armored Troops, Red Army; and G. S. Isserson, Brigade Commander, Chief of the Operations Directorate, Red Army Staff, and author of <u>The Basic Elements of the Deep Operation</u> (1933).
2. N. V. Ogarkov, <u>Always Ready to Defend the Homeland</u> (Moscow: Military Publishing House, 1982).

Chapter 1
Introduction to the Soviet Ground Forces: An Operational Assessment

Many recent books stress the numbers of Soviet tanks and planes and their armament and capabilities. This book examines the way the Soviets intend to use their equipment. It is an operational assessment. The authors have spent most of their adult lives, a total of 90 man years, appraising Soviets' points of view, both through direct contact with Soviet military personnel and units and through Soviet writings.

This assessment is analogous to painting a moving train. Growth of the Soviet armed forces and development of the Ground Forces' organization and its position within the armed forces structure have been continuous. The period from 1975 through 1985 has witnessed a greater increase in the capability of the Soviet armed forces than any period other than that of World War II. At the same time, the Ground Forces' relative position in the Soviet hierarchy has diminished as the Strategic Rocket Forces (SRF), Navy, Air Defense, and Air Forces have grown even more rapidly in relation to the Ground Forces.

Nevertheless, some things have remained relatively constant: the attitude of the Communist Party toward the armed forces and their place and role in society and the "defense" of the USSR, particularly the place of Ground Forces in the armed forces; the organizational philosophy of the Ground Forces as primarily offensive forces; and, the deep strike concept introduced by Marshal Tukhachevskiy in the 1920s.

The Soviet Ground Forces are one of five components of the armed forces and would operate in any major war in western Europe in conjunction with all the other components. While coordination is certainly close between the Ground Forces and Strategic Rocket Forces, particularly at front level, it is more pervasive with the Air Defense and Air Forces. Once the initial coordinated attack has been launched, continuing phases of the strategic offensive will be carried out by close cooperation of three elements: the air operation, the air defense operation, and the ground force operations. Of these three, there is an independent character to the air operation and the air defense operations that will be touched on lightly in this introduction, then only alluded to thereafter -- not because they are unimportant to the success of the ground force operations but because they are properly the subject of separate studies. They will be covered in detail to the extent that there is direct interaction with the Ground Forces.

Naval and marine (Naval Infantry) operations will be a coordinated element of the initial attack to assure Soviet control of areas such as the Danish Straits. The steady growth and improvement in quality of Soviet maritime forces make such operations entirely possible today.

Operations of the Strategic Rocket Forces and offensive air operations probably will constitute the opening strike of a major offensive, either nuclear or conventional. Because the Soviets want to seize the productive capacity of western Europe in as serviceable condition as possible and apparently believe that NATO will not use nuclear weapons first, they have built and maintained massive conventional ground forces that are the subject of this study. Soviet uncertainty about when and how NATO might employ nuclear weapons has been and remains the principal deterrent to offensive action in Europe.

NATO command and control, air, and theater nuclear forces are all threatened by Soviet surface-to-surface missiles (SSM's) -- SS20s, SS21s, SS22s, and SS23s -- and by aircraft. Conventional capabilities of air and Strategic Rocket Forces are the accepted substitute for an initial mass nuclear strike and will be used to obtain air superiority and an initial favorable correlation of forces on the battlefield. NATO ballistic and cruise missiles, as well as airfields with aircraft capable of delivering nuclear weapons, will be the first targets. Air defenses and command control communications also will be high priority targets. Attacks by Soviet special forces and airborne forces will supplement missile and air strikes.

The favorable range/payload characteristics of Soviet aircraft allow them to mount operations from widely dispersed bases in the USSR's western military districts and occupied areas of Germany and eastern Europe. This will improve the possibility of achieving surprise by making it unnecessary to move aircraft forward during the crisis period preceding hostilities. With or without surprise, however, the Soviets will mount airfield attacks continually since NATO relies on a small number of main operating bases (MOBs) and Soviet aircraft can deliver enough ordnance in any weather to persuade Soviet commanders that they can keep the bases closed.

To achieve mass in their air operations, the Soviets probably will drive corridors through the NATO air defenses and maintain them free of NATO's PATRIOT and HAWK air defense missiles. That will allow them to attack the PATRIOT belt from the rear and hit MOBs with impunity. The overwhelming emphasis on suppression of air defenses will continue until NATO air forces are defeated. Thereafter, offensive air support and heliborne forces can operate as described in Chapter 5 with relative safety.

Soviet air defense forces expect to contribute to the defeat of NATO air power by destroying penetrating aircraft with coordinated, integrated activities of Soviet and Warsaw Pact air defense networks. Initially, the Soviet forces operate under an air defense system that has been emplaced over the years, integrating Warsaw Pact national systems with microwave data links and broad band telecommunications. This provides for sophisticated command and control of both surface-to-air missiles (SAM's) and air defense aircraft.

The tactical air defenses described in Chapters 3 and 4 are designed to move out from under the protection provided by this system and continue to cover the forces as they advance to the Channel. The combination of the counter air battle described above and these air defenses is expected to keep NATO airpower from seriously affecting the operations of the Soviet Ground Forces.

While the Soviet Strategic Rocket Forces, Navy, Air, and Air Defense Forces have been improving steadily their position relative to the Ground Forces, the Ground Forces themselves have been modernized and strengthened continually since 1965. They have received 50 percent more artillery, much of it self-propelled, more and radically improved tanks, and have virtually mechanized their entire infantry force. The infantry, called "motorized rifle" since World War II when most of them walked have, in the intervening years, acquired trucks, then armored personnel carriers and recently mechanized infantry fighting vehicles.[1] Not only is the infantryman armored, but he has also been provided sophisticated antitank and anti-aircraft weapons at the squad level and his personal weapon, the AK47/74, redesigned in 1974, is one of the finest in the world.

The assessment that follows is presented in five parts. In Chapter 2, John Erickson examines how the Red Army, which marched the road to Stalingrad and then to Berlin, has evolved as the Soviet army until present. In Chapters 3 and 4, Colonel William P. Schneider, USA (Ret.), presents the results of a BDM study of Soviet army operations in terms of the norms the Soviets have set themselves.[2] Colonel Lynn Hansen, USAF (Ret.), presents in Chapter 5 the air force role in Ground Forces operations. Chapter 6 is a joint assessment of the Soviet capability to meet their own standards followed by prognostication of how the Ground Forces might develop in the rest of this century.

Certain threads can be seen to carry through all the material in spite of organizational changes prompted by the massive input of new and improved equipment.

Although there have been modifications and equipment modernizations over the past 40 years, the tank division still has the same basic organizational form as in 1946. New tanks with bigger guns, better armor, more maneuverability, greater range, and easier maintenance as well as amphibious tanks and armored personnel carriers, entered the tank divisions (TKD) as the force evolved, but the essential structure was unchanged although organic artillery and additional support and additional motorized rifle support is new. A comparable pattern applies to the later evolution of the motorized rifle division (MRD). Their structures are shown in Figures 1.1 and 1.2.

The maneuver regiments have been and continue to be organizationally analogous to the division. They are composed as follows:

(1) MRR (Of MRD and TKD) (2) Tank Regiment (TKR) (Of MRD and TKD)
    Regt Hq   Regt Hq
    3 MR Bn   3 TK Bn

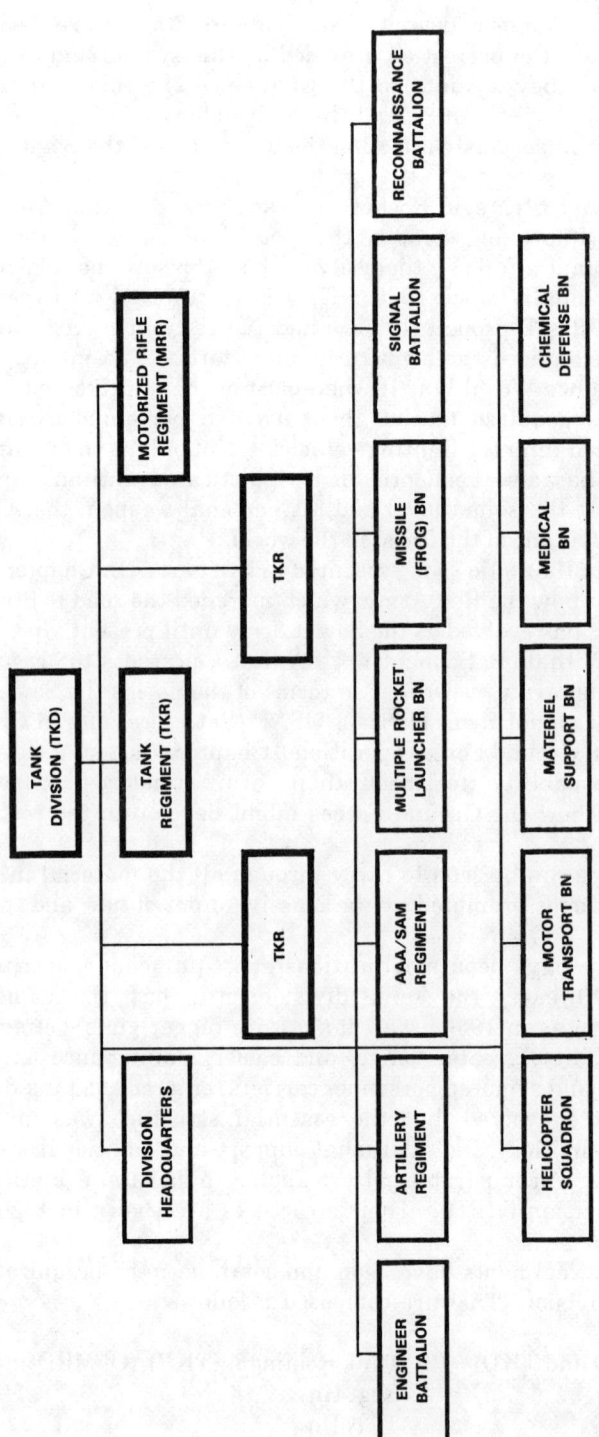

Figure 1.1. Type Motorized Rifle Division (MRD)

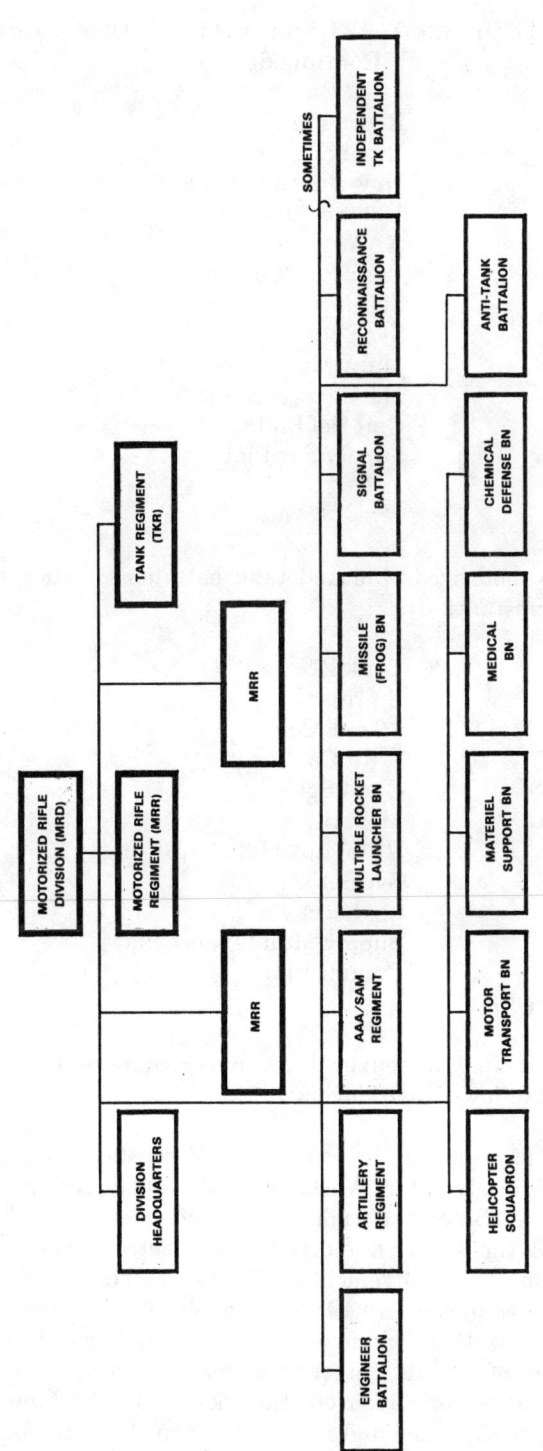

Figure 1.2. Type Tank Division (TKD)

(1) MRR (Of MRD and TKD) (2) Tank Regiment (TKR) (Of MRD and TKD)
    (Continued)   (Continued)
    1 TK Bn   1 MR Bn
    Cmbt Spt   Recon Plat/Co
    Mortar Btry /   Cmbt Spt
      How Btry/How Bn   How Bn (Btry 1977-1979)
    AAA Btry   120 mm Mort Btry
    Recon Plat/Co   AAA/AD Btry
    ATGM Btry   Engr Plat/Co
    Engr Plat/Co   Sig Co
    Sig Co   Svc Spt
    Svc Spt   Maint Co
    Maint Co   MT Co
    Med Co   Cml Def Plat/Co
    Motor Transport Co   Supply/Svc Plat
    Cml Def Plat/Co
    Supply/Svc Plat

The pattern applies to motorized rifle and tank battalions. They have an organization which is substantially:

(1) MR BN   (2) Tank BN
    Bn Hq   Bn Hq
    3 MR Cos   3 Tank Cos
    1 Tank Co   1 MR Co
    Cmbt Spt   Cmbt Spt
    Mortar Btry/or Plat   Mort Btry
    How Btry   (Plat until late 1970s - early 1980s)
    AT Plat   Svc Spt
    Svc Spt   Med Sect
    Comms Plat   Supply/Maintenance Plat
    Med Sect   Comms Plat
    Supply/Maintenance Plat

The pattern of three principal maneuver units supported by tank or infantry troops as appropriate is followed at all levels.

While the pattern of organization has remained constant, the numbers have changed. Immediately after World War II, the forces dropped in numbers and readiness. Since the 1960s the trend has reversed. After Czechoslovakia in 1968, there were five divisions in Central Group of Forces plus supporting aviation. US involvement in Southeast Asia, along with the Sino-Soviet border clashes in the late 1960s, made for a quite rapid buildup along that border. Organizational changes were not abrupt or radical in this period, but the numbers of Ground Forces unit were increased. By the late 1960s and early 1970s, it became apparent that Soviet Ground (and tactical air) Forces were being reorganized and their equipment holdings increased.

New units were activated and upgrading and modernization programs pursued over this somewhat extended period (1968 to 1975). MRD strength went from 10,000 to 12,500; the tank division went from 8,000 to 9,800. Beginning in the mid 1960s, the number of tubes in division artillery regiments increased from 48 to 54 in MRDs and from 36 to 54 in TKDs. Reductions made during the 1950s were restored and division artillery regiments enlarged in strength by 50 percent. Motor- Rifle Regiments (MRRs) began upgrading in the early 1970s. From an organic artillery battery of 6 guns, they moved to a battalion of 18 guns. Armored personnel carriers (APCs) in the MRDs increased from 200+ to more than 300. The independent tank battalion appeared in MRDs with about 40 tanks and in some cases with as many as 51. The tank battalion in MRRs went from 31 to 40 vehicles. Thus, tank strength in an MRD expanded from 188 in 1964 to 284 in 1972. Later evidence showed tank divisions had organic motorized rifle units in their tank regiments.

Since 1969, air units have increased in numbers of fighters and fighter-bombers from 110 to 130, transitioning into a new third generation of aircraft with increased maintenance capabilities. By 1979, all fixed-wing tactical aircraft in Central Europe had entered service within the preceding decade.

NOTES

1. In this book the term motorized rifle (MR) will be used hereafter to translate the Soviet term *motostrelkoviye*. The Soviet Encyclopedic Dictionary (Moscow: Military Publishing House, 1983, p. 465) compares the Soviet motorized rifle forces to infantry, motorized infantry, and mechanized troops of the US, UK, and FRG.

2. The BDM International Corporation is a professional services company located in northern Virginia, USA. Soviet Army Operations was a technical report prepared for the Defense Nuclear Agency by Dr. J. V. Braddock, W. P. Schneider, W. R. Bell, F. D. Conant, and others.

Chapter 2
The Evolution of the Soviet Ground Forces, 1941 - 1985

THE GREAT PATRIOTIC WAR

In the early hours of June 22, 1941, Hitler's *Wehrmacht* launched Operation Barbarossa, the massive surprise invasion of the Soviet Union that opened the greatest land campaign in the history of the world. The Red Army (Workers-Peasants Red Army: RKKA) was engulfed in merciless combat that raged for 1,425 days. After the Soviet-German war ended in May 1945, Soviet forces conducted a brief 23-day *blitzkrieg* campaign in the Far East against the Japanese Kwantung Army.

The staggering statistics of the Soviet-German war, known in the USSR as the "Great Patriotic War of the Soviet Union," reflect the magnitude of sustained fighting through which the Red Army passed from the first calamitous defeats of 1941-42 to its final victories in 1945. It emerged on the morrow of these triumphs as the Soviet Army.[1]

The Soviet-German war was waged along battle fronts ranging in length from 3,000-6000 kilometers. The 47 months of war fall into three distinct phases. The first (June 1941-November 1942) involved desperate attempts to stem the German advance deep into Soviet territory, marked by the shock to German arms delivered before Moscow in December 1941 and the mighty reverse that sent the German Army reeling back from Stalingrad. The second phase (November 1942-December 1943) saw the huge blood-letting battle of the Kursk salient in 1943 and the ultimate Soviet success in breaking the offensive power of the German armies in the East. In the third period (January 1944-May 1945), the Red Army moved across Soviet frontiers into southeastern Europe, central Europe, East Prussia, and the glittering prize of Berlin itself, the "lair of the Fascist beast".

The intensity of warfare in these three periods bears some investigation. The first phase lasted for 516 days, 485 or 94 percent of which saw the Red Army fully committed operationally, leaving only 31 days of relative quiet. The second phase included the only period of extended pause throughout the war, the 66-day lull that preceded the massive armored clash of German Panzers and Soviet tanks in the Kursk salient during the high summer of 1943. The third phase lasted for 500 days, 451 or 90 percent of them operationally active. In all, the Red Army was fully engaged 88 percent of the time, with only 145 days of relative quiet.

Measured in terms of manpower and human sacrifice, no less than 70 percent of total German strength was committed to the Soviet-German front in 1941 (153 out of 217 divisions), a proportion that remained more or less constant until the end of 1942. In 1943, the number of divisions increased to 196, rising to a peak of 201 in January 1944, though the percentage of German divisions on the eastern front fell to just over 60 percent and then to 57 percent in January 1945. The Red Army destroyed or took prisoner 290 enemy divisions and 25 brigades, with 93 divisions surrendering at the end of the war when Soviet Armed Forces numbered 11,365,000 men. Just over 6,000,000 German soldiers were killed, wounded or missing in the *Ostfeldzug*. The pitiless scale of Soviet battle losses -- though never precisely calculated -- soared past 12,000,000, with 10,000,000 perhaps lost forever. Some 10,000,000 civilians were enslaved, massacred, or simply hapless victims of a gigantic war. The heaviest military losses came during the first 20 months of battle including the staggering number of prisoners taken by the German Army in the late autumn of 1941.

Weapons and equipment were consumed at a colossal rate, confirming Stalin's view that war would be won or lost in the machine shops. The Soviet Union, aided by American Lend-Lease, won this industrial war, with (Figure 2.1) 104,000 tanks and self-propelled (SP) guns (78,000 tanks and 16,000 SP guns went to the field armies); 110,000 lorries; 10,000 armored cars and 30,000 motorcycles; 17 billion rounds of small arms ammunition; 427,000,000 artillery and mortar rounds; 13,000,000 tons of fuel; 40,000,000 tons of food; and, 73,000,000 army tunics. The six Soviet tank armies, the first of which[2] was almost destroyed in 1942 but lived to fight another day and became the pride and joy of the Red Army, participated in 64 offensive operations at Front (Army Group) level or acted as "mobile groups" attached to Soviet Fronts.

YEAR	TOTAL TANKS/ SP GUNS	TYPES			TANK DIESEL ENGINES
		HEAVY	MEDIUM	LIGHT	
1941	6,590	1,358	3,014	2,218	4,867
1942	24,719	2,553	12,578	9,588	16,890
1943	24,006	1,423	17,192	5,391	22,955
1944	28,983	4,762	17,066	7,155*	28,120
1945	15,097	3,030	8,505	3,562	14,498
TOTALS	99,395**	13,126	58,355	27,914	87,330

* SP Guns Only.
** Representing Only Tanks/SP Guns Accepted from Factories.
For Details of Soviet Tanks/SP Guns, see German Military Documents (GMD). *Genstdh/fho (IID) Reports to Chef Der Heerestrustung; T-78/Roll 478.*

Figure 2.1. Soviet Tank/SP Artillery Production: 1941-1945 (to June)

ARMY	OPERATION	NO. OF TANKS/ SP GUNS INITIAL	DURATION (DAYS)	TOTAL UNITS	RECYCLING RATE: % INITIAL STRENGTH	TOTAL LOSSES NOS.	'WRITE-OFF' % OF INITIAL STRENGTH
1 GDS TK A	BELGOROD-KHARKOV	562	29	1,040	185	289	51.4
	PROSKUROV	549	36	1,317	240	523	95.2
	LVOV-SANDOMIERZ	419	12	429	102.4	121	28.8
	E. PRUSSIA	584	8	149	24.6	49	8.4
2 GDS TK A	OREL	371	9	415	111.8	78	21.9
	VISTULA-ODER	838	16	302	36	84	10
3 GDS TK A	VISTULA-ODER	922	19	520	56.4	183	19.8
4 TK A	OREL	735	10	551	75	252	34.3
	LVOV	464	14	456	98	112	26.3
	VISTULA-ODER	750	13	423	56.4	18	15.7
5 GDS TK A	E. PRUSSIA	585	25	421	72	210	35.9
AVERAGES:		613	17	547	89.2	184	30

Figure 2.2. Loss Analysis/Tank Army Operations

There is no better illustration of the transformation in Soviet capabilities than the rapid growth of armored striking power and Soviet employment of the armored offensive, *tankoviy udar*. Out of a grand total of 67 operations conducted by Soviet tank armies, only 11 were during 1942-43, with 236 "operational days" of tank army operations (Figure 2.2). In 1944-45, Soviet armor mounted 56 operations (including the Far Eastern offensive with 6th Guards Tank Army) amounting to 1,081 "operational days," expended by the "homogeneous" (*odnorodniy sostav*) tank armies. These armies consisted of one or two tank corps and a mechanized corps with 35,000-50,000 men and some 550-700 tanks. In 1945, the Soviet command had about 15,000 tanks and self-propelled (SP) guns.

The same process of expansion and diversification -- above all, the increase in fire-power -- affected the entire Red Army, making it a startlingly different military machine at the end of the war than it was in 1941. At first sight huge and seemingly formidable, the Red Army was grievously flawed. It discovered to its enormous cost in 1941, that the rifle division, with 14,483 officers and men, was too cumbersome, lacking both mobility and effective communications. Though committed in theory to "maneuver warfare", it was wholly unfitted for such a role (Figure 2.3). Worse still, no proper "rear services" (logistics) organization existed at the outbreak of war. Staffs handled both operations and supply. The armored forces were in little better shape, though Soviet plans called for creating 20 mechanized corps that would have needed 30,000 tanks, including 16,600 new KVs and T-34s plus 7,000 armored cars, a build-up that would have taken four to five years in the opinion of the Soviet General Staff. Like the rifle formations, the mechanized elements suffered a drastic shortage of transport (lorries, tractors, and motorcycles).[3]

DATE	1941 – 1945 ESTABLISHMENT
APRIL 1941	14,483
JULY 1941	10,859
DECEMBER 1941	11,626
MARCH 1942	12,795
JULY 1942	10,396
DECEMBER 1942	9,435
JULY 1943	9,380
DECEMBER 1944	11,706
JUNE 1945	11,780

Figure 2.3. Rifle Division Establishments (Manpower)

A battered and bloodied Red Army nevertheless summoned up sinew enough to deal the Wehrmacht a stunning reverse in the winter of 1941-42, thrusting the German divisions back from Moscow. Corps administrations had been reduced to only six, but the number of combined armies had grown from 27 to 58, with an army fielding an average of five to six rifle divisions (Figure 2.4). To provide mobility, the Red Army put 82 cavalry divisions in the field, while the armored forces proper consisted of seven tank divisions (four in the Far East), 76 independent tank brigades, and 100 independent tank battalions. In the winter of 1941-42, the Red Army acquired its first experience in conducting large-scale offensive operations, which weakened but did not mortally damage the German Army in the east.

OPERATION	ARMY	LOSSES (IN%) DUE TO				
		ARTY. FIRE	MINE	AIR ATTACK	'FAUST-* PATRONE'	VARIOUS
OREL (43)	2 TA	76.0	14.0	10.0	-	-
	4 TA	68.5	8.0	17.7	-	5.8
KIEV (43)	3 GD TA	94.8	2.0	0.5	-	2.7
LVOV-SANDO-MIERZ (44)	3 GD TA	80.0	6.0	14.0	-	-
	4 TA	91.8	3.0	3.4	-	1.8
VISTULA-ODER (45)	3 GD TA	88.5	2.0	9.5	-	-
	1 GD TA	63.1	5.3	10.5	20.0	1.1
	2 GD TA	79.5	2.0	1.5	-	17.0
	4 TA	78.5	9.5	1.0	6.2	4.8
BERLIN (45)	2 GD TA	58.7	5.8	6.6	24.0	4.9
	3 GD TA	67.1	6.6	10.3	16.0	-

* BAZOOKAS / *PANZER-FAUST*

Figure 2.4. Distribution/Characteristics of Tank Army Losses (Offensive Operations)

THE RED ARMY REBUILDS

In the spring of 1942, the Red Army slowly expanded and diversified, re-introducing the tank corps and the rifle corps (34 of the latter existed at the end of 1942, including Guards rifle corps and Guards rifle armies). Rifle formations also were receiving tank regiments and independent tank breakthrough regiments with 21 heavy tanks as infantry support. The number of guns and mortars rose from 44,900 to 77,800 and tanks from 3,900 to 7,350.

Soviet tank forces slowly clambered back with more powerful tactical units. In March 1942, four tank corps were reformed, each with two tank brigades, though these new units still lacked "operational-tactical self-sufficiency". In May-June 1942, the first Soviet tank armies appeared on the scene (Figure 2.5), together with the refurbished mechanized corps.

TANK ARMY: ESTABLISHMENTS 1943 - 1945			
	1943	1944	1945
PERSONNEL	4,000	48,000	50,000
TANKS	40-560	450-620	700
SP GUNS	25	98-147	250
GUNS/MORTARS	500-600	650-750	850

TANKS CORPS: ESTABLISHMENTS 1942 - 1945				
	1942	1943	1944	1945
PERSONNEL	7,800	10,977	12,010	11,788
TANKS (TOTAL)	168	208	207	228
LIGHT	70	-	-	-
MEDIUM	90	208	207	207
HEAVY	-	-	-	21
SP GUNS	-	49	63	42
TANKS AND SP GUNS (TOTAL)	168	257	270	270
GUNS	12	12	36	56
MORTARS	18	48	94	94
MRLS	8	8	8	8

Figure 2.5. Tank Army and Corps Establishments

Though of "mixed" establishment (rifle, tank, and cavalry divisions, plus artillery and multiple rocket launchers) and in spite of being roughly handled by the *Panzers* in the summer of 1942, the new tank armies proved their worth in the Soviet counteroffensive at Stalingrad in the winter of 1942. At the same time, the Red Army began to concentrate and expand its artillery resources, introducing the artillery division in November 1942 with eight regiments and a total of 168 guns. It was an innovation that justified itself during the Stalingrad counteroffensive, leading to accretion of the vast artillery reserves of the "Supreme Command" (*RVGK*), which added massive firepower to the "shock power" so ardently desired by Soviet commanders.

Artillery support came increasingly to the fore, with the concept of the "artillery offensive" making its appearance in 1942. It was designed to correct previous weaknesses by massing fire resources, furnishing fire support for the assault to the full depth of enemy positions, and providing planned fire support when mobile formations were introduced into a breach in the German defenses. Improvements in the course of 1942-43 brought in the long-range artillery groups (at army level), together with heavy bombardment groups, multiple rocket launcher (MRL) divisions, and antiaircraft groups. At divisional level, artillery support for the rifle elements was distributed among the first echelon rifle regiments. The "artillery offensive" usually lasted for some 70 to 80 minutes, with the heavy bombardment phase (neutralization and destruction shoots) increased from 20 to 65 minutes, while rolling barrages were extended to a depth of 1.5 kilometers to give greater support to the infantry attack. Artillery support for the mobile groups (tank formations) was assigned to the long-range artillery groups operating to a depth of 10 to 12 kilometers. As artillery resources grew in the later stages of the war, army artillery groups were split into subgroups to facilitate cooperation with rifle troops, while the appearance after 1943 of heavily fortified and substantially engineered German defensive systems brought the Soviet heavy bombardment/demolition artillery group *gruppa artillerii razrusheniya* into existence. However, it was not until 1944 that the various artillery groups at regiment,[4] division, corps, and army level were given standardized organization, based mainly on their operational-tactical roles. The decisiveness of artillery in the combined arms battle became justifiably something of an article of faith.

Better understanding of the role of tactical air support led to the organization of frontal aviation (*frontovaya aviatsiya*) in a move away from the early, primitive scattering of air elements throughout combined arms armies. The advent of the air army (*vozdushnaya armiya*) in 1942 helped to stabilize the situation, but allocation of the air effort needed urgent resolution. Too often tactical bombing assigned to targets in the depth of the enemy defenses bore little relation to and lacked coordination with "direct support" (close air support). Before 1943 the air effort was usually planned to cover only the first day of offensive operations, largely ignoring the organization of air support as the attack developed through the depth of the enemy positions. Later in the war the "air offensive" was standardized into two phases: the "air preparation" (*aviatsionnaya podgotovka*) was followed by "air support" (*soprovozhdeniye*) during the course of the offensive. An army would have from three to five air divisions for support, while the mobile group was supported by one *shturmovik* (ground-attack)[5] air division and one fighter division. Bomber divisions also were used in support of Front and Army operations.

THE BEGINNINGS OF COMBINED ARMS

The essence of the "combined arms" battle became, in theory at least, fire, shock power/attack, maneuver. Soviet efforts, therefore concentrated continuously on increasing the "tactical densities" (*plotnost'*) involved in the combined arms mix of infantry, armor, artillery, SP guns, engineers, and communications. During the latter stage of the war (1944-45), breakthrough operations used five to seven rifle battalions, 200 to 250 guns, 20 to 30 tanks, and two to four combat engineer companies concentrated for each kilometer of the attack sector. Similar densities were used for both the meeting engagement and defensive actions. The 1943 FSR (Field Service Regulations - *Polevoy ustav/1943*) stipulated that inter-arms cooperation and coordination should be managed in the interests of the infantry, though it became increasingly plain that fire (*ognevoy boy*) was becoming the arbiter of the battlefield, whether the action was defensive or offensive. Without massive artillery and air support, the tank/infantry team could not carry out its mission to any depth; for all practical purposes, fire (*ogon'*) came to exercise total sway over the battlefield. The diversification of the combat arms, however, inevitably complicated the interaction/coordination process, which added to the significance of both maneuver with firepower (*manevr ognem*) and troop maneuver, all culminating in the fusion of maneuver with assault/attack.

At the beginning of 1944, in preparation for the "ten decisive blows" about to be rained on the German army, the Red army mustered 5,987,000 men (Figure 2.6) (419,000 of them held in reserve) with 92,650 guns and mortars (5,000 in reserve), 5,357 tanks and self-propelled guns (271 in reserve), 461 rifle and motorized rifle divisions, 76 artillery/mortar divisions, and 124 aviation divisions (more than 8,000 combat aircraft.) In June 1944, Red Army strength topped the 6,000,000 mark, the tank inventory had grown to 7,753 (including SP guns), the reserves had 2,323 combat machines, and the strength of combat aircraft had risen to 13,428. To direct these formations and units, the vast network of Soviet training establishments turned out some 317,000 officers in 1944. Front commands now consisted of six to nine combined arms armies, one air army and, not infrequently, one or two tank armies, while the combined arms army itself (Figure 2.7) expanded to include three to four rifle corps (nine to twelve rifle divisions), one to three tank brigades, and the possible addition of a tank or mechanized corps for particular operations (Figure 2.8). Artillery strength continued to increase though more than one-third of the divisions and brigades were held as "Supreme Command reserves", facilitating the centralized direction and

FRONT-LINE AND RESERVE STRENGTH JANUARY 1944

	FIELD ARMIES, FLEETS	STAVKA RESERVE	TOTAL
RED ARMY	5,568,000	419,000	5,987,000
AIR FORCE (INCLUDING LONG-RANGE AVIATION, *ADD**)	331,000	77,000	408,000
NAVY	266,000	–	266,000
AIRBORNE TROOPS	–	75,000	75,000
	6,165,000	571,000	6,736,000
DIVISION/BRIGADES			
RIFLE, MOTOR-RIFLE CAVALRY, AIRBORNE DIVISIONS	461	19	480
INDEPENDENT BRIGADES	38	17	55
'FORTIFIED DISTRICTS'**(*URs*)	32	–	32
TANK/MECHANIZED CORPS	23	12	35
INDEPENDENT TANK BRIGADES	42	4	46
ARTILLERY/MORTAR DIVISIONS	76	4	80
AVIATION DIVISIONS	124	4	128
WEAPONS			
GUNS AND MORTARS	92,650	5,040	97,690
TANKS AND SP GUNS	5,357	271	5,628
AIRCRAFT	8,506	312	8,818

FRONT-LINE AND RESERVE STRENGTH JUNE 1944

	FIELD ARMIES, FLEETS	STAVKA RESERVE	TOTAL
RED ARMY	5,691,000	386,000	6,077,000
AIR FORCE (INCLUDING LONG-RANGE AVIATION, *ADD*)	337,000	70,000	447,000
NAVY	357,000	–	357,000
AIRBORNE TROOPS	–	58,000	58,000
	6,425,000	514,000	6,939,000
DIVISION/BRIGADES			
RIFLE, MOTOR-RIFLE CAVALRY, AIRBORNE DIVISIONS	453	23	476
INDEPENDENT BRIGADES	17	–	17
'FORTIFIED DISTRICTS'***URs*	19	–	19
TANK/MECHANIZED CORPS	22	15	37
INDEPENDENT TANK BRIGADES	36	1	37**
ARTILLERY/MORTAR DIVISIONS	72	11	83
AVIATION DIVISIONS	132	21	153
WEAPONS			
GUNS AND MORTARS	92,557	4,493	97,050
TANKS AND SP GUNS	7,753	2,232	9,985
AIRCRAFT	13,428	1,359	14,787

* *Aviatsia Dalnevo Deistviya.*
** *Ukreplyonniy Rayon, UR,* Firepower Equivalent to a Rifle Division.
***Including 2 SP Gun Brigades.

Figure 2.6. Soviet Strength: January - June 1944

ARMY	MANPOWER	GUNS/ MORTARS	AT GUNS	AA GUNS	MRLS	TANKS	SP GUNS	AIRCRAFT
30A (41)	72,000	303	77	25	19	21	–	–
20A (42)	70,000	444	79	4	40	96	–	–
6A (42)	101,000	1,004	149	55	24	445	–	145
11 GDS A (43)	135,000	2,652	468	255	144	615	33	–
53A (43)	77,000	1,698	390	80	48	291	11	–
1 GDS A (44)	122,000	2,087	192	148	360	293	191	–
3A (44)	93,000	2,108	370	78	232	319	225	–
2 SH A (45)	102,000	1,910	327	104	388	306	125	–
5 GDS A (45)	81,000	2,400	217	124	456	420	217	–

Figure 2.7. Combined-Arms Armies: 1941-45

maneuver of enormous artillery fire power and enabling the Soviet command to mass artillery in the requisite densities on decisive sectors and axes of advance.

	1942	1943	1944	1945
PERSONNEL	13,559	15,018	16,442	16,318
TANKS (TOTAL)	175	204	183	183
LIGHT	75	42	-	-
MEDIUM	100	162	183	183
HEAVY	-	-	-	-
SP GUNS	-	25	63	63
TANKS AND SP GUNS (TOTAL)	175	229	246	246
GUNS	36	36	80	80
MORTARS	54	72	154	154
MRLS	8	8	8	8

Figure 2.8. Mechanized Corps: Establishments 1942–1945

COMMAND AND CONTROL

Centralization, strict centralization, was (and remains to this day) the dominant mode of command and control. Operational direction of the field armies devolved on the *Stavka* (General Headquarters) of the High Command, with the General Staff acting as the "operational channel" to the fronts and Front Commands. This super-centralization, however, even with regionalized "high commands" as an intermediate echelon, proved to be too inflexible, while the *Glavkoms* (the regional "high commands") lacked adequate staffs and communications facilities. In effect, higher staffs were mere information-collecting agencies passing information upwards to the *Stavka*, which became overloaded as it struggled with strategic decisions, operational questions, and even tactical decisions. Coordination and communications broke down. Five Fronts were activated in June 1941 but within a matter of months, the *Stavka* was wrestling with a battle front that had expanded from 2,000 to 4,000 kilometers, involving eight Fronts and four independent armies. The intermediate high command echelon (*Glavkoms*) did not endure throughout the war, though it was revived briefly for the Far Eastern operations in 1945. Stalin kept the tightest grip on both strategic and operational matters. As a means of strengthening centralization, the General Staff sent its own representatives to field commands, down to divisions, in many instances. At the same time the *Stavka* also dispatched *predstaviteli*, representatives with enormous authority and sweeping powers, to Front commands to coordinate the operations of several Fronts. That procedure soon earned the label of the "flying circus" as Marshal Zhukov, Marshal Vasilevskiy, or Artillery Marshal Voronov descended on Front commanders with specific *Stavka* directives, reporting directly to Stalin and steering Front and Army commanders towards particular operational decisions and solutions that fit the prime directive.

In the first phase of the war, as the high command struggled to develop a wartime system of command, control, and coordination, combat performance was affected by shortage of weapons and equipment, lack of available reserves (or reserves heedlessly squandered), the inadequacies of hastily improvised "mobile groups", and the lack of tactical skills at lower levels. Armies and divisions were simply expended wholesale in defense and attack. Overtasking, brute expenditure of major formations without reinforcement, and total attrition over time, plus calamitous losses among junior officers, accelerated defeat in the field.

Providing and maintaining adequate tactical densities in men and weapons could reduce losses, as well as preserve the cohesion (*kompaktnost'*) of formations operating on divergent axes of advance and with open flanks. Special attention was directed to maintaining the cohesion of the small units even in the face of heavy losses and, above all, the integrity of command and control, *upravleniye voyskami*. It was the latter that was perhaps one of the most critical measures of performance and effectiveness. The Soviet aim was to coordinate all the elements of a full combat deployment (*boyevoy poryadok*). This involved coordinating the first echelon with the second or with a combined arms reserve, and with the antitank (artillery) reserve and artillery groups; internal coordination between infantry and artillery, armor and combat engineers; the battlefield "interaction" of the infantry/tank team with artillery and tactical air; and cooperation with neighboring units, all to effect the rapid exploitation of the fire assault.

After a calamitous start, the Red Army made a remarkable recovery. While many of its victories were won in bludgeoning fashion, that should not obscure the skill that Soviet commanders showed at all levels or the quality of Soviet weapons and the sturdiness of their equipment. In many respects, Soviet performance was a paradox: centralization and inflexibility giving way to improvization and rapid adaptability, doggedness to deftness, the unimaginative and the stolid to boldness and even dash. For all its shortcomings, the Red Army proved to be no mean precursor to the modern Soviet Army, which became at once the beneficiary of experience, tradition, and competence so dearly bought.

GROUND FORCES STRUCTURES AND SOVIET MILITARY POSTURE

The Soviet Army, successor to the victorious but battle-scarred Workers-Peasants Red Army (*RKKA*), formally came into existence in 1946 during the post-war phase of demobilization and reorganization. Appraisals of its size and functions are bedeviled by both great confusion over numbers[6] and by the savage politics of Stalin's post-war handling of the Soviet military command. The "purge of the victors" apparently inflicted not only terrible losses on the officer corps but also intensified internal disputes over the nature of modernization and reorganization in the Soviet Army.

According to Soviet figures, total strength dropped from 11,365,000 in 1945 to 2,874,000 in 1948. At the beginning of 1945, the Soviets report, the field strength of their armed forces (including *Stavka* reserves) was 7,109,000 men with 6,289,000 in the Ground Forces. There were reportedly 488 rifle divisions[7] and 35 armored corps (tank and mechanized) supported by 155 air divisions with an inventory of 15,100 tanks and SP guns and 15,815 aircraft. The Soviet command had deployed a total of 80 "combined arms" armies plus six tank armies throughout the wartime period.[8]

It is impossible to arrive at a firm upper figure for Soviet wartime strength but it probably hovered around the 11,000,000 mark. If we accept the Soviet assertion of a two-thirds cut by 1948, active field forces would total about 2.75 million and the entire armed forces about 4,000,000. The absence of a clear baseline for the field forces or the total establishment[9] has led to gross discrepancies in Western estimates. This is no mere pedantry, for we have as yet been unable to either fix the size of the Soviet Ground Forces with accuracy or to account for the enforced reductions brought about by modernization. For example, in 1946 Soviet divisions in East Germany, while being properly counted as divisions in the formal order of battle, in fact amounted to little more than regiments as a result of reorganization.

We do know that the post-war demobilization (completed in 1948) reduced the gross tally of some 500 Soviet divisions to 175, of which one-third were retained or reorganized as armored strike forces, divided between tank and mechanized divisions. In this first response to wartime experience, the mechanized division was stabilized at a strength of some 12,000-13,000 men with three mechanized and two tank regiments, while the tank division was reduced to 10,500 men equipped with three medium tank regiments. The rifle division remained at about 11,000 men, but was motorized, making it fully mobile. All the transport in a mechanized division was also motorized, and the tank division was equipped with enough motorized infantry to supply its own protection and to hold the ground taken by the tanks. The Soviet command also retained the wartime artillery division with 9,000 men, a field gun brigade, a howitzer regiment, and a medium-gun regiment, plus an "antiaircraft division" with a strength of 2,500 men included within the numbers of artillery divisions.

Numbers alone, however impressive, did not represent the full scene. The Soviet Army, the mainstay of the Soviet military system at that time and Stalin's "deterrent" against the American nuclear monopoly, was undergoing major restructuring, incorporating both the lessons of the recent war and advances in military technology. The rifle (infantry) component of the Soviet Army was based on the "combined arms army" (*obshchevoyskovaya armiya*), and armored forces were reorganized into mechanized armies (*mekhanizirovanniye armii*), replacing the wartime tank armies. The highest tactical entity within the combined arms army became the rifle corps, and the basic tactical entity, the rifle division. Tank and mechanized corps were now reorganized as tank and mechanized divisions. The corps echelon disappeared in the armored forces, producing a mechanized army consisting of two tank divisions and two mechanized divisions. The combined arms army could include three rifle corps with each corps having three rifle divisions, or two rifle divisions and one mechanized division. A brief profile of these post-war Soviet divisions[10] demonstrates the degree to which wartime lessons were being absorbed:

(1) Rifle Division. A far more mobile division with replacement of horse-drawn transport by motorization, etc. (Figure 2.9).
(2) Tank Division. A highly mobile formation of 252 medium and heavy tanks with adequate motorized infantry to hold ground seized by the armor and to provide protection for the armor plus one more medium tank battalion than the mechanized division though fewer rifle units.
(3) Mechanized Division. A fully motorized formation, embodying the lessons of the "infantry/tank team" of the war. The mechanized regiment contained three rifle battalions and one tank battalion, while the medium tank regiment and the heavy tank/SP gun regiment each had a motorized rifle battalion.
(4) Artillery Division. Also a motorized unit, varying in manpower from 9,000 to 12,000 (for the heavy "breakthrough" divisions), with artillery complements to suit the particular operational assignments-- a light gun brigade, a howitzer brigade, a medium howitzer regiment, a medium gun regiment, an MRL brigade and a heavy mortar brigade in various combinations--nearly all towed by trucks or tracked vehicles.
(5) Antiaircraft Divisions. 2,500 men and four regiments were included in the tally of artillery divisions.
(6) Cavalry Divisions. Retained on strength but not developed, and phased out in 1955.

Clearly the emphasis was on mobility and firepower, with the tank and mechanized divisions receiving more tanks and greater artillery resources. The rifle divisions were reinforced with more tanks, SP guns, prime movers, and transport. All this was reflected in the revised postwar table of organization:

(1) Rifle Division. Manpower: 11,013
   - Three rifle regiments,[11] medium tank/SP gun regiment, gun and howitzer regiment
   - 52 medium tanks (T-34/85)
   - 18 SU-76 (SP), 16 SU-100 (SP), 36 122mm howitzers, 12 160mm mortars, 18 120mm mortars
   - 162 medium machine guns, 511 light machine guns, 6,208 rifles, 279 antitank rifles
(2) Tank Division. Manpower: 10,659
   - Three medium tank regiments, heavy tank/SP gun regiment, motorized rifle regiment, light AA and mortar regiment, howitzer

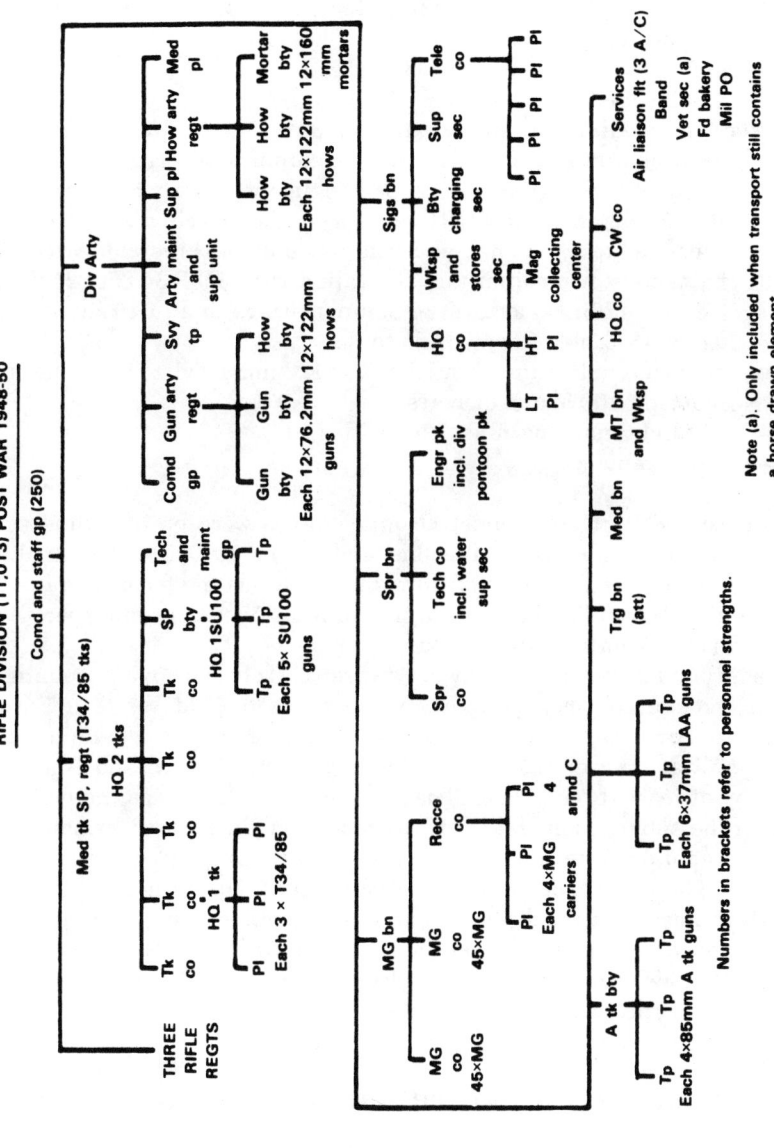

Figure 2.9. Rifle Division (11,013) Postwar 1948-1950

battery (the medium tank regiment consisted of 65 tanks with 3,660 men.)
- 44 heavy tanks, 208 medium tanks
- 21 heavy SP guns, 12 122mm howitzers, 42 120mm mortars, 52 82mm mortars
- 405 light machine guns, 6,112 rifles
- 1,362 vehicles

(3) Mechanized Division. Manpower: 14,485
- 3 mechanized regiments, one medium tank regiment, heavy tank/SP gun regiment, howitzer regiment, mortar regiment, light AA regiment and MRL battery (the mechanized regiment consisted of 2,711 men and was made up of three motorized rifle battalions, a medium tank battalion with 35 T-34/85s, 257 vehicles, six 120mm mortars, 30 82mm mortars, and 1,510 rifles.)
- 21 heavy tanks, 183 medium tanks
- 44 heavy SP guns, 8 MRLs, 24 122mm howitzers, 54 120mm mortars, 100 82mm mortars
- 611 light machine guns, 7,645 rifles
- 1,667 vehicles

In general composition, the Soviet Ground Forces were built around some 50 to 60 tank or mechanized divisions and 80 to 100 rifle and artillery divisions. One hint of the shape of things to come was the formation in July 1946 of the first Soviet "rocket troop unit," (a multiple rocket launcher, MRL regiment) formed from a Guards mortar regiment.[12]

Soviet ground forces in Europe were at first the sole and obvious counter to the American nuclear monopoly. The effect was to hold Western Europe "hostage" to American restraint by the presence of overwhelming conventional military power that outnumbered British, French, and American divisions by at least three to one. The same military force was the principal element in the subjugation of Eastern Europe, including East Germany. The threat of a rapid drive to the Atlantic was the first and rudimentary Soviet "deterrent." The sense of preponderance was summed up in the saying that all the Russians needed to reach the Channel was boots.[13] The ground forces in Europe, stripped for a while during the first reorganization phase, were soon equipped with new weapons (improved tanks and SP guns); their mobility was enhanced, and tactical air power expanded.

EVER INCREASING TEMPO – THE BREAKTHROUGH

Inevitably Soviet commanders saw their operational-tactical requirements through the prism of the recent war. Offensive operations assumed top priority, with major offensives to be conducted by groups of Fronts, where a Front might consist of three to four combined arms armies or mechanized armies with an air army in support. An encirclement operation would normally be carried out by two Fronts with a third committed in the final stage. Combined arms armies were assigned to break the enemy line on the flanks of the force to be encircled, with mechanized elements moving through the gap and completing their pincer movement, followed in turn by rifle divisions forming an inner perimeter while the mechanized forces drove outward to set up the outer perimeter--the "double encirclement" operation. A Front would breach the enemy defenses at a number of points, with armor committed once "operational depth" had been attained, the armor striking to a depth of 200 miles.

Leaning on wartime "superiority norms," the Soviet Army turned to improving upon them in the postwar period, envisaging tactical densities of three to four rifle battalions, 180 to 240 guns, and 20 to 30 tanks (or SP guns) for each kilometer of the breakthrough sector. Above all, the number of tanks had to be increased, hence the inclusion within the rifle division of a tank/self-propelled gun regiment and the addition of a mechanized division to the rifle corps. Similarly, the frontage for offensive operations of a division was increased to four kilometers; that of a regiment to two kilometers. Deep echeloning became the order of the day as the equipment piled up. Tanks and SP guns, mobile groups and combat engineer groups deployed in echelons, though advanced detachments (*peredoviye otryady*)[14] now assumed greater importance as small, combined arms, mobile elements, all this with an eye to increasing tempo.

The war also had indicated that committing tank and mechanized formations to complete breaching the main defensive positions appreciably increased tempo, though these forces suffered substantial losses in the process; postwar practice, therefore, assigned this task to the rifle corps suitably reinforced with a mechanized division. In sum, postwar operational-tactical doctrine envisaged: 1) expanding in depth the simultaneous neutralization of the defensive system and a general "spatial" expansion of the battle; 2) increasing the role of tactical air in providing fire resources; 3) augmenting the "shock power" and mobility of divisional and corps second echelons; 4) using these elements on the lines of army "mobile groups;" and 5) developing the means to conduct offensive operations off the march. Nor did Soviet tacticians neglect defensive operations, with special emphasis on increasing depth, "densities," and antitank measures.

It was assumed that Front offensive operations would begin with breaching prepared defenses, or with a breakthrough into hastily prepared defensive positions, breaking into "fortified districts", though meeting engagements either at the outset or during the course of these operations were not excluded. Breaching the enemy defenses was assigned to the rifle divisions, with tank and mechanized divisions in the first echelon only where the defenses had been hastily (*pospeshno*) erected. The assault would be initiated with infantry support tanks, artillery, and ground-attack (close support) aircraft, with mechanized divisions forming the second echelon of the rifle corps and assigned to complete the breakthrough of the main defensive positions. The second defensive line should be taken off the march. Enemy tactical defensive positions would be breached on the first day of offensive operations. The breakthrough into "operational depth" would be effected by the Front "mobile group" consisting of a mechanized army, which would be committed on the second day of the offensive on a frontage of eight to twelve kilometers and operating with artillery and air support. Properly supplied with combat engineer support, the mechanized army would break away from the main assault force, smash enemy reserves, and close the encirclement ring in cooperation with other Front mobile groups and with airborne forces. Airborne troops in divisional strength might well be employed to seize bridgeheads and key river crossings, sections of coastline, road junctions, airfields, and command/communications centers.

POST-STALIN PERIOD

Soviet and non-Soviet sources agree on the dating and importance of the second stage in postwar evolution of the Ground Forces. Beginning in 1953-54 with the death of Stalin and the revision of Soviet military doctrine, the Soviets began to recognize the importance of surprise and the reality of nuclear war, which led them to begin restructuring the air defense forces and reorganizing the Ground Forces into their modern form. With Zhukov at the helm as Defense Minister from February 1955 to October 1957, the Ground Forces were given a leaner and more mobile look, accompanied by manpower reductions in 1955 advertised by Khrushchev as part of a unilateral Soviet move towards disarmament. On completion of the State Treaty with Austria in 1955, the Soviets announced transfer to the reserve of a number of men equal to the troops to be withdrawn from Austria. That number was estimated at 50,000, the equivalent of one to two divisions. They were moved into Hungary which thereafter became the main base for the Soviet "Southern Group of Forces." During 1955-57, 1,840,000 men were released from the armed forces. Later, Khrushchev revealed that total Soviet strength was 5.7 million before this demobilization, thus disclosing a very substantial mobilization during the Korean war period.[15] Soviet announcements intimated that 63 divisions and independent brigades had been disbanded, though no hint was offered as to the manner in which this affected the order of battle.

THE ADVENT OF NUCLEAR WEAPONS

Nuclear weapons thrust themselves to the forefront of Soviet attention, demanding changes in structure and tactics from 1954-59. Marshal Koniev had again assumed command of the Ground Forces in 1955, but the master plan for radical change was developed and implemented by Marshal Zhukov himself. The reduction in manpower, whatever its political and economic advantages, assisted appreciably in this new rationalization and further modernization. For the nuclear battlefield, Zhukov required more mobile and flexible formations, eliminating the corps as an intermediate echelon between army and division and restructuring Soviet rifle and armored/mechanized formations. The mechanized army and the mechanized division disappeared, the latter apparently being too unwieldy for the fast moving operations envisaged by Zhukov. Henceforth, the Ground Forces would consist of only two main types of division: the motorized rifle division (MRD), *motostrelkovaya diviziya*, and the tank division, with tank armies comprised of three to four tank divisions and combined arms armies formed with three to four motorized rifle divisions and one tank division. Air support for both types of army came from tactical air resources under Front control. The tank came to predominate as never before, with a combined arms army having more than 1,000 tanks and the tank army almost 1,500.

With nuclear weapons fully admitted into the Soviet arsenal and their effects generally recognized, tactical requirements were drastically revised, particularly the relationship between fire, "shock power" and maneuver. Hitherto, maneuver had been largely a matter of rapidly positioning forces to mount their own blow or to parry an enemy blow. Nuclear weapons employed on the battlefield now transformed maneuver into a process of exploiting to the fullest the nuclear strike in order to make the deepest possible penetration into enemy defenses, or conversely, to "counter-maneuver"[16] by moving Soviet troops out of range of an impending nuclear strike. In brief, the battlefield had expanded, increasing attack frontages, the depth of assigned missions, and the tempo of offensive operations. The radiation environment became a factor of great importance, thus amplifying the role of reconnaissance and altering the tactics of operating in an irradiated battlefield. In offensive operations, the breakthrough could now be effected not only from a position of direct contact with the enemy, but also off the march, where tactical densities of men and weapons were appreciably reduced. Artillery and air support would be combined into a single mode of fire preparation, though the duration of this support would inevitably decline.

Tactical deployment also had to be reviewed against the requirement for maximum exploitation of both the nuclear strike and conventional fires. This did not preclude the general principle of mounting a massive fire assault through the depth of enemy defenses and constantly intensifying the weight of the assault. Tank formations were singled out for special attention since they could fill gaps torn in the assault forces or take over the role of a first echelon decimated by nuclear strikes. Equally, "forward detachments" and airborne units could be used to exploit the nuclear strike with the "tactical air landing operation" designed either to eliminate enemy mass destruction weapons or to close breaches that had been opened by enemy nuclear strikes.

THE FLUID BATTLEFIELD

The meeting engagement[17] now became a focus of Soviet attention, since it could develop in the course of all types of military operations. It was essential to organize combat groups able to forestall the enemy's recourse to either nuclear or conventional weapons, the deployment of the main body of his forces, and the launching of an attack. "Forward detachments" should, under these circumstances, be reinforced with tactical airborne forces in line with standard Soviet doctrine that in the meeting engagement the enemy forces were best eliminated "in packets." Both frontal and flank attacks should be directed against those gaps in the enemy lines already opened by nuclear strikes.

Under modern nuclear conditions, the meeting engagement would be marked by substantial dispersion in combat deployment and in the order of march, the use of tactical airborne forces, and a reduction of time available for organizing the operation and implementing "interaction" (*vzaymodeystviye*). There was increased reliance on frontal attack as the most effective way of winning time and splitting enemy forces into separate pockets. As for defensive tactics, Soviet practice presupposed extending defensive frontages (including battalion and even company "defensive sectors," prepared positions, and trenches dispersed to reduce losses), deepening and dispersing the echelon system, and developing the stability of "anti-nuclear defense."

Although Zhukov was abruptly removed from the scene, Malinovskiy, his successor, continued Zhukov's policy in most essentials and proceeded to reduce the strength of the Ground Forces to some 140 divisions. He deployed the new tank armies and motorized rifle divisions, the corps having vanished as the echelon between army and division, established the division itself as the basic tactical entity, and gave the regiment greater self-sufficiency. These changes in organization were accompanied by an unequivocal total emphasis on the strategy of offensive, based on seizing the initiative and exploiting the surprise factor. The Ground Forces (together with the Navy and tactical air units) would, in the event of war, strike out as far and as fast as possible against the enemy, committing him to "close battle" under conditions of Soviet choosing and thus denying him the opportunity to use nuclear weapons at will. At the same time, this forward thrust would move Soviet forces out of the hinterland threatened by nuclear bombardment and would preserve Soviet war-fighting capability.

The fortunes of the Ground Forces, however, dipped sharply after 1960 when Khrushchev introduced his own strategic "new look," downgrading traditional arms and relying on strategic (missile) delivery systems, all within the concept of the short spasm war. This approach disrupted the existing military organization by throwing the relationship between theater and strategic warfare into the melting pot. Not surprisingly, there is some confusion in Soviet analysis over the exact chronological progression of these "phases," a problem compounded by the fact that radicalism and conservatism went hand-in-hand during this period of Khrushchev's preeminence.

He continued the policy of fitting out the Ground Forces for nuclear warfare in addition to their conventional role, and maintained a substantial, modernized force deployed forward in the European theater. The nub of the plan, nevertheless, was the "fit" between strategic war and theater war. Khrushchev's solution was to use the Ground Forces to "prolong" the effect of an initial nuclear strike. The subsequent struggle over this concept centered on manpower levels and on the "long war/short war" controversy, or the need to preserve a continuing capability for combined arms operations, which would require retention of a multi-million man army.

The form and future of the Ground Forces were at the eye of the storm in the late Khrushchev period. Limited reduction of manpower was apparently acceptable to the military during the early phase of Khrushchev's policies; drastic cutbacks, however, even the "hollowing out" of the Ground Forces from the inside by eliminating their cadre structure, was not acceptable. Khrushchev's military policy suffered from two fatal flaws: it appeared that in terms of strategic weapons his position could lead only to permanent strategic inferiority, and his "missile mania" seriously endangered the "creative development" of other arms and thus ran counter to Soviet military theory at large, which placed no reliance on "one-weapon" system as a war-winning instrument. Differences persisted over what type of war the Soviet Union should prepare for -- a "land war" or a fundamentally new kind of war in which the principal means of solving strategic tasks would be missiles and nuclear weapons. And how did theater operations throughout the Eurasian land mass fit, or connect, with global strategic operations? What, then, would be the duration of this "war" -- long or short? The answer crucially involved the role of the Ground Forces.

During the later period of his tenure, Khrushchev tried unsatisfactorily to attain a balance by arguing that strategic nuclear strikes, aided by improvement of the Ground Forces' attack capability resulting from the introduction of modern weapons, would mean a "short" war. To counterbalance this, he endorsed the "combined arms" doctrine, which, while acknowledging the key role of the strategic missile forces, stressed the need for combined action by other arms in order to consummate military victory and, above all, invest enemy territory. Within the combined arms concept of the viability of particular weapons in the Ground Forces mix, proponents of the tank found themselves facing strong opposition. The Soviet "antitank" debate dates back to this period.

Modernization of the Soviet Ground Forces, which has extended over almost three decades, proceeded in circumstances that were both uneasy and turbulent, due in no small degree to the personality and the policies of Nikita Khrushchev. In 1956, as "de-Stalinization" began to bite, the Soviet Army was flung into limited conventional warfare in Hungary, crushing the revolution which had begun with the severe military reverse inflicted on two Soviet mechanized divisions. At Zhukov's command, Soviet forces returned in force to stamp out popular resistance in a bloody bout of fighting. Here was both tragedy and irony, for it was only months before, in May 1955, that the Warsaw Treaty had been signed, ushering in the framework of a "Socialist military alliance" under the aegis of the Warsaw Pact, with the Joint Command headed by Marshal Koniev. Khrushchev's mind, however, was scarcely fixed on "Socialist military integration." Launching the first Soviet ICBM and the first ever artificial satellite (the famous Sputnik in 1957), implanted in him the notion of the primacy of nuclear weapons and strategic missiles. Finally, he unveiled the military "new look" in January 1960. At the same time, within the confines of the *Politburo*, he succeeded in displacing

Marshal Zhukov, stripping him simultaneously of his Central Committee membership and replacing him as Defense Minister with Marshal Malinovskiy. A. A. Grechko, hitherto Commander in Chief of Soviet forces in Germany (GSFG), took over the Ground Forces.

THE BREZHNEV ERA

In September 1964, Khrushchev, in one of his last acts, eliminated the Ground Forces as an independent command and placed them under the direct control of the Ministry of Defense, in effect leaving them in suspended animation. Three full years elapsed before the Ground Forces reemerged as an integral command, demonstrating that here was no case of Khrushchevian eccentricity but rather a protracted reappraisal of the role and organization of the Soviet Army, all against the background of a thorough examination of Soviet military policy as a whole.

Essentially, Brezhnev tackled the same issues, but treated them more patiently. He rejected the concept of "one-variant war" -- nuclear war and nothing short of it--on the ground that it imposed unacceptable inflexibility on Soviet policy and was based on the unrealistic assumption that conventional Soviet military means were incapable of attaining Soviet objectives. The "nuclearizing" of the Soviet Ground Forces, when carried to extremes, would leave them dangerously deficient in all-round capabilities. The possibility of the Ground Forces in a nuclear straitjacket disquieted many senior Soviet commanders, but, in fact, Brezhnev had no such intention. Rather, he developed for the first time a genuine dual capability within the Ground Forces. While the strategic missile force was built up to parity with the United States, the Ground Forces were undergoing their own transformation. This was first unveiled in 1967 in Exercise DNIEPR with its conventional backdrop while, almost simultaneously, the 1967 law on military service further reduced manpower.

Brezhnev's policy has for the most part prevailed effectively over the past decade and a half, from the mid-1960s to 1970 and from 1971-72 to the present time. The fortunes of the Ground Forces are themselves a commentary on Soviet military policy as a whole.[18] The build-up of the Ground Forces, particularly those deployed forward in Europe, followed the pattern of matching capabilities more precisely to objectives and moved closer to the "combined arms" concept. The Soviet command brought major new systems into the Ground Forces: five new battlefield air defense systems, five artillery systems, new infantry combat vehicles, and improved battlefield engineering and logistics equipment. The build-up assisted appreciably in eliminating inadequacies perceived by the Soviet command: absence of a genuine dual capability, shortage of mobile air defense for moving columns and of conventional artillery and ammunition stocks, and the lack of infantry on the axes of armored advance.

During the post-Khrushchev period, the Ground Forces, as a "theater force" for operations in Europe, accepted a nonnuclear phase of operations, though this did not amount to envisaging a conventional campaign in toto. The most prominent of these changes were strengthening of conventional artillery components in Soviet divisions; widespread introduction of the T-62 main battle tank; introduction of the BMP, an infantry combat vehicle; inclusion of a motorized rifle division within the tank army; an increase in the mobility and capability of organic air defense systems; and improvements in logistics in the areas of fuel and ammunition. This pronounced upgrading of conventional weapons systems was accompanied by the introduction of helicopters and of modern aircraft for tactical air units, and the expansion of medium- and short-range airlift. However, the Soviet move toward "flexible response"--*Gibkoe Reagirovaniye*--by no means reduced their main emphasis on nuclear weapons. It was simply an additive, making it possible for the Ground Forces to conduct military operations with or without the use of nuclear weapons. To over-estimate nuclear weapons meant under-estimating conventional weapons. If anything, the conventional mode could actually assist in exploiting nuclear weapons. They were not regarded as mutually exclusive, and neither could be isolated from the other. The "combined blow" by aircraft, artillery, armor, and infantry without the use of nuclear weapons did, however, place the greatest importance on coordination, particularly between armor and infantry with an expanded role for airborne forces.

THE RESURRECTION OF MASSED ARMOR AND ARTILLERY

The technicalities of ground forces modernization have, in short, added to the "armament norms" of the several formations but have not increased the nominal order of battle in terms of deployment on the ground. To put it another way, the present 20 divisions in Group of Soviet Forces Germany (GSFG) (one of which is an artillery division) have the capability of some 25 or 30 divisions of a decade ago. The most striking change has occurred within the motorized rifle division (Figure 2.10 and Figure 2.11), whose tank strength has recently increased from 188 to as many as 266 in some cases, bringing these motorized rifle divisions within measurable distance of a tank division proper. In addition, the organic tank battalion of a motorized rifle regiment now has 40 tanks, and an additional independent tank battalion in several of the motorized rifle divisions (MRDs) has more than 40 tanks.

Towed artillery in an MRD has increased from 105 to 165 pieces and in a tank division (Figure 2.12) from 36 to 70 pieces. Both divisions are incorporating self-propelled guns. The increase in multiple rocket launchers (MRLs) in divisions leaped from 192 tubes to 720. Both tank divisions and MRD's have increased manpower from 9,000 to 11,000 in the former and from 10,500 to 13,500 in the latter. Much of this is "self-correction" resulting from the perception of previous shortcomings in capability and performance. The MRD is now only a little behind the tank division in tank strength making the MRD a multi-purpose formation. The tank division has increased its artillery component for direct fire support and has added a rifle company to each tank regiment. Flank cover for the attacking column has also been increased, along with organic air defense and the defensive antitank component, reinforced by the antitank capability of the BMP itself.

	1967 MR REGIMENT	EARLY 1970s MR REGIMENT BTR-60	1976 MR REGIMENT BMP
PERSONNEL	1,800 (OFFICERS & MEN)	2,400	2,300
AFVS	3.T-54/55	40 T-62	40 T-72
PT-76	3	3	5
BMP	–	–	102
BTR-152	66	–	–
BTR-60	–	105	28
BRDM	10	34	28
ARTILLERY	NIL	18 122-MM TOWED	3 X 6 = 18 122-MM SP
MORTARS	9 82-MM	18 120-MM	
ORGANIC AIR DEFENSE	NIL	4 ZSU 23/4	4 ZSU 23/4 ALSO SA-8

Figure 2.10. Organizational Change: The Motorized-Rifle Regiment as an Example (1967-1977) General Evolution of the MR Regiment: (1967-1977)

For all the importance of these changes, which continue to increase "armament norms" the ground forces were benefited even more substantially by the major transformation resulting from the successful conclusion (from the Soviet standpoint) of the SALT-I and SALT-II agreements. Codifying strategic "parity" intensified Soviet interest in general purpose forces, whose function began to change in the new strategic environment. For the first time, the Soviet command could think of some degree of diversification as opposed to the highly specialized forces it had previously been obliged to assemble. Once again, the "fit" of the theater campaign with strategic war was reappraised and has produced for the first time something akin to an "independent" theater option involving a more extended phase of conventional operations, as well as theater nuclear war. It has led to the development of what Professor William van Cleave has called "various boundaries", all within a new-found Soviet flexibility and "a new confidence in their ability to prosecute war at various levels successfully, without escalation beyond the bounds consistent with Soviet political and strategic objectives".[19]

Professor van Cleave correctly points out the ambiguities in these concepts, for the Soviet command is presently treading unfamiliar ground. It is relevant to note that, after 1972, "received doctrine" within the Ground

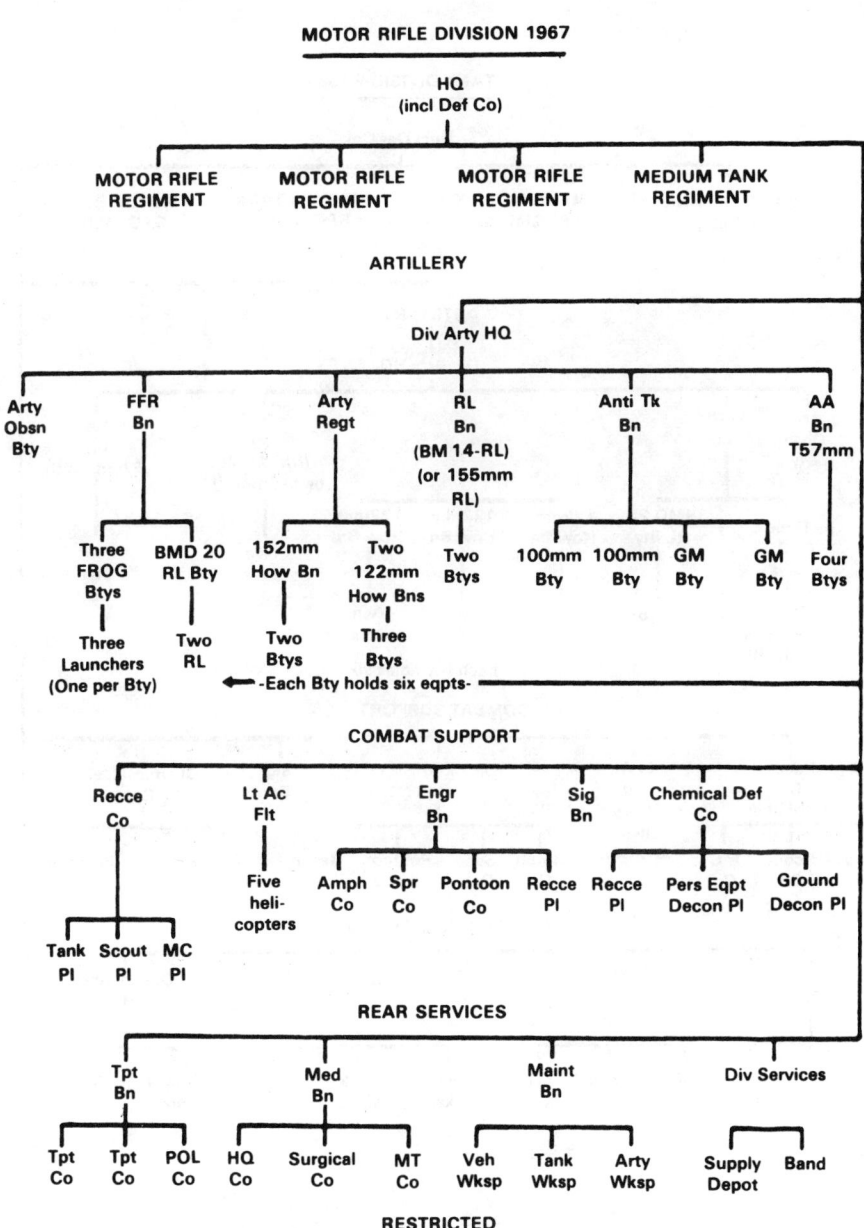

Figure 2.11. Motor Rifle Division 1967

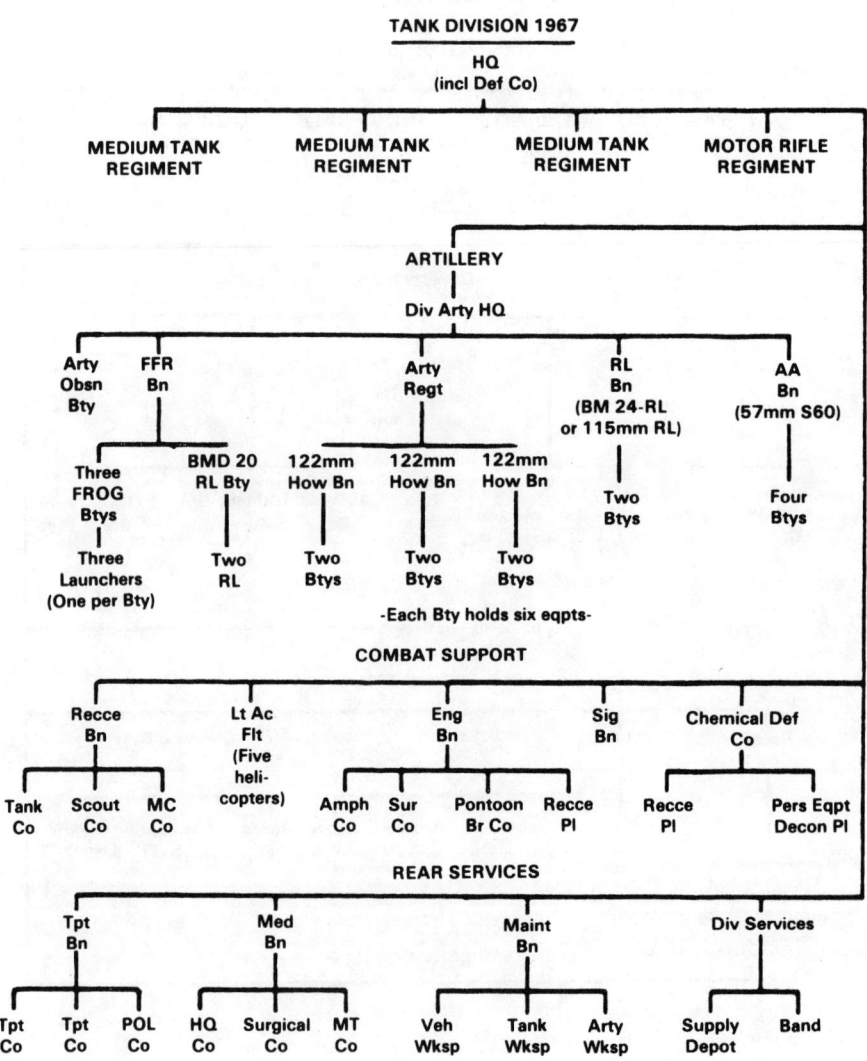

Figure 2.12. Tank Division 1967

Forces contemplated using conventional weapons only during the initial phase of operations and for some extended period. It did not envision a campaign conducted exclusively with conventional weapons but rather one opening in this mode, and the initial phase of operations has always been a critical consideration in Soviet military thinking. Conventional artillery holdings and ammunition stocks have been built up, the MRD has been strengthened so that it can be useful in first-echelon high-speed breakthrough operations, and advance rates have been more realistically adjusted to some 30 kilometers per 24-hour period in non- nuclear conditions and to 50 kilometers for nuclear operations.

The main objectives of a theater campaign in Europe are to destroy NATO's nuclear means and defense capabilities early, rapidly occupy a large area of NATO territory, and "seal off" Europe from its US ally. These objectives would apply under conditions of general war as well as in any "independent" campaign that was limited not by the weapons employed but by the the nature of its political goals. This is a return to the "hostage" concept vis-a-vis Europe, although in a positive mode, decoupled from major deterrence and limited by its political relevance to Europe alone. A hypothetical example might be the "enforcement" of nuclear-free zones in Europe.

SUSTAINABILITY-VIABILITY-ZHIVUCHEST'

Inevitably, the "long war/short war" controversy has reared its head again, both with respect to a general war and to any major theater campaign or to both in combination. In a sense, this has always been a circular argument for the proponents of substantial ground forces insisted that in either contingency, a short or a protracted war, a large force is necessary. However, the ground has shifted to a narrower appreciation of "sustained combat capability", or sustained combat viability, *zhivuchest'*, affecting both the strategic scene and the general purpose forces. Political propaganda apart, the Soviet command seems to be unsure that an initial Soviet missile strike on the United States would both disarm the opponent and cause the rapid collapse of capitalist society. A "more protracted" general war demands preparation for sustaining not only Soviet military capability but also the productive capability of Soviet society; hence, the offensive/defensive "mix", including large-scale civil defense measures. The ground forces have begun to examine their own "viability doctrine" afresh, planning for "sustained combat capability" in more extended operations instead of a short war of high-speed maneuvers, a revised approach that would be applicable to both the European and Far Eastern (China) theaters.

Soviet investigation of their own "armament norms" and their evaluation of "viability" has brought strategic forces into closer balance. One example will suffice. Using Soviet figures, it is apparent that a Soviet MRD committed to high-intensity operations would be completely expended after 5 days and anticipated loss rates of 20 to 30 percent per day in armored formations would greatly reduce their combat capability.

This review of the evolution of the ground forces, necessarily somewhat perfunctory, does, nevertheless, establish a certain framework. Excluding the immediate postwar demobilization phase (1946-1948), five main stages emerge: 1949-1954 (Stalin), 1955-1964 (Nuclear Study), 1965-1967 (Eclipse), 1967-1971 (Nuclearization), and 1972-1985 (Brezhnev). The last stage continued at least through the Andropov/Chernenko interregnum. When the new First Secretary, Gorbachev, has consolidated his authority, he may make changes. A generation younger than his predecessors (born in 1931), he did not participate in the revolution, the Civil War, the Finnish War of 1939-1940, or the Great Fatherland War (World War II). His attitude toward the military services has been formed in completely political surroundings, and the traditional tank-infantry, or nuclear-conventional relationships, may have new meanings. Each of these stages can be identified with a specific formulation of strategic policy, or a minor reappraisal of it, as in 1967-1970.

At each point the ground forces linked decisively with those policies: as a "deterrent" force in its own right in the late 1940s; as a nuclearized adjunct to strategic nuclear forces; as an increasingly important component in a "mix" of strategic/general purposes forces for waging and winning war at any weapons level; and, most recently, as the main instrument of a potential "independent" or decoupled theater campaign option in pursuit of prescribed political objectives (e.g., Afghanistan and Poland). The Ground Forces were at the very center of the persistent "long war/short war" controversy. Now, they are deeply involved in the urgent debate over developing "sustained combat capability" for all operational contingencies.

The Ground Forces always have participated in arguments over the "harmonious development" of the entire Soviet arsenal and military organization. The "combined arms" concept is now deeply rooted in the notion that such diversity is necessary for final victory if war continues much beyond the initial exchange. This does not deny a "decisive" role to the Strategic Missile Forces but it recognizes the indispensability of Ground Forces' capabilities. In sum, there is no reason to expect that the combined arms concept will be suddenly terminated. On the contary, we are now entering another phase of discussion of what kind of war the Soviet Union would wage and what provision it should make for sustained and diversified combat capability.

FORCE LEVELS AND FORCE STRUCTURES: DEPLOYMENT AND ORGANIZATION

How have the Ground Forces been deployed over the past three decades (short of military operations beyond Soviet-Warsaw Pact boundaries) in order to implement military policies? Deployment patterns are certainly only one part of the story. The little explored significance of modernization cycles, although they are highly relevant to Soviet views of operational-tactical requirements, is another. Nor should we ignore the overt political aspects of Soviet policy, particularly with respect to Europe, the Soviet Far East, and Central Asia (Afghanistan). The political utility of the Ground Forces is by no means unconnected with specific patterns of their deployment.

The postwar Stalinist period established at least one major principle of deployment: maintaining high minimum forces levels in the forward area in East Central Europe. In East Germany (DDR), GSFG has consistently maintained a force of some five to six field armies, with about 400,000 troops manning a minimum of 20 divisions (one is an artillery division), supported by a powerful tactical air arm (previously the 24th, then the 16th Air Army, and now the Front Air Forces, GSFG).[20] The present GSFG order of battle is laid out in the accompanying diagrammatic map (Figure 2.13). To this force must be added the several "Groups of Soviet Forces": the Northern in Poland; the Central, formerly in Austria, now in Czechoslovakia; and the Southern (Figure 2.14) in Hungary.

The early postwar deployment pattern gave the Soviet army a forward force of some 29 divisions, backed by 50 reserve divisions in western Russia. Another feature of the Stalinist period after 1946, however, was the deployment of Soviet forces not merely as occupation troops but also as covering troops throughout the length of a vastly extended perimeter. This "linear" deployment, much of it in pursuit of the specious theory of *aktivnaya oborona* (active defense) and rationalized on the grounds of Stalin's confidence in the superiority of the "permanently operating factors" in modern war, placed immense strain on Soviet resources. Undoubtedly, the physical presence of the Soviet Army in East Europe appreciably assisted in the process of implanting Communist regimes, an enormous political gain. Soviet military presence also was "legitimized" by the need for "lines of communications" troops stretching from the Soviet frontier to Berlin and Vienna. The only conspicuous failure occurred in Yugoslavia, where military coercion did not bring the dissidents to heel.

The rationale for this deployment pattern is not difficult to assess. Manning a protective belt covering the Soviet Union's western frontiers obviously made sense. It also reduced the possibility of serious disturbances in East Central Europe. It is apparent (if the "Kaplan papers" mean anything) that Stalin kept a wary eye on US military involvement in Europe and increasingly feared American-led consolidation of the European continent. At the same time, in view of the American nuclear monopoly, there was every reason to emphasize the Soviet Union's potent conventional force, to augment its "visibility", and to accompany this with continual assertions of the superiority of the Communist world's military- political ethos.

The modernization programs of the early 1950s certainly increased the mobility and firepower of the Ground Forces, particularly the formations in GSFG, but it had to wait for the advent of Khrushchev and the initial acts of his revised foreign policy to rationalize some Soviet policies. Treaty settlements were concluded with Austria and Finland, and in the Far East, exposed Soviet garrisons were reduced. The "state of war" with Germany was formally ended, thus also ending the occupation status of Soviet forces.

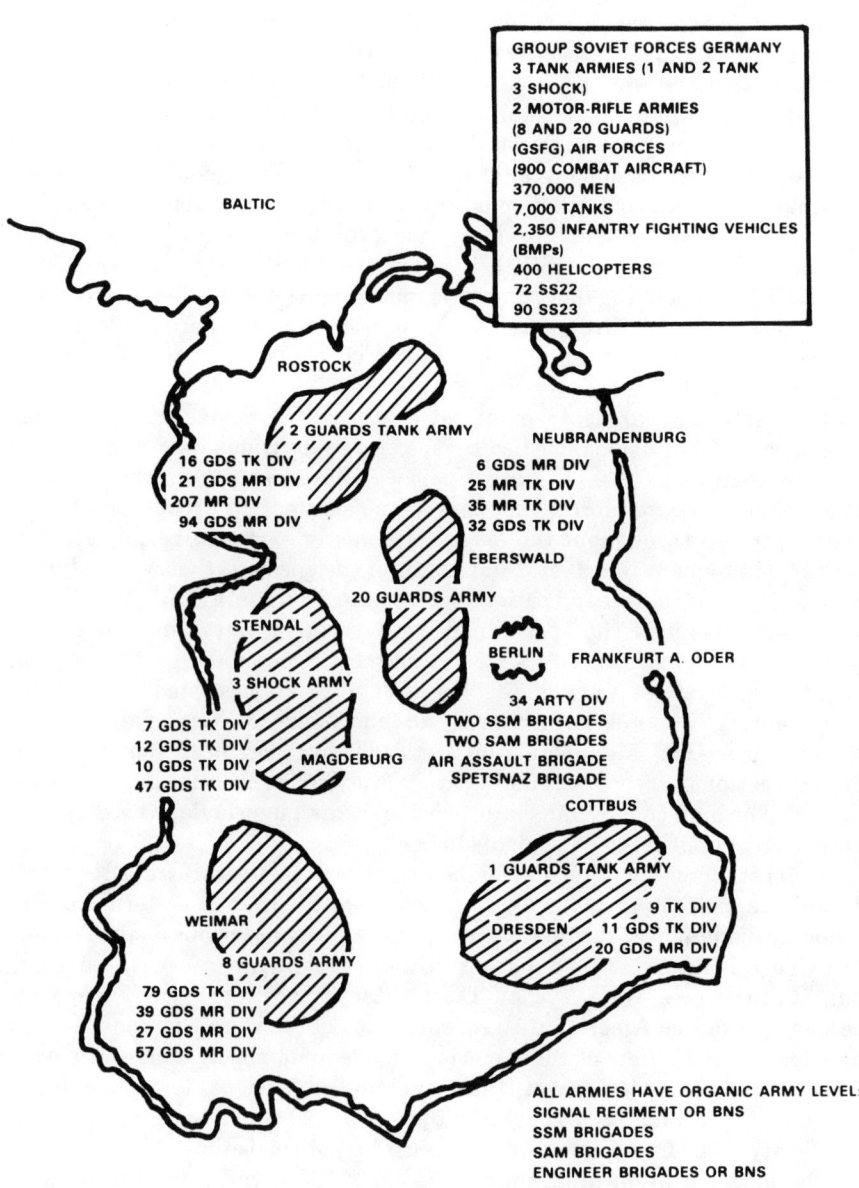

Figure 2.13. Soviet Forces in East Germany

FORCES ARE CONSTANTLY BEING IMPROVED AND REDEPLOYED -- THIS IS AN APPROXIMATION

	1ST ECHELON
GSFG	SEE MAP HQ ZOSSEN-WUENSDORF FIVE ARMIES, ONE ARTILLERY DIVISION, 19 DIVISIONS, AIR FORCES
NORTHERN GROUP (POLAND)	HQ (TRANSFERRED FROM LEGNICA) AN AIR ARMY OF THE SOVIET UNION AND TWO TANK DIVISIONS
CENTRAL GROUP (CZECHOSLOVAKIA)	HQ MILOVICE FIVE DIVISIONS AS FOLLOWS: AN MR & A TANK DIVISION, WESTERN GROUP 2 MR DIVISIONS AND A TANK DIVISION, EASTERN GROUP
SOUTHERN GROUP (HUNGARY)	HQ BUDAPEST AN AIR ARMY OF THE SOVIET UNION FOUR DIVISIONS AS FOLLOWS: 2 TANK DIVISIONS AND MR DIVISIONS
	2ND ECHELON
CARPATHIAN MILITARY DISTRICT	ONE ARTILLERY DIVISION 8TH TANK, 13, 38 ARMY WITH 13 DIVISIONS INCLUDING: 3 TANK DIVISIONS AND MR DIVISIONS
BALTIC MILITARY DISTRICT	TWO ARTILLERY DIVISIONS 11 GDS ARMY WITH TEN DIVISIONS INCLUDING: 3 TANK DIVISIONS 7 MR DIVISIONS AND AN AIRBORNE DIVISION
BELORUSSIAN MILITARY DISTRICT	ONE ARTILLERY DIVISION 7 TANK, 5 GDS TANK, 28 TANK ARMY WITH 12 DIVISIONS INCLUDING: 4 TANK DIVISION 3 MR DIVISIONS, AND AN AIRBORNE DIVISION

Figure.2-14. Distribution of Soviet Forces in Europe (1985): 1st and 2nd Echelons

Preparations were made for creation of the Warsaw Pact, legalizing Soviet military presence in Eastern Europe. The lines of communication, the Soviets conceded, were no longer justified. To compensate for this, the 10th Section of the General Staff, hitherto the supervisory agency for the bilateral treaty system and for East Germany, now worked on the military coordination implicit in the "Warsaw Pact". Theater warfare in Europe meanwhile retained its primacy in the allocation of Soviet resources, and the Zhukov modernization programs enhanced the mobility, firepower, and shock power of the Ground Forces in East Central Europe. With the withdrawal of Third Guards Tank Army[21] from GSFG in 1958, Soviet forces in East Germany took on a shape that they have retained basically to the present day. Marshal M. V. Zakharov, Commander in Chief of GSFG from 1957 to 1960, supervised these significant changes in the combat capability of this key command, building to some extent on the foundations laid by Marshal Grechko and his rigorous training program.

In mid-1961 the Berlin crisis reached a sudden climax when Khrushchev used the threat, and the visibility, of force to win his ends. Two Soviet armies, including 20th Guards were deployed to cover Berlin, and Marshal Koniev was most ostentatiously sent to assume temporary command of GSFG. In spite of Khrushchev's subsequent onslaught on the gigantism of the Ground Forces, the "nuclearization" of Soviet forces in Europe proceeded apace resulting among other things in a protracted dispute about the role of tactical aviation vis-a-vis the tactical battlefield missile. However, the development of growing tensions in the Sino-Soviet relationship intruded in the early 1960s to force a change in Soviet deployment patterns. Where force levels had been maintained since the 1950s with a meager 15 to 16 divisions committed to guarding a 4,000-mile Sino-Soviet frontier, an additional 30 divisions had to be deployed.

Much mystery attends the hiatus from 1964-1967 in the history of the Ground Forces. There is a certain irony in the fact that manpower, and possibly cost, rationalization introduced by the 1967 Law on Military Service should have coincided with over-extension resulting from commitments to both East and West. The Soviet invasion of Czechoslovakia in 1968, while a test of sorts for the newly emerged Ground Forces, added a further Group of Forces, the Central Group, to the pattern of forward deployment. Indeed, forward deployment was very much a problem since the Soviet Ground Forces filled the gap which had opened with the onset of the "Prague Spring" and finally deployed some five to six divisions in Czechoslovakia, thus straining both manpower resources and morale as admitted by Soviet officers. The eruption of armed clashes between the Russians and Chinese in the Far East came shortly after the Czechoslovak crisis and demanded reinforcement and reorganization in the Far East. Here was an echo of the situation of the 1930's, when the Red Army was heavily committed to both East and West. The immediate solution recalled the expedient of 1941; then the Far Eastern forces were strengthened by local mobilization in the eastern military districts (MDs) to hold troop levels constant.

Toward the end of the decade, Soviet conventional power was brandished in the face of China. It was used to cow the Czechs and to impose a military reoccupation reminiscent of 1956 in Hungary, and it established a military deployment pattern that persists to the present day. Some 27 Category I Soviet divisions were deployed in the East Central European staging area (GSFG, Central, and Northern Groups), supported by the immediate reserves in the Baltic and Belorussian MDs. In this connection the Carpathian MD should not be forgotten for it forms an important part of this provisional order of battle, as we shall see shortly. This deployment pattern was accompanied by a marked increase in the manpower of the Ground Forces during the 1970s and first half of the 1980s. Between 1970 and 1985 manpower increased from 1,450,000 to 1,900,000, a growth of nearly half a million.

Numbers by themselves, however, are not enough. Some exploration of quality as well as quantity is needed. The ground order of battle, unlike that of tactical air, has remained nearly static since 1969 to 1970 in East Central Europe, but both ground and air units have been "packed" with additional weapons and manpower so that by one German estimate the present 20 divisions (including 1 artillery division) of GSFG are the equivalent of 25 or 30 of decade or so ago. Out of the present tally of 199 divisions in the ground forces, 40 percent (80 divisions) are of Category I type--that is, maintained with upwards of 75 percent of their manpower and full war equipment, needing only to be "topped up" with specialists and support troops. Of this number, at least half are deployed forward in the European theater and are supported by 50 Category II divisions (formations with just over half their manpower, full "command staff" of officers, NCOs and specialists, and much of their war equipment) in Poland and European Russia. Thus, the Soviets are capable of fielding 105 fully manned divisions within a short period of time. Among these active-service divisions, a further 20 must be counted within the Far Eastern order of battle. Over the past decade, the number of divisions in that area has increased from 15 to a nominal 53, but an appreciable number are divisional headquarters staffs and probably would fall in the Category III type, with many tanks stored and equipment inferior to that of the Category I and II formations in European Russia and Eastern Europe.

The deployment pattern throughout the 16 military districts of the USSR, assumes the shape of a lopsided dumbbell. The main strike force is poised in East Central Europe (with five divisions in Southern Group of Forces in Hungary), a mix of 14 MRDs and 16 tank divisions. The Carpathian MD, which plays a key role as a military junction and reinforcement pool that can provide rapid movement to follow up Central Group as it moves forward, has a strength of 11 divisions (eight MRDs and three tank divisions). The Baltic MD to the north has ten motorized rifle divisions and one airborne division. The Leningrad MD reaches into the northern flank with 10 divisions (eight of them MRD's) and an airborne division. The three prestigious MDs of European Russia, Belorussia, Moscow, and Kiev, have almost 30 divisions among them, 10 in Belorussia including an airborne division, seven in Moscow, and 12 in Kiev. Moscow and Kiev, however, have a high proportion of guards formations which do not seem to redeploy on any scale, and the

Belorussian MD serves mainly as reinforcement strength available to forces deployed forward.

Moving south, the dumbbell bulges somewhat, with the Odessa and Caucasian MD's maintaining a strength of 26 divisions, including quite strong tank forces, airborne troops, and artillery divisions. These impressive forces not only secure a vital staging area for Middle East support, but also Soviet preoccupation with "local adversaries". The Turkestan MD with its nine divisions, including an airborne division and a tank division, must be considered totally preoccupied with the Afghan problem.[22] The stem of the dumbbell is provided by the two hinterland MD's, Volga and Ural, which act as central reserve with six divisions, three in each MD.

The other counterbalancing weight is along the eastern border, four MDs (Central Asian, Siberian, TransBaikal and Far Eastern) plus a Soviet force deployed forward in Outer Mongolia. The grand total for these Soviet forces in the East is 52 to 53 divisions, a nominal order of battle made up of seven divisions in the Central Asian MD, four divisions in the Siberian MD, nine in the TransBaikal MD, and 22 in the Far Eastern MD, with at least two MRDs and a tank division deployed forward in Outer Mongolia. The Far Eastern MD force consists of 19 MRDs, two tank divisions, and an airborne division.[23] Including the TransBaikal MD, this gives only four to five tank divisions in the order of battle facing China. There has been a steady movement toward permanent garrisoning of the Far East, a long-term policy recommended by Marshal Zakharov during the crisis days of 1969.

An examination of the Soviet pattern of deployment shows at least considerable strain on Ground Forces' resources if not over-commitment. Assuming that MD forces in the reinforcement and frontier areas are already earmarked for operational tasks, not more than a dozen divisions from the 104 to 105 formations that are in a reasonable state of readiness are excess to operational requirements at the present. The 64 Category III divisions vary appreciably in their availability for mobilization, ranging from those maintaining the standard one-third of manning with a full complement of weapons and vehicles to others with little more than skeleton staffing. This point may be clarified by looking at first echelon forces available to the Soviet command. Assuming an in-place unreinforced attack, the forward-deployed forces in East Central Europe could field 20 divisions from GSFG (including the artillery division) with 370,000; 7,000 main battle tanks (many of them new T-72s and T-80s), 2,350 modern infantry combat vehicles, and 400 helicopters for assault landings and fire support. The Front (GSFG) Air Forces would come to full strength at 1,200 aircraft, topped up with light bombers and reconnaissance elements, without the need now for extensive preattack marshaling. Linked with the Central Group, GSFG could field about 200 battalion-size combat groups providing the resources for some eight to ten breakthrough sectors and at least one corps-size Operational Maneuver Group (OMG).

This is the measure of the Soviet effort to "compress" maximum fire- and shock-power into its forward-deployed formations, using Category I and topped-up Category II divisions as an immediate reserve for the first assault echelons. Nominal order of battle has hardly changed since 1968-1969, but internal reorganization has increased firepower considerably. The reduction of support elements to a minimum enables a Soviet motorized rifle division to field 18 maneuver battalions for a divisional strength of a little more than 13,000. However, not much more can be squeezed from the lemon and optimization has probably been achieved. Significant changes now pending in the area of logistics support are shifting the emphasis from heavy breakthrough fighting to sustaining protracted operations in both the European and Far Eastern theaters.

ALLIANCE COHESION AND MILITARY INTEGRATION: THE WARSAW PACT

Optimization may well be only part of the Soviet goal. Military integration within the Socialist alliance system is also of major importance for Soviet policy as a whole, and here the Soviet Ground Forces have a major role.

The Ground Forces (with select air elements) provide the preponderance of military muscle within the Warsaw Pact. But how important is the Warsaw Pact to the Soviet Union and what contribution does it make to overall Soviet capabilities? Essentially, the Warsaw Pact does not of itself guarantee Soviet security interests in East Central Europe. These interests are anchored in a complex network of bilateral mutual assistance treaties, not only between the Soviet Union and Warsaw Pact members but also with non-Soviet states. Since the 1949 to 1953 period, the Soviet Union has pursued a form of military multilateralism, albeit in very limited form and with continuing attention to the general expansion of the indigenous non-Soviet military establishments. The first step in the process of attaining Warsaw Pact adherence to Soviet patterns of organization, equipment, tactics, and training, was much assisted by the presence of large Soviet military missions and by the introduction of Soviet-trained Army officers (their non-Soviet names and origins notwithstanding) to senior command posts, all under the eagle eye of the Soviet General Staff, with its special section for East Germany.

Sovietization produced considerable strains within these diverse establishments, which had been coupled by Nazi Germany into the status of enemy. "The liberal attitude towards bourgeois military theory" obviously hid a multitude of sins, even as the steady re-equipment of these non- Soviet forces resulted in numerically impressive military establishments-- something on the order of 1.5 million men. Although there was close Soviet supervision, the Soviets made few attempts at integration, save for some preparatory work in the air defense field, which demands a degree of integration in order to function in an effective manner. After 1953 a Communized officer corps came into greater prominence in the East European armies, and Russified Poles, not to mention Rokossovskiy himself, held the reins in Poland.[24] In May 1955 the Warsaw Pact came into existence. This formal alliance system established, in theory at least, a joint command and a political consultative committee. Senior Soviet Ground Forces officers continued to occupy the top command positions, from Marshal Koniev up to Marshal Kulikov or his successor at the present time.

Military relations between the Soviet Union and its East European allies is a highly complex and controversial subject, further complicated by the risings of 1956 in Hungary, the invasion of Czechoslovakia in 1968, and the turbulence in Poland in 1981. But in general, save for those who perceive a dire threat to national existence, the East European military elites have remained consistently loyal to Moscow. Both the bilateral treaties and the Warsaw Pact itself are designed to circumvent any true national control of national armies. The political control devices under general Soviet direction reinforce Soviet domination.[25]

One particular feature outside formal treaty arrangements and the devices of political control was the personal relationships established by virtue of shared wartime experience between Soviet and East European senior officers. In the postwar period there was, as a result, a small coterie of senior officers who could work together with some empathy and a sense of shared aims, which was destroyed when the Soviets invaded Czechoslovakia.

After 1955 the Soviet military assistance program grew apace and included a carefully controlled but extensive program of indigenous military production on a "division of labor" principle, an arms cartel of distinctive proportions. The modernization program, which brought in more major items of Soviet equipment, was accompanied in the late 1950s by a planned reduction of manpower. The result was a recognizably modern total order of battle of some 53 divisions within the participant non-Soviet countries.

The Warsaw Pact, in a political sense, lay inert for most of its first decade. It was the Soviet High Command, Grechko himself, who began to insist on a more positive form of military integration. Only when Khrushchev's attempts at politico-economic integration using the mechanism of the Council for Mutual Economic Assistance (COMECON), failed, did he, too, look more attentively at closer military cooperation as a promising avenue to his political ends. In the early 1960s, the East European military establishments were further modernized with the new T-54 and T-55 battle tanks, modern artillery, and improved tactical aircraft (MIG-21s and SU-7s), as well as short-range battlefield missiles minus nuclear warheads. What could be called the "re-professionalization" of the East European officer corps also began with a certain amount of Soviet help. The non-Soviet elements of the Warsaw Pact began to move into the "northern tier", East Germany, Poland, and Czechoslovakia, and the "southern tier", including Bulgaria and Rumania. Of immediate operational importance was the consolidation of the air defense systems, which in 1964 were publicly identified as coming under the command of a Soviet air commander, Chief Marshal of Aviation Sudets, Commander-in-Chief of *PVO Strany*, National Air Defense. That arrangement remains in effect.[26]

With the support of Grechko, joint Soviet/non-Soviet military exercises began in 1961 and have now assumed considerable importance in both military and political contexts. Although the modernization program had introduced tactical missiles, this did not prove to be the prelude to nuclear sharing, either in principle or in practice. The Soviet nuclear hegemony remained, and still remains, inviolate. Continuing joint exercises, command conferences, and the work of the Soviet military missions with the various national establishments nevertheless encouraged Soviet interest in building up the military effectiveness and promoting the military efficiency of the Pact's northern tier.

The evolution of the Warsaw Pact military establishments provides some clue to present Soviet policy. During the 1960s the Soviets seemed to repose a certain faith in integrated military capabilities. The total number of East European divisions (taking the northern and southern tiers together) reached 62 in the second half of the 1960s, with 35 divisions located in the northern tier. Well over half of the available combat aircraft (1,700 of 2,400) were East European, and naval forces were contributed by Poland and East Germany with its light surface combat units. By the mid-1960s the combat capability of some 30 to 40 East European divisions may have been raised to something approaching Soviet standards. This was probably the heyday of Soviet enthusiasm for fuller military integration. It was followed by what might best be described as "selective integration", not merely by national contingents but by particular national formations.

In the ensuing years, from 1968-69 to the present, the Soviet command and the Soviet political leadership have steered a careful course between re-structuring the Pact on selective lines as the East Germans prescribed, and a return to the bilateralism of earlier years. What may be described as "selective integration" was the result of balancing the requirements of Soviet theater force effectiveness with certain promising tendencies in non-Soviet Pact military establishments. This was accompanied by a cosmetic change in Warsaw Pact organization which gave the appearance of affording non-Soviet Pact members a greater share in the management of Warsaw Pact affairs in order to "further perfect the structure and command organizations".

It is important to remember in this context that the Warsaw Pact has neither an operational command organization nor a mobilization system. It is essentially an administrative organization to supervise peacetime routines and training. How then does it work? The Soviet chain of command does not exist in any formal sense, but it would be naive to suppose that the Ground Forces have not addressed this problem. Both the organization of the Groups of Forces and the Warsaw Pact are peacetime administrative entities, incompatible with the highly centralized operational direction envisaged by Soviet doctrine. Nominal order of battle means less than appears on paper; the key lines in the General Staff "battle staffs" assigned to shadow operational groupings could be "combined battle groups" included in non-Soviet formations. The *TVD, Teatr Voyennikh Deystviy* (Theater of Military Activities) is the basis of organization for combat.

Under selective integration the Soviet command could count on earmarked non-Soviet Warsaw Pact formations without recourse to full mobilization. Three tank divisions, three MRDs, the Polish airborne division and the marine brigade from the Polish nominal OB of fifteen divisions; four Czechoslovak divisions from the nominal OB of ten divisions; and the six East

German divisions would be available and could be "corseted" within the Soviet formations and retained to repel a "counterattack" on Berlin. For the thrust along the Baltic, a Front could come under the command of a Polish general utilizing a "combined battle group" of Soviet-Polish troops with some East German support from specialists. Aside from these special formations, the Polish army has a markedly "defensive" look both in deployment and equipment. It has the T-72 tank but does not have the T-80 for prestige reasons. The Polish army and air force do seem to receive most-favored-nation treatment from the Soviet Union, much to the annoyance of the East Germans and a certain derision on the part of the Czechs.[27]

Select Czech ground formations could be used for a limited time with the first echelon as expendable elements until Carpathian MD forces had fully taken over from Central Group Soviet divisions, a process taking two to three days. Non-Soviet Warsaw Pact air elements, in cooperation with Soviet Air Defense (PVO) operations, would be used primarily in the defensive role. It appears that some Polish air force units have been committed to ground-attack/ground-support roles[28] perhaps to replace the Czechoslovak regiments that had earlier been earmarked for this purpose. Polish naval aviation as well as surface and submarine units would presumedly come under the operational command of the Soviet Commander/Baltic Fleet.

This system would enable the Soviet command to judge more precisely which non-Soviet commanders and their staffs they might rely on for "combined battle groups". The persistent "socialist emulation" or "socialist competition" pressures also enable the command to have a better idea of how well-trained and operationally ready are the various formations and units. "Deployment by exercise" would not be difficult under these circumstances and would eliminate the need for extensive mobilization procedures. The "in-place, unreinforced offensive" could be managed in a similar style should circumstances so warrant.

Some evidence to support the existence of this type of deployment/mobilization pattern is supplied by the reported presence of various Warsaw Pact "Fronts", which shadow wartime organization with regional headquarters and Army staffs, including three in Poland, and two in Czechoslovakia. The "first echelon" could operate with three "Front" staffs: (1) GSFG and Northern Group, (2) the Southwestern Front (Central Group and Czechoslovakia HQ Tabor),[29] and (3) the "Danube Front" using Soviet Southern Group[30] elements for flank cover and even westerly operations. What additional changes Marshal Kulikov, the Warsaw Pact Commander-in-Chief, will institute in the organization and operational readiness of the Pact we do not know; but, already he has supervised the dramatic modernization described and has suggested that a greater effort must be made to revitalize military doctrine in the Pact and to develop doctrine more closely tailored to indigenous requirements. The Soviet Minister of Defense, Marshal Sergei Sokolov, has also made his tours of inspection. Inspection tours, of course, signify little or nothing, but there is no doubt of continuing Soviet interest in maintaining certain levels of military viability in the Warsaw Pact, in retaining control of its military mechanism, and in persisting with a variety of control devices that keep national control out of national hands. This is so even if "supranationalism" has not quite succeeded. In any event, Marshal Sokolov's latitude for real improvement is probably somewhat limited. His main contribution may well be to speed up and intensify the professionalization of the various non-Soviet military establishments. Particularly is his latitude limited by Marshal Ogarkov's authority in the TVD and his avowed intentions to improve readiness even further!

NOTES

1.   The designation *Raboche-Krestyanskaya Krasnaya Armiya, RKKA*, The Red Army (and the general abbreviation of *Krasnaya Armiya*), spanned the years 1918-1946. The term Soviet Army, *Sovyetskaya Armiya, SA*, was introduced in 1946, the postwar reorganization defining three branches (*vid*) of the Soviet Armed Forces: the Ground Forces (*Sukhoputniye voyska*), Air Force (*Voyenno-vozdushniye sily*) and Navy (*Voyenno-morskoy flot*). It is worth noting that "Soviet Army" is frequently used to denote the Soviet Armed Forces at large.

2.   The first tank armies (with "mixed" establishments, including rifle troops) were raised between May 1942-January 1943. The 5th Tank Army in this phase was twice constituted -- in May 1942 and again in August 1942. The first of the "homogeneous" tank armies (comprising tank and mechanized corps) was the 2nd Tank Army raised on January 28, 1943, followed two days later by the 1st Tank Army. The last of these tank armies, the 6th, was established in January 1944.

3.   The mechanized corps was made up of two tank divisions and one motorized division: the tank division of two tank and one motorized rifle regiment; the motorized division two motorized rifle and one tank regiment.

4.   RAG: regimental artillery groups; DAG: divisional artillery group.

5.   Equipped primarily with the IL-2 Shturmovik but later with some lendlease US aircraft. To this day Soviet air marshals remember the P-39, Bell "Airacobra," which they used to devastating effect in the ground attack role.

6.   We urgently need a study of the immediate postwar history of the Soviet military establishment, not least to establish these disputed figures.

7.   This includes also cavalry and airborne formations.

8.   The German military intelligence figures for August 1944 cite a total of 510 rifle divisions, 109 infantry brigades, 173 tank brigades, and 129 air divisions. See the comprehensive study, *Truppen-Uebersicht und Kriegs Gliederung: Rote Armee* and also *SU Fliegertruppe*, February 1944.

9.   The total Soviet establishment, according to Western estimates, amounted to some 4,000,000 to 5,000,000 (plus 400,000-600,000 security troops): the Ground Forces were set at between 2.5 and 4.5 million men, and how the Ground Forces could nearly equal in number the entire Soviet establishment seems something of a mystery. It is obvious that these figures

need some rigorous re-working, if only to accommodate the Air Force and the Navy.

10. Airborne forces were subordinated in June 1946 directly to the Armed Forces Ministry, with parachute and air-landing (glider) elements forming airborne brigades and select rifle divisions.

11. As Soviet sources point out, the rifle regiment now included a battery of six SU-76 SP guns. Otherwise the rifle regiment consisted of 3 rifle battalions (1,688 men), with a total strength of 2,106 men, 194 vehicles, 27 82mm mortars, and 1,263 rifles.

12. This was at the insistence of M.I. Nedelin, Chief of Staff/Soviet Artillery, who selected the best artillery specialists from wartime days and particular Guards mortar regiments to form further "missile units," as well as setting up a special staff to study the problems of organization and operational use for the new weapons.

13. While the Soviet Union assiduously fostered this sense of preponderance, the so-called "Kaplan papers" refer to actual planning in 1951 for a "pre-emptive offensive" against Europe in order to forestall the consolidation of American power. This can be connected with the upheavals in the Soviet command and the displacement of Shtemenko, whose competence was called into question when drawing up major offensive plans. This is a highly complex story which needs much more investigation, but the Ground Forces were at the center of the furor.

14. Also translated as "forward detachments", or "advanced detachments", or even "spearheads". See Capt. Stephen Shervals, Jr., USAF, "'Forward Detachments and the Soviet Nuclear Offensive", Military Review, April 1979, pp. 66-71.

15. This is to assume that the 1948 figure for the Soviet military establishment was, in fact, correct at 2,874,000 men.

16. "The anti-nuclear maneuver stands out separately among the known forms of maneuver as the newest form of maneuver, consisting of organized movements of troops to take them out of range of the enemy's nuclear attack and give them freedom to perform their missions", Maneuver in Modern Land Warfare, p. 35.

17. Note the two terms, *vstrechniy boy* and *vstrechnoe srazheniye*, the former tactical (and comparable to the hasty attack), the latter at the operational level (Armies, Fronts). The tactics rely upon rapid deployment from the line of march with artillery and antitank reserves well forward, providing a firm fire base, the object being to deploy and defeat the enemy before he can deploy his forces into attack formation.

18. The mid-1960s also are distinguished by a burst of important publications on Ground Forces organization and operation, confirmation of a kind that even when this branch was in "suspended animation", there was furious activity behind the scenes.

19. Laurence L. Whetten, The Future of Soviet Military Power (New York: Crane-Rusak, 1976), pp. 66ff.

20. Twenty divisions, counting the 34th Guards Artillery Division stationed at Potsdam. While the 6th Guards Tank Division had not, in 1985,

been replaced in Luther's town of Wittenberg, the total number of troops in Soviet occupied Germany has remained nearly constant since 1976.

21. <u>Not</u> Third Shock Army--Third Guards Tank Army went to cadre status in 1957-58 and left GSFG in the early 60s.

22. Best estimate of forces in Afghanistan in early 1985--an Army headquarters 3 MRD, 1 Abn Div and an additional MRD equivalent, approximately 2 Air Assault Bde equivalent--appears in "Afghanistan Forces: How Many Soviets are There?" <u>Jane's Defence Weekly</u>, 22 June 1985.

23. Plus two artillery divisions at Slavyanka and Polrovka.

24. The study, *Marszalek dwoch narodow,* Warsaw, 1976.

25. Christopher D. Jones, <u>The Warsaw Pact: A Political or Military Alliance</u>? Airlie House Conference, April 1977.

26. With the recent reorganization of Soviet Air Defense forces, the organization of Warsaw Pact Air Defense is not yet clear. See further discussion Chapter 5.

27. It is too early to predict the effect of Soviet reaction to the Polish trade unions' efforts at freedom with the now banned Solidarity movement.

28. The Polish Air Force received the SU-20/SU-17 before other Pact air forces.

29. See the important discussion of Southern Group by Graham H. Turbiville, "Warsaw Pact Force in Hungary: A Key Element in Pact Contingency Planning", <u>Rusi Journal</u>, December 1976, pp. 47-51, suggesting an operational role in a southerly thrust through Austria. Southern Group strength presents something of a problem, for it does vary, but what has been seen of the Soviet divisions in Hungary suggests that most are near Category I establishments or could be very rapidly brought up to that strength.

30. These would operate, presumably, under the Western Theater of Military Operations (*Teatr Voyennikh Deistviy - TVD*).

Chapter 3
Soviet Operational Procedures

"In the land theaters, the mission of the armed conflict will be resolved primarily by the offensive", says Marshal Sokolovskiy.[1] The Soviets consider the offensive the basic form of combat action, playing a decisive role in achieving victory. The aim of the offensive is complete destruction of the enemy in the shortest possible time and the occupation of his vital regions. The Soviets recognize defense only as something the enemy does, or as a temporary local measure to prepare a successful offensive. How the nation and the armed forces will be readied for war and how they will carry on the offensive are the subjects of Soviet military doctrine, science, art, and tactics.

DOCTRINE

Soviet military doctrine represents the officially accepted views on the nature of contemporary wars, the use of armed forces, and the requirements for war preparedness.

Soviet military doctrine specifies the structure of the Soviet armed forces, allocates industrial resources and output, and orients research and development to support armed forces. The two essential components of military doctrine are political and military-technical. Military doctrine is the blueprint drawn up by the highest Soviet political leaders that specifically describes the shape and utilization of the armed forces. Military doctrine also governs the component of military science called "military art", or the theory of the art of war.

Military science studies the theory of the organization of the armed forces, military geography, military history, the theory of training, military technical science, and military art in order to develop war-fighting ability at three levels: strategic, operational, and tactical.

The strategic level of military art, as developed by military science, applies at a global, national, or theater level (*teatr voyni-TV*). The General Staff plans and directs two forms of strategic military operations: strategic-global and strategic groupings of operational (*operativniye*) formations. The strategic level is manifested in campaigns phased by objectives and time.

The objectives of each phase are met by simultaneous and successive operations.

At the operational level, that is, operational formations of Fronts and Armies, a Front is the basic formation, and an Army is the basic combined arms formation. In a campaign, operational art governs the preparation and conduct of operations at the level of Fronts and Armies within a Theater of Military Operations (*teatr voyennykh deystviy – TVD*). In the Soviet view, operational art is the basis of military art. Operational art is the connective link between strategy and tactics operating within the requirements of strategy. It determines the means of preparing for and conducting operations to achieve strategic aims. It also provides the initial data for tactics--organizing for the preparation and conduct of battle.

At the tactical level, which is below the Army, combat activity is by large tactical units, which are divisions (*soyedineniye*), regiments (*chast'*), and tactical subunits, battalion or smaller size (*podrazdeleniye*). Military tactics govern the conduct of combat within an operation at the divisional level and below.

Two recent authoritative books on Soviet tactical doctrine have reinforced the Soviet position that the maneuver battalion is the basic tactical unit on a nuclear or conventional battlefield.[2] In the first book (a Frunze Military Academy text), Sverdlov, writing principally on battalion-level tactics, expects maneuver to be used to exploit nuclear strikes. Maneuver to the Soviets includes not only the movement of personnel and equipment but also the movement of firepower, both nuclear and conventional. He directed his attention to a Western European environment, and the rapid maneuver advocated was basically vehicular rather than dismounted, executed by forward detachments and tactical airborne forces landed by helicopter.

The second Frunze Military Academy book (Reznichenko's replacement for his 1966 text) is a manual for the reinforced motorized rifle or tank battalion operating on an independent mission. Helicopters, automated troop control systems, tactical airborne landings, electronic warfare, and night operations were mentioned repeatedly. Normal battalion attachments are listed as artillery, mortars, AT/AA weapons, and engineers.

PRINCIPLES OF SOVIET MILITARY ART – DOCTRINE

> The principles of the military art are historical. They change both in content and form with a change of condition and character of armed struggle. Principles born of former conditions lose their meaning and new ones appear in their place . . . the diversity of conditions in conducting combined arms combat is responsible for the variety of its principles.[3]

In Soviet literature varying lists of principles pertaining to military art, in general, and tactical doctrine, in particular, are presented. General Reznichenko's comment echoes other Soviet remarks that such listings are always subject to change because of the ongoing "revolution in military affairs." One such set of principles became somewhat standardized after the potential impact of nuclear weapons had been considered by Soviet military scientists.[4] These seven principles are said to be applicable to all combat--strategic, operational, and tactical. They are:

(1) Mobility and High Tempo of Combat Operations: The basic requirement is to achieve and sustain rapid movement of combat forces. The principle includes battlefield mobility of maneuver forces, maneuverability of fire support, and mobility of logistics elements.

To the Soviets, the principle also implies any action that might contribute to rapid accomplishment of the mission.

High tempo is the relentless prosecution of an operation without pause and is particularly critical on the nuclear battlefield. Applying constant pressure will keep the enemy off balance and prevent his forming an effective defense. Additionally, it will allow maximum effectiveness in exploiting the effects of one's own nuclear strikes.

(2) Concentration of Efforts. This principle applies in two major areas: the deliberate attack, and tactical employment of artillery.

An essential feature of the deliberate attack is the concentration of troops and weapons on relatively small frontages to achieve superiority at the point of attack. Note, however, that concentration for this type of attack is a carry-over from World War II tactics, and, in the present view, a deliberate attack would only be used when success of a hasty attack cannot be foreseen. One should recognize, however, that deliberate attack is almost inevitably more costly in men and equipment. Also, any concentration for attack requires additional time for planning and execution, must result in some loss of momentum, and may violate requirements for nuclear survivability.

(3) Surprise and Security. Considered from the strategic viewpoint, surprise may be achieved through integrated plans for military, political, and psychological operations. Tactical surprise comes from undertaking an action when and where least expected. It is not considered essential that the enemy be taken wholly unaware--only that he become aware too late to react effectively. The Soviets consider security to be an integral part of surprise, and they go to great lengths to ensure the security of their plans and operations.

(4) Combat Activeness. This is in effect the principle of the offensive and is expressed in terms of boldness and decisiveness in all combat operations. The major objective of this principle is the constant attempt to seize and maintain the initiative. The attack basis of the principle is carried over to defensive operations in which the Soviet defender will hold large tank elements in reserve for the inevitable counterattack and resumption of the offensive.

(5) Preservation of the Combat Effectiveness of Friendly Forces. This principle refers not only to conserving fighting strength through the use of sophisticated combat vehicles equipped with chemical and nuclear protection devices, but to a medical system geared to

returning casualties to combat rapidly. From the point of view of staff planning, it is using the minimum forces necessary to accomplish a specific task.

(6) Conformity of the Goal. The goal or purpose of an operation must conform realistically to the actual combat situation. The goal is taken from the combat mission received from the senior commander, which is the starting point for developing a concept of operations.

Clarification of the combat goal is a vital element in Soviet troop-leading procedures at all levels. The importance of clarification is determined by its central role in the entire process of fulfilling the decision of the higher commanders. A commander is guided from initial data to the final solution--finding the most appropriate type of action in a given situation. A commander may seek clarification of the orders even while the senior commander is giving the order. In any case, he must completely understand the goal of the senior commander and, in particular, his concept. The commander must know the enemy positions or fire means, which will be destroyed or suppressed by the senior commander in support of his unit. The conclusions of a commander, based on this clarification, form the basis for his own decisions. Clarification, of course, must not interfere with his own analysis of the situation.

Since a realistic estimate of the situation is the basis for applying the principle, the Soviets warn against two hazards. The first is overestimating friendly forces and underestimating the enemy. This leads to the assignment of impossible missions. The second is underestimating friendly forces and overestimating the enemy. This leads to losing an opportunity to defeat the enemy. A combat mission invariably carries interrelated elements:

(a) Destruction or capture of enemy personnel;
(b) Seizure or destruction of his combat means; and
(c) Seizure of terrain held by the enemy. (The defeat of the enemy and seizure of terrain are considered to make up a single interrelated process.)

The mission must be completed at the time prescribed. Even though the enemy may be defeated and the terrain taken, the mission is not successful if its completion is delayed.

(7) Coordination. Coordination allows rapid exploitation of success and the effects of nuclear strikes, in particular. It requires the coordination of commanders, not only in planning the initial attack but in carrying through to the depths of enemy defenses. In the Soviet army, all elements of the combined arms and services operate together in battle. Coordination of effort entails reviewing the strong and weak points of combat and supporting units, mutual assistance between these and adjacent units, and continuous teamwork for the duration of battle. If this coordination is destroyed, subordinate commanders are

expected to assume the initiative. They must in that case act without orders to regain contact with adjacent units or headquarters and coordinate ongoing action.

SUMMARY OF PRINCIPLES

Soviet military principles have a degree of flexibility because they can be amended to reflect current conditions. As stated by Colonel Savkin,[5] "Principles are formulated by people as a result of perception of reality." The current enumeration of principles has been influenced by three stages of development of Soviet armed forces: the Stalin "mold", the Zhukov "face lift", and the Khrushchev "new look".

The Stalin mold involved developments based on war experiences, including considerations for adding more sophisticated conventional equipment to improve mobility and firepower. Under Zhukov, emphasis shifted to training for more realistic nuclear conditions. Khrushchev's new look meant that a contemporary war would be fought with both conventional weapons and weapons of mass destruction. Brezhnev did not visibly alter Soviet military principles although he was responsible for extensive growth and modernization during his long tenure.

As discussed in the previous chapter, nuclear weapons had a considerable effect on the organization and tactics of the Ground Forces and the strategy employed by the Soviet government. The Soviets view nuclear, chemical, and biological armaments as weapons of mass destruction. They have demonstrated capabilities to employ nuclear and chemical weapons and the potential for biological munitions. Military literature emphasizes nuclear weapons. Limited open discussion of chemical warfare, concerned almost entirely with protective measures, is misleading. Soviet military forces are the best equipped in the world for the use of gas, including its offensive employment in exercises. Biological warfare is dismissed in the Soviet Military Dictionary with "bacteriological warfare is forbidden by international law and is condemned by all progressive mankind". There is, however, convincing evidence that the Soviets have used both chemical and biological agents in Afghanistan and Southeast Asia.[6]

Since the use of nuclear and chemical weapons does not eliminate the simultaneous use of conventional weapons, the term "complementary warfare" describes a situation in which both conventional weapons and weapons of mass destruction are employed. Soviet tactical doctrine assumes that tactical operations will take place on a nuclear battlefield, or on one that may become nuclear at any time. When conditions of complementary warfare are anticipated, there will be different force requirements, rates of advance, and depths of objectives. The need to anticipate complementary warfare requires consideration of the material basis of battles; that is, the availability of highly sophisticated equipment, arms, and armaments. With a modern array of such materials, specifically weapons of mass destruction, tactical principles and procedures must be refined to consider their employment.

Several refinements are pertinent:

(1) Force balances. In past wars, the numerical relation of opposing forces in a particular sector could be changed only by a slow process of providing more men and equipment. Weapons of mass destruction can now bring a sudden change of great magnitude in the balance. Their use can change ratios of forces and means on any axis of advance and to the entire depths of the enemy's dispositions.
(2) Mobility. Dynamic changes in force correlation bring a new meaning to the mobility now held by exploiting forces. High rates of advance are promoted when enemy fires can be reliably suppressed by weapons of mass destruction. The ability of Soviet combat vehicles to move through contaminated areas, using collective filtration protective systems, and the increased emphasis on use of air-landed forces in the combat areas enhance this capability.
(3) Preservation of Troop Combat Effectiveness. Formerly considered routinely as one of the commander's duties, preservation of troop combat effectiveness is elevated to the status of a principle in view of the potential for sudden huge losses of personnel. Tactics must be adjusted to reduce the risk of instantaneous disabling of major troop elements and loss of fundamental organizational structure.
(4) Concentration of Effort. The principle is necessarily changed in interpretation and application. Potential nuclear attacks by the enemy make concentration, in its old sense, inadmissible. At the same time, the availability of friendly nuclear strikes reduces the requirement for massive artillery formations. Greatly improved troop mobility (especially large quantities of self- propelled artillery) permits both the rapid concentration and quick dispersal essential to complementary warfare.

OFFENSIVE OPERATIONAL PROCEDURES

Offensive operations in a Theater of Military Operations (TVD) are conducted by one or more Fronts supported by Long Range Aviation and, if required, by Strategic Rocket Forces. The objective of theater level operations is the absolute, uncompromising physical and political destruction of the opponent. In this context, the final objective of a Front offensive operation is the seizure of key political and economic centers deep in the opponent's rear areas, with the concurrent destruction of the military forces defending them. The structure of a Front or *TVD* will be determined by the General Staff. Combat and support elements will be assigned in accord with the General Staff's visualization of how the Front is to undertake component tasks in meeting the objective.

Planning a Front operation always includes nuclear planning, with special attention to the potential for a transition from conventional to nuclear warfare. The need to anticipate the enemy's use of nuclear weapons is equally important. The readiness to deliver an initial nuclear strike must be preplanned, but the plan will be changed or refined as the situation develops. It is essential to destroy the enemy's nuclear delivery systems, even during the conventional phase; thus, planning includes continuing reconnaissance to target and destroy those systems.

The basic features of planning operations at this level will be essentially the same in nuclear and conventional operations: establishment of objectives, allocation of forces, designation of main and supporting attacks, and identification of axes of advance. The scheme of maneuver and the plan of fire support will, however, differ. In conventional operations, there will be successive intermediate operations prior to reaching the objective. Regroupment of forces may take place as the operation continues. Frontal air units are relatively more important, because only they can reach enemy targets in substantial depth. Artillery will be the primary means of neutralizing enemy combat and support forces directly opposing the Soviet combined arms forces.

In nuclear operations, the number of phases in the maneuver scheme will be at a minimum, reflecting to a greater degree a sustained, single, high-speed operation on multiple axes of advance, exploiting the nuclear fire plan to reach Front objectives. Planning must also be based on an assessment of the balance of forces and means between attacker and defender. The planners consider the ratios of divisions, total manpower, tanks, antitank weapons, field artillery and mortars, nuclear delivery means, and combat aircraft.

Front plans must support the requirements of conducting deep operations. The successive operations to be conducted by its assigned Armies are of two types. (See Figure 3.1).

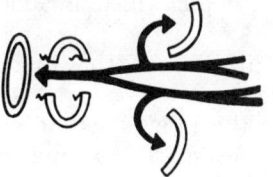

Attack along one or more axes to split the defenders into separate or isolated groups. These are to be destroyed in detail, with concurrent further attacks toward the enemy's rear depths.

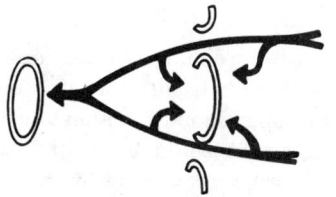

Attacks along converging axes to envelope sizable enemy forces. Surrounded forces are to be destroyed as concurrent attacks continue to the depths.

Figure 3.1. Types of Successive Operations

The phasing of operations is regulated by two related Soviet concepts of defining operational progress. These are, first, the categorization of "depths" and, second, delimiting objectives at each operational level. (See Figure 3.2.)

Depths	Front Objectives	Inclusive Limits
Tactical	–	To enemy's Corps rear area
Immediate Operational	Immediate	Into the enemy's Corps rear area
Operational	Long Range	Into the enemy's Army Group rear area
Strategic	Final	Remaining rear forces; logistical, political, and economic centers

Figure 3.2 The Categorization of Depths and Delimiting of Objectives

Following these concepts of "depths," the designation of objectives involves analysis and planning for the following sequence of actions as shown in Figure 3.3:

(1) Penetration of the enemy's forward defending brigades;
(2) Overcoming the echelons of the tactical depth which includes the forward-defending divisions' reserve;
(3) Destruction, disorganization, or neutralization of the immediate operational depth, which includes corps reserves;
(4) Seizing terrain that permits introducing the Front's second echelon armies, usually in the role of exploitation forces. The second echelon armies attack strategic reserves of the enemy's army group and theater reserves, and strike for the Front final objective--the strategic depth.

For both attack and defense the Soviet units probably will be deployed in one or two (sometimes three) echelons[7], with or without a combined arms reserve, strike group, mobile group, or operational maneuver group. (Figure 3.4). A typical echelonment for a Front could be a first echelon consisting of one combined arms army and two tank armies with a second echelon of one combined arms army and one tank army. The Front reserve could consist of a motorized rifle division. The Front might also have a tank army or a corps as a strike group or operational maneuver group.

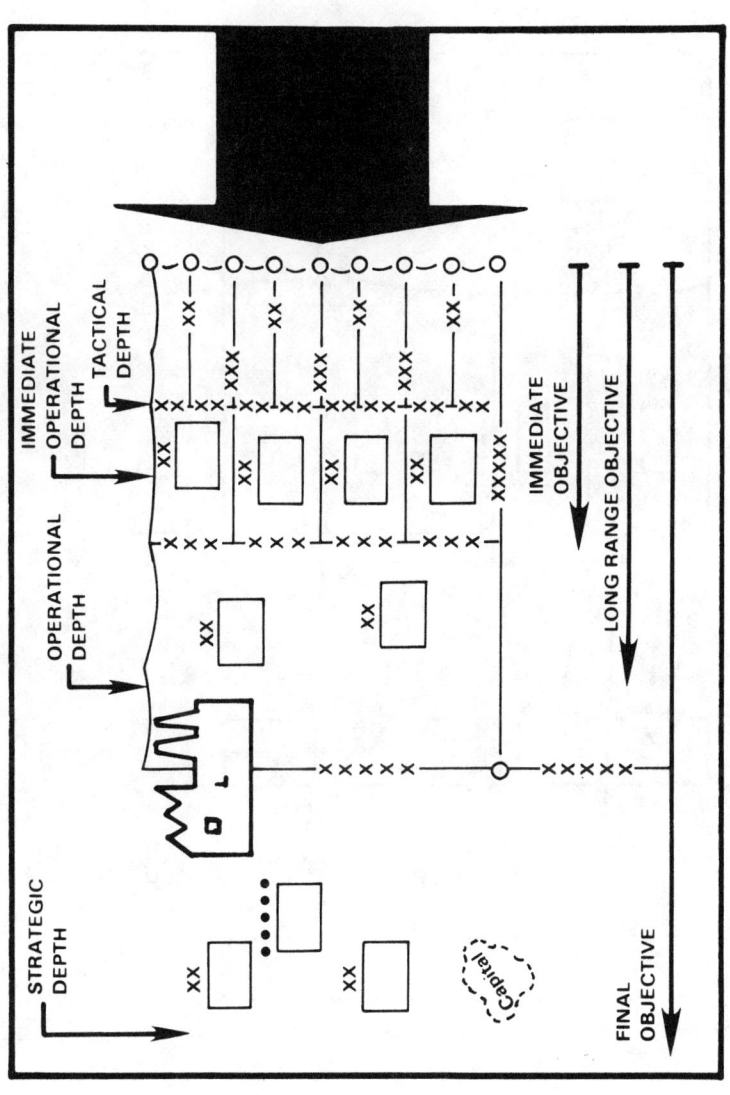

Figure 3.3. Depths and Objectives

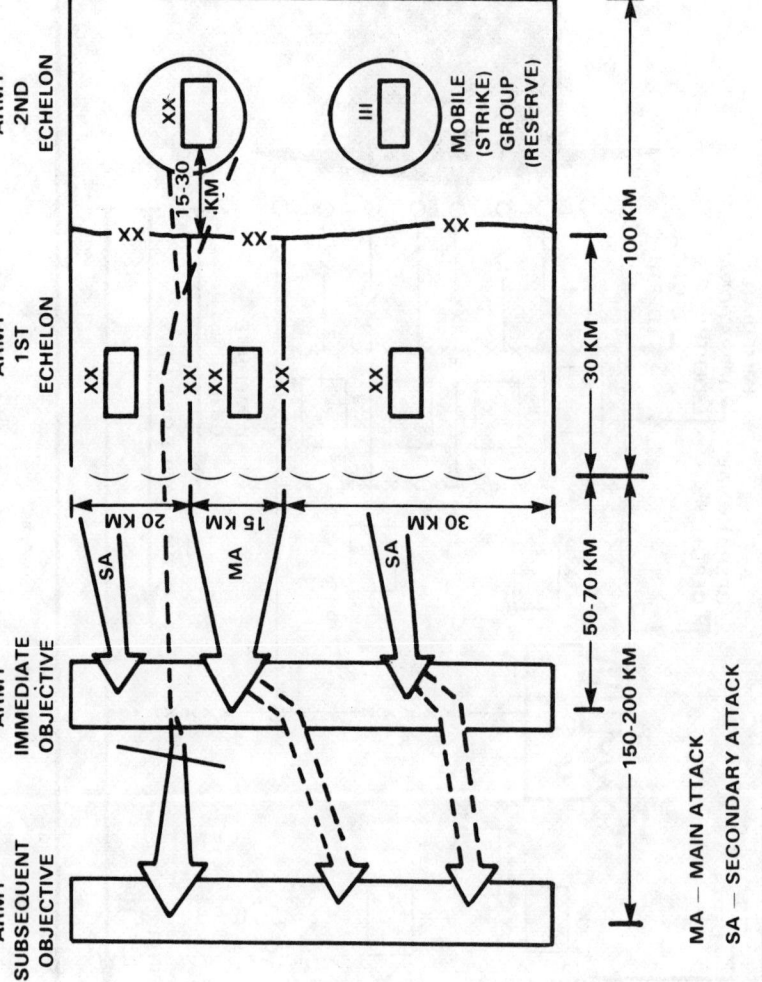

Figure 3.4. Type (Army) Deployment for Offensive Operation

There can be many variants depending on the nature of the defense and the nuclear situation. Tank armies may be placed in the first echelon to obtain greater speed when terrain and other conditions permit. A Front might attack with four armies in the first echelon and one army in the second echelon. With reliable nuclear suppression of a relatively shallow defense, a Front might attack in one echelon, holding several divisions as reserve and strike groups. The first echelon of the Front will penetrate enemy defenses (either splitting the defense or on converging axes) and will, as a general rule, attack through the enemy's immediate operational depths to the defender's corps rear boundary.

Preparatory fires for the attack are coordinated and controlled by first echelon armies and are included in the Front fire plan. Nuclear weapons, if used, normally would be delivered immediately prior to the nonnuclear preparation, thus shortening the duration of the nonnuclear preparation. If nuclear fires are not used, the preparation may last from 30 minutes to an hour or more. The Front commander may have airborne forces up to division strength allocated for an operation. Either in the initial stage of the operation or subsequently, these forces may be used to seize important areas in the defensive depths. Smaller airborne forces may be assigned long-range reconnaissance or sabotage missions. Second echelon armies of the Front may be directed to the most appropriate of these missions:

(1) When the first echelon forces achieve objectives rapidly and have promise of continued success, they may bypass pockets of enemy resistance to be dealt with by the second echelon forces. As a general rule, first echelon forces will bypass large urban areas.
(2) When initial success of the first echelon is followed by reduction in its momentum, the second echelon may be assigned the exploitation mission (Figure 3.5). This would be the ideal time for employment of an Operational Maneuver Group if available.
(3) Lack of success by first echelon forces could require that second echelon forces assume the attack or attack in a new direction.
(4) Enemy nuclear strikes could damage first echelon forces to the degree that they must be replaced by the second echelon.

In any of these cases, the commitment of the second echelon is supported by an intense fire preparation. The fires are delivered by the artillery of in-contact first echelon forces. Nuclear fires may also be delivered at this time.

METHODS OF INITIATING THE ATTACK

Two methods for initiating the attack are attack from positions in contact and attack from the march. Attack from the march is expected to predominate, particularly in nuclear war. In making the transition from the march to the offense, units make successive deployments from assembly areas to assault positions. At designated lines they deploy into battalion columns, company columns, and platoon columns. The successive stages are called march formation, pre-battle formation, and battle formation.

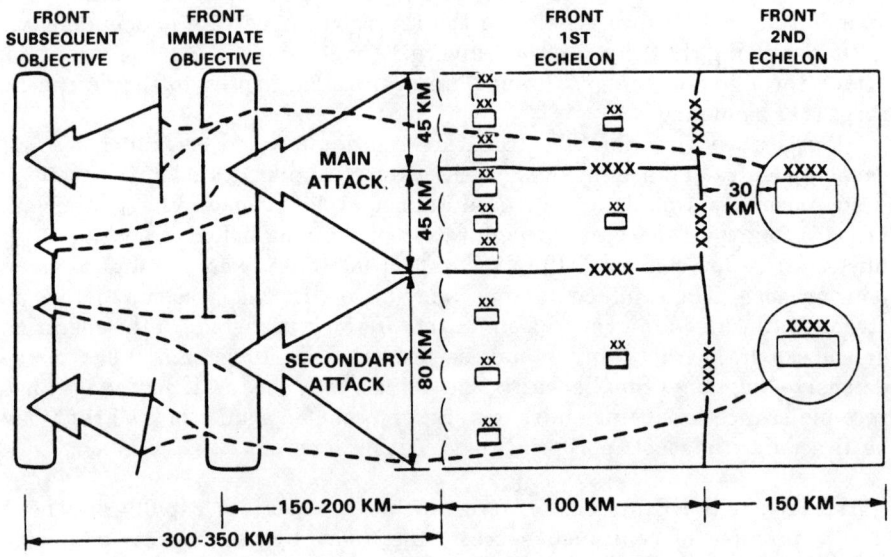

Figure 3.5. Type Front Deployment for Offensive Operation

Attack times are so coordinated that units deployed from the march attack simultaneously with those attacking from positions already in contact with the enemy. Selection of the method used to convert to the attack depends on the senior commander's concept of the operation, the degree to which the enemy defenses can be neutralized, the nature of those defenses, and the terrain. The advantages and disadvantages are shown in Figure 3.6

THE MARCH TO CONTACT

Any movement of a column or unit in a *TVD* must be governed by the assumption that contact with the enemy is possible. A march to contact may occur at the outset of a war when columns move from a concentration area to cross a border or when units move through or between friendly units in the direction of the enemy. When a force that has penetrated enemy defenses is ordered to pursue a withdrawing enemy, that also can be a march to contact, as it is when a force must relocate to meet a probable counterattack. A march to contact may be required in any type of offensive action or when making the transition from defense to offense. When both sides are moving to contact, a meeting engagement is the expected combat action. (Some special considerations for the meeting engagement are covered in the next section.) In any march to contact, the problem facing the Soviet commander is the proper disposition of his combat elements within the column so that the enemy can be defeated with the smallest redisposition of the column. To ensure proper disposition of combat elements, the column must be organized prior to starting the march. This minimizes or precludes any reorganizing before commitment.

METHOD	ADVANTAGES	DISADVANTAGES
Attack from the March	• Provides best protection since units lie initially in assembly areas behind friendly lines • Avoids long stay in range of enemy artillery • Increases chance of surprise • Increases capability for dispersion and establishment of air defense	• Requires detailed planning and coordination for a simultaneous attack • Creates difficulty in coordinating nuclear and conventional fires in support of maneuvering forces • Requires more engineer support • Traffic control is very difficult • Requires more terrain study
Attack from Positions in Contact	• Allows thorough study of terrain and defense • Permits more refined organization of the battle • Eases coordination of the assault	• Places units under threat of attack while organizing • Lessens chance of surprise • Requires preparing and occupying attack positions under possible observation

Figure 3.6. Advantages and Disadvantages of Types of Attack

In whatever form the actual engagement may take, the commander faces a multitude of decisions and potential hazards. A commander must examine his mission in light of orders he has received from the senior commander and the missions of the units in his force. He then calculates the time available for planning and organizing so that all the necessary measures to permit crossing the initial line at the required time are accomplished. One of the commander's first actions is to issue warning orders to his subordinate commanders so that preparations for the march can be initiated.

Planning the march is carried out in as much detail as time and information will permit. If at all possible, a route reconnaissance is conducted to determine route conditions, locate contaminated areas, identify constricted areas or obstacles, and determine requirements for engineer or decontamination support. Next, he divides the march route into segments based on the terrain, estimates the permissible rate of march over each segment and the times required for rests and halts, and thus determines the time to complete each segment. With these calculations, he can determine the control measures for conduct of the march and the times associated with each control measure. Control measures include the starting or initial line or point, control lines and points, halts and rests, and the line for deployment. Figure 3.7 shows an organization for the tactical march of a motorized rifle division. Not shown in this figure are the security detachments comprised of an advance party, a rear party, and flank parties, which for a division might be of company or platoon size depending on the situation.

The terms "Forward Detachment", "Advanced Detachment", or "Spearhead Unit" do not refer to a formation that is an integral part of the tactical march. Such detachments are a reinforced combined arms formation of company, battalion, possibly regiment, or an even larger size that is sent out ahead of the march column to seize and hold important lines and objectives, major road junctions, mountain passes, and bridgeheads until arrival of the main force. On the defense, such a formation may be sent out to conduct operations in the security zone. In some cases, Forward Detachments are sent 50 kilometers or more ahead in order to seize key terrain features or other objectives that will facilitate a favorable development of the battle.

Frequently, the first security element (other than reconnaissance) meeting the enemy will be the advance guard. The advance guard of the leading regiment may be 20 to 30 kilometers ahead of the regimental main force. This allows the main force commander approximately an hour to make his decision and to deploy.

The organization of a tank division for a march to contact is very similar to that shown for a motorized rifle division. A division can march on three routes, two routes, or even a single route. It should be noted, however, that the major elements depicted vary greatly. Forces from Front or Army may be attached to the division for early employment; likewise, the commander's concept of echelonment could change the location of entire regiments. Major attention is given to security on the march both for protection from enemy attack and for enhancing chances of entering into battle under advantageous conditions. Security considerations include: intelligence and reconnaissance,

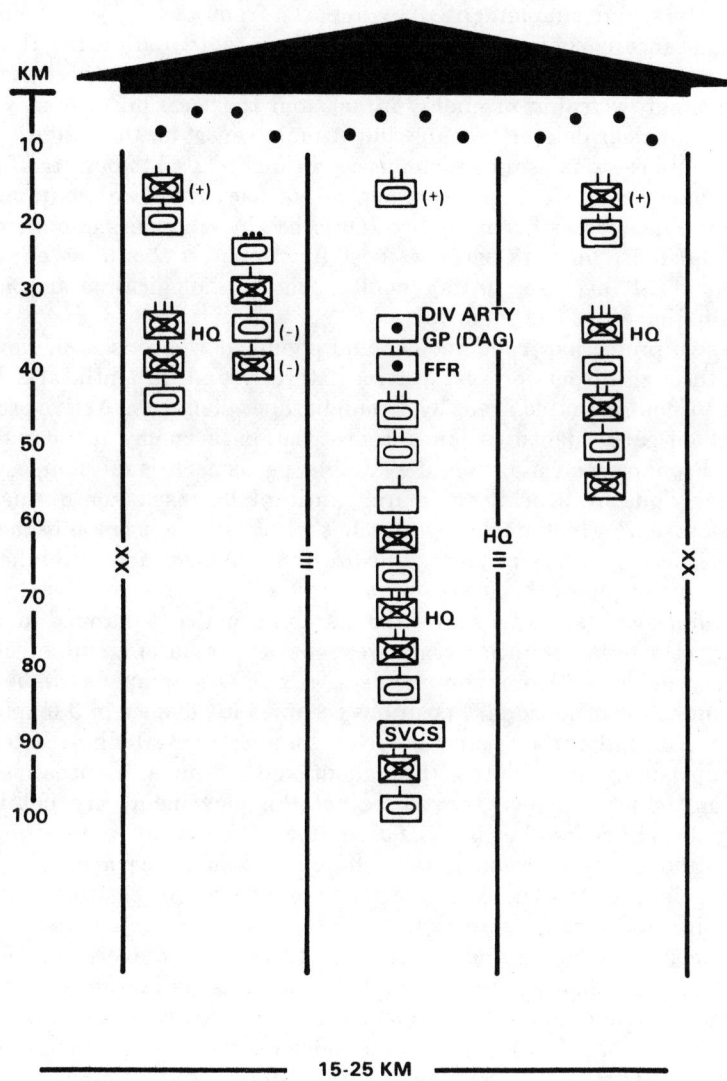

Figure 3.7. Tactical March of Motorized Rifle Division

chemical defense, antitank defense, air defense, concealment, engineering support, logistical support, and organization security.

At the tactical level, intelligence is generally provided by higher headquarters and supplemented by reports from tactical reconnaissance. Reconnaissance is continuous along the march route and on the flanks and may be conducted by air or by ground patrol. Not only must reconnaissance provide timely warning of enemy attack and the location of enemy forces, especially nuclear delivery means, but it must report on the condition of the route. Route reconnaissance includes conditions related to both trafficability and the presence of chemical, radiological, or bacteriological contamination. Reconnaissance forces normally are reinforced by engineers and elements of chemical defense units to perform these functions. It should be emphasized that chemical defense units monitor for radiological and biological contamination as well as chemical.

Passive protection from nuclear and chemical weapons is achieved primarily through dispersion of the force laterally and in depth, and through warning of contaminated areas by reconnaissance elements. Active protection can include early identification and destruction of enemy nuclear delivery means. Front or army aviation, if available, performs this mission, especially in the early phases. During the march, antitank defense is maintained by an antitank reserve which normally marches with the first echelon of the march unit. It is based on the unit's organic antitank element and is reinforced, as required by the enemy threat, with tanks and self-propelled artillery.

Column cover (air defense) for the march normally is planned in advance and includes organic antiaircraft weapons and aviation and air defense weapons provided by senior commanders. Air defense weapons can be located in the column or in stationary positions occupied in advance in a leapfrogging manner. Normally, when marching to contact in potentially hostile territory, the weapons are distributed throughout the columns. Concealment and deception, which enhance the secrecy of the movement, are obtained by moving at night or in other periods of limited visibility, by maintaining radio silence, and by special masking techniques such as corner reflectors or screening fences constructed along roads or in front of positions to protect against infrared or radar detection.

Engineer support for the march allows the force to overcome or bypass areas that would disrupt the march. In addition to the presence of engineers with reconnaissance and security elements, there are two distinctive engineer organizations that facilitate column movement: the movement support detachment (*Otryad Obyespecheniya Dvizheniya (OOD)*) and the mobile obstacle detachment (*Podvizhniy Otryad Zagryazhdeniya (POZ)*). In the task organization of the force, engineer-sappers will be attached to maneuver units to assist in obstacle clearance after contact is made and will lay mines as necessary.

Logistic support of the march is divided into two phases: prior to the march and during the march. Prior to the march, supplies are replenished, maintenance work is performed, and the wounded and sick are evacuated. Rear service elements are brought forward to conduct these activities. If the march is behind friendly lines, refueling and maintenance elements are sent forward to halt or rest areas to establish refueling points. Every attempt is made to replenish fuel reserves for vehicles to prepare for combat. During the march, logistic support is performed in areas of halts or rests. Vehicles that break down between these areas are repaired on the spot, wounded and sick are given medical aid in place, and seriously wounded are evacuated.

Traffic control platoons that are organic to tank and motorized rifle regiments assist movement and enforce march control at the planned control lines, halts, and rests. Motorized rifle and tank divisions have an organic traffic control company. These units provide traffic regulators who guide, direct, and control the column. When possible, routes are marked in advance and traffic regulators are posted at critical points along the route. These techniques are obviously more suitable for use behind friendly lines. When marching at night or during conditions of limited visibility, night signaling devices and night marking devices supplement other communications means.

On the march, command posts are located in this manner:

	Division	Regiment
Forward	Head of main force, main axis.	Advance guard main force.
Main	Head of second echelon regiment or rear of main force of lead regiment.	Head of regimental main force.
Rear	Head of column of rear services units.	Head of column of rear services units.

Two possible methods of crossing zones of radioactive contamination are immediate movement across the zone from the march and movement across the zone after waiting for a reduction in radiation levels. An immediate crossing is led by tanks, since their armor gives them protection against radiation. Units mounted in carriers and trucks follow. The crossing assisted by *OOD*s or *POZ*s, is made on primary routes to ensure high speed and control, unless it is necessary to reduce the distance traveled or to bypass areas of very high radiation. Enemy forces may be positioned to interrupt movement, forcing stops in the contaminated area. To preclude this, a reliable means of fire suppression must be available--an ideal role for self-propelled artillery. Reconnaissance elements and forward detachments assist in forewarning of enemy capabilities.

To make the transition from the tactical march to the attack, Soviets pursue two successive deployments: tactical march to prebattle (approach march) and then to battle (attack). These deployments are practiced in standard battle drills. The drills include variations that could be required by terrain, limited maneuver space, urbanization, or forestation. All drills are based on dual requirements of placing maximum firepower on the enemy while retaining maximum security for the attacking force. It must be kept in

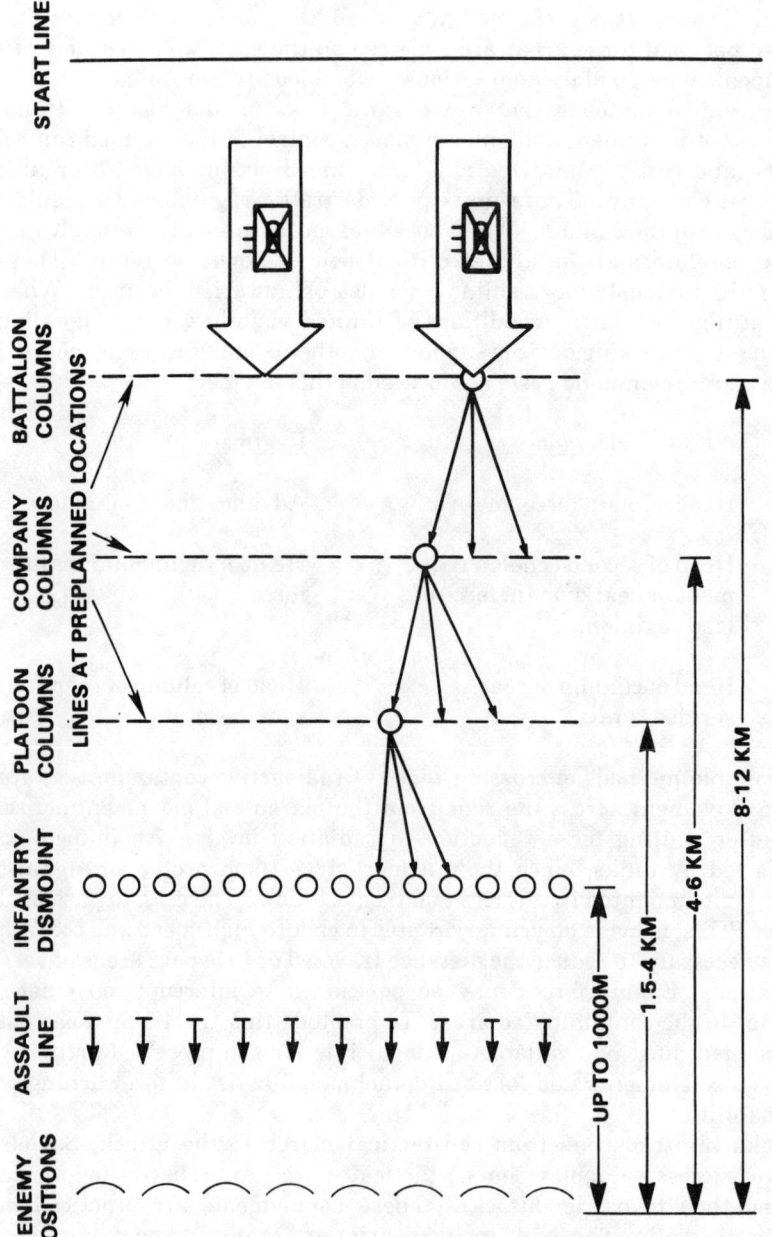

Figure 3.8. Deployment for Attack from the March

mind that forces deploy only when battle is imminent, and for larger forces, deployment is made only by that part of the force required for attacking the enemy.

The formation of a battalion approach march consists of company columns with supporting forces, separated in frontage and depth, arranged in wedge or line. At the prearranged line for deployment into battalion columns (Figure 3.8) the regiment moves on to several routes with battalions marching in column formation. They may all be on line or arranged in an order that suits the plan of the regimental commander. At the line for deployment into company columns, the battalions assume an approach march formation. Task-organized companies, marching in column formation, may be arranged as in one of the formations illustrated in Figure 3.9.

The final element of the approach march is the assault. When attacking an enemy defense, the company deploys from its approach march (pre-battle formation--platoon columns) into a battle formation for mounted attack, which is the preferred mode. When attacking dismounted, at the dismount line the attacking units form a line, a wedge, an inverted wedge, or an echelon right or left; the carriers support the assault from the rear of the dismounted troops.

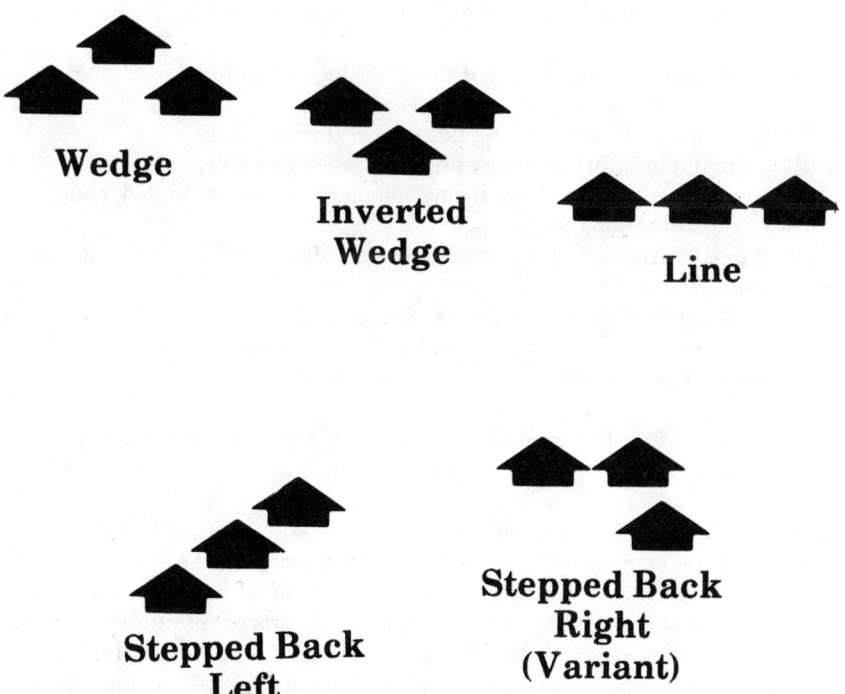

Figure 3.9. Various Formation Arrangements

THE MEETING ENGAGEMENT

The Soviets consider the meeting engagement to be the offensive operation that, in a future war, may be the most likely form of encounter at all echelons in either nuclear or nonnuclear war. Dynamically enhanced mobility and firepower have significantly increased the probability of meeting engagements. More and better tanks, personnel carriers, and helicopters permit a greater degree of mobility. The increased lethality and range of modern weapons, especially nuclear-armed missiles, have expanded the area, intensity, and fluidity of the modern battlefield. Command and control equipment and procedures now make more manageable the complexities of this high-tempo combat situation.

The meeting engagement may occur under widely differing circustances, either offensive or defensive; circumstances, in turn, influence combat formation and conduct of the engagement. Four probable circumstances are shown in Figure 3.10.

The meeting engagement unfolds as follows:

(1) March to contact and activities of forward reconnaissance elements;
(2) Initial combat contact and its development by the advance guard;
(3) Maneuver and engagement of the Main Force with supporting arms;
(4) Termination and transition to subsequent actions;

The principal characteristics of the meeting engagement are:

(1) Extemporaneous planning because of limited time;
(2) Continuous effort to seize and retain the initiative;
(3) Deployment into combat from the march column at high speed;
(4) Lack of detailed intelligence;
(5) Rapid situational changes, demanding redirection of combat deployment;
(6) Development of actions on a wide front;
(7) Probable presence of open flanks of each opponent;
(8) Both sides seeking enough maneuver room.

General Radzievskiy, then Commandant of the Frunze Academy, had the following to say about the meeting engagement:

> One of the most important tendencies in the development of the meeting engagement is the ever greater tendency for the premeditated initiation of the meeting engagement instead of its accidental arising. As a result of the depths of action and the means of reconnaissance of modern armies, obscurity of the situation more and more is losing its meaning as a characteristic. Commanders of both sides more often then not already, far before the meeting, will have some indication of the strength and fire means of the enemy and, hence, the decision for

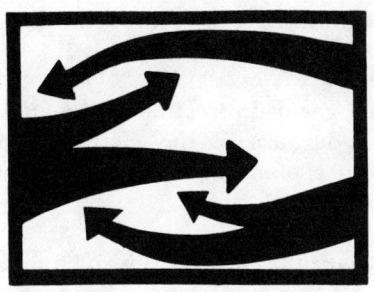

Beginning of a War
Could also occur at the outset of any attack when opposing forces are not in initial contact, and both assume the offensive.

After Penetration of Enemy's Front Line Defense
Would involve the penetrating force meeting the defender's advancing reserve elements.

During Pursuit
Meeting engagement likely during counter-attack by either side.

During Counterattack
Strong probability that the counterattacking force could be met head-on or from the flanks by the enemy.

Figure 3.10. Meeting Engagement Circumstances

the meeting engagement will be taken as a result of real assessment...[8]

A military commander advancing in the general direction of the enemy must anticipate a meeting engagement. Because of the distinguishing characteristics listed above, the commander, in planning his decision, must consider the need for:

(1) Continuous and thorough reconnaissance by his own means and the correct interpretation and use of reconnaissance information furnished from higher echelons;
(2) Speed in his troop-leading procedures--the making and transmitting of decisions;
(3) Anticipating of enemy air and artillery strikes, nuclear or nonnuclear, and the use of such information in gaining fire superiority;
(4) Achieving of the initiative through immediately responsive deployment of maneuver forces;
(5) Adequate flank and rear security.

Success in a meeting engagement comes from the combination of timely command direction, decisions, and attaining combined arms fire superiority. Current weapon systems, particularly if nuclear weapons were employed, make it possible to delay or destroy an advancing enemy even before an encounter with ground forces. Any delay of the enemy will gain time for the commander to organize his attack plans. Timely supporting fires, both to delay the enemy and support the actual engagement, contribute directly to the basic aims; namely, seizing and holding the initiative and maintaining the high tempo of the advance and the momentum of the offensive.

Because of the stress placed on both the meeting engagement (one of the most important forms of combat in a modern war) and artillery support for such an engagement, it is important to examine the capabilities and methodology for supporting this concept logistically. Can it actually be supported with the required rate of fire to attain artillery superiority at the critical point?

The rate of ammunition expenditure will be governed during the course of the meeting engagement by two primary factors discussed below: the means of target acquisition that come into place sequentially, and the decreasing artillery effectiveness per mission as enemy units deploy and as artillery fires shift from primarily observed fires to a combination of observed and unobserved fires. (Calculations indicate that observed fires are more effective per mission than unobserved.)

Early in the meeting engagement, target acquisition by the advance guard is limited to that provided by reconnaissance patrols and forward observers. This may be supplemented by higher echelon means such as aerial observers. Initially, the targets will be hastily deployed maneuver units close to the line of contact for units moving forward. Technical target acquisition-- including counter-battery, and radio and radar intercept elements from the regiment and division reconnaissance units--will become operational, starting at about two hours after the initial contact. As a result, deeper targets such as command posts and active artillery batteries will be vulnerable.

The arrival of additional target acquisition capabilities, coupled with the developing tactical situation, creates new targeting situations. As the enemy deploys, the targets become difficult to locate and defeat. Because artillery effectiveness will decline as observed fires are replaced by unobserved fires, the use of ammunition increases. Consequently, the Soviets place heavy emphasis on the early decisive use of fire support, with enemy artillery and antitank weapons receiving the highest priority. Organic transportation is adequate for the immediate ammunition requirements. The meeting engagement is expected to be of high intensity and relatively short duration. In the first two to three hours of contact, the arrival of ammunition in organic transportation will exceed normal expenditure. Thereafter supplies will decline rapidly unless there is resupply from the rear.

The essence of the meeting engagement (intensive fire power in conjunction with rapid troop maneuver) remains the same in nuclear or in nonnuclear war. In a nuclear environment, however, the likelihood of the occurrence and the tempo of action would be increased. Dispersion would necessarily be increased among the troop formations in immediate contact with the enemy, in the space relationship of units supporting the combat, and in corresponding defensive deployments. The general aim of such dispersion would be to eliminate the probability that more than one unit of a specific type--company or battalion, for instance--would be destroyed by a single nuclear strike. The long range of missiles permits strikes into rear depths. A concentration of nuclear fires can instantly bring major changes in the balance of opposing forces in a critical area. The complete motorization of maneuver units permits rapid movement in depth and laterally, which can also quickly alter force ratios. As the yields and frequency of employment of nuclear weapons increase, nuclear fires could saturate the battlefield. Any maneuver could risk prohibitive losses. The first side capable of exploiting firepower, either nuclear or nonnuclear, has an overwhelming advantage. To meet their own commitment norms (see NORMS, Chapter 4) for a meeting engagement, the Soviets would have to accept some risks because excessive dispersion of units, either on the march or in deployment, would limit the high-speed commitment of units and fire superiority in the meeting engagement.

A carefully planned march is the key to success. Proper organization permits the timely commitment of the advance guard's combat power and the subsequent deployment of the main forces. In formulating his decision for the march, the commander must ensure a firm understanding of the mission of his unit as it relates to the higher commander's plan. Basic factors of march planning include:

(1) Mission of the march to include areas to be secured;
(2) Time available;
(3) Friendly forces situation, including missions of adjacent units;

(4) Attachments and supporting units;
(5) Armor threat;
(6) Radiation and chemical situation;
(7) March route and nature of terrain;
(8) Time of day and weather;
(9) Areas of likely enemy encounter along the route and the concept of operation at each point;
(10) Reconnaissance and column security; amd
(11) Control measures for the march and entry into combat.

Having determined the march order and distribution of forces in the columns, detailed calculations for the movement are in order. These include total march distance, speed of movement over each sector of the route, location of control lines and rest stops, and the times for elements to reach and clear the control points.

The organization of the march column will vary with the size of the Main Force (division or regiment), the enemy situation--particularly the nuclear and chemical situation--and the number of routes available. Doctrinally, the division rarely would advance on a single route with regiments in columns, since this formation would slow the overall forward movement and would delay deployment in battle formation if strong resistance were encountered. A division could, however, be forced onto a single route by lack of adequate road nets, as in mountainous, swampy, or forested terrain or when approaching a river crossing. At the other extreme, a division seldom would advance on four routes with regiments abreast, except when the weakest of resistance is expected. In practice, however, units have been frequently observed using a single route.

A regiment leading a division march can be designated the advance guard of the division. In turn, such a regiment would organize itself into the basic components of an advance guard and a main force. The advance guard, in either case, would be approximately one-third of the main force's total combat power.

As a rule, the advance guard has the task of ensuring unhindered movement of the main force, establishing suitable conditions for its commitment, warning it of surprise attack, and preventing penetrations of the main force by enemy reconnaissance. The advance guard usually will be reinforced with artillery, tanks, chemical, and air defense elements. These elements are distributed among the components of the advance guard.

In front of the advance guard there generally will be either division reconnaissance elements, regimental reconnaissance elements, or both. The advance guard will, nevertheless, establish a combat reconnaissance patrol perhaps as large as a platoon in front of its advance party. The mission of the advance party, moving about 10 kilometers behind the combat reconnaissance patrol, is to advance at maximum speed and engage lead enemy elements. Through use of its mobility and firepower, it will seize and retain a line for subsequent commitment of the advance guard's main force. From within this element, the commander will dispatch a platoon-size patrol with chemical and engineer reconnaissance personnel up to a kilometer ahead. Fire support commanders (artillery and antitank) will move at the head of the main column with the motorized rifle company commander. Typically, the advance guard main force will consist of somewhat less than one-third of the entire force. Its mission is either to eliminate enemy opposition, thereby permitting continuation of the march, or to fix the enemy force in place so that deployment and maneuver of the main force can proceed. Fire support and tanks are placed forward in the column. In the event of a threat from the flank, artillery and tanks may be placed in the middle of the column.

The main force, representing two-thirds of the combat power of the march formation, will maneuver to destroy enemy formations that cannot be quickly overcome by the advance guard. Its composition will vary, but emphasis will be given to the location of fire support elements and antitank reserves. The commander normally will be located at the head of the main force column, followed in rapid succession by the antitank and engineer elements of the column. Next will come a tank unit, then a motorized rifle unit, followed by the artillery and anti-aircraft elements (less those that may be spaced throughout the column), and finally the rear element of the column. Rear parties up to platoon strength normally will be positioned up to three kilometers from the advance guard and the main force. Depending on the nature of the enemy threat, flank parties up to platoon strength are dispatched as far as three kilometers from the column. The principles and considerations governing planning a tactical march in anticipation of the meeting engagement are generally applicable to the conditions of a meeting engagement occurring during a counterattack or pursuit. The same requirements for column security, timely fire support, and the delivery of decisive blows on the enemy, must be met.

INITIATION AND CONDUCT OF THE MEETING ENGAGEMENT

The initiation phase of the meeting engagement is that period of active combat from enemy encounter by the leading element (the combat reconnaissance patrol) to the commitment of the main force. Thus, the initiation phase usually will be carried out by elements of the advance guard. The subsequent employment of the main force will depend on the outcome of the initiation phase. With current reconnaissance capabilities, the initial encounter by the combat reconnaissance patrol and its reporting of enemy dispositions may permit employment of long-range artillery and air support fire to inflict damage on the enemy and to delay his advance. A one-hour delay could permit the further advance of the march column by 25 or 30 kilometers. The combat organization of the advance guard, while flexible, is tailored to meet the norms of staying power for the time the commander requires (Chapter 4, NORMS).

The actions of advance guard elements are indicated in the following tables. The buildup of combined arms firepower, based on a typical organization for each element, is also shown. The actions of the lead element (the combat reconnaissance patrol) ahead of the advance party by as much as 10 kilometers, would be:

Buildup of Firepower	Action
	• Report contact to advanceguard commander.
Time: zero minutes	• Attempt to penetrate to enemy main force by bypassing his advance elements.
Soviet forces committed:	
3 BMPs (infantry combat vehicle), each with 73mm gun and SAGGER ATGM (Anti-tank Guided Missile)	• Perform chemical and engineer reconnaissance.
	• Collect all information on the enemy that will expedite the commander's decision.

Actions of the advance party of the advance guard moving in column behind the combat reconnaissance patrol by approximately 10 kilometers (10 to 20 minutes of travel time) would be:

Buildup of Firepower	Action
Time: plus 20 minutes	• Advance at maximum speed.
	• Develop the situation.
Soviet forces now committed: 10 BMPs 6 mortars, 120mm 6 howitzers, 122mm, self-propelled 4 tanks 2 antitank weapons, SAGGER 2 antitank weapons, SPG 9	• Seize and hold position until arrival of the advance guard main force.

At the time of initial contact, the advance guard main force will be moving in march column 5 to 10 kilometers behind the advance party and a total of 15 to 20 kilometers behind the combat reconnaissance patrol. The commander will define the combat plan for engagement.

Buildup of Firepower	Action
Time: plus 60 minutes	• Issue new orders to the commanders of the combat reconnaissance patrol and advance party.
Soviet forces now committed:	
31 BMPs 13 tanks 6 mortars, 120mm	• Move forward with the artillery commander at maximum speed to an observation point.
18 howitzers, 122mm, self-propelled 5 antitank weapons, SAGGER 2 antitank weapons, SPG-9	• Issue orders for the deployment
2 antiaircraft (ZSU-23-4) weapons	• Launch the attack.

The attack by the motorized rifle and tank units may or may not be coordinated; time will not be sacrificed trying to achieve a coordinated attack. Artillery and antitank weapons will be deployed to support the maneuver, firing by battery when ready.

As the forward elements of the advance guard encounter the enemy, the regimental commander will be at or near his main force some 20 to 30 kilometers to the rear of the advance guard. This deliberate spacing is calculated to give the commander a period of 60 to 90 minutes for planning and execution of his battle commitment.

When the advance guard becomes engaged, the main force will continue its forward movement. The ultimate deployment of the main force will depend on the outcome of the advance guard action. Four possible outcomes of advance guard action are:

(1) Attack by the advance party of the advance guard is successful.
(2) Enemy element is destroyed.
(3) Advance guard resumes march.
(4) Main force of regiment does not deploy.
(5) No immediate success by the advance guard.
(6) Advance guard continues agressive action by probing flanks.
(7) Main force continues to march forward and prepares to deploy.
(8) Enemy Forces deny further offensive action by the advance guard.
(9) Advance guard shifts to defense and directs maximum fire on the enemy.
(10) Advance guard repels counterattack.
(11) Main force deploys and attacks.
(12) The advance guard is unable to hold enemy.
(13) Main force defends on best available ground.
(14) Advance guard withdraws and joins defense.
(15) Follow-on division forces committed.

When the outcome of the advance guard action requires the deployment of the main force, the commander makes his decision on the form of maneuver to be used. He has three basic choices: envelopment, flank attack, or frontal attack. To achieve surprise and maintain momentum, envelopment or flank attack is preferred. In some cases, however, the frontal attack will be required.

The major contributing factors to a successful envelopment are:

(1) Effective real-time intelligence to locate the enemy and counter-intelligence capability to screen one's own movements;
(2) Effective utilization of terrain;
(3) Coordination between forces and, in the case of the flank attack, mutual fire support;
(4) Appreciation of enemy tactics and capabilities;
(5) Capable, ingenious leadership.

While the envelopment or flank attack is preferred, a frontal attack may be required in certain circumstances; for example, when reconnaissance feedback is not sufficient to give an adequate base for planning an envelopment, when insufficient time is available for planning and coordination, or when maneuver space is inadequate.

The preceding description of the meeting engagement has focused on the actions of a motorized rifle regiment. Unless the regiment has been assigned an independent mission, such as in a pursuit or acting as a forward detachment, it will be marching as part of a division force. Consequently, the development of the battle might require commitment of the follow-on elements of the division. The procedures are substantially the same as in the example of the lead regiment. This pertains whether the division is a motorized rifle or a tank division. A tank regiment can lead a division march and form an advance guard with a reinforced tank battalion.

The follow-on forces of the division may be advancing on one route or on multiple routes, as was depicted in the description of the march to contact. Before his lead regiment is fully engaged, the division commander, with his forward command post, normally will be near the head of the main body of the division force, most likely with the next following regiment. He monitors action of the lead regiment and, after its engagement, moves his command group to the best location to control subsequent deployments. Doctrine for the meeting engagement emphasizes that the disadvantage of a hastily planned attack is more than offset by the advantage of a quick strike against the enemy before he has sufficient time for his own preparation. A division's hastily coordinated attack from the march can be made within five to six hours of the initial contact by lead elements of the advance guard. Follow-on forces can be fully engaged in less then three hours after the lead regiment's main force is engaged.

The employment of division follow-on forces will be dictated by the progress of the lead regiment's initial actions. If the attack by the lead regiment is successful, that regiment exploits the success, or resumes the march. Depending on the assigned mission and the degree of success, units could consolidate positions and await orders, or resume advance in a new direction.

If the enemy establishes a hasty defense, the lead regiment initiates a quick attack and, by fixing the enemy force, facilitates commitment of division follow-on forces. Depending on availability of maneuver space, follow-on regiments flank or envelop the hasty defense to destroy the enemy. Artillery fire is increasingly centralized in order to control effectively the fires of the division. Helicopter assault forces are employed if practical and appropriate. If follow-on forces succeed, exploitation or pursuit may be carried out. Alternatively, the position may be consolidated, forces regrouped, and the march resumed.

If the lead regiment is forced to establish a hasty defense, it will hold, pending arrival and deployment of the follow-on forces. Follow-on forces counterattack and attempt to envelop the enemy. If they are successful, subsequent actions are as above. Follow-on forces may be required to augment the defense.

Should the lead regiment be unable to contain the enemy attack, follow-on forces conduct a counterattack. If they are successful and the enemy withdraws, exploitation or pursuit is initiated. Alternatively the position may be consolidated and regrouped and the march resumed. Follow-on forces establish defensive positions, to or through which the lead regiment withdraws. The division holds, pending commitment of Army follow-on forces and the meeting engagement continues, or the meeting engagement terminates and planning for other forms of offensive, such as attack from the position in contact, is initiated. If additional combined arms firepower is available to the division commander, nuclear or chemical strikes from the division's FROG tactical rocket battalion may be employed. Such chemical or nuclear strikes will be allocated to the division from Army. Air support and helicopter attack sorties are allocated to the division or are available on call to supplement division helicopter resources. Army and frontal long-range artillery and missiles will be used to reinforce fires.

In addition to the variations described, there are, of course, many other possibilities as formations move on a fluid battlefield and encounter one another. The meeting engagement will not always unfold in the sequence of encounters by reconnaissance elements, advance elements, and main bodies. Neither will it invariably begin with a head-to-head meeting. It may arise from direct encounter by main bodies or from oblique encounters of the many possible variations. One example will serve to show the flexibility of division employment. A division could be assigned the mission of acting as an operational maneuver group (OMG) for an Army advance. In such a case, having penetrated the line of contact, it might move with three regiments roughly abreast on a wide front. Each regiment would have the role of a lead regiment. The division commander would have to respond to the scale of an initial encounter with substantial enemy forces. In this linear formation, a regiment making the first major encounter would become the fixing force, and the other regiments would move to the attack laterally, not directly forward, to destroy enemy forces from the flanks, by encirclement or by fire. Whatever the patterns and conditions, the Soviet's formula for successful meeting engagement requires surprise, rapid execution of decisive employments, and concentrated fires against the enemy.

The meeting engagement terminates under any of the following conditions:

(1) The advance guard or the main force has succeeded in destroying the enemy and resumes the march.
(2) The main force has shifted to the defense, pending initiation of another form of offensive action.
(3) The main force is required to withdraw.

ATTACK OF A DEFENDING ENEMY

The essential aims of Soviet offensive combat at any level are to destroy enemy forces and to seize important terrain. They are generally realized by following a course characterized by rapid buildup of forces, echelonment of forces, massing forces and fires in the "decisive direction," and continuous development of the attack by intense combat.[9] Attack operations follow a basic pattern that includes advancing to an attack line, assaulting while exploiting concentrated fire, anticipating and defeating counterattacks, striking through the depth of defense, and exploiting any first echelon success.

First echelon forces attack to destroy any opposing enemy troops that survive the initial suppressive fires and to create favorable conditions for second echelon forces to exploit. Massive suppressive fires that enable the "strike" into the key points and full depth of an enemy's defense are exploited through the vigorous sustained forward movement of attacking troop formations. Attacking forces will attempt to bypass strong points and envelop defensive positions. The maneuvers used will vary with the situation; they range from the frontal attack to deep or close envelopment, either alone or in combination. Attacks will attempt to exploit gaps in a defense and to maneuver against its flanks and rear. Attack operations stress firepower, mobility, maneuver, and continuous momentum, underscored by speed of execution. For this purpose, the attack from the march is favored. The importance of surprise in offensive combat receives particular emphasis and close study. Feints and ruses will characterize the planned deception prescribed for Soviet ground force attacks.

Suppressive fires by artillery and air will precede an assault by maneuver units and support their subsequent combat actions through the depth of the defense. The attack may be carried out by bringing up forces to pass through units already in contact with the defense (i.e., an attack from the march) or following required regroupment by a carefully planned, well-coordinated attack from positions in contact. This kind of deliberate attack will require a substantial concentration of forces and massive fire support, which consumes considerable time. The Soviets prefer a rapid attack to reduce risks and vulnerability to nuclear weapons, maintain a high tempo of action and rate of advance, limit losses, and, where possible, exploit the lack of enemy preparations for defense. If practicable, the Soviets may attack a defense directly from the march.

Nuclear capabilities and vulnerabilities make the need for mobility in attacking the defending enemy a crucial requirement. In a nuclear environment, time is critical for mounting and executing an attack, meeting the requirements for "continual continuity of combat"; conducting preliminary and continuing reconnaissance and intelligence gathering, arranging essential coordination, and maintaining effective command and control. Nuclear weapons are the element that can most suddenly and acutely change the course of battle. Soviet attack planning takes this potential into careful account. Soviet capabilities for using weapons of mass destruction are significant and substantial. If their use is authorized, tactical forces are prepared to exploit the effects.[10] An apparently effective organization, extensive training, and specially designed equipment such as collective protection breathing equipment in tanks also helps shield them from nuclear attack by the enemy.

Soviet operational level (*operativniye*) offensive plans may direct tactical level attacks along particular axes as part of a large-scale maneuver. They frequently prescribe in detail how combat actions will be carried out: to split an enemy defense, to destroy specific enemy forces in a prescribed sequence, or to seize terrain objectives within a planned period of time. The suppressive fire plan and the allocation from higher headquarters of various combat support units and resources may govern how tactical attacks will be executed as part of the larger offensive. They may also establish time and space limits for planning the combat actions to be carried out by divisions, regiments, and battalions in attacks against a defending enemy. For a division attack, normally one main axis and one secondary axis are selected. The entire division may be concentrated along the main axis if that is necessary to achieve force superiority. Regiments and battalions usually attack on a single axis.

Soviet doctrine distinguishes between quick attacks and deliberate attacks. A general spectrum of these types and distinguishing characteristics is shown in Figure 3.11. A quick attack from the march against a prepared enemy position or a hasty defense may be mounted by a division within about an hour. A deliberate attack against a well-prepared position may be staged from an assembly area. If an assembly area is used, the stay will be limited to the time necessary to assign missions to subordinate units, check preparations, and organize combat formations. The assembly area will be far enough forward for first echelon regiments to move to their lines of deployment, normally during the hours of darkness, and to reach their attack lines during the artillery preparation.

The Soviets usually will concentrate the forces necessary to achieve desired local superiority for any attack. Divisions committed to main effort attacks may reduce frontages to as small as four kilometers compared with the nearly 15 kilometers in secondary attack areas.

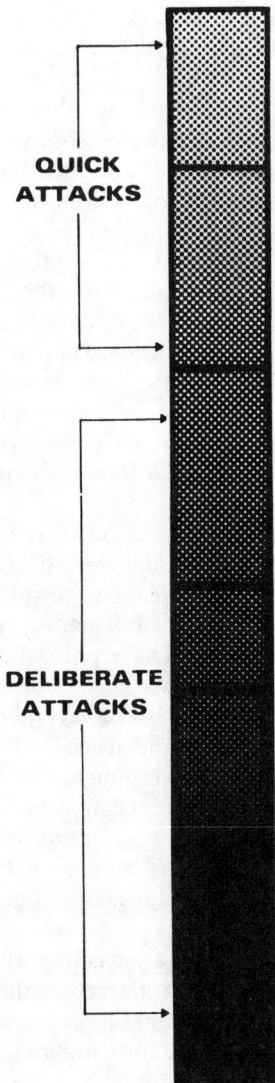

QUICK ATTACKS

Quick Mounted Attack in Advance Guard Action
- Combines frontal, flanking attacks and available fire support; comparable to the meeting engagement

Quick Mounted Attack from the March, Broad Front, Against Hasty Defense
- Rapid, minimum-necessary coordination
- Immediately available or on-call suppressive fire support

Mounted Attack from the March Against Enemy in Prepared Positions
- Rapid Deployment
- Attack maintained without halt
- Support by forward-deployed artillery

Dismounted Attack Against a Defense Having a High Density of Anti-tank Weapons

DELIBERATE ATTACKS

Deliberate Attack Against Prepared Defense (Mounted or Dismounted)
- Systematic but rapid planning and coordination
- Stong fire support
- Forces concentrated; organized in two echelons

Deliberate Attack Against a Fortified Position
- Meticulous planning
- Thorough coordination
- Heavy fire support
- Concentration and deep echelonment

Figure 3.11. Spectrum of Attack Tactics

BREAKTHROUGH

The breakthrough is a form of attack employed when the enemy occupies a well-organized defense. The Soviets do not expect this maneuver to occur very frequently in modern war. They would plan to surprise NATO forces and therefore would attack at a time and place where NATO forces are not properly organized for the defense. If a nuclear war should evolve, it is expected that continuous lines will, in general, not exist; however, this form of warfare has not been completely ignored by the Soviets.

The Soviets see three ways of achieving the concentration of forces required to break through a continuous well-organized defense line:

(1) Concentrating forces "on the ground" in the event that nuclear weapons are not expected to be used, especially by the enemy;
(2) Concentrating forces "in time" to bring forces on the march into combat rapidly, thus minimizing their concentration time and making them relatively immune to attack by nuclear weapons;
(3) Employing weapons of mass destruction (nuclear or chemical) which, upon their sudden and unexpected use, would create large gaps in a continuous defensive line of the enemy.

Only a few words will be said about concentration on the ground, since that is a method the Soviets think is unlikely.[11] Concentration in time achieved, in general, by introducing second echelons (Figure 3.4), mobile or shock groups, or operational maneuver groups will be discussed more fully. Finally, the use of weapons of mass destruction--a special case of concentration in time--will also be examined briefly.

A breakthrough operation against a stiff forward defense would be carried out in the classical Soviet manner, using heavy conventional suppressive fires and the timely application of the "massive blow," followed up with supporting echeloned forces. Soviet doctrine calls for using these techniques in the face of a prepared or heavy defense, especially when Soviet attempts at deception and surprise have failed and NATO's forces have been positioned properly to deal with an expected Soviet attack. The Soviets had considerable World War II experience in breaking through prepared defenses. In a nonnuclear conflict they would expect to draw on that experience, which has been described extensively and can be a useful body of knowledge.

Along a small sector of the defense, the Soviets' suppression, maneuver, logistics, and air defense are massed and focused against the opposing forces. The means of suppression include artillery (guns, missiles, multiple rocket launchers, and mortar's), helicopter artillery and close air support. If required, conventional suppression can be augmented by weapons of mass destruction delivered by missiles and aircraft that reach out to include not only front line units but if possible, reserves, especially those committed to the defense. The artillery will attack targets up to 20 kilometers behind the line of contact. Protection for this concentration of force elements is provided by a mobile air defense umbrella made up of a number of gun and surface-to-air missile systems having significant overlap and depth. Logistic support is provided using operational concepts that can place Army and Front assets in direct support of the assaulting divisions.

A good mobile defense in depth, however, cannot be defeated without the direct fire of maneuver units. Assaults carried out by lead motorized rifle and tank elements are directed against platoon strong points, which are expected to fall after they have been partially attrited by artillery fire. Soviet offensive doctrine calls for lead elements of the first echelon units to penetrate defenses to as great a depth as possible. Following on their heels to maintain momentum are elements of the second echelon unit.

Organizational problems encountered in building up the number of vehicles needed to accomplish a breakthrough are enormous. The hundreds or thousands of vehicles might extend many kilometers rearward from the line of contact. Buildup starts with front line security forces and their artillery, logistics, and engineering support, all protected by air defense. Maneuver elements are programmed to come in on the run. Soviet doctrine calls for entering the attack directly from march formation. This accomplishes two goals: first, it maintains momentum once the attack is begun; second, it minimizes the time those elements that cannot disperse are exposed to attack. The risk of massing maneuver units is countered by minimizing the amount of time they remain massed, and by suppressing the enemy's nuclear battlefield capabilities. When the first echelon elements of the attacking unit have seized their primary objectives, second echelon units are brought into combat to exploit the new severely attrited defense and to move forward to seize the unit's primary objectives.

As noted above, the key element in the breakthrough is the second echelon unit, which attacks at the right moment to destroy the attrited enemy units. For this reason, the employment of second echelons will be discussed at length. A second echelon unit receives its mission at the same time as the first echelon unit. If the situation alters radically after that, the commander normally will either issue a new order or clarify the original. The main direction of advance, the objectives, or the times of attack are easily revised. Soviet literature also suggests that sometimes mobile groups, shock groups, or operational maneuver groups may be substituted for second echelon units but the usage frequently appears to be identical.

The second echelon unit enters into combat in one of three ways (Figure 3.12). Most commonly, it will be introduced between two first echelon units that either have moved apart in order to make a space or have suffered attrition so that space exists between the two units (A). Under these circumstances, the second echelon unit will receive fire support form the two units on either side. The second method is by sending the second echelon unit around an open flank (B). Here, fire support comes only from the one side, a less desirable situation. Moreover, open flanks are not expected to be that common. The least common method of introducing the second echelon is by passing through a unit in combat (C). There are a number of drawbacks to such an operation, it must be very carefully controlled, it presents a vulnerable target for either nuclear or conventional weapons at the time of actual pass-through and, at best, even a carefully controlled passage of lines is organizationally extremely complex.

The introduction of second echelons is achieved only by very careful prior planning with adjacent units. Liaison officers from the adjacent units usually will spend the night before an operation with the penetrating unit and return to their command post immediately before the attack. Almost universally, the second echelon unit enters combat from the march, possibly screened by a forward detachment that will seize important terrain such as bridges or high ground, or will block the approach of enemy units. Fire support will come from units adjacent to the introduction point; there will be close air support and perhaps the use of nuclear or chemical weapons.

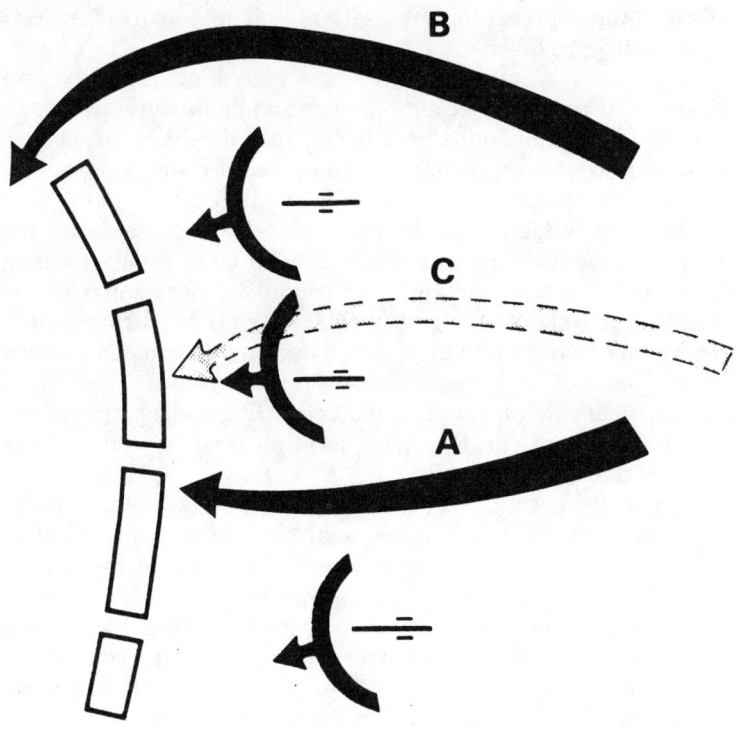

Figure 3.12. Introduction of the 2nd Echelon into Combat

The most usual roles for second echelons are the accumulation of force in the direction of the main attack and the breakthrough to immediate and subsequent intermediate objectives. Second echelons have secondary missions, such as repelling counterattacks, covering open flanks, creating an external front for surrounding a unit, and replacing units of the first echelon that have suffered serious losses in the offense and are unable to continue the advance. In general, the Soviets never plan to reinforce a unit that is in trouble with a second echelon unit. In normal operations, however, introducing a second echelon unit into combat is planned with several variations. Mobile groups or reserves, as a rule, are expected to fulfill such tactical missions as:

(1) Completely destroying the enemy in the tactical, as well as the operational, depths of the defense;
(2) Cutting off the enemy's retreat, with the aim of completely destroying him;
(3) Destroying approaching reserves and seizing important objectives and enemy defense lines.

In all cases, introducing second echelons and mobile groups into combat is supported by the major units' artillery with densities of perhaps 60 to 80 weapons per kilometer, Front aviation, and Front engineer troops. In preparing for the operation, second echelon divisions usually are located between 30 and 100 kilometers from the line of direct contact with the enemy (Figure 3.4). This allows the units to be hidden from enemy reconnaissance and keeps them relatively immune to his ground artillery and rocket weapons, while at the same time allowing for a relatively short entrance into combat. The assembly areas and surroundings are thoroughly combed to discover and destroy any air assault or parachute troops that may be dropped into the area. Intensive efforts at misinformation and camouflage will be made in order to confuse the enemy as to the true location and intended direction of employment of the second echelon.

If Soviets believe that NATO forces will not be able to establish an adequate defense in depth, an operational maneuver group (OMG) may be employed. The Army OMG, typically a reinforced tank or heavily reinforced motorized rifle division, will be used somewhat like the "normal" second echelon. An OMG, however, might be committed before a gap is opened by first echelon forces if the commander judges that he has weakened the defensive line adequately. The commander of an OMG will be allowed greater latitude in time of attack and will be given mission-type orders for continuation of his attack deep in enemy defenses.

Typically, the plan will call for the OMG to operate much as the Forward Detachment does at lower levels. It is expected to seize key terrain or destroy operationally significant enemy installation; e.g., NATO's wartime headquarters or a major theater nuclear force depot. Because it is expected to be committed while defensive forces are still intact, the OMG will need fire support of the maneuver elements during movement from the assembly area to and through the area of commitment. The use of air and missiles is required to attack those elements beyond the range of the OMG. Typically the OMG will require additional command, control, and communication to support the additional fire and maneuver resources attached from Front resources.

For the properly organized introduction of a unit into combat, the commanders of the units to be introduced are moved forward to the initial line with a group of staff officers and with reconnaissance means. There, directly on the terrain, they firm up the combat formations for entrance into battle and coordinate with the units of the first echelon. Committing second echelons to combat is dependent on thorough organization and coordination, both the evening before and immediately prior to the operation. Coordination also includes engineer support and the careful use of traffic regulators on the march routes. Proper organization of fire support by the adjacent units of the first echelon and by Army and Front units in support of the unit to make the breakthrough can be decisive.

One of the most important decisions is the moment for introducing the second echelon into combat. Soviet experience shows that the best time is when the second echelon will cause a decisive break in the course of combat in favor of the offensive. In order to achieve a cumulative effect on the enemy, the second echelon must be introduced before the first echelon has lost its momentum and slowed the tempo of its offensive. Committing an element of the second echelon too early would lead it to assume the mission of the first echelon, thereby jeopardizing the overall mission. In contrast the OMG takes on the mission of destroying forces in place whether or not the first echelon was to have destroyed them. The second echelon must not come too late since that would allow the enemy to prepare a counterattack.

When the second echelon unit is ready to enter combat, the unit commander clarifies its mission by explaining to the second echelon commander the character of the enemy action, what objectives or strong points on the route of main attack have been destroyed by artillery, what are the conditions near the initial line, and the exact time set for reaching the initial line. He also specifies the time for seizing the immediate objectives and the direction of further advance. He makes necessary changes in the reinforcing means and assures that coordination with elements of the first echelon and adjacent units is perfectly clear. Should a unit be introduced into combat from an unplanned initial point, changes in orders for subordinate units usually will be made by radio. Prior to launching the attack, there usually will be a short artillery preparation against enemy strong points, including direct artillery fire against tanks and antitank weapons.[12] Upon approaching the initial line, the unit making the attack will deploy from march formation to combat formation in the manner previously described.

A nuclear weapon might be used to create an initial opening for the breakthrough. In some circumstances, the entire breakthrough might be achieved with a group of nuclear weapons. Soviet doctrine is heavily weighted in favor of using nuclear weapons preemptively. Once the enemy's continuous line has been broken, introducing a second echelon unit will proceed as described above.

Units responsible for main axis attacks will be augmented and reinforced to meet prescribed superiority norms and attack requirements. Their combat formations will include units of the combat arms and the augmentations needed to accomplish the combat mission.

Forces will be appropriately organized and echeloned in depth for their assigned combat tasks. Just as their assigned missions may vary, so may the combat composition and organization differ at successive levels. Units as small as motorized rifle or tank battalions will be augmented with reinforcing artillery, air defense artillery, tank, antitank, engineer, or chemical units. Regiments fight as combined arms units, and their organization for combat builds on their organic capabilities. A typical combat organization for motorized rifle and tank regiments is shown in Figure 3.13.

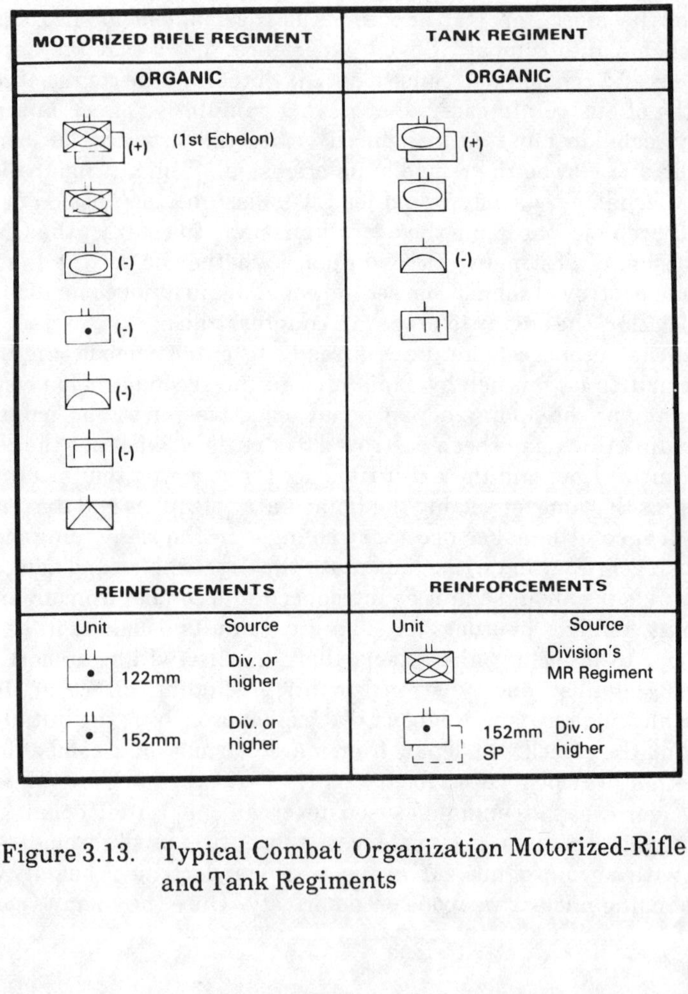

MOTORIZED RIFLE REGIMENT	TANK REGIMENT
ORGANIC	ORGANIC
⊠ (+) (1st Echelon)	◯ (+)
⊠	◯
◯ (-)	△ (-)
• (-)	冊
△ (-)	
冊 (-)	
△	
REINFORCEMENTS	REINFORCEMENTS
Unit Source	Unit Source
• 122mm Div. or higher	⊠ Division's MR Regiment
• 152mm Div. or higher	• 152mm SP Div. or higher

Figure 3.13. Typical Combat Organization Motorized-Rifle and Tank Regiments

These capabilities will be reinforced and supported for an attack, depending on the nature of the terrain and enemy capabilities. In addition to its tank battalion, the motorized rifle regiment includes in its basic organization an artillery battalion and organic reconnaissance, air defense, antitank, and engineer elements. The motorized rifle regiment will also be augmented by artillery allocations from higher levels.

The tank regiment of the motorized rifle division provides a force available to the division commander for exploiting the results of attacks by the reinforced motorized rifle regiments. Battalions of the tank regiment also may augment first echelon motorized rifle regiments; if the tank regiment is committed later, its battalions will revert to regimental control. Similarly, the motorized rifle regiment of the tank division may not always fight as a unit since its battalions may be attached to tank regiments. The tank regiment contains about 100 tanks. While in the past this unit had no organic motorized rifle troops, it now includes at least a motorized rifle company. It may receive a battalion of motorized rifle troops from the tank division's motorized rifle regiment. It has no organic artillery but, when committed to battle, normally will be allocated one or more battalions of division artillery, tactically organized for its support.

A Soviet division, in addition to the fighting strength of its combat regiments, may receive, for example, reinforcements from Army and Front resources as follows:

(1) Two to four artillery battalions;
(2) One combat engineer company;
(3) One engineer construction company;
(4) One pontoon bridge company;
(5) One engineer amphibian company.

Such augmentations significantly extend the capabilities of division forces which, in some cases, already include an independent tank battalion in the motorized rifle division. Other Army and Front augmentations to the division may include additional air defense, communications support, signal intelligence resources, medical support, chemical defense, and motor transport.

In organizing for combat, artillery groups are formed and specific units are allocated to them on the basis of the importance of the tasks to be carried out by the combined arms force at regiment and division level. In a division attack, at least half of the divisional artillery will be in support of first echelon regiments. Each first echelon regiment may have an artillery group organized for its support. Depending on its mission, a first echelon division may receive additional artillery in allocations from Front and Army. That artillery may be organized into artillery groups at the division level or allocated to support first echelon regiments.

Principal considerations for forming artillery groups are the availability of artillery and ammunition and the requirements of the mission. At division and regiment levels, an artillery group usually will be formed if more than one artillery battalion is available to support the attack. Specific allocations of artillery for support and attacks are made on the basis of careful assessment and calculation of the numbers and types of targets expected to be encountered in the course of the attack through the entire depth of the enemy defense. If nuclear and chemical weapons are not used, conventional artillery will be employed on a larger scale. Allocations of artillery to attacking units will be in keeping with their roles and missions in the planned attack. A first echelon division artillery group (DAG) might be allocated three or more battalions of Front and Army artillery. A division might have several DAGs. A first echelon regiment on a main axis might have an additional one to two battalions to form a regimental artillery group (RAG). A maneuver battalion in the first echelon attack force often will have an artillery battalion in support. In a deliberate attack, control of available artillery will be centralized. The division commander will act to continue or discontinue the assignment of units to artillery groups as appropriate to the developing situation.

A balance will be sought between the need for nuclear dispersion and the requirements for local superiority through rapid concentration of forces on the main axis. Within the assigned zones of action, actual attack frontages will be established by commanders concerned, depending on the type of attack formation to be used. Determining the width of an attack front will be guided by prescriptions that such frontages:[13]

(1) Must provide for superiority over the opposing enemy force at the start of the attack and to the depth of the assigned objectives;
(2) Must allow effective employment of organic and attached unit personnel and weapons without congestion; and,
(3) Must permit development of favorable conditions for maneuver by first echelon units and second echelon elements when committed.

In preparing for the attack, the commander is expected to follow troop-leading procedures very much like those discussed earlier. Having made an assessment of the situation, the commander makes his decision and issues his orders. In his decision, he spells out the plan of attack, designating targets for nuclear, chemical and conventional suppressive fires; states immediate and subsequent missions; assigns combat tasks to subordinate units; and details the measures to be used for coordination and control. The established form of the Soviet combat order permits subordinate commanders to understand fully the attack concept, their specific combat mission, and organization for combat. When time is limited, especially during an active combat phase, the commander may issue abbreviated instructions instead of a formal combat order. Combat instructions indicate the combat tasks for subordinate units and subunits, planned fire support, and the time troops are to be ready. These instructions may also specify the methods of attack and the mission of adjacent units.

The depth of attack objectives is determined by the depth of the defensive positions, location of enemy forces, and the objectives of higher headquarters.

Divisions and regiments are assigned an immediate and a subsequent mission or objective. First echelon battalions are assigned an immediate mission and direction of further advance. The immediate mission of a battalion in the attack usually calls for destroying enemy personnel and weapons in the strong points of the defender's first echelon battalions. Subsequent objectives will then be assigned. The objectives of any unit in the attack will correspond with those of the next higher commander. Thus, a regimental commander may have an immediate objective for his leading battalions, between which his second echelon will pass to gain the subsequent objectives. Thereby, he achieves the division's immediate objective.

Other measures to make ready for an attack will include:

(1) Concentrating reconnaissance activity in the direction of the planned main effort;
(2) Checking the operational readiness of communications;
(3) Coordinating arrangements for artillery allocated from higher headquarters;
(4) Organizing other support (this may include, for example, obstacle clearing, tactical air support, etc.);
(5) Assigning and appropriately deploying reconnaissance resources, engineer and artillery units, and control elements and facilities at required locations; and
(6) Supervising deployment, replenishment and supply activity, and concealment discipline.

A division's reconnaissance screen will operate forward of the leading elements of the division advance guard. it will consist of the division reconnaissance battalion augmented by engineer and chemical/radiological reconnaissance personnel. Other tactical reconnaissance measures such as ground, air, radio/electronic, and artillery, will be organized to provide current information. Organization and concentration of reconnaissance against the defensive sector planned for deliberate attack will employ observation, monitoring by listening post, patrolling, raids, and ambushes. The divisional radio and radio-technical reconnaissance company will be deployed directly behind the combat units of first echelon regiments to conduct radio intercept and direction finding as part of the reconnaissance mission.

The Front commander allocates tactical aviation[14] support to armies and divisions for specific operations. To plan an air assault operation as part of an attack, there is a time-consuming requirement for detailed coordination with higher echelons to arrange airlift, ensure suppression of enemy air defense, and provide for fire support. Even more significant, planning air strike missions as part of suppressive preparatory fires, and arranging close air support for the continuing attack must be closely integrated with the division's missile and artillery fire plan and the advance of the maneuver force. Coordinating air and artillery strikes is of major importance, with the artillery preparation concentrating on enemy artillery, strong points in the defense, and command posts, while air strikes are directed at deeper targets, such as airfields and other tactical nuclear delivery means. Increasingly, Soviet attack helicopters will participate in fire support and close air support missions planned for tactical attacks.

The artillery fire plan will include specification of the time of reassignments, regroupings, and displacement of artillery. Fragmentary orders provide details concerning the missions of designated artillery units and identify the location of observation posts and unit areas for firing positions. Deadlines for units to be ready to fire will be announced. Artillery units will be among the first combat forces to deploy.

Artillery units allocated by higher echelons will join the designated elements of the attack force, if necessary, in the assembly area or will link up on the march. Artillery designated to support or reinforce the attack will take up firing positions early enough to be ready to cover the advance of the division in an attack from the march several hours before the attack is to be launched. Artillery attached to maneuver regiments usually moves at the head of the main forces. Based on requirements of the artillery fire plan, the designated artillery will move forward at a speed that will permit it to occupy new positions about an hour-and-a-half before the maneuver force is deployed for the attack.

Nuclear fires may be planned as an integral element of the basic fire plan for attack. Where surprise is a major consideration, both nuclear and chemical fires may be employed in conjunction with or instead of conventional artillery and air attacks. Conventional fires may follow to support the planned ground attack. Fire planning, being highly centralized, will integrate conventional artillery and air strikes as well as missile strikes and possible nuclear or chemical fires. For the attack, the fire planning, which is conducted in the first echelon regiments and divisions, is based on the scheme of maneuver and fire support plan of the division and higher echelons.

The Chief of Rocket Troops and Artillery (CRTA) at division level receives instructions from and advises the division commander on nuclear fires allotted to the division and plans for integrating nuclear, chemical, and conventional fires and available air strikes; fires to create passages through obstacles and obstructions; priorities of sectors of the enemy defense that are to be neutralized; and starting time, duration, and phases of the fire preparation. The CRTA also advises the division commander on methods of supporting the attack, plans for partial decentralization of artillery control during the course of battle and the scheme of reinforcement of the assault units with accompanying artillery, and the plan of support for commitment of second echelon forces and reserves. The division fire plan is based on the Army fire plan. The CRTA incorporates planned fires of the artillery groups into the Army plan, including them in the division fire plan. The completed division plan is forwarded to Army for approval and incorporation into the Army plan.

Fire planning is basically designed to suppress enemy defensive capabilities, including artillery (except nuclear artillery, where the requirement is destruction), and to cover the deployment and initial assault of the attacking maneuver elements. High priority is given to neutralizing enemy antitank defenses and to preparing for the engagement of possible counterattack forces. Fire planning also provides for suppressing enemy strong points on the flanks of the attack zones. Doctrine stresses the importance of concentrating artillery weapons in attacks. Planners will attempt to achieve the necessary densities of weapons for artillery in support of an attack. Relatively high numbers of artillery weapons per kilometer of attack frontages are desired. (These are discussed in Chapter 4, NORMS.)

If nuclear or chemical strikes are to be made, they will be planned for the beginning of the preparatory fires in order to achieve surprise, generally about thirty minutes before 'H' hour. There would be no pause between the end of the preparatory fires and the start of fire support for the attack. Fire planning will provide for continuity of fires with regular shifts of firing batteries, battalions, and observation posts. Normally, artillery is held under centralized division control for more rapid response during the preparation. The fire plan may provide for partial decentralization of control when the attack begins.

Troops will be dispersed in assembly areas, with their attached reinforcements, and will be grouped by battalions. Their movement routes, with prescribed control and deployment lines, will permit rapid, effective movement to the attack line. The attack lines will be designated in the combat order and planned to be as near as possible to the forward positions of the enemy defenses so as to provide cover against antitank and machine- gun fire.

CONDUCT OF THE ATTACK

If the attack is to be from the march, without prior contact, a division commander may first have to drive back or destroy enemy covering forces. Forward detachments and advance guard units, usually reinforced companies and battalions, will be used in the attack of covering forces. First echelon regiments will attack the main defensive positions after the covering force has been driven back and the outline of the defensive positions established. In the Soviet view, a defensive covering force generally will have relatively light strength and will occupy a defense in the security zone only on the most important avenues of approach of the attacker. As a basic rule, a delaying action will be fought by the covering force. On that account, the Soviets generally commit limited attack strength to driving out the covering force and will attempt quickly to establish the current location, outline, and strength of the main defensive positions for attack by the main force.

Forward detachments will try to outflank the covering force. If necessary, they will attack from the march after a brief artillery preparation of 10 to 20 minutes, but will avoid prolonged contact. After bypassing the covering forces, they leave the attack in the security zone to advance guard units of about reinforced battalion strength that attempt to clear the axes of advance for the main force. To minimize delay and rapidly overcome the defense in the security zone, the Soviets will strengthen the advance guard with engineer and artillery support. Whenever possible, the advance guard will attempt to assault the forward edge of the forward defensive area directly from the march. Rapid deployment into company and platoon columns will follow the basic deployment as the main part of the advance guard attempts to assault the main defense position. Depending on the situation and their mission, advance guard units may attempt to breach the defense at a weakly defended area, bypass strongly defended positions, or fix the enemy in place. Even before the main attack, Soviet forces will be trying to envelop enemy defensive strong points and penetrate the defense to support the deployment and commitment into combat of the main body. If appropriate, the Soviet advance guard may be a regimental size force and operate more deliberately, including the use of attack helicopters, to uncover the defense. Following strikes by fixed- wing ground-attack fighters and artillery preparation for the attack, attack helicopters will provide close fire support for the advance guard by sustaining the suppressive fires and attacking enemy armor as targets of opportunity. With the advance guard in contact and diversionary attacks fixing the enemy defensive force, first echelon forces will then move rapidly to assault critical parts of the main line of resistance.

Whenever possible, the Soviets will attack from the line of march, using all available routes and tracks or, if necessary, by moving tactical columns cross-country. If an enemy defense is weak or ill-prepared, units may attack in platoon or company columns. Battalions will deploy into company columns. Against a strong defense, all first echelon assault units are expected to cross the attack line at the same time so they can reach the objective together. If tanks and artillery fire support have neutralized the defense, infantry will remain mounted for the attack. Dismounted attacks will be used against strong, continuous defenses, particularly in nonnuclear conditions. If necessary or appropriate, attacking units will move from deployed combat formations back to column during the course of the attack. When assembly areas are occupied by division units before an attack, first echelon regiments will move to their lines of deployment for the attack during hours of darkness or under conditions of restricted visibility. If attacking directly from the march, division main body forces may attack within two hours. The next higher commander specifies the start time for moving out, the line of deployment into company columns, and the line and time for the attack. Unit movement to the attack line will be covered by an artillery preparation which will fire its heaviest concentrations at the end of the preparatory phase.

During the move to attack positions, engineer units will open lanes and passages through obstacles, mine fields, or wire, in front of the forward edge of the enemy defense. The number of passages or lanes will depend on the number of columns required for the attack and on the terrain. Ideally, the Soviets visualize one lane per assault platoon. If necessary, the leading tanks in the assault will clear paths and and deal with mine fields, using mine plows and explosives.

Artillery support will provide a pattern of fire about 200 to 400 meters ahead of troops advancing on foot as part of the preplanned fires of the attack.

Fires will lead advancing tanks by about 100 meters. Fires like the "rolling barrages" of World War II are unlikely, but fires on successive concentrations or on successive fire lines will be provided. "On call" fires are delivered as needed. Control of fire remains centralized. The regimental commander directs artillery and tank fire against enemy strong points and attempts to neutralize or destroy enemy tanks, artillery, and antitank guided missiles by concentrated fire. Successive concentrations of fire may be used along the main axes of attack if enough artillery is available. Leading assault elements will move closely behind such fires as they shift from the forward edge further into the depths of the enemy defense. As the attack begins, artillery fires will be shifted to successive fire lines, and attacking forces will make a rapid assault against the forward edge of the defense to penetrate the position before defending forces can effectively recover. The Soviets anticipate that enemy troops in a prepared defense could man their positions effectively within two to three minutes after suppressive fires have been lifted.

After breaking into the forward edge of an enemy defense, attacking forces will attempt to destroy enemy personnel and weapons and project the attack further into the depths of the defensive position. Enemy strong points and blocking positions that cannot be reduced immediately may be bypassed. If this is impossible, an attack will be made against them, with, if needed, a short, intense artillery preparation. Successive neutralization and suppression will be a continuing artillery and air support mission. Separate attacks of varying scale may be needed through the depth of the defense to the objective. Close and continuing fire support by massed fires, by fires on individual targets, and by direct and indirect fires against counterattacks will be employed. Self-propelled artillery may be used in close accompaniment to advancing motorized rifle troops. Smoke and flame weapons may be used on a sizable scale against strong points.

Part of the attack force will meet any counterattack head-on while the main strength of the attacking unit strikes the defender's counterattack on the flanks and rear. Artillery fires will be brought in rapidly. Regimental and division antitank reserves will move forward and lay hasty mine fields. If necessary, the attacking force may temporarily take up the defense to defeat counterattacks before it resumes the offensive.

When the regiment's first echelon battalions have achieved penetration, the attack plan may require that the area of penetration be widened for exploitation by second echelon forces, or it may provide that first echelon attacking units continue the attack further into the enemy position. Maneuver and surprise may mark this phase of the attack. Attack units may revert to an approach formation and advance rapidly to deny enemy movements of reserves and supplies and to prevent the organization of defense on new positions. Actions of the regiment's first echelon maneuver battalions also may include consolidating gains, widening the gap and holding the shoulders of a penetration, or attacking in a new direction.

The Soviets visualize that an enemy will throw all his forces and means into the battle from the immediate depth, commit other forces to restore his defensive position, attempt to assess rapidly the direction and weight of the main attack, and relocate available defense forces in an effort to defeat that attack. For such reasons, the regimental commander will be particularly alert for enemy counterattacks as the first echelon attack battalions move to their subsequent tasks. Regimental success may provide the basis for the division's exploitation. A first echelon regiment that has successfully penetrated the enemy forward defenses may commit its immediate reinforcement capability (its own second echelon) to the attack or establish the gap through which the division follow-on force will attack. The first echelon regiment may become a forward detachment and be tasked to move ahead of the division to seize important objectives in depth. Often such actions will take place in cooperation with heliborne forces. Regiments may themselves send out forward detachments of battalion strength, following initial success. With a motorized rifle division, the independent tank battalion, if present, is likely to be used in this role. The actions of all forward detachments employed by the division are coordinated by the division commander.

The division's second echelon is, ideally, committed on completion of the division's immediate task in order to intensify the thrust on the main axis (Figure 3.14). This commitment must take place before the first echelon regiments are exhausted so that the momentum of the advance does not slacken. The second echelon may be committed as an enemy counterattack is repulsed by the initial assault force. The division's second echelon will move forward in march formation and deploy on its "line of commitment" protected by antitank reserves and divisional air defense subunits. Movement will normally be from prepositioned locations along a main route.

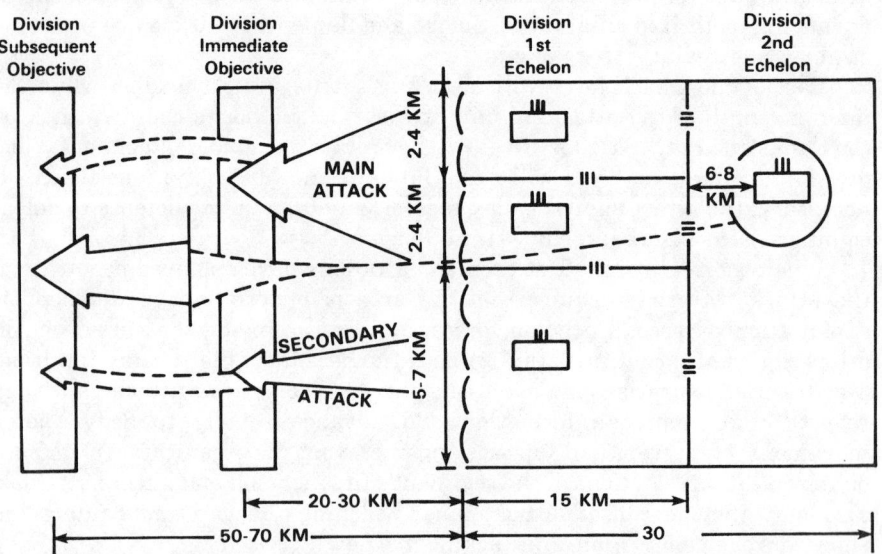

Figure 3.14. Type Division Deployment for Attack of a Defending Enemy

A gap of some two to five kilometers between first echelon regiments is required for a second echelon regiment to pass through, unless it deploys to a flank. If the enemy is withdrawing, second echelon regiments could, however, pass through in columns. The commitment of the second echelon probably will be marked by an intensification of reconnaissance and increased artillery support. Lacking direct contact, second echelon forces will need information on the organization of enemy positions, antitank barriers, command and control of the defense, support and coordination of the fires. Air strikes will be intensified to support commitment of the second echelon. The second echelon usually attacks from the march, especially if it is to make a quick attack. The second echelon regiment will approach the enemy defense either in march, approach march, or combat formation. If moving immediately to the attack, the frontage will be wider than in other attack situations because of a greater possibility that the enemy will use nuclear weapons. The advance guard of the second echelon regiment will attack into the gap created by the first echelon, which will permit the main body to move rapidly into the enemy's rear.

If nuclear weapons have been used against enemy reserves, second echelon forces of the leading assault elements will attempt to bypass surviving centers of resistance. They will develop the attack and attempt to deny the enemy the chance to bring up fresh reserves, reinforce the defense, or prepare counterattacks. Surviving centers of resistance will be attacked by follow-on forces or destroyed by concentrated forces of artillery attack helicopters, and tactical aviation. Hastily occupied positions or lines deep in the enemy defense will be attacked by advancing second echelon forces directly from the march in mounted formations; a dismounted attack may, however, be required if mine fields are present or a plethora of antitank weapons survives.

As a basic rule, second echelon units will attempt to remain in column for ease of control and rapid advance, unless confronted by an effective antitank defense. First echelon regiments, assisted by the second echelon, will continue the attack on the main axes and expand the breaks in the prepared defense to envelop and isolate enemy units. Intensified reconnaissance, artillery and air strikes, and rapid local attacks will be used to locate and destroy enemy nuclear systems and reserves.

OFFENSIVE TANK OPERATIONS

Tank units, possessing high maneuverability, great firepower and resulting shock force are capable of moving rapidly to the defensive lines of the enemy and can attack from the march. Developing the offensive at a high tempo, they can break through gaps between strong points and deal decisive blows on the enemy's flanks and rear. The tank, basic shock power of the Ground Forces and a powerful means of armed combat, is designed to accomplish the most important missions in various kinds of combat.[15] Tanks are the best vehicle for intensive and rapid maneuvering combat actions following the use of nuclear weapons or other weapons of mass destruction.

The tank division's mission, when used in the first echelon, is to penetrate enemy defenses, exploit gaps created in the enemy defenses, destroy the continuity of the defense, and assist in securing the army's objectives. Only when the terrain, enemy troop dispositions, or time dictate, will the tank division undertake a coordinated, deliberate attack against prepared defenses. The tank division will exploit gaps created in the enemy defenses by the initial thrust of a motorized rifle division, attack to destroy or isolate remaining enemy forces, or bypass enemy resistance to destroy the enemy corps reserves. Its operations are directed primarily toward preventing the enemy force from reconstituting an organized defense or making an orderly retrograde movement. At the first sign of an enemy withdrawal, the tank division will start pursuit.

When the forward defenses are passed, the tank division overruns and destroys isolated enemy groups. If resistance is too great, the assault is broken off, containing forces are left to await the arrival of motorized rifle units, and the tank forces move on. Crossroads, bridges, and other terrain features whose seizure would result in cutting off enemy forces are seized. Enemy command posts and logistical installations are overrun, weapons seized, and lines of communications severed as deep in the enemy rear as possible. Every effort is made to retain the initiative and maintain the emphasis of the attack. The tank division concentrates on rapid attacks and leaves the destruction of strong centers of resistance to the motorized rifle divisions. If the enemy commits sizable reserves, the tank division blocks them with motorized rifle forces or by requesting nuclear fires, and continues the advance. In the exploitation phase, tank divisions frequently are involved in a series of meeting engagements.

A tank division in the second echelon normally would be employed in a similar manner after it is committed; the tank division is the unit of choice Army level for the OMG role. Division artillery that has been supporting the attack reverts to division control. The division deploys at an assigned line of commitment and enters combat through a gap between the first echelon divisions or from an exposed flank. Usually attacking from the march, the tank division may attempt to penetrate the enemy's deeper defense zones. The division may also be assigned a mission of defeating counterattacks. It will occupy areas selected for that purpose with a minimum of forces while the bulk of the division is maneuvering against the enemy from flank or rear.

TACTICAL BREAKTHROUGH

The breakthrough at the tactical level is an extremely important phase of the offensive.[16] The principal aim of a breakthrough is the destruction of enemy forces in a specific sector of a front by artillery fire, air strikes, tank attacks, and motorized rifle forces, with further development of the action into the depths and flanks of the enemy. Depending on the scale and the goals of the offensive, as well as the forces taking part in the operation, a breakthrough can have either tactical or operational results. (The operational breakthrough was dealt with earlier.) The result of a successful breakthrough at any level will be a pursuit operation.

PURSUIT

The Dictionary of Basic Military Terms, A Soviet View defines a pursuit as follows:

> An attack on a withdrawing enemy, undertaken in the course of an operational battle for the purpose of finally destroying or capturing his forces. Destruction of a withdrawing enemy is achieved by hitting his main body with fire strikes, by relentless and energetic parallel or frontal pursuit, by straddling his withdrawal route, and by attacking his flanks and rear. Pursuit features swift and deep movements with short deployments of small forces to strike the enemy's most vulnerable areas. For deep penetration into the enemy's withdrawal route, tank troops are used in the first instance, but airborne assault forces may also be employed.[17]

Soviet writings on the pursuit stress maintaining "a high tempo." By this they mean a high rate of advance, maintaining momentum, and especially an intense and relentless application of combat actions. If both sides are heavily mechanized, a pursuit can be expected to develop into a contest of mobility and initiative. Contact in the pursuit must be maintained from the outset, beginning with attacks from screening forces that disrupt orderly withdrawal and lead ultimately to attacks on flanks and rear. Normally, the regiment is the lowest command level to order initiation of pursuit, however, commanders at all levels are expected to move independently into pursuit when indicators of withdrawal are seen.

The scale of a pursuit is governed by the size of the force involved and is categorized as either tactical or operational. Tactical pursuit is that conducted by a regiment or division. In the case of a regiment, pursuit would probably begin about 10 to 20 kilometers in the enemy depths; in the case of a division, from 20 to 30 kilometers. Operational pursuit is that conducted by Army or higher echelon on a broad front and may extend to a depth of several hundred kilometers. The three basic requirements for a successful pursuit are: good planning and organization, timely detection of the withdrawal, and maintaining a high tempo.

Tentative planning for pursuit is included in the initial attack plan. The amount of detail depends on the enemy's anticipated actions, the echelonment of attacking troops, and the amount of planning time available. Planning considerations include:

(1) Possible enemy route of withdrawal;
(2) Determination of the scheme of maneuver best suited to the situation, considering availability and condition of pursuit routes, the forces

available and the critical terrain features (high ground, road junctions, river crossing areas, bridges, defiles);
(3) The feasibility of using forward detachments and helicopters or assault forces,
(4) Allocation of nuclear weapons and delivery systems; and
(5) Combat support resources.

Timely detection of the withdrawal is essential to a successful pursuit. Active reconnaissance, appreciation of enemy tactics, and up-to-the-minute knowledge of the tactical situation are required in discerning indicators of the enemy withdrawal. Once a pursuit has been initiated, a rapid advance with continuous application of force is necessary. Methods and resources for enforcing this momentum are elaborated in the following paragraphs.

The forms of pursuit are frontal, parallel, or a combination of the two. The preferred and most effective form is the combination of frontal and parallel. It hinders disengagement and leads to flank attacks and cutting enemy withdrawal routes. Generally speaking, the main pursuit force moves parallel to the withdrawing enemy while a smaller force pursues directly, maintaining constant contact. The frontal pursuit conducted by forces in contact is the most likely type at the beginning of the enemy withdrawal. It is usually undertaken at night, often over terrain where it is difficult to overcome obstacles or where off-road maneuver is limited. It applies constant pressure on the enemy and limits his freedom of maneuver, his ability to take up defense positions, and his capacity to disengage. The frontal pursuit forces the enemy to accept combat under unfavorable conditions and delays the withdrawal. Maneuver and flank attacks, though limited, are also conducted. Frontal pursuit is not decisive since it only pushes the enemy back on his approaching reserves.

The parallel pursuit is employed when the pursuing force can advance on routes parallel to the withdrawing enemy. High-speed parallel pursuit may permit either an attack on the enemy flanks or cutting his main withdrawal routes. Under threat of flank attack, the enemy may be required to split his force and delay withdrawal while defending against the pursuer's attack. Unless accompanied by frontal pursuit, this method gives the enemy some opportunity to maneuver for a counterattack.

Based on the assessment of available indicators, a timely and correct decision to initiate pursuit is critical to its success. If the enemy is able to begin an undetected withdrawal, he avoids the constant pressure that disrupts his actions. Further, if the enemy can gain a safe distance in his withdrawal, the attacking forces are vulnerable to tactical nuclear strikes. The enemy will attempt to choose an advantageous time for withdrawal, usually at night. Early actions must be taken to ensure that contact is maintained. Each Soviet unit in contact moves immediately after the withdrawing force, using its existing combat deployments to prevent disengagement. Organic fire support, long-range weapons, and air support are used to harass and disrupt the withdrawal. In the initiation phase, efforts are made to establish conditions that will permit placing tank and motorized rifle pursuit on routes parallel to the enemy withdrawal. This leads to establishing the combination frontal and parallel method of pursuit. Maintaining the tempo in pursuit is not based on application of unique tactics or the establishment of special means of support. Established tactics and the use of support elements must, however, be adapted to meet the requirements of successful pursuit. Measures to maintain the tempo are discussed in the following paragraphs.

Units in contact initiate frontal pursuit immediately upon the detection of the withdrawal, moving from whatever formation they have at the moment. As the situation permits, they will form into march column or approach-march formation and, when required, into attack formation. The actions of the frontal pursuit force are aimed at facilitating the commitment of a parallel pursuit, which will preferably be weighted with tanks. The parallel force, with security elements in the lead, will also use march column or approach march formations until deployment for the attack is required. In the pursuit, the commander attempts to employ all available combat troops. Pursuit is conducted in a wide zone--up to 30 kilometers for a division. The commander retains the tactical options of converging on the most important axis or redirecting his effort on a new axis. He also has this flexibility when engaging advancing enemy reserves or counterattack forces.

Pursuit is characterized by centralized planning and decentralized execution; preservation of control is a primary concern in such a fast moving situation. Continuity of control is achieved by several means:

(1) Designating direction of advance, routes or zones of advance, phase lines, and objectives;
(2) Fixing times for completion of specific missions;
(3) Altering missions as subsequent developments require;
(4) Augmenting normal radio communications with aerial relays;
(5) Using two command groups with the commander at an observation post behind the leading combat elements and the second group, headed by the chief of staff, with the main force; and
(6) Designating phase lines from which the artillery must be prepared to fire by specified times.

As the pursuit is developed, reconnaissance elements provide information on the disposition of retreating enemy formations and on the forward movements of his reserves. Because of the potential depth of the operation, aerial reconnaissance may be the primary means of identifying significant threats to pursuit forces. This intelligence is vital at the point when a pursuit force faces the risk of becoming overextended. It could be the basis for termination of the pursuit.

Prior to or during the pursuit, forward detachments may be designated to move ahead of main pursuit forces and to operate independently to take critical terrain features. These detachments will outdistance pursuit forces by avoiding engagement to the extent possible, until they reach their assigned objective. Their missions might include concurrent reconnaissance reporting, seizing critical points on withdrawal routes, destroying the enemy's means of nuclear attack, and linking up with tactical airborne or helicopter assault landings. Forward detachments could be formed from units having the greatest success.

Helicopter or parachute assault forces may be assigned missions similar to those described for forward detachments, although air insertion permits operations much deeper into enemy territory.[18] The obvious advantages of using forward detachments and tactical airborne forces to cut withdrawal routes are frequently pointed out in Soviet commentary; however, the risks of having such forces defeated before linkup can be effective must also be considered. When pursuit is initiated, the formation of the parallel pursuit force will normally be from uncommitted second echelon formations. As the pursuit develops and main forces link up with forward detachments or air assault forces, these smaller elements may revert to second echelon or reserve status.

At the start of a pursuit, the control of artillery is decentralized to maneuver battalions. Batteries and even individual guns move with lead elements to deliver direct fire. Artillery elements are also a normal component of forward detachments. Artillery missions during pursuit include: fire on columns and concentrations at road junctions, defiles, bridges, and crossings; repelling enemy counterattacks; destroying or delaying enemy reserves; and destroying enemy means of nuclear attack.

Air support complements other fire support in the destroying and disorganizing the retreating enemy, particularly his mobile targets. When the situation during the course of a pursuit becomes obscure, air reconnaissance is an important factor in the success of the pursuit. Air reconnaissance is used to determine:

(1) The beginning of the withdrawal of rear area forces;
(2) The composition of withdrawing forces and the direction of movement;
(3) The composition and direction of movement of reserves moving forward; and
(4) The nature of obstacles and intermediate defensive positions.

Air cover for pursuit forces would be expected from frontal aviation.

The pursuing force (in conjunction with forward detachments, and air, land, and sea forces) creates priority nuclear targets, which include: approaching reserves; main groupings of retreating forces; enemy concentrations at critical areas (bridges, road junctions, defiles); and nuclear attack systems.

The distribution of organic air defense weapons gives priority to protection of fire support elements. Surface-to-air missile support would include mobile division units and semi-mobile army units (e.g., SA-6, SA-13, SA-8 and SA-4). Units under air attack attempt to maintain their forward progress using organic weapons for defense as opposed to using a grid or area defense provided by higher formations.

Movement support detachments (*OOD*s) and mobile obstacle detachments (*POZ*s) provided by engineer troops are important in sustaining the rate of advance. Their missions include breaching obstacles and mine fields in the initiation phase, then operating from forward positions; providing bridging and road repairs; and blocking withdrawal routes of bypassed energy units with mines, demolitions, and obstacles.

With maximum commitment of forces, requirements of fuel, ammunition, and maintenance will increase. The depth of pursuit may be governed by the capability for logistic support. Priority of support will be given to units having the greatest success. One yardstick for sustaining pursuit is the expectation that, in a large-scale offensive, a tank division with reinforcing transportation units should be self-sufficient for about six days.

Situations under which pursuit would be terminated, or under which the immediate commander might recommend termination, include destruction of the enemy, inability of logistic support to keep pace with the pursuing force and danger that the pursuing force may be cut off. When pursuit ends, units are regrouped from decentralized missions, and forces are deployed to subsequent operations.

DEFENSIVE OPERATIONS

The Soviets emphasize that the offensive is the only means of achieving victory.[19] The constant repetition of offensive themes in exercise scenarios, after only a short defensive plan (Dnieper, Nieman etc.), further confirms its importance in Soviet doctrine; however, defensive doctrine has not been totally overlooked. Grounded in the history of World War II and the great defensive battles of Stalingrad, Moscow, and Kursk, the Soviets' doctrine now is also mindful of recent technological developments, such as antitank guided missiles (ATGM's) and nuclear weapons. In the Soviet view, reasons for going to the defense are:

(1) To consolidate gains of advance elements;
(2) To await additional resources when temporarily halted by the enemy during the course of an offensive;
(3) To protect the flanks of a formation;
(4) To repulse an enemy counterthrust;
(5) To regroup after severe losses suffered from nuclear weapons;
(6) To free resources for other elements of the formation that are on the offensive; and
(7) To await logistic support.

In most of these cases, the defense is clearly temporary and will end in resumption of the offensive. The two major forms of defense are the deliberate defense and the hasty defense, adopted in the course of an offensive. A hasty defense may ultimately turn into a deliberate defense if conditions and availability of resources do not favor resumption of the offensive in that particular sector.

The defense at Front and Army level may involve the entire formation during the initial stage of hostilities, where an enemy attacks across international boundaries or in a sector where no offensive action is planned. More likely, only a portion of the formation will be on the defensive while the remainder undertakes offensive action. During World War II, entire theaters were on the defense and extremely dense defensive positions were developed. These defenses consisted of three or more static defensive belts, with the majority of the combat forces deployed in the first belt.

The advent of nuclear weapons forced modification of this tactic and increased the value of the security echelon and the reserve. Modern defensive doctrine continues to stress defense in depth, but rather than multiple continuous belts, the defensive area now consists of clusters of strong points. At both Front and Army level, the key is stubborn defense of the forward edge by motorized rifle forces deployed in depth, and decisive counterattacks by highly mobile tank-heavy forces of the second echelon and reserve. The increased fluidity of the situation has required an increase in the size of reserves. Under current defensive doctrine, the reserve and second echelon may make up more than half of the total force. While second echelon divisions of the Army will occupy defensive positions, their major tasks will be to counterattack and destroy enemy forces penetrating the forward defenses. The first echelon divisions, however, hold the forward edge of the Army and Front positions, and it is at this level that we find all the principles of defense employed. Therefore, the remainder of this portion will examine the defense as conducted by a first echelon division.

The security zone is that portion of the battlefield forward of the main defensive area. It is occupied by a force whose mission is to delay the enemy and deceive him as to the location and deployment of the main defensive elements. The security force engages the enemy at the greatest possible range and attempts to force him to deploy prematurely. The security zone may extend to a depth of 30 kilometers at Front level and 16 kilometers at division level. It will be at least far enough forward to prevent aimed directed fire from being placed on the main defensive area.

The security force will delay on the most advantageous terrain in order to inflict maximum damage on the attacking enemy. Mines and barriers will be used extensively. In addition, the Soviets rely heavily on fire, "fire sacks" (*ognevye meshki*), or killing zones, to damage or destroy the enemy force. When the enemy is well supplied with tanks, tank ambushes are also planned and executed. When faced with encirclement or decisive engagement, the forces of the security zone will attempt to withdraw under the cover of artillery fire and return to the main defensive area.

The main defensive area may appear as bands or belts or layers, but it is simply a defense in depth. Today, as in World War II, defense in depth is still a critical element of the deliberate defense. The basic element of the main defensive area is the company or platoon strong point. This is established on terrain that is key to the defense and must be retained at all costs. The unit occupying the strong point prepares an all-around defense with alternate and supplementary fire positions for all weapons. Fires are planned to be mutually supporting as well as to provide for fire sacks and kill zones. Vehicles are dug in, and a network of communication trenches is constructed, linking weapons positions with supply, command and control, and fighting positions. Everything that can be dug in and given overhead protection is dug in, even wire lines that provide the primary means of communication. Minefields and barriers are emplaced and covered by fire.

Fires are planned to cover all approaches to the position and, finally, the entire position is camouflaged. This includes the use of dummy positions to draw fire and to deceive the enemy as to the true location of the defenses. Battalion strong points are then linked together by other forces until a defensive area or belt is formed. This occurs at every echelon, forming multiple belts. Included in these belts and in between them are headquarters, logistic facilities, reserves, and combat support forces. Each of these elements is responsible for its own local security and, as with forward forces, will be dug in with overhead cover and camouflage.

Minefields are placed forward of the defensive position to slow the enemy and force him to concentrate. Fires are planned to attack these concentrations and to prevent or delay breaching operations. They are also designed to force the enemy into fire sacks where concentrated fires of all weapons may be brought to bear. Minefields are designed to break up the enemy's assault and strip away his supporting armor. Within the main defensive area, minefields are placed to confine the enemy within fire sacks, to create kill zones for antitank weapons, and to facilitate the employment of the reserves.

In conjunction with these deliberate minefields, the Soviets plan to use hasty minefields emplaced by engineer mobile obstacle detachments (*POZ*'s) using mechanical mine layers or possibly by helicopter delivery. These hastily laid minefields normally are used in conjunction with the antitank reserve to counter enemy tanks that may have penetrated the depths of the defense. Barriers, like simple minefields, are used to slow, disorganize, and canalize the enemy force. They are used alone or in conjunction with minefields and concentrated fire areas. The utilization of natural barriers, such as lakes, rivers, marshes, and densely forested areas, is stressed. Artificial barriers, including antitank ditches, wire entanglements, abatis, antiheliborne and antiairborne stakes, may also be emplanted.

The Soviets, who acquired considerable vicarious knowledge of antitank warfare during the various Arab/Israeli wars, have adopted six principal methods of combating tanks: the use of tanks, still the most powerful antitank weapon; anti-tank guided missiles (ATGMs); massed artillery fires (and potentially nuclear weapons) directed against tank formations, conventional artillery used in a direct fire role to destroy individual tanks; helicopters (not only a powerful antitank weapon but also a powerful ally of friendly tanks.)[20] and obstacles of all types to hinder tank advances.

In their book, <u>Antitank Warfare</u>, G. Biryukov and G. Melnikov state:

> A system of antitank defense is built on the basis of all antitank weapons, their coordination with nuclear attacks, and with each other, and must envisage their grouping and maneuver with due regard for

enemy action and maximum utilization of the protective features of the terrain.[21]

Such a system of antitank defense may include company strong points containing well-sited antitank weapons. Tank ambushes are usually set up throughout the defense. Antitank reserves placed to respond to any enemy tank thrust are a fundamental part of the defense, and tanks of second echelon units may be used to bolster the first echelon or to counterattack. *POZ*s and *OOD*s are responsive to the needs of the defense.

Artillery in the direct fire role, particularly self-propelled, both in forward positions and from positions in the depth of the defense, is the mainstay of the antitank defense. Antitank obstacles are covered by fire and are complemented by the maneuver of fires and forces. Antitank guns and antitank guided missiles are concentrated by platoon and battery. They employ multi-layered cross fires, long-range fires, and all-around fires.[22] Cooperation between guns and ATGM systems is considered essential to adequate antitank defense.

As with all facets of Soviet doctrine, the integration of combined arms is considered paramount. Ground attack helicopters mounting rockets and antitank missiles are used as mobile, quick reaction antitank reserves and are of particular use in combating armor penetrations or flanking maneuvers.

In a defensive situation, the reserve has been increasingly emphasized in recent years. Reserves are located so as to undertake multiple missions: blocking, counterattacking, reinforcing, and providing rear area security. A reserve at battalion level might consist of the tank element supporting the defending motorized rifle battalion. At regimental level, both a maneuver reserve in the form of tanks and an antitank reserve in the form of ATGM vehicles may be found. Reserves at division and higher echelons are predominantly tank-heavy formations.

CONDUCT OF THE DELIBERATE DEFENSE

As an enemy approaches the security zone, he will be engaged at long range, 2000 meters or more, with air, artillery, ATGM, and tank fire. As he comes closer, all weapons will be brought to bear against him and under the cover of smoke and artillery fire, the security forces will disengage and move to secondary positions. If the enemy does not appear strong, local counterattacks may be mounted. This action is designed to slow the enemy's advance, strip his infantry of armored support, and deceive him as to the true location of the main defensive area. Ambushes, dummy positions, fire strikes, obstacles, and barriers will be used to the maximum by the security zone forces. Some elements of the security force will stay behind after the force withdraws to the main position. They continue to harass enemy columns and to report any enemy buildup that might signal the direction and timing of the main attack.

As the enemy nears the main defensive area, he will come under increasingly heavy fires from artillery, tanks, and long-range antitank weapons. Doctrine calls for frequent shifting of forces to alternate firing positions in order to confuse the enemy and reduce the effectiveness of his counter-fires. Strong points are held at all costs, even when encircled and cut off from the other positions. Infantry and tank weapons fire in prearranged zones and, when directed, concentrate their fires in fire sacks in order to annihilate an enemy that has been forced into these areas. Reserves are committed at the most opportune time to complete the destruction of the enemy force or to reinforce strong points when necessary. These reserves are normally tank heavy and, as such, are used primarily in the counterattack. Antitank reserves are committed to destroy or disrupt enemy armored formations and to support the maneuver of the reserve.

The Soviets perceive several problems associated with night defensive combat. These include reduced effectiveness of aimed fires and increased difficulty in maneuver, coordination, and maintenance of battlefield surveillance. These problems are to be overcome by detailed planning and thorough training. Reduced effectiveness of aimed fires at night may be overcome by using detailed fire plans, night vision devices, and battlefield illumination. Difficulties in maneuver may be alleviated by driver training, night driving devices, and rehearsals. Coordination problems may be reduced by thorough staff planning and aggressive leadership. The problem of maintaining adequate surveillance of the battlefield may be met by detailed surveillance plans, active patrolling, use of illumination, night vision devices, electronic surveillance equipment, and a high state of readiness of combat forces. Despite the problems of night combat, the Soviets insist that by using modern technology and with adequate training the Soviet soldier can be as effective at night as in the daytime.

While, in general, the Soviets treat defense of cities or other built-up areas as a normal part of defensive combat, some adaptations are required. First, a built-up area should be defended not within the area, but outside it. This is done in the same manner as the deliberate defense. Counterattacks are conducted outside built-up areas by highly mobile, mechanized, or armored forces. Every effort is made to stop the enemy short of the city; however, it is realized that a determined enemy may gain a lodgement within the built-up area and that this will lead to fighting within the city itself.

Soviet experience in Stalingrad, Brest, Berlin, and many other large cities during World War II has provided a wealth of data on combat in cities, and this is reflected in Soviet training programs. Forces within the perimeter of a city will be organized into key strong points, such as major street intersections, large building complexes, bridges, choke points, and areas where killing zones can be established. Engineers are used extensively in preparing for the defense, clearing fields of fire, and preparing positions for tanks, artillery pieces and antitank guns within and next to buildings. Since ruins are more easily defended than standing buildings, many structures will be demolished in advance.

Artillery is used extensively in a direct fire role, and as much as 50 percent of the divisional artillery may be attached to defending companies. Fires of all weapons are coordinated; a combination of flanking and interlocking fires is used by all direct fire systems, including artillery. Communication problems within the confines of a built-up area are eased by reliance on wire and messengers. Where possible, sewer systems or other underground tunnels are employed as lines of supply and communication. If the size of the sewers permit, reserve forces may use them to move about without being exposed to enemy fire.

SUPPORT OF THE DEFENSE

Artillery fire support of the defense is divided into several phases: counter-preparation, support in the security zone, and support to the main defensive area. The principal effort in counter-preparation is destruction of the enemy artillery. Artillery will be targeted as soon as observed, and particular effort will be made to destroy nuclear-capable artillery systems. In support of the security zone, fires are planned to support security positions, cover the withdrawal of the security forces, and support counterattacks. Artillery elements will be assigned to the security force to augment those that provide support from locations within the main defensive area. The defense of the main defensive area, using counter- preparation fires, static barrages, mobile barrages, and massed fires, is planned to cover barriers, minefields, defilades, and the defensive positions themselves. Fires are also planned within the defensive positions where they could support a withdrawal.

Artillery is not only expected to suppress or destroy enemy infantry, but also to destroy armored vehicles. Artillery and antitank guided missile batteries are integrated into the overall fire plan with the mission of destroying the enemy's armor anywhere on the battlefield, but particularly in preselected fire sacks. Every artillery weapon is expected to fire in the direct fire role when necessary. The final phase of artillery support is fire in support of a counterattack. This fire is, for all practical purposes, offensive fire support, as has been discussed earlier. Air defense will be expected to prevent air attacks on high priority targets, such as command posts, nuclear delivery means, and reserves. In addition, moving columns, such as those conducting counterattacks, will be provided cover by SA-6, SA-7, SA-8, SA-9, SA-11, and SA-13 surface-to-air missiles and ZSU-23-4 mobile anti-aircraft guns.

Engineers will be used extensively in preparing a deliberate defense the same as in the defense of a city. Engineer heavy equipment will be used to assist maneuver forces in constructing field fortifications and in digging in armored and other vehicles. Command bunkers, artillery revetments, and medical facilities (although assigned a lower priority) will probably also be dug in by engineer equipment. Natural obstacles will be supplemented by wire, mines, and other devices. In addition, antitank ditches will be prepared and tied-in to natural obstacles. Route preparation and maintenance is another important part of the defense. While deception is a normal feature of

Soviet life, it has been developed to a fine art by the engineers who provide and use dummy equipment, fences (for concealment) and anti-radar devices.

Chemical support of the defense is both offensive and defensive in nature. Chemical reconnaissance units monitor for enemy use of chemical weapons. Chemical decontamination units counter the enemy's use of chemical weapons, either at central decontamination sites or, more likely, at the contaminated positions themselves. The Soviets have the capability to decontaminate terrain as well as individuals, vehicles, and equipment. The use of chemical munitions and mines is a command responsibility executed by the maneuver forces and the artillery, and not a function of chemical defense units; however, chemical defense units may be called on for technical assistance in target evaluation. The Soviets train for and can be expected to use gas in any combat situation, as they have demonstrated in Afghanistan. In Soviet usage smoke is considered a chemical agent, whether or not it is toxic. They use both kinds of smoke effectively.

Radioelectronic combat (REC) plays a large part in the defense. False nets are established as part of the deception plan to mislead the enemy. Radio direction finding locates targets for the artillery, and signal intelligence provides valuable information as to the intent of the enemy forces. Jamming enemy command and control frequencies is planned for the most critical part of the battle, while jamming bombing navigation equipment and surveillance and target acquisition radar will be continuous. Command and control communications are critical to the defense. Wire and messenger will be used to the maximum; radio will serve as a backup and will be the primary means of communication during counterattacks. Command and control sites will be hardened, including the use of hardened antennas. Wire lines will be laid below ground, and multiple wire lines will be employed with alternate switching to avoid interruption at critical points. In addition, command posts are duplicated, along with their communications, to ensure continuity of command.

In general, supply, recovery, maintenance, and medical support will be provided as far forward as possible. Supplies will be delivered to the point of intended use, and casualties will be evacuated from the battle area by medical personnel sent to search for the wounded.

When a unit is forced into a hasty defense, offensive actions may be necessary to gain defensible terrain. Where possible, a defense will be established to the rear of the fighting area and then a withdrawal made to that line; for that reason, a reverse slope defense is often chosen. Forces will be left in contact with the enemy on the forward slope while the remainder of the force prepares the position on the reverse slope. Where possible, both forward and reverse slopes will be defended to take maximum advantage of the terrain. Since the force going over to the defensive frequently will be in contact with the enemy, it will be difficult, if not impossible, to establish a security echelon. If one is established, its depth will not be nearly as great as the forward defense. Long-range fires will not play the part they do in the deliberate defense. Also, deception will be difficult to achieve as the friendly forces may be under direct observation of the enemy. Barriers and minefields will be deployed in depth, but will not be as extensive as in the deliberate defense. Engineer mobile obstacle detachments (*POZ*) play a critical role in laying mines rapidly across critical avenues of approach. Helicopter mine layers are expected to be particularly helpful, and armored mine layers will also be of assistance.

WITHDRAWAL

Inasmuch as withdrawal is usually the outcome of an unsuccessful defense, it is not emphasized in Soviet training. The complicated nature of the withdrawal indicates that it will be used only where absolutely required. When it does become necessary, the Soviets will resort to deception, movement at night, and secret preparation to avoid alerting the enemy. It would be carried out only by the order of the next higher commander in a deliberately organized manner, with emphasis on strict secrecy and security. The mission is to relocate the force in a timely and organized fashion from one position to another without sacrificing the combat capability of the unit. The main force, the bulk of the force to be withdrawn, is charged with disengaging and secretly withdrawing, under cover of darkness or adverse weather if possible, and elaborate deception schemes may be planned to deceive the enemy as to the true nature of the operation. The rear guard will cover the movement from one location to another and delay the enemy should he attempt pursuit. The covering forces are the elements left in position to deceive the enemy and to cover the disengagement and withdrawal from the initial position. Units along the forward edge of the defense normally will consist of a reinforced platoon from each company supported by specially selected artillery units. A rear guard is charged with delaying the attacking enemy independently of the main force or the covering force. It will consist usually of tank units reinforced with motorized rifle, artillery, and engineers.

The initial stage of the withdrawal is the disengagement. This is the critical point when the force is most vulnerable, especially to attack from nuclear weapons. Maximum use is made of dummy positions, the weather, and covering fires to ensure the enemy does not detect the disengagement. In some cases, limited-objective attacks may be conducted to deceive the enemy. Unengaged forces including the second echelon and reserves are withdrawn first; next, artillery and first echelon forces, except for the covering force. All the covering force will then withdraw suddenly, departing at the same time, and will rejoin the main force in the new area after completion of the mission. The rear guard is prepositioned on lines selected by the force commander to cover the withdrawal of the main force. Subsequent positions are selected at sufficient distance from each other so that the enemy will be forced to pause and reorganize before attacking the next line. Forces are withdrawn to the subsequent defensive lines by leapfrogging with mutual fire support maintained throughout the action; ambushes and barriers are used extensively. Engineer POZ's with a rear guard lay minefields, destroy bridges, and construct barriers to assist in delaying the enemy. Artillery forces of the rear guard open fire at maximum range on road junctions, defiles, and crossing points to slow enemy movement. Artillery units also withdraw by leapfrogging while ensuring continuous fire support. If the enemy does not pursue the force or attempt to envelop it, the rear guard may form march columns and return to the main body under protection of its own security forces. After arrival of all the elements in the new area, the force will be reorganized in accordance with the plan for future combat actions. The unit will be refueled, rearmed, and all repair and replacement of damaged equipment and personnel will be accomplished. As soon as this is done, the unit is available for future combat actions.

OPERATIONS IN "SPECIAL CONDITIONS"

This section, deals with "special conditions" such as mountains, cold, and desert. Some special conditions are expected to be encountered with considerable frequency in the European theater of operations: combat at night, in cities, in forests, and river crossings. The Soviets believe their normal motorized rifle and tank units are well suited for all these special operations and conditions. They recognize the need for certain specialized equipment in extreme cold and desert environments and for the river crossings. They believe that regular troops given special training for a period of days or weeks immediately prior to any one of these types of operations will be able to fulfill their duties in exemplary fashion. The Soviets have had the advantage of combat in Afghanistan, which has provided an opportunity to train in actual combat in mountains and desert. Most of the fighting has been of a counterinsurgency nature, and, because of language requirements, large numbers of Central Asians have received actual combat experience.

MOUNTAIN OPERATIONS
(NOT COUNTERINSURGENCY)

The Soviets had considerable combat experience in a variety of mountain terrain during World War II, from the Alps to the Khingan Range in Manchuria. This experience can be summed up in the phrase, "whoever takes the passes has the mountains." Tactical deployment for the attack will be governed by the nature of the terrain, which may range from foothills to medium or high mountains or to upland plateaus. In all cases, deployments are aimed at controlling the passes, the road junctions, any built-up areas, and the high ground adjacent to these areas.

Tactical actions are designed to bypass defensive positions, attack the enemy from the flanks and rear, and break up coordination between the defending units. Offensive operations in mountains are expected to be conducted by regiments or smaller units operating on separate axes along roads, valleys, or ridges. Attacks will usually be made from positions in contact, as contrasted to the general preference for attacking from the march.

Flanking units will use gaps to seize and control critical areas. It is increasingly probable that helicopters will carry these detachments over the rugged or impassable terrain and to the flanks and rear of defenders. While mountains are basically an obstacle to attacking forces, they may provide concealed avenues of approach, particularly if the terrain is forested. Mountain terrain tends to restrict tank movement to valley roads; consequently, the principal fighting forces in difficult mountain terrain will be motorized rifle troops. Special attention is given to destroying antitank and other direct fire weapons. Without their elimination, obstacles cannot be cleared and supporting tanks cannot advance. Should a tank battalion be required to operate independently, it would be reinforced with motorized rifle troops, engineers, and artillery. Tanks would lead attack formations in broad valleys, depressions, or on the slopes of small hills; motorized rifle units would lead along defiles or ravines with tanks spread out to the rear. Tanks may give overwatching fire from halted positions. Seizure of heights and slopes may be assigned to tactical airborne forces, which would be landed from helicopters, since in the mountains there are very few terrain sectors suitable for parachute assault. The helicopter is also a valuable asset for reconnaissance, command and control, resupply, and evacuation in the mountains.

Special difficulties are encountered in command and control, engineer and artillery support, and in the use of nuclear weapons. Control tends to be difficult in mountain areas because of difficulties encountered in radio communications. Mountain terrain adversely affects VHF and UHF bands, particularly during the second half of the day. Vehicles carrying radio equipment may not be able to reach the commanding heights necessary for effective use. Laying wire lines requires considerable preparatory effort in route reconnaissance and preparing crossing points over mountains, rivers, and across gorges. Frequent detours increase wire consumption, and rock falls damage lines. Special techniques and equipment have, however, been devised to overcome these limitations, including portable remote control equipment, transmission parallel to ridges or along gorges, aerial relays using helicopters, and foot messengers. Mountain operations will require considerably greater and more difficult engineer support than normal missions. Roads are typically narrower, steeper, and more crooked; reconnaissance is more difficult; and obstacle clearance is usually a serious problem. There will be crossings required, not only over water gaps with high rates of flow, but also over dry gaps.

To support maneuver forces in the mountains, artillery usually must be more decentralized than in other areas. Firing by battery or even by platoon may be usual; firing positions often must be located immediately adjacent to available roads. To best cover dead spaces, mortars and howitzers are placed near the forward edge of the enemy defense, while flatter trajectory guns are located at the flanks. Direct fire at maximum range will be used. All methods of fire adjustments must take into account the environmental complications of variations in atmospheric pressures and temperatures, as well as the frequency of dead spaces created by terrain masking. The same dead spaces shield sound and electromagnetic waves and provide multiple reflections of echoes from mountain sides.

Should nuclear weapons be employed in the mountains, the dead spaces form protected areas that would reduce the casualty zone. Shock wave propagation would be intensified in the narrow valleys and defiles opening in the direction of the burst. The danger of casualties resulting from rock falls, avalanches, and landslides, which could occur a considerable distance from ground zero, is increased. Reverse slopes greatly attenuate the shock wave effect when the height of burst does not exceed the height of the ridge. It is not expected that a nuclear weapon would be used if the burst would impede the advance of friendly troops.

Defense in mountains is notable for its exceptional variety of organization and great irregularity in the distribution of manpower and equipment along the front and in the depth of the position. Natural obstacles of mountain terrain permit quick organization of the defense with relatively smaller forces--recognizing that mountain defense positions may be vulnerable to bypassing, to envelopment, or to a helicopter assault. The defense prescribed is in depth and, to the extent possible, mobile. Motorized rifle troops organize platoon strong points with antitank weapons, mine fields, and obstacles covering avenues of approach. Battalions and companies maintain small reserves with relatively larger counterattack forces held at regiment and division. Tanks are positioned in tiers on both forward and reverse slopes, normally within platoon strong points. If there is an area with a trafficable route, armor may be held in reserve for counterattack or to block penetrations. If not, tanks will be placed in the most vital areas. Artillery is usually attached to forward units where it fires from covered positions, possibly dug back into a hillside, and may use direct fire on penetrating tanks. Artillery delivers planned fires on gaps, river crossing sites, and open approaches.

OPERATIONS IN EXTREME COLD

Soviet training for winter operations is extensive. It begins in grade school where nearly all Russians learn to ski as a regular part of their physical training. In the army, soldiers have at least one major field training exercise per enlistment scheduled under winter conditions. All personnel are taught to move on skis behind tanks, to serve as tankborne infantry, and to fire while moving on skis. Training covers how to prevent frostbite, care and cleaning of equipment, and camouflage techniques for snow conditions. Drivers are trained in the operation and maintenance of vehicles in extreme cold.

No special organizations are known to exist for winter or arctic warfare; the Soviets would deploy normal tank and motorized rifle units. Those units stationed in the far north during peacetime would be the prime units to undergo any additional training for winter missions. Special equipment includes cold weather clothing and foot gear, protective goggles, warming tents, heating and lighting equipment, and special lubricants.

Attack frontages are increased in snow conditions because of the difficulty in maneuvering, and for this reason, reserves are often larger. A battalion operating in deep snow may attack in one echelon and maintain a company in reserve. In nonnuclear conditions, troops may attack on skis towed behind tanks. Upon reaching the assault line, the troops release the tow ropes or cables, form an assault line, and attack in coordination with the tanks. If the snow is deep, troops may attack mounted on tanks with the squad leader maintaining communication with the tank commander using the tank's intercom. At the appropriate time, the squad leader tells the tank commander to slow down and orders his squad to dismount and form a skirmish line.

Snow depth and cold affects not only the offense, but also the defense. The forward defensive perimeter is positioned close to natural obstacles in deep snow; above-ground trenches are built with ice walls facing the enemy. The strongest defensive positions are located along the most likely avenues of approach, namely roads and areas of light snow. Populated areas and forests provide shelter and often are used as strong points. Obstacles, including minefields covered by fire, are constructed in gaps between a system of strong points to delay the attacking enemy and deny him shelter. No more than one-third of the fighting personnel occupy firing positions, permitting the majority of the defensive force to be at peak efficiency in the event of an attack. Limited counterattacks may be launched against the enemy's flanks and between his attacking elements by small ski or armor units.

OPERATIONS IN THE DESERT

Desert warfare concepts and techniques are of longstanding as well as current interest to the Soviets and are a major feature of the training of forces stationed in areas of the Soviet Union containing desert regions-- Turkestan, Central Asia, Mongolia, and the Far East military districts. Afghanistan has provided the opportunity to greatly improve this training. Because of environmental considerations, the planning and preparation for movement in the desert becomes a critical task. Preparation requires reconnaissance, obstacle clearing, route marking, and grading of elevations and descents. The difficulty of orientation in open terrain with few landmarks, complicated by reduced visibility, requires marking with stable signs that have good day and night visibility. The signs must indicate the route and also warn of dangerous locations. Soviet traffic regulators are specially trained to cope with these kinds of problems.

Tactical operations will be characterized by broad frontages, wide gaps between units, and frequent independent operations by regiments or battalions. To cope with the environment, control measures for movement must ensure security for flanks and rear, and communications must be supplied to cover the wide dispersals. Locations of water, fuel, and supply points become critical when moving off roads.

In any advance, the basic method of land navigation is movement on an assigned azimuth, supplemented by reference points, elevations, and rare identifiable features such as wells, canals, and structures. Soviet combat capabilities include vehicles equipped with directional gyroscope systems (land navigation systems) that permit holding the required direction for one-and-a-half hours with an error no greater than two degrees. With careful adjustment the gyros can be used up to five hours without reorientation.

Attacks in the desert are carried out from the line of march at high speed. Battalions deploy to company columns at 12 to 15 kilometers, while companies deploy to platoon columns at three to five kilometers from the assault position. Tank formations are generally used in the first echelon and may attack in a single echelon.

The tactics of the attack are basically those described in earlier chapters; however, frontages are generally wider (with gaps being accepted) and objectives are at greater depths. Regiments attack on separate axes and are reinforced with sufficient artillery to enable them to operate independently. Flanking detachments usually are employed to penetrate gaps in the defenses and to carry out harassing tasks in the rear. If they are available, parachute and helicopter assaults are used to seize objectives in depth. Airborne assault units may cover the flanks of the main attacks.

The defense is organized in depth with the bulk of the forward troops covering main axes and probable enemy objectives. Strong reserves, consisting mainly of tanks, are held in greater depths than normal and could be used to forestall enemy enveloping and encircling movements. Battalion frontages in the forward area are similar to those in the normal defense but divisions and possibly regiments may operate independently with wide intervening gaps. Gaps, mined sectors, and areas of limited trafficability are lightly defended. They may be covered only by obstacles and mobile patrols during the day, and possibly occupied by small standing patrols at night.

Some penetration is accepted but it is quickly counterattacked. The defensive forces try to mislead the enemy by such practices as leaving tracks leading to dummy positions and erasing tracks leading to actual positions, performing maintenance on equipment behind dummy positions, and sending false radio messages from dummy positions.

COMBAT IN URBAN AREAS, FOREST, AND AT NIGHT

Urban areas, forest, and night operations, also present special problems for an attacker; in the Soviet view, however, these situations must be dealt with routinely so as not to slow the tempo of the general offensive.

Urban Area Operations

While doctrine recommends avoiding combat in built-up areas, a war in western Europe inevitably would require attacks on cities, since many urban areas serve as important axes of advance. They may be attacked directly or following envelopment. Seizing the city by attack from the march to envelop the area may be attempted under the general condition of fluid, open warfare, and the threat of nuclear weapons. This form of attack seeks to forestall an enemy from establishing an effective defense, cut the enemy's line of communication, bypass isolated groups to gain critical areas or lines, and attack from different approaches simultaneously.

Simultaneous attacks will be conducted along different avenues of approach or, as the least desirable alternative, the city may be taken "by storm." The location of the city and the terrain on its approaches will be significant factors in determining whether this form of attack will be employed. Political objectives may dictate the method of attack. If, for example, the city is inhabited by citizens considered disaffected and ready to join the communist cause, every effort will be made to avoid forcing the enemy into a house-to-house defense.

In any attack against an enemy defending a built-up area, problems of troop maneuver control and the use of various weapons and equipment will arise. The conditions and methods of attacking in urban areas differ significantly from ordinary field conditions. Specifically, city fighting demands larger forces, slower pace and tempo of attacks, longer duration of commitment, and longer preparatory fires.

Basic features of the seizure of a city involve the main force bypassing the city entirely, if possible. Second echelon forces will execute holding attacks and attacks from the rear. Forward detachments operating in advance will have seized critical bridges, junctions, or installations. Probing attacks will be made to determine the location of defensive positions in the city. Withdrawal routes will be blocked by tank elements or air-landed forces, and a tank reserve will be held to engage enemy counterattacks.

The conduct of the attack itself will include attempts to drive back defensive outposts and to surround the built-up area. The plan of attack will divide the city into battalion areas and the attack will be preceded by artillery preparation and suppressive air strikes. The reinforced motorized rifle battalion is the basic assault team, attacking in a column organized as shown in Figure 3.15.

Large tank units will be held in the second echelon (reserve), although tanks of the motorized rifle regiment will be attached to companies, or even down to platoons in a fire support role. Tanks will be protected by a group of three or four riflemen and small size engineer elements equipped with mine detectors and explosive charges. A defender should expect the Soviet use of tanks in areas considered virtually impassable.

Forests

A discontinuous front in forested areas can be exploited by a combination of penetrations and flanking movements executed either to bypass or attack from the rear. Where practicable, helicopter assault units may seize critical

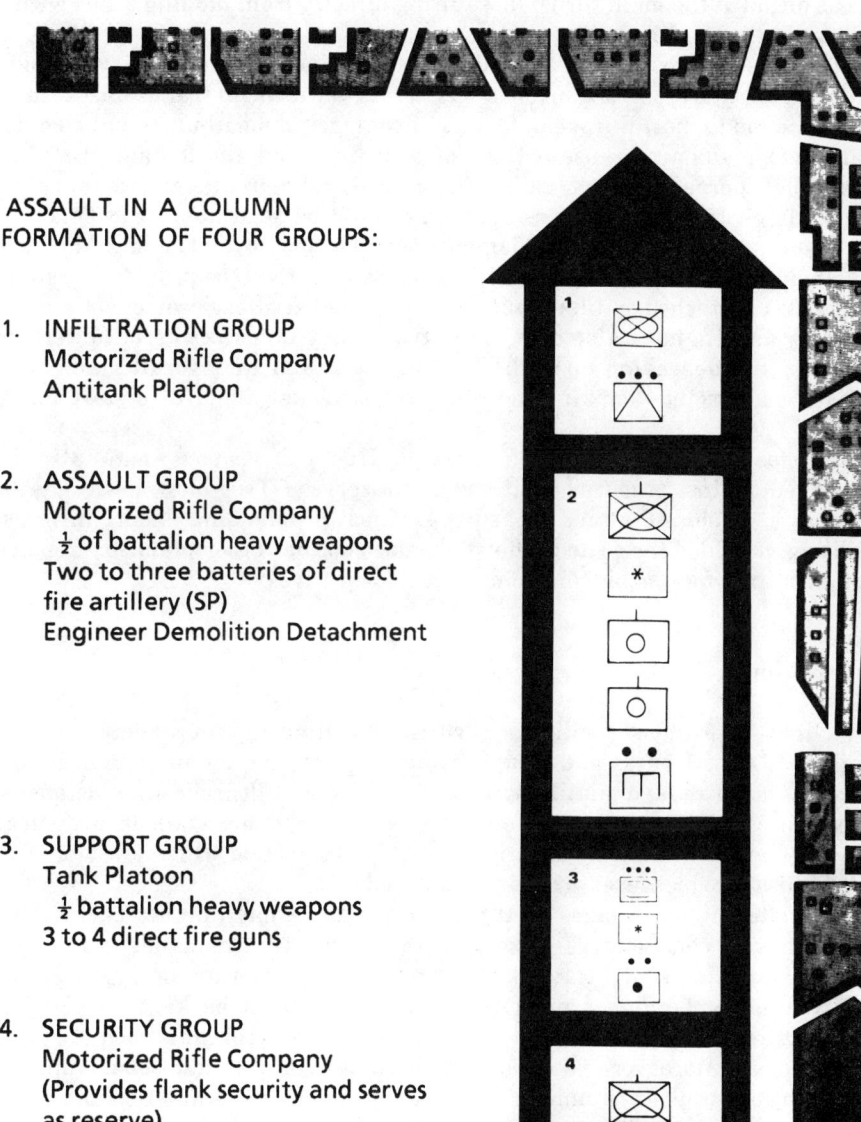

ASSAULT IN A COLUMN
FORMATION OF FOUR GROUPS:

1. INFILTRATION GROUP
   Motorized Rifle Company
   Antitank Platoon

2. ASSAULT GROUP
   Motorized Rifle Company
   ½ of battalion heavy weapons
   Two to three batteries of direct
   fire artillery (SP)
   Engineer Demolition Detachment

3. SUPPORT GROUP
   Tank Platoon
   ½ battalion heavy weapons
   3 to 4 direct fire guns

4. SECURITY GROUP
   Motorized Rifle Company
   (Provides flank security and serves
   as reserve)

Figure 3.15. Assault Formation of MR Battalion in City Attack

areas ahead of the main thrust, assaulting directly from landing zones within or adjacent to the forest.

Attacks in forests are executed at the battalion or company level. Small units necessarily use the normal crisscross pattern of trails and natural breaks found in most European forests. Frontages of small units will be quite narrow--a platoon may use a front of 50 meters, but the distance between available approaches may widen the overall unit frontage. Platoons will normally be 150 to 200 meters apart and could be separated by as much as 500 meters. Reconnaissance elements will be 300 to 500 meters ahead of advancing platoons. Direct and indirect fire support will be provided by small elements of attached artillery, with self-propelled artillery protected by small infantry and engineer elements. Air strikes may be used where the terrain permits, and depending upon the type of forest and the overall plan, those strikes may include napalm and other fire attacks intended to start forest fires.

Nuclear strikes and other mass destruction weapons may also be employed against prepared positions and reserves. Tree blow-down may be used as a deliberate attack measure to defeat a defending enemy in forest fighting, provided the scale of the strike does not bar other planned offensive action or the timely achievement of planned objectives.

Operations at Night

Night operations facilitate surprise by limiting an enemy's reconnaissance effectiveness and complicating his targeting for mass destruction weapons, aircraft, and missile strikes. They also may degrade other defensive capabilities. Night operations may be particularly important in a nuclear environment, when enemy aviation is highly active, and when new technical reconnaissance measures are being employed.

Despite the advantages of trying to sustain a daytime attack into the night, Soviet commanders anticipate that competing demands will arise. Before launching a night attack, comprehensive, wide-ranging preparations and thorough planning are required. Planning must be kept simple, but detailed, and arrangement must be made for possible reorganization of attack formations. Moreover, detailed coordination requires additional support, including a significant number of special measures for illumination and night vision equipment. To carry out the attack, troops with a high level of discipline, training and effectiveness are essential. For these reasons, major offensive operations at night probably will occur rarely. Small-scale attacks that continue operations begun in daylight are more likely.

When night operations are undertaken, battalion-level attack formations normally will comprise a single echelon made up of a tank/infantry team with a small advance guard. Companies advance with platoons on line. If resistance is light, the attackers may remain mounted. The attack may be made either from the march or from positions in contact. Routes of advance to assembly and deployment areas will be marked, and the routes from assembly areas to the line of departure outlined by luminous markers, traffic regulators, and guides. If possible, deployment areas are occupied secretly during twilight.

The direction of an attack will be marked periodically during its course by aircraft, artillery, and mortar fire. Illumination will be designed primarily to reveal objectives and to delineate unit boundaries; searchlights and flares may be used. Soviet artillery will be prepared to suppress enemy illumination. Included in the plan of fires will be provisions for using smoke. An artillery preparation is usually carried out, but may be omitted during an initial assault for the sake of surprise. Generally, artillery will be well forward to support the attack. Regimental artillery groups (RAGs) will support the attack by lead battalions and companies.

ASSAULT RIVER CROSSINGS

A Soviet study has estimated that forces in Western Europe would encounter water obstacles up to 100 meters wide every 35 to 60 kilometers and obstacles between 100-300 meters wide every 250 to 300 kilometers. The Soviets therefore have developed and deployed large stocks of bridging and assault equipment for river crossings, designed and deployed numerous amphibious combat vehicles, and emphasized river crossing tactics in Soviet and Warsaw Pact training exercises. Although the Soviets have a significant line of communications (LOC) bridging capability, we will cover only the tactical application of assault river crossings.

Soviet doctrine calls for hasty assault crossings on a wide front in order to maintain a high rate of advance. Forces do not stop to consolidate bridgeheads, but continue the offensive. Keys to the successful crossing of water barriers are adequate planning and reconnaissance. Generally, the Soviets will seek to seize crossings of water obstacles by sending detachments of airborne or heliborne forces forward of the advancing main elements. The Soviets have practiced using helicopters to deliver and emplace bridge sections and to transport troops to seize the far bank and establish blocking positions. A battalion-size landing force could be emplaced 20 to 30 kilometers ahead by the division's forward elements, where it would be expected to defend for four to six hours before linkup with the main force.

The forward detachment will attempt to secure undefended crossing sites while avoiding contact with enemy forces deployed in blocking or screening positions on the far bank. Forward detachments receive their fire support from attached artillery, helicopters, and tactical aviation. If bridging is unavailable, forward detachments will plan to cross the water barrier using amphibious vehicles, and by snorkeling or ferrying their tanks.

Once the far bank is secured by surprise or assault, snorkeling, bridging, and ferrying operations can begin. Bridging is preferred because it will handle a much greater volume of traffic. Units will proceed from assembly areas several kilometers from the river's edge to the bridge or ferry site under control of a crossing commander. Soviet units have been seen to bridge the

Elbe river in 10 to 15 minutes. Bridging equipment is capable of carrying medium tanks, and an entire motorized rifle battalion can cross within four to five minutes.

Snorkeling is a unique Soviet stream-crossing method used when the enemy can still deliver observed fire on the crossing site and when reconnaissance determines that bottom conditions and depths (no more than 5.5 meters) are acceptable. Attaching the snorkel and sealing tanks takes place one to five kilometers from the water barrier after the far bank has been secured. Some tanks are assigned to provide fire support for the crossing and artillery is used for both direct and indirect fire. Efficient traffic control is essential. Tanks cross under water in a column formation at approximately 30-meter intervals without shifting gears, halting, or changing direction of movement. (A Soviet tank battalion crossing a river under water with only the snorkels and exhaust plumes showing is an eerie sight.) Tank crews can fire the main gun immediately upon emerging from the water. Once motorized rifle and tank elements have crossed, artillery and air defense elements are brought over by tracked amphibians and ferrying until the bridge is erected. Crossing may take place by either day or night.

The only essential difference between a hasty assault crossing and a deliberate river crossing is in the artillery preparation prior to the crossing. Once enemy defenses have been neutralized, the crossing is, for all practical purposes, the same as the hasty assault, with reserves committed to exploit success by pursuit of withdrawing enemy forces. A standard technique, observed in field training exercises, for reducing the defenses on the far shore is the use of nuclear weapons.

AIRBORNE AND AIR-LANDED OPERATIONS

The airborne assault is an integral part of Soviet combined arms doctrine for both nuclear and conventional warfare. Projecting combat troops by air to secure objectives forward of advancing ground forces directly supports the Soviet concepts of surprise, mobility, deep penetration, and rapid exploitation. Parachute assault operations using transport aircraft are primarily associated with deep objectives on the strategic and operational levels. Helicopter assault operations are mainly at the tactical level and are necessarily limited in depth by the operating radius of helicopters.

Strategic airborne assault operations may involve one or more airborne divisions under Ministry of Defense control. Strategic objectives may be at considerable depth and could include air bases, sea ports, or other targets vital to the success of theater operations. Under conditions short of war, this type of operation could be used to project Soviet power and presence outside the Eurasian land mass.

Operational airborne assaults in support of a Front offensive may involve up to division-size parachute assault forces at depths as great as 300 kilometers. Potential missions include securing bridgeheads, air- landing or river crossing sites, seizing key terrain, leapfrogging contaminated areas to exploit the results of nuclear strikes, encircling enemy forces, and destroying enemy nuclear delivery systems.

Tactical airborne assault operations, involve primarily helicopter assault forces of brigade or lesser size used against forward enemy objectives. Tactical missions are essentially the same as operational, but with a reduction in depth of employment, size of force, and level of control.

Special purpose airborne assault operations are conducted by either parachute or helicopter assault forces of company size or smaller, organized as reconnaissance or raid groups. Parachute assault forces may be targeted at either tactical or operational depths. Missions include target reconnaissance and other intelligence collection; destruction of nuclear delivery means; destruction of command, control and logistic functions; and rear area harassment.

"SPECIAL OPERATIONS" – CONCLUSIONS

Soviet tactical attacks will vary in their particulars according to the strength of defensive positions and the conditions and circumstances of offensive operations. Fighting in built-up areas or attacking an enemy defending on a river line will differ considerably from the general pattern of other attack operations. Maneuver and mobility may be constrained in special operations that may be required as part of the attack against a defending enemy. The Soviets also anticipate variations in the scope and intensity of combat in various phases of an attack. The overriding tactical requirement of the assault forces in all phases of an attack is to maintain high speed and continuous momentum. Aggressive, sustained combat action in keeping the initiative is sought through realistic planning and thorough preparation, exploiting success, ensuring mutual cooperation and coordination of the combined arms, and attacking through the entire depth of the defense.

The depth and character of the objectives vary depending on the terrain, enemy dispositions, and whether nuclear weapons are employed. Governing the initial determination of prescribed attack objectives will be the capabilities of available Soviet forces and the degree to which the enemy has been neutralized. In a basic sense, the objective of tactical attacks is to destroy the enemy found in the unit's zone of operations, get into the rear of enemy defenses, and destroy the forces and reserves committed to the defense. Overcoming an enemy defense also will facilitate destroying his nuclear attack resources, another continuing Soviet combat objective. As part of a larger offensive, tactical attacks contribute to operational success.

LOGISTICS REQUIREMENTS

Soviet logistics requirements are determined by numerically large forces heavily armed with high technology weaponry and expected to move at high rates of speed over fairly long distances. These requirements are very demanding.

During World War II, the Soviet ground forces were made up of foot soldiers armed with rifles or submachine guns, mortars, artillery, rockets, and T-34 tanks. They were supplied principally by animal-drawn transport, supplemented by a relatively small number of trucks. During the four-year war these forces covered great distances and consumed massive amounts of fuel, food, and ammunition, and material. (See p. 10). The Red Army, which began the war with approximately 3.5 million men, grew to 20,000,000 by the end of the war. During the course of the war, the Army lost 137,000 aircraft and 100,000 tanks but when the war ended, the Soviet armed forces were equipped with 16,000 aircraft and 15,000 tanks. The economy succeeded in producing this huge amount of materiel despite the loss of approximately one-third of its production capacity at the beginning of the war, the transfer of another one-third to new sites, and the construction of new plants. The Soviet Union now is vastly more powerful, both economically and militarily, than when it entered the war in 1941.

Complicating the logistic problem is the fact that the Soviet Armed Forces now have a far greater variety of equipment--several types of tanks and self-propelled artillery pieces, an assortment of armored personnel carriers and armored scout cars, four kinds of self-propelled antiaircraft guns and 13 types of SAMs to take a few examples. Soviet equipment is good and its quantity is overwhelming. Chapter 4, NORMS, includes a discussion of the numbers required by Soviet norms to provide the force ratios they believe necessary for victory. Here only the philosophy underlying the Soviet logistics organization is dealt with.

The Soviet military logistics system is based on the principle that the several arms and services are responsible for supplying and maintaining their functionally subordinate units. The supply interrelationships for the national directorates are shown in Figure 3.16. An example of a military arm and the type of equipment it must supply is the missile and artillery directorate. The Chief of the Main Missile and Artillery Directorate is responsible for the delivery, storage, and repair of artillery weapons, mortars, antitank guided missiles, air defense weapons, and small arms to all artillery units at all levels, i.e., Army artillery divisions artillery regiments, motor rifle regiment mortar companies, etc. The Directorate also supplies tank guns to tank factories and repair units and is responsible for all types of ammunition and for lubricants and cleaning materials used in maintaining weapons. The other major supply directorates are the Main Tank Directorate, Central Motor Vehicle-Tractor Directorate, Engineer Troops, Signal Troops, Chemical Troops, Military Transportation Service, Food and Clothing Directorates, Fuel and Lubricant Supply Directorate, Central Military Medical Directorate, and the Chief of Veterinary Services. Each of these directorates or branches of troops is not only responsible for providing the material, but also for training troops to use the material in combat.

The person responsible for supply, i.e., for reporting needs up to the directorates and seeing that they are filled at lower levels of organizations

(Front, Army, Corps division, brigade and regiment) is the Chief of the Rear Services or the Deputy Commander of the Rear. He is the senior logistics officer, directly responsible for the day-to-day administration and management of the military logistic system. He exercises control through a staff of officers from the combat arms and technical services. At the regiment level, the Deputy for Technical Affairs oversees the ordering, storing, distributing, and maintenance of all weapons, vehicles, and technical equipment associated with his arm or service.

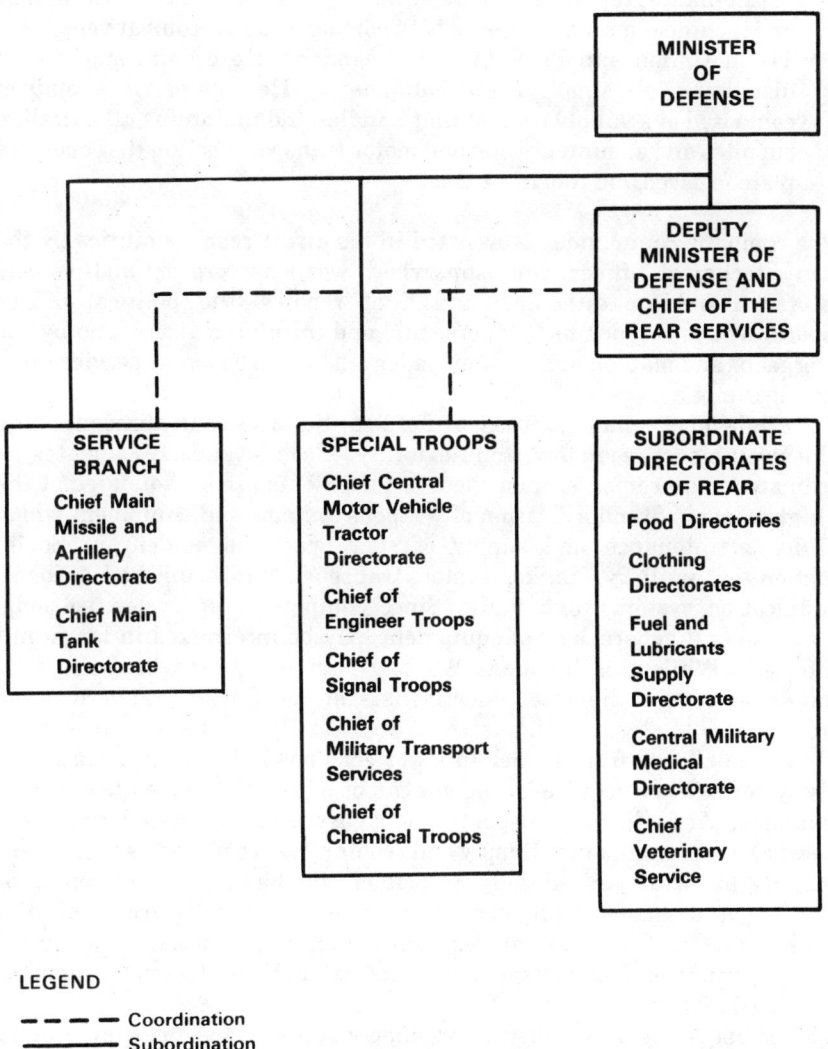

Figure 3.16. Ground Forces National Level Logistical Organization

In tank and motorized rifle units, all aspects of logistics are the responsibility of the commander. At the battalion level, for example, he is assisted by:

(1) The chief of battalion staff (battalion executive officer). As primary organizer and administrator of battalion rear services, he must know the status of weapons availability, combat equipment, and transport vehicles, as well as the status of on-hand battalion supplies.
(2) The battalion technical officer. He organizes and controls maintenance, repair, and salvage, and is responsible for serviceability and technical maintenance for both combat and non-combat vehicles.
(3) The battalion supply platoon commander. He orders, stores, and distributes all supplies and equipment. He commands a platoon composed of a supply section that handles and maintains all battalion supplies and an ammunition and motor transport section that operates platoon cargo and lubricant trucks.

The company commander is assisted in his direct responsibilities by the company technical officer who supervises weapons, crews, and vehicle operators in field maintenance and light repairs, the political officer (*Zampolit*) who is responsible for personnel and training matters, and by the first sergeant and platoon and section leaders. There are no rear service units within the company.

At each level of command, the Chief of Rear Services centralizes planning to achieve efficiency, economy, and flexibility. Each level daily computes its subordinates' requirements, then these requirements are consolidated at the next higher level. Standardization of weapons systems and equipment which simplifies maintenance and supply of spare parts is evident in Soviet production of artillery, tanks, motor transport, tank-launched bridges, communication systems, and POL. Since equipment life cycles are long, however, several generations of equipment may be intermixed in large unit inventories. While this broadens Warsaw Pact equipment holdings, it is beginning to reduce the total effectiveness of the Soviet standardization programs.

Forward delivery from higher to lower echelons is the foundation of the supply system. When required, echelons can be bypassed to expedite delivery; for example, Army-level transport can bypass division installations and deliver directly to regiments. Supply and repair sites are placed as far forward as possible to ensure expeditious arrival of supplies and rapid repair or evacuation of damaged equipment. Priorities of supply are: missiles (warheads and fuels); ammunition; petroleum, oil, lubricants; weapons, equipment, and technical parts; rations; medical and non- technical supplies; and captured materiel.

The Soviet Army uses a distinctive supply-account measuring system for quantifying requirements. Key elements include the following:

(1) *Unit of fire*: The number of rounds or metric tons of ammunition assigned to each type weapon, based on current allowance norms.

(2) *Refills*: The internal and auxiliary fuel tank capacity of a tracked vehicle or the average consumption rates and established cruising range norms for wheeled vehicles, both measured in liters.
(3) *Daily Ration*: The amount of food, by weight, required by daily mess-norms.
(4) *Set*: A group of specific items needed to meet a functional requirement.
(5) *Charge*: The quantity of gases, fluids and/or granular materials loaded at one time into a specialized apparatus or container, such as flame thrower or fire extinguisher.

The minimum total amount for each type of supplies to be held is specified in regulations for material allowance norms (Chapter 4 - NORMS).

ORGANIZATION FOR BATTLEFIELD SUPPLY

Installations providing logistic support are shown in Figure 3.17. The Front main supply base will be located near railroad lines some 150 to 200 kilometers from the rear boundaries of subordinate areas, and will contain branch depots for each of the arms, services, and special-troop directorates. When delivery distances become excessive, the base may be moved forward, or Front supply base sections may be established. Similarly, the Army supply base, smaller than the Front supply base, is located about 100 kilometers behind the line of contact. When necessary, mobile Army advance supply bases will be established immediately behind division sectors.[23] Preferably, both Army supply facilities will be serviced by a railroad line to expedite deliveries from the Front supply base.

Forward delivery of division supplies normally will be made by Army-level trucks. The division mobile supply base is commanded by a logistics officer who is assisted by branch depot chiefs; the base is subordinate to the division Chief of the Rear. At division level, supplies are generally maintained on board vehicles, although ammunition may be stored on the ground when extended periods of preparation fires are planned. The division mobile supply base is approximately 25 to 40 kilometers behind the line of contact.

Normally, regiment supplies are "up-loaded" on vehicles at the regimental mobile supply point, located 10 to 30 kilometers behind the line of contact. The installation is supervised by the regimental Chief of the Rear who functions without branch depot chiefs.

Supplies are maintained by the battalion supply platoon at the battalion supply point and are transported on organic vehicles. Prescribed norms are held for all classes of material and are replenished before a combat mission from regimental and division stocks.

Company supplies held by platoon section and crew chiefs are of two types: expendable, for use in assigned missions; and emergency reserve

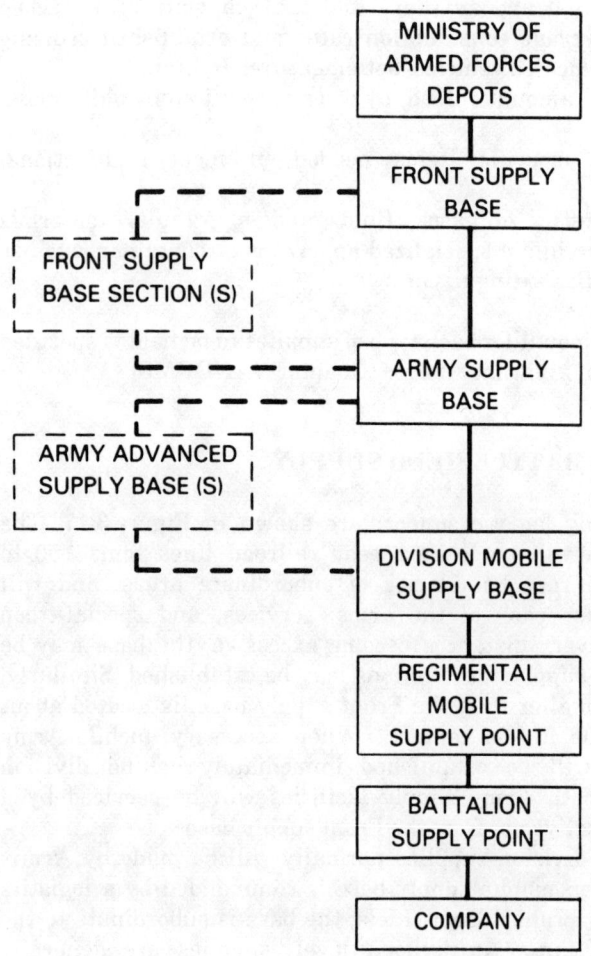

From Armed Forces Depots to Army Advanced Supply Bases, transportation may be by road, rail, air, pipeline, or inland waterway. Road transportation is usually used to lower levels.

The forward delivery system normally uses higher echelon transport to deliver to lower: however, from regiment to Army Supply Base, transport from the lower echelon may be used as available. From regiment down to company, delivery is always higher to lower.

Figure 3.17. Supply Installations

(*neprikosnovennyy zapas*), which may be used only with higher authority approval.

The logistics buildup prior to an offensive includes:

(1) Stocking the Front supply base and Army supply base;
(2) Establishing and stocking Front supply base sections and Army advanced supply bases as required;
(3) Checking regimental and division stocks;
(4) "Up-loading" allowance norms for battalions and companies; and
(5) Placing additional ammunition at firing positions.

Similarly, technical units (engineer, chemical, signal, and medical) attached to combat units, similarly, usually are supplied technical equipment by separate supply channels within each branch, from Front to regimental level. The unit to which they are attached may augment basic supplies, such as ammunition, fuel, and rations.

A division has enough organic transportation to carry about five days' supply of ammunition, POL, and rations. Development and large-scale production of fixed-wing and rotary-wing cargo aircraft indicates an effort by the Soviets to exploit aerial resupply capabilities.

During an offensive, supplies are moved forward when needed. Additionally, Army mobile supply columns follow the assault divisions. Refueling and supply of ammunition is carried out before the combat mission and at the end of each day; if required, emergency resupply can be made during battle. In a mounted offensive, combat units arrange a rendezvous point with the battalion supply platoon and escort trucks to company positions, where supplies are transferred direct to combat vehicles. In dismounted operations, supplies are hauled to a company supply point and picked up by ammunition bearers or vehicles from the combat unit, and transferred to firing positions. In fast-moving situations, such as in the pursuit, refueling is carried out during halts, first from on vehicle auxiliary tanks, then by calling on battalion fuel supply trucks.

In defensive situations, there will be many cases in which supplies will be offloaded for ground storage in pits or earth bunkers. Most deliveries will be made during the hours of darkness or under conditions of limited visibility.

RECOVERY AND MAINTENANCE

The forward repair concept is aimed at effective support for high tempo offensive operations. Front line units have limited maintenance capability and depend on higher-level maintenance units to provide direct and backup support. Above battalion level, maintenance responsibility is done by type of equipment, with a staff officer at each level responsible for a particular type such as tanks or artillery. Service is provided by mobile repair shop complexes that extend the forward repair capability.

To ensure prompt recovery and repair during battle, a Technical Observation Point (*TNP*) (*Technicheskiy - Nablyudatel'niy Punkt*) is formed in the forward area of each combat battalion. The purpose is to monitor the battlefield for damage, help crews, and call repair or recovery teams. The *TNP* is headed by the battalion's deputy commander for technical matters, and includes company deputies, extra vehicle operators, radiomen, and combat engineers. Radio contact is maintained with retriever crews and the repair shops. When it is not possible to observe the entire battalion area, company *TNP*s may be established. Vehicles needing repair beyond regimental capability will be evacuated by division to its damaged vehicle collection point. When divisions cannot make the repairs, vehicles are taken to Army or Front facilities. If necessary, vehicles may be left on evacuation routes to await mobile maintenance teams providing direct or backup support. The higher level units' team will remain to complete repairs as the lower unit moves out in support of front line operations.

MEDICAL SUPPORT OPERATIONS

In wartime, the Soviet Army medical service will be able to draw freely on the civilian medical establishment for personnel, equipment, services, and training facilities. The high casualties, both civilian and military, that probably will occur in any future war will be dealt with through coordination of military and civilian medical services and the civil defense system. The battlefield mission of the Soviet Army Medical Service is to bring forward aid to the wounded and sick and to provide quick evacuation to a facility capable of proper care. The service is also responsible for general preventive medicine, dental care, epidemic control, sanitation, medical supply, and inspection of food and water. Doctors, assisted by nurses, are of officer rank. Medical assistants (*feldshers*) are warrant officers. They are trained to perform minor surgery and treat minor ailments and are also the principal administrators of medical units. Medical orderlies or NCOs provide troop training and carry out administrative duties. Medical assistants perform supporting routine duties.

At Front and Army level, the Chief of the Directorate of Rear Services administers medical activities through his subordinate Directorate of Medical Support. This directorate operates various types of hospitals. A division medical station is operated by an organic medical battalion. The battalion operates a field hospital consisting of a receiving section, a surgical section, and a medical section. The field hospital provides major surgery and can process about 400 patients every 24 hours on a sustained basis. It is located 12 to 20 kilometers behind the line of contact. At regiment and battalion levels, a medical post provides a dressing station and pre-medical treatment to the wounded. The company aid man and his assistants establish aid stations and casualty collection points. Traveling in their own vehicles or in combat vehicles, they locate casualties, administer first aid, carry casualties to the aid station, and arrange for evacuation to battalion. They are also responsible for organizing burial of the dead. Evacuation procedures are shown in Figure 3.18. Casualties and the dead from Afghanistan, however, are being regularly evacuated by air for hospitalization and burial in the Soviet Union.

PERSONNEL REPLACEMENTS

A unit may be replaced when its combat capability has been seriously impaired. Replacement will depend on the unit's mission and the ability of the higher commander to provide a new unit. When a unit cannot be replaced in entirety, an organizational alternative may be used. The remaining forces may be consolidated into a smaller structure; for example, reduction of the number of companies in a battalion or battalions in a regiment. Branch specialists (positions requiring lengthy training), may be replaced from reserve forces, from pools of surviving crews and hospital returnees, or by personnel not fully trained. Officer replacements may come from reserve units, hospital returnees, or from military academies, schools, and training courses.

COMMAND, CONTROL, AND COMMUNICATIONS C^3

Marshal Ogarkov, in his now famous "Always Ready to Defend the Homeland," several times reemphasized the problems and importance related to command, control, and associated communications (C^3): "The revolution in technology is bringing about changes in the form of military operations at an ever accelerating pace; in any future armed conflict the basic operational entity would no longer be the Front, but a form of military operations of much greater scale. ... Command and control systems have become more complex, requiring a fundamentally new approach to the organization and deployment of senior command systems."[24]

The Soviet concept of troop control (*upravleniye voyskami*) includes not just communications but all battle management to include staff organization and procedures, planning, decision making, and computer automation. In this chapter we shall deal with command at tactical levels, but the Soviet C^3 System at all levels is larger and more complex than the US counterpart, primarily because they have paid more attention to providing redundancy that we have, but also because they have a force ten times the size of ours with considerably more artillery and vastly more missile capability. Add to this the fact that they have a truly combined arms concept which requires survivable effective C^3 to succeed.

The Soviet philosophy of unity of command (*edinonachaliye*) requires that the commander communicate his concept of the operation to everyone through his staff and subordinates to insure that his will is done. This centralization is frequently seen as a weakness but it is also a strength in the chaos of modern combat, especially if it is nuclear. The central command structure of the

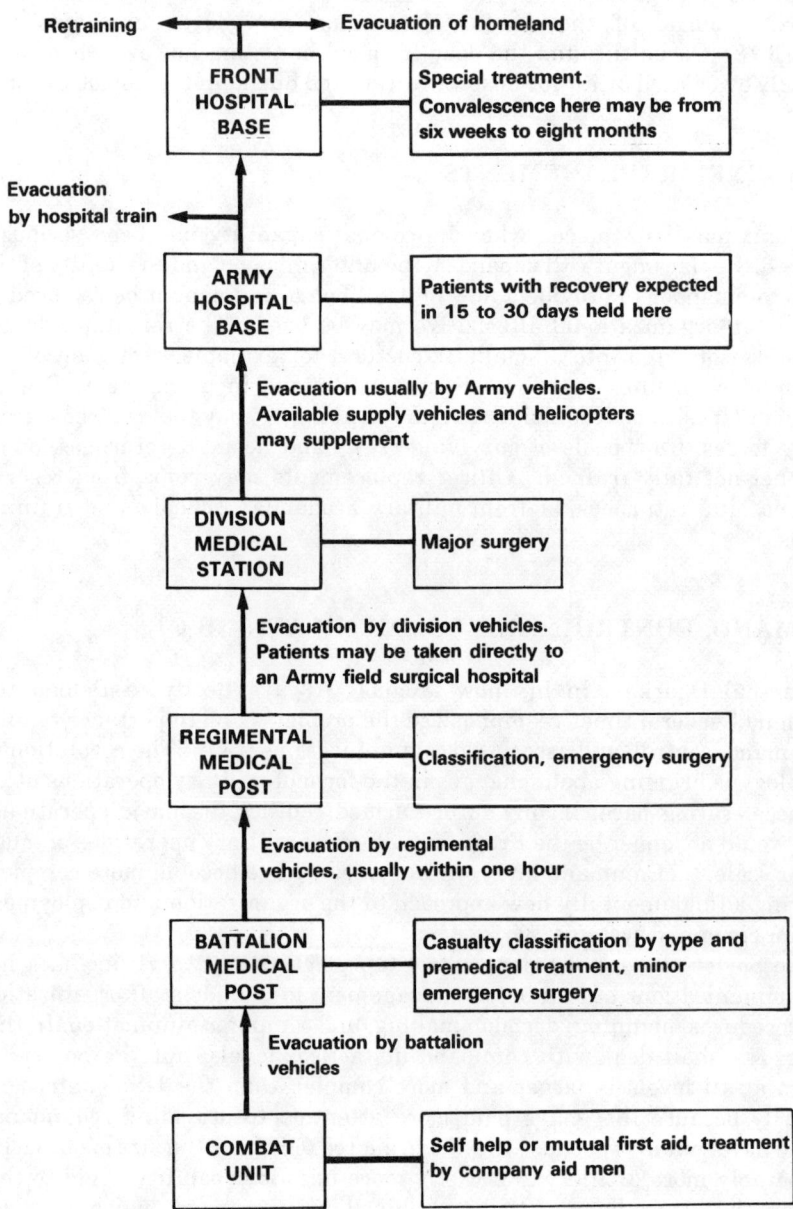

Figure 3.18. Medical Evacuation and Treatment

party/High Command insures that its will is done by providing KGB signal units down to division level. These units communicate regularly with Moscow and are additionally responsible for encrypting and decrypting traffic out of all division and larger size units (*soyedinyeniya*). Soviet efforts to improve their command and control procedures will be mentioned in Chapter 4 (NORMS), but the general outlines of their system are as follows. All headquarters, division and higher, are organized in the same basic manner, although they vary in size. For example, a division staff is approximately one-third the size of an Army staff. The staff, under supervision of the chief of staff, directs the tactical operations of subordinate units in accordance with the commander's plan. Staff elements are responsible for operations, intelligence, cryptographic communications, training, air defense, and administration.

The Political Directorate, a department of the Central Committee of the Communist Party, is responsible for propagating party policy throughout the armed forces; all elements of communication media and educational cultural activities are used. Political officers are assigned at all levels of the Soviet Army down to the company. They conduct troop education and indoctrination, assist the commander in maintaining troop morale and motivation, and advise him on non-operational matters. The political officer does not now participate in military decisions, as was the case in World War II; he does, however, exert considerable influence on general policy and political direction of the unit.

The senior officer of each arm is also an advisor with direct access to the commander. For example, tank, artillery, air defense, engineer, signal, and chemical troop directorates are each responsible for the technical aspects of their own arm. The Soviet commander at every level is charged with overall responsibility for his forces. Under Soviet doctrine, it is preferable for a tactical commander to be free as much as possible from concerns not directly related to current and future tactical situations. The Chief of Staff, therefore, is given a strong role in conducting the day-to-day operations of the command. The Soviets emphasize that in fluid warfare, during the course of planned operations, a commander is required to develop a battle scheme on his own initiative without recourse to a higher level. All commanders are required to be conversant with the general situation and the intentions of the senior commander.

Control is exercised by the establishment of a series of command posts. The distance between them is planned so that not more than one may be put out of action by a single medium-yield nuclear weapon. The number of command posts and the size of each depends on the level of organization. Five basic types of command posts are:

(1) Forward command post (*peredovoy komandniy punkt [PKP]*). A command post deployed near the first echelon troops, from which the commander controls the troops in action, especially on the main axis or sector. It is used by division-level or higher commanders when control is difficult from the main command post or when the main

command post is moving or has been put out of action. A division *PKP* would be located up to 5 kilometers from the line of contact.

(2) Main command post (*komandniy punkt [KP]*). A main post for the control of troops and units, formations, and major field forces, from which consistent direction is maintained leading to the successive accomplishment of objectives. A division *KP* would be located 5 to 15 kilometers from the line of combat.

(3) Alternate command post (*zapasniy komandniy punkt [ZKP]*). A post established, with reduced staffing, to ensure continuity of control should the main command post be put out of action. A division *ZKP* would be located 5 to 15 kilometers from the line of contact and at least 5 kilometers from the main command post.

(4) Rear services control point (*tylovoy punkt upravleniya [TPU]*). A control point organized to direct the rear services activities of a major field force or strategic formation or unit. A division *TPU* would be located 10 to 30 kilometers from the line of contact.

(5) Command observation post (*komandno-nablyudatel'niy punkt [KNP]*). A post established by units and sub-units in order to direct the combat actions of their elements. It is normally an armored command vehicle, infantry combat vehicle (or APC) or a tank. It is the only command post at regiment level and below.

The commander decides where the command posts are to be established and the axes along which they will move. Front and Army headquarters are generally sited in depth in order to maintain control of their entire respective areas. During lengthy moves, command posts may leapfrog forward along different routes. They are preceded by small reconnaissance parties that select the new locations and act as traffic guides. While on the move, command posts maintain continuous radio contact with subordinate units, higher headquarters, and flanking units. Normally the alternate command post moves behind the main command post, prepared to take over control if required. At halts command posts are dispersed in areas furnishing cover and concealment and are camouflaged if necessary. Radio stations and special vehicles are located some distance from the actual command center. All headquarters have an administrative element that provides local defense and traffic control. Air defense of these headquarters receives a high priority. Due to dispersion in a mobile environment, there are times when headquarters are responsible for their own local ground defenses.

Command and control of a unit in combat calls for carrying out all measures necessary to ensure complete preparation, through the organization and conduct of combat actions. It includes sustaining the morale and combat readiness of units, making decisions and issuing orders to subordinates at the proper time, preparing units for combat action, organizing and maintaining continuous coordination, uninterrupted control to ensure fulfillment of the mission, and furnishing subordinate units necessary assistance. The high intensity and rapid maneuver of combat action and the rapid changes in the situation demand of all commanders firm but flexible and continuous command and control of their units.

Where opposing forces are not completely out of balance, success in battle depends on clarity of purpose and the commander's will, initiative, determination to see that decisions are carried out accurately and on time, and his ability to mobilize subordinates for the complete execution of the mission.

Flexible command and control is ensured by continuous knowledge of the situation, rapid reaction to changes, and an established system of cooperation and coordination. A decision should be carried out only so long as it corresponds with the situation. When a situation changes and there is no possibility of immediate instructions from a higher level, a commander must take responsibility for making a new decision and carrying it into action. He must, however, immediately report his decision to his superior and inform his adjacent commanders.

In combat the commander is required to personally observe the field of battle so that he can issue orders to subordinate units that will exploit the results of nuclear explosions and artillery fire. He also must make full use of all his own fire means to defeat the enemy in the shortest possible time.

The basic command and control element for a unit is the decision of the commander. To make sound decisions, the commander must thoroughly understand his mission and properly evaluate the situation and conditions on the battlefield. He must understand the role and place of his unit in the mission to be fulfilled by the higher headquarters and the results the senior commander expects of his unit. He must know which enemy forces (particularly on the axis of advance of his unit) will be destroyed or suppressed by nuclear weapons and by other means of the senior commander. He must remember which means of reinforcement will be assigned to his unit, what support will be provided by other units, and the times for meeting with their commanders.

Commanders are expected to make full use of their staff's knowledge and experience, but must accept full responsibility for their own decisions. A commander briefs his staff on the concept, organization for combat, axes of advance, battle tasks for major units, and command and control organization. The chief of staff prepares an order including:

(1) Intelligence on enemy forces;
(2) The operations plan (from the commander);
(3) Boundaries;
(4) Missions of flanking units;
(5) Missions of combat support and service units;
(6) The air defense plan;
(7) Coordination (timing of the attack); and
(8) Deployment of command posts.

During the course of battle, these orders may be supplemented by battle instructions containing additional tasks. At division and lower levels, battle orders are commonly issued verbally; written confirmatory notes and overlays may be issued subsequently.

COMMUNICATIONS

Communications requirements and capabilities reflect the overall concept of control indicated by Marshal Ogarkov above. Emphasis is on top down control, with limited flexibility at lower organizational levels; the communications arrangements reflect to a great degree this philosophy. The Soviets know that the enemy has the means to interrupt and intercept electrical transmissions, a threat that requires redundancy in modes and means.

The organization of communications that meet immediate tactical requirements is a responsibility of the commander at each tactical level. At the division level, communications authority is delegated to the chief of staff; at regimental level, to the deputy commander. Unit signal officers are charged with establishing and maintaining continuous communications throughout an operation.

The following principles are applied in organizing tactical communications:

(1) Responsibility for command communications is from higher to subordinate headquarters; however, if communications are not established by the higher headquarters, the subordinate headquarters must provide them using their own equipment.
(2) Communications with supported units are the responsibility of the headquarters of the supporting units.
(3) Lateral communications are normally established from right to left, but if such communications are not established by the unit on the right, the unit on the left must do so.
(4) Radio is the principal means of communications, especially when in contact with the enemy; messengers and other liaison services are used for augmentation and security.
(5) Wire is used extensively in the defense and in the preparatory phase of offensive operations.
(6) Operator discipline is strict, operating procedure is of a high order, and security precautions are observed minutely.
(7) Command nets are designed to provide communications with subordinate units two echelons down, in a "skip echelon" manner. This allows, for example, division to control a battalion, or regiment a company, should the situation require.

Soviet communications equipment ranges from simple, easy-to-operate electronic devices to complex, vehicular-mounted equipment that requires highly skilled operators. Radio (single channel radio and/or multi-channel radio relay) is the principal means of communications except in those static situations where wire can be efficiently employed.

Collectively, Soviet Ground Forces radios consist of low power, frequency modulated (FM), and amplitude modulated (AM) sets of the usual manpack and vehicular-mounted types; medium power high frequency (HF) radio sets of a heavy mobile variety; and two basic types of multi-channel radio relay equipment. Standardized Ground Forces field telephones are used in connection with automatic switching capabilities. Switchboards are provided down to company level. Teleprinter communications are provided down to regimental level.

There are several types of communications nets adding up to an estimated 40,000 different radio nets expected to be established across the front in a hypothetical Soviet attack on NATO. These are:

(1) Command nets used by the commander primarily to pass combat orders. These channels are generally direct from a superior to his next immediate subordinate, but they also are designed to permit skipping echelons. The arms and services have separate circuits, similar and parallel.
(2) Staff nets used by the chief of staff for directing other staff elements at his level and for keeping subordinate and superior staffs informed of his commander's intentions. The chief of artillery at Front, Army, and division has his own staff communications for control of units subordinate to him and to direct the operations of similar forces at the next lower echelon. The chiefs of engineer and chemical troops must use the main staff communications network.
(3) Liaison nets established between ground force units operating in coordinated action, and from supporting units to supported units. Each liaison officer provides his own communications equipment to operate with his parent unit.
(4) Coordination nets established between commanders to insure mutual understanding and unity of purpose and action with adjacent units.
(5) Other nets – warning, air defense, and special purpose nets. The warning nets are used to warn subordinate units of impending air, tank, nuclear, and chemical attack and to disseminate meteorological information. Air defense nets include air surveillance nets to radar sites, air warning nets, and air defense control nets connecting higher and lower staffs and air defense units. Special purpose nets are those established between main command posts and selected units.
(6) Control communications used by a combat commander to maintain direct control of his forces, usually established at lower echelons, e.g., company, battalion, and regiment. Fire control, operations, and liaison communications at battalion and lower levels are defined as control communications.
(7) Logistics/administrative (rear) communications used by rear echelon elements for control of supply, transport, medical, and other administrative and support services at all echelons from Front

through battalion. The nets are used for internal control by the chief of the rear, as well as for the control of rear service elements at the next lower level. More reliance is placed on cable and wire circuits for these nets than for the other type nets.

Signal units are assigned at all levels from Front to battalion to provide for internal headquarters operations and to establish communications with higher, subordinate, and adjacent units.

At the tactical level, each division has a signal battalion, each regiment has a signal company, and each maneuver battalion has a communications platoon.

As an example, Figure 3.19 shows the net diagram of a typical tank battalion radio net. Company nets can be established by limiting communications with the battalion commander to the R112 net. Should a tank company be placed in support of a motorized rifle battalion, the company commander uses the R123 to communicate with the supported motorized rifle battalion commander, and he can communicate with his tank battalion commander with the R112 also. This can all be facilitated using the preset frequencies available on the various radios.

In addition to radio communications, various other forms of communications are available to small unit commanders. Wire has been mentioned. It is reliable and relatively secure and is used extensively. Especially in mobile situations where time does not permit establishing wire communications, the use of visual and audio means is included in the signal plan. These include arm and hand signals, semaphore, and flares.

Soviet technicians are known to have an excellent capability in all phases of electronic warfare, both offensive and defensive. Soviet writings and conversations with Soviet communicators indicate that the Soviet capability is roughly equivalent to that of NATO, but their equipment is far more lavish. The term radioelectronic combat (REC) is a direct translation of the Russian *radioelectronicheskaya bor'ba (REB)*, but the term "REC" is widely used in NATO to describe this effort. Included in REC are communications and electronic reconnaissance, electronic countermeasures (ECM) (jamming and deception), and electronic counter-countermeasures (radio silence and other security measures, redundancy, system design characteristics, frequency hopping, etc., and training operators).

The Soviets have treated their electronic counter-countermeasure (ECCM) efforts far more openly than other aspects of REC. Writings on electronic warfare are included under broader topics such as security, command and control, reconnaissance, air defense, and camouflage. This treatment of electronic warfare in the context of routine operations is an indication that the Soviets consider electronic warfare to be integral to all combat operations.

Soviet technical writings have dealt with these EW means:
(1) Electronic reconnaissance to include detection and location of radars, command posts, communications centers, and nuclear delivery systems.

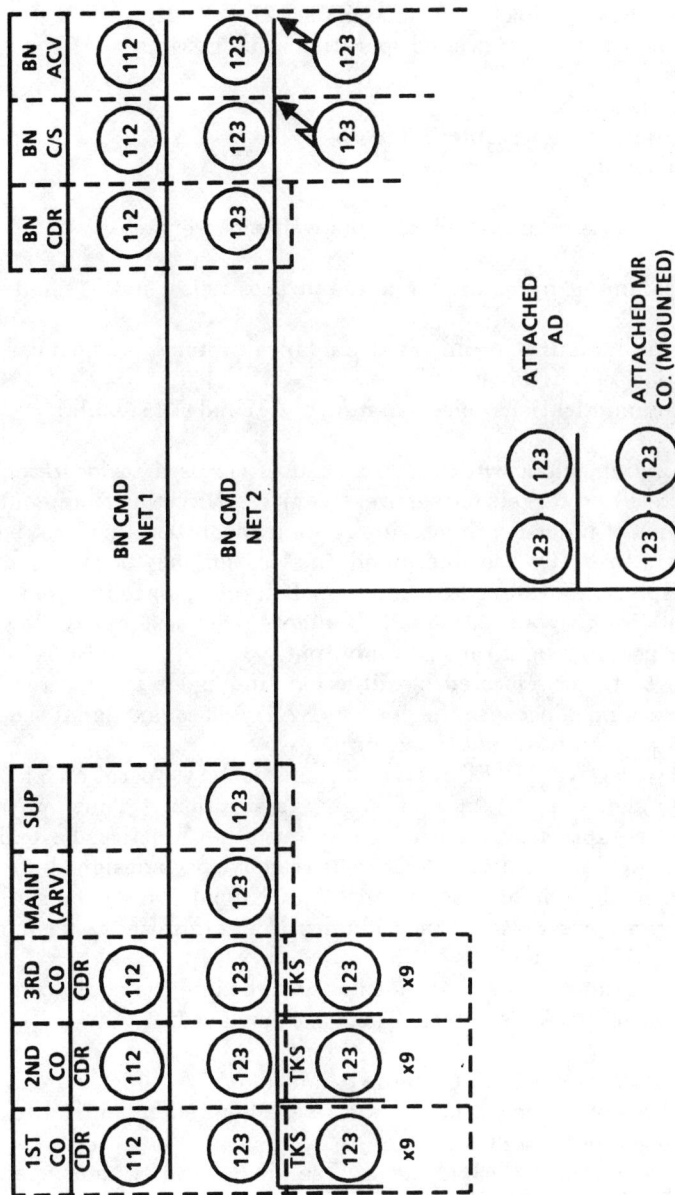

Figure 3.19. Reinforced Tank Battalion Nets

(2) Jamming in support of air defense operations, suppressing:
   (a) Radar bomb sights,
   (b) Radio navigation equipment, and
   (c) Radio control links for ASMs, SSMs.
(3) Jamming in support of ground operations, suppressing:
   (a) Radars,
   (b) Command posts,
   (c) Communications centers, and
   (d) Nuclear delivery systems.

The principal systems discussed in Soviet writings are:

(1) Radar jamming by using barrage and spot noise, pulse, chaff, and decoys;
(2) Electronic jamming of command guidance systems using pulse and simulation techniques; and
(3) Radio communications noise jamming of AM and FM signals.

Direction finding, along with other measures, is used to locate enemy electronic emitters and targets for suppressive fires. Direction finding alone, because of its lack of precision in locating radio transmitters, may not be the basis for artillery fires. On the other hand, the location may be sufficient for the use of multiple rocket launchers against soft targets, since they deliver a high volume of fire in wide dispersal. Jammers are most easily detected because of their peculiar signal and power output.

In addition to targets located by direction finding, it is expected that others will be developed because the enemy (NATO) uses lax signal security and poor electronic counter-countermeasures.

The Soviet objective for ECCM is the satisfactory operation of their electronic equipment in the face of enemy disruption. Thus, physical protection of the equipment is included, as well as other practices beyond the scope of western ECCM. Modern ECCM features have been designed into the newer air defense equipments used in the Yom Kippur War. The greatest emphasis, however, has been on individual and organizational techniques that can be applied in the field.

The Arab air defense system provided an insight into the equipment and ECCM techniques of the Soviet forces. Their use displayed:

(1) ELINT security. The radars of the SAMs and AAA, which were moved forward to cover the initial assault, were kept silent until after the initiation of the assault.
(2) Frequency spread. Each of the diverse air defense systems operated within separate radar frequencies, so that no one jamming system could operate simultaneously against all.
(3) Frequency diversity. The ability of the tracking and guidance radars to change frequencies to overcome jamming.

(4) Multiple and interchangeable guidance. Some systems worked on pulsed radar, others on continuous wave. Some of the radar tracking systems also had optical tracking for continued operations in a high ECM environment. Other systems used infrared homing.
(5) Mobility. All tactical air defense systems were extremely mobile and capable of quick change of position after firing or being spotted by reconnaissance.

Each Soviet tactical air army will have several organic support squadrons with aircraft equipped to conduct electronic warfare missions. These units can conduct electronic reconnaissance missions and ECM against radar, electronic guidance, and communications systems. The most common air ECM operations are spot or barrage jamming and dispensing chaff directed against enemy air defense early warning and fire control radars.

Bombing operations of the tactical air armies will be protected or camouflaged by aircraft using ECM in either a stand-off or escort role. Jamming equipment, with an effective range up to 200 kilometers and covering frequencies used by NATO air defense radars, is installed in these ECM aircraft. They may also eject chaff to achieve jamming, deception, and camouflage. Individual aircraft may carry self-screening jammers and chaff dispensers.

NOTES

1. V.D. Sokolovskiy, Military Strategy (*Voyennaya Strategiya*) (Moscow: Military Publishing House*, 1962, 1963, 1968), p. 341.
2. V. G. Reznichenko, Tactics (*Taktika*) (Moscow: Military Publishing House, 1984), and F. D., Sverdlov, Tactical Maneuver (Moscow: Military Publishing House, 1982).
3. V.G. Reznichenko, Tactics (*Taktika*) (Moscow: Military Publishing House, 1966), p. 76.
4. In the USSR, institutes of higher learning award degrees of Doctor of Military Science. V.D. Sokolovskiy, op. cit., p. 2.
5. V.Ye Savkin, The Basic Principles of Operational Art and Tactics (Moscow: Military Publishing House, 1972).
6. "Unequivocal Proof of Yellow-Rain Weapons" (The Wall Street Journal, 4 November 1985, p. 24) summarizes four studies on yellow rain [Soviet chemical/biological warfare] that were published in peer-reviewed scientific journals from 1982 to 1985 that give detailed evidence of Soviet use of chemical/biological weapons: Journal of the Association of Official Analytical Chemists (Vol. 66, No. 6, 1983); Biomedical Mass Spectrometry (Vol. 9, 1982); Fundamental and Applied Toxicology (Vol. 4, 1984); and Journal of Forensic Science (April 1985).

*Military Publishing House = *Voyenizdat*

7. A.A. Grechko, "The Science and the Art of Victory," *Pravda*, 19 February 1975, p. 3.

8. A.A. Radzievskiy, Tactics in Combat Examples - Division (*Taktika v Boyevykh Primerakh - Diviziy* (Moscow: Military Publishing House, 1978), p. 27.

9. A.A. Malkov, Soviet Military Encyclopedia (*Sovyetskaya Voyennaya Entsiklopedia*) "Attack" (*Ataka*) Vol 1. (Moscow: Military Publishing House, 1976), p. 308 ff.

10. A.A. Sidorenko, The Offensive (*Nastupleniye*) (Moscow: Military Publishing House, 1970), p. 109.

11. A.A. Radzievskiy, The Breakthrough (*Proryv*): Experience of the Great Fatherland War (Moscow: Military Publishing House, 1978).

12. A.A. Sidorenko, op. cit., p. 119.

13. Considerations governing frontages will be discussed in Chapter 4, NORMS.

14. See Chapter 5, THE AIR COMPONENT

15. V.G. Reznichenko, Tactics (1984), p. 14.

16. A.A. Sidorenko, The Offensive, p. 62.

17. Dictionary of Basic Military Terms, A Soviet View, USAF Soviet Military Thought Series (Washington D.C.: US GPO, 1976).

18. M. Byelov, "Airborne Operations," Red Star, 19 August 1975, p. 7.

19. V.Ye. Savkin, Military Herald (*Voyennyy Vestnik*), #3, March 1974, "Characteristics of Modern Warfare" (Moscow: Military Publishing House), p. 25.

20. V.G. Reznichenko, "Tactics Development Trends" Red Star, 5 October 1976, p. 3.

21. G. Biryukov and G. Melnikov, Antitank Warfare. Translated by David Nyshne. (Moscow: Progress Publishing House, 1972), p. 4 (published in English).

22. A.A. Radzievskiy, Army Operations (*Armeiskiye Operatsiya*) (Moscow: Military Publishing House, 1977), p. 213.

23. One of these is the *PRTB* (*Podvizhnaya Raketnaya Tekhnicheskaya Baza* - Mobile Rocket Technical Base) responsible for maintenance and supply of nuclear warheads.

24. N.V. Ogarkov, Always Ready to Defend the Homeland (Moscow: Military Publishing House, 1982).

Chapter 4
Norms

PLACE OF NORMS IN SOVIET LIFE

This chapter covers some of the ways that norms are used and how they are calculated, examines in considerable detail norms as they relate to the capabilities of the Soviet Ground Forces and evaluates the ability of the Soviet Ground Forces to meet the norms they have set for themselves.

The first definition of norm in the <u>Large Soviet Encyclopedia</u> (Volume 18, p. 123), is "a minimum or limiting quantity of something which is allowed by rule or by plan (for example, time norm or sowing norm)." Later, under the heading of "Establishing the norms for the expenditure of material resources," norm is described as "the establishment (in socialist countries) of planned measures of material into expenditures for the units of production or the volume of work." Norms of the expenditure of material resources characterize the measure of production, the use of raw materials, semi-processed materials, fuel, and other elements of production.

In order to understand the importance of norms in the Soviet military forces, it is necessary first to appreciate the place norms occupy in Soviet life. Virtually every Soviet activity is regulated by norms in one way or another.

Norms govern the distribution of all forms of material, the various aspects of Soviet life. They are used not only for the allotment of raw materials, finished products, fuel, and electrical energy, but also to control their use. Norms of expenditure must be scientifically established, progressive, and dynamic, and they must be systematically reviewed at each level of production. Norms are created for the amount of work that a factory, any branch of the factory, or any individual in the factory must perform. They also are developed for the amount of time any particular process should take. There are norms for the five-year plan, annual norms, and current norms.

Essentially norms are established in one of three ways: by analytical calculations, by production experience, and by statistical methods. In contrast with the Western belief that analysis supplements experience, the Soviets consider that their analytical method is the most progressive and scientific; experience and statistical norms are secondary. Norms, in general, are calculated by the supervisors of the people for whom the norms are intended. Establishing a norm is generally a two-step practice that involves, first, a calculation and, second, a trial of the calculated figure in order to confirm the norm. The English word <u>norm</u> is used to translate two Soviet concepts. The distinctions are fuzzy in Russian and after this brief introduction, both words will be represented by "norm."

NORMS IN MILITARY PRACTICE

The Soviet Military Encyclopedia defines Norms (military) (*normativy (voyen.)*) as:

(1) operational-tactical numerical quantities used to characterize space and time factors for operational or tactical activities of forces and the areas in which they take place. Space factors include: depths of objectives, widths of sectors, dimension for combat formations-- widths depths, etc. Time factors include: the time to fulfill every mission, complete marches, or maneuvers, etc. These are developed based on the make-up of Soviet formations, their capabilities, enemy capabilities, combat and exercise experience, level of training, results of special research studies, terrain, weather, and time of day. The basic operational-tactical norms are reflected in regulations and directives [emphasis added].
(2) timeliness, quantitative, and qualitative factors for fulfillment by service-persons and small units [usually battalion and smaller] of specified tasks, methods or applications of weapons or technology in the course of combat preparation. Norms ensure a uniform and objective approach to the determination of times for the fulfillment of [combat] actions and for the evaluation of the level of training of service-persons and units [up to regiment] as a whole. (Vol. 5, p. 636).

Norms (*normy*) are listed under four headings: financial, supply, exploitation, and expenditure. The first three are essentially logistical while the last is both logistical and operational. The norms cover all material requirements for military personnel, units, and formations in both peace and war. In combat, norms establish, for example, how many artillery rounds are needed to destroy a given target and how many guns, planes, or tanks will be required for a kilometer of front in a conventional situation.

Soviet military norms were in use at least as early as 1929, when Marshal Tukhachevsky, included them in one of the earliest sets of Soviet field service regulations. Since then they have become all-pervasive in Soviet military practice. There are norms for consumption of food, temperatures of barracks, amount of sleep, the number of hours of training, the number of hours of instruction in party doctrine, etc. Training to meet norms and the development and testing of norms are the major activities in which soldiers and officers engage during the normal work week. Staffs calculate the norms, and soldiers and officers then test the norms and determine the proper level at which they should be set.[1] Norms, then, are used to describe how much, how far, how fast, how wide, and how deep the Soviet Army is expected to operate. The norms also dictate how much ammunition, fuel, and food will be carried by every unit. These norms appear in the field service regulations and in military writings at all levels. Since they reveal so much about the Soviet Army, most of the norms are classified and are revealed only on a need-to-know basis.

Because the Soviet Ground Forces have not been involved in combined arms warfare with the equipment they now have, norms for actual combat can only be calculated. It is safe to assume, however, that the norms have been checked in Afghanistan and against client army combat activities in the Middle East, Angola, and other places to determine their accuracy.

CALCULATIONS USING NORMS

There are essentially three types of calculations that can be made using norms, or for improving and creating new norms. First are direct calculations in which one starts with the number of troops and weapons, then examines a variation of a plan using these forces. In this case, it is possible to determine the effectiveness of a particular variant of the plan and then to examine other variations. Second, there are reverse calculations that start with an assumption of the desired result, such as a certain number of tanks to be destroyed, followed by an examination of a variation of the plan, using the calculations to determine the number of troops and fire means required to obtain the desired results. Finally, there are calculations to achieve the optimum plan. Here, the number of troops and weapons and the conditions for their use are the starting point from which the optimum variant is determined.

Four principal methods are used to make calculations using norms:

(1) Direct application of norms in mathematical formulas and tables derived from them;
(2) Relation of norms to other variables in nomograms;
(3) Critical path method; and
(4) Analog instruments, mechanical or electrical.

All of these methods can be speeded up with electronic calculators, which are now being introduced in quantity into the Soviet forces.

An example of a formula and the calculations performed using engineer norms for preparation of a position is shown in Figure 4.1. We find from this table that 230.55 man days are required and 46.3 machine hours or, in a two-day period, 115 men and one bulldozer are required to fortify the given area.[2]

Fill-in charts similar to this are used extensively in artillery units to calculate the amount of artillery ammunition needed for a given target. Using an expected number of targets, the day's expenditure of ammunition can be calculated and the required amount up-loaded.

The use of nomograms is illustrated by the following nomogram for determining the quantity of antitank weapons required versus the possibility of destroying armored targets (Figure 4.2).[3]

Nomograms such as these frequently are made by a unit as it moves into a combat position to compensate for terrain peculiarities. The use of this particular nomogram is explained by the directions on the diagram for determining the required number of antitank rounds needed to destroy not

Formula: $N_L = \sum_{i=1}^{n} K_i \cdot P_i$; $N_M = \sum_{i=1}^{n} K_i \cdot m_i$; $K_L = \dfrac{N_L}{t} = \dfrac{K_M}{20t}$

N_L - where required work expenditure for the planned fortification in man-days.

K_i - number of fortifications of a given type.

P_i - norm (normativ[sic]) for a human labor for each fortification of a given type

N_M - required expenditure of machine time on construction of the planned fortifications in machine-hours.

m_i - norm (normativ) of machine time for a single fortification of a given type.

K_L - required number of men.

t - time determined for fortifying the area, days.

K_M - required number of machines.

Item	Description	No.	Time Norms (Nomy[Sic])		Required Expenditure	
			Man Days	Machine Hrs	Man Days (3)x(4)	Machine Hrs (3)x(5)
(1)	(2)	(3)	(4)	(5)	(6)	(7)
15	Cover for GAZ-69, GAZ-66	6	1.5	1.1	9	6.6
16	Cover for ZIL-157	4	3	2.7	12	10.8
17	Cover for BTR	5	2	1.4	10	7
18	Total in columns (6) and (7)				230.55	46.3

Figure 4.1. Basic Formula and Blank for Calculations of Norms

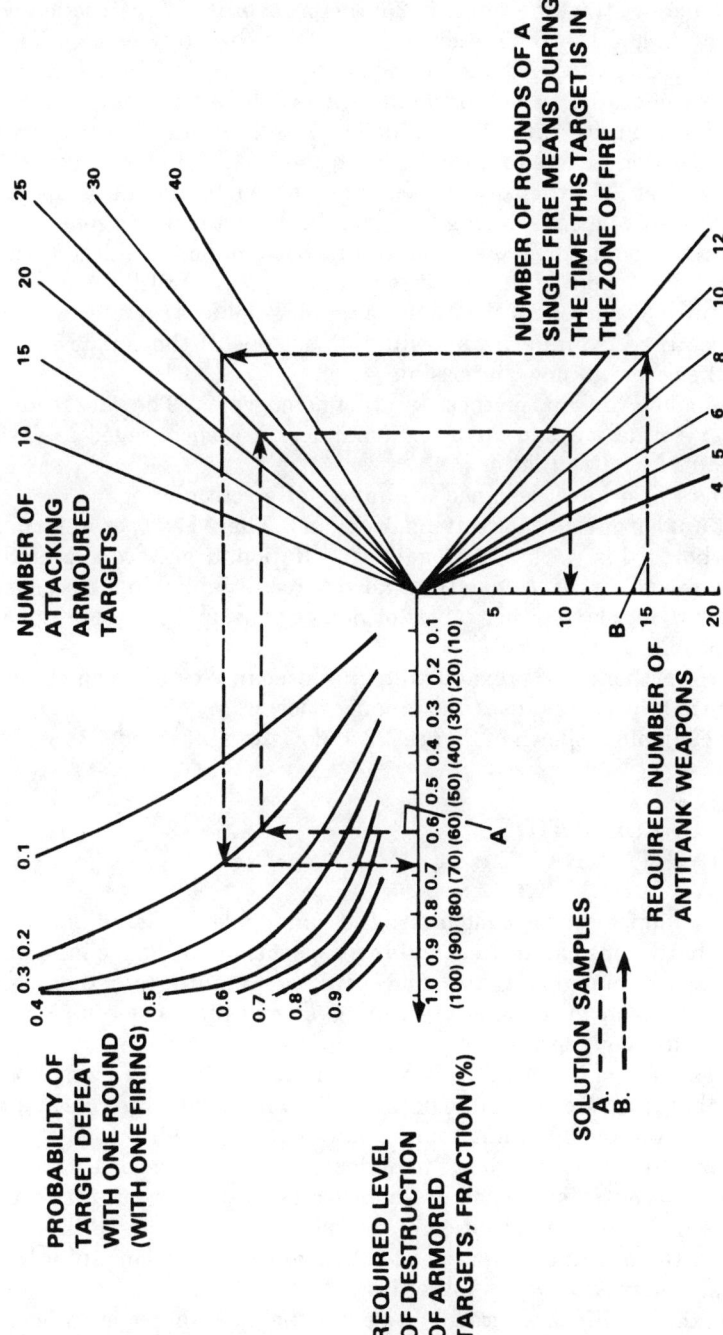

Figure 4.2. Nomogram for the Calculation of Required Quantity of Antitank Means

less than 60 percent of the attacking enemy tanks. In Solution Sample "A" the expected number of attacking tanks is 25, the probability of destruction with one weapon is .2, and the time of exposure is approximately enough for ten rounds. Using variant "A," from the number "60" (or six- tenths) on the scale "Required level of destruction of armored targets," draw a perpendicular line to meet the curve "Probability of target defeat with one round" at two-tenths. Then draw a horizontal line to intersect with the line "Number of attacking armored targets" at "25," then drop a vertical line down to the line "Number of rounds of a single fire means during the time this target is in the zone of fire" at "10." From this point, draw a horizontal line back to the "Required number of antitank means," and find the result to be ten. Thus, to fulfill the mission-- the destruction of 60 percent of the attacking tanks--not less than ten antitank rounds are required. Similarly, knowing all but one of the unknowns, the solution for the other unknown is possible.

There are many variants on these kinds of nomograms. They are made for virtually every situation and Soviet commanders are encouraged to design new nomograms for new situations.

The Soviets also have designed a number of electronic means (not calculators, but analog devices) for solving problems. There is a special term for the people who do this work: "rationalizer." Rationalizers are expected to invent various means of calculating norms (or establishing the norms themselves) without using either tables or nomograms, and to find pragmatic solutions to problems of all sorts.

The critical path method is exactly like that used in Western armies, other than the fact that the process uses and produces norms.

A Soviet example is shown in Figure 4.3 and Figures 4.3a and 4.3b.

TACTICAL CALCULATIONS: ORGANIZING THE BATTLE

Among the number of basic measures the commander and staff undertake to organize a battle, one can include making the decision to engage in combat, the planning of the combat activities, and seeing to it that they are thoroughly carried out. Decision making by the commander is the most complex and responsible act in troop control.

The process of working out a decision begins, as a rule, with sizing up the assigned combat task. To do so, it is necessary to understand the role and the place of one's unit in the upcoming combat activities and the intended plans of the higher commander. One also has to understand where the basic forces are going to be concentrated, what influence the resources of the senior commander will have, the activities of neighboring forces in fulfilling the assigned task, the amount of time needed to make preparations in order to fulfill the assigned task, as well as other issues.

To more thoroughly and broadly size up the task, a Soviet officer is expected to use various kinds of calculated data. For example, when organizing offensive combat, he must consider the effectiveness of the activities of the forces and assets employed by his senior commander, as well as any opportunities for reinforcement and support units. The results of the calculations on the effectiveness of the means of destruction available to the senior commander in guiding the activities of the units allows the commander to have a more precise concept of the nature of the task and the conditions available to fulfill it.

---

1. Determine and identify steps in process.

2. Layout, label (below line), and number (upper quadrant) steps.

3. Enter time for each process - norm, experience, or intuition (above line).

4. Accumulate time required for process if norm followed.

5. Recalculate process times based on need to launch attack in two hours
$\frac{150-120}{120} = .2$ = fraction of reduction e.g. $15 \times (1 - .2) = 12$.

6. Enter calculation back from attack time (last event to first) in right quadrant.

7. Calculate reserve time, if any (right quadrant minus left quadrant), in lower quadrant.

8. Determined critical path - connects "0" extra time.

Figure 4.3. Eight Steps in the Development of a Soviet Critical Path Chart to Determine the Earliest Time an Attack Could be Made (Figures 4.3a and 4.3b)

After sizing up the assigned task, the commander produces a timing calculation, organizes reconnaissance, and makes the necessary preliminary instructions to prepare for combat activities.

To quickly and correctly calculate the time needed to complete all the measures to organize the battle, one can successfully use a modified critical path method for planning and control. In using it, the Soviet officer is expected to preserve logic, meaningfulness, and consistency in carrying out measures and one optimizes the spread of allocated time for each job so that the entire organization for the battle is completed in the established timeframe. In organizing reconnaissance, he has to factor in the capabilities of available forces, the means to detect objectives, and the anticipated effectiveness of the reconnaissance tasks being completed.

Another major purpose tactical calculations achieve is evaluate a situation. The results of a situation evaluation make it possible to determine the ways in which troops will operate, most fully conform to assigned tasks, and display the conditions for their fulfillment.

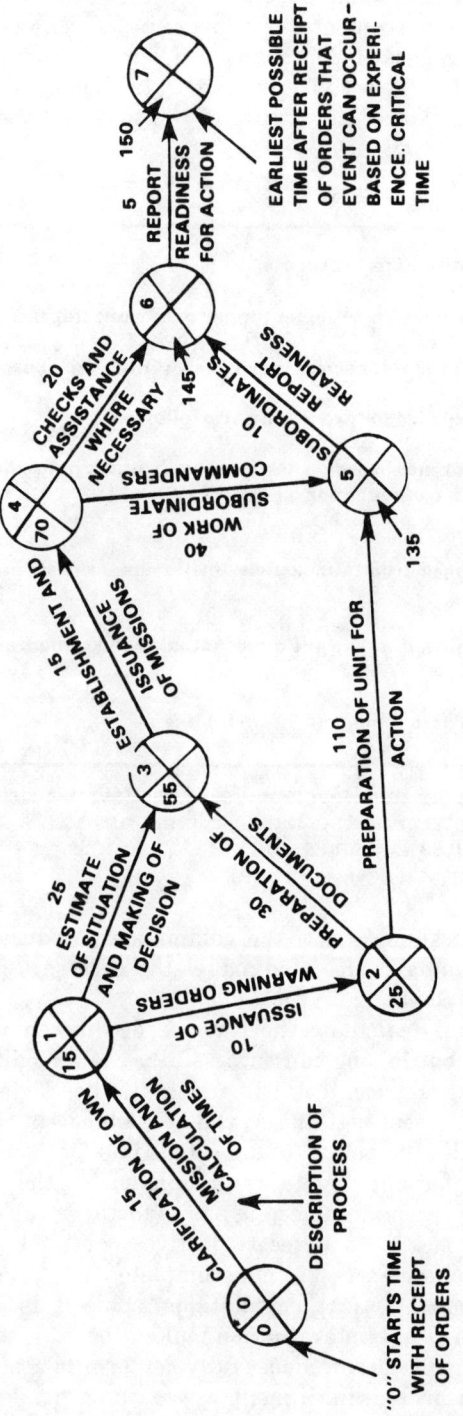

Figure 4.3a. A Soviet Critical Path Chart (Steps 1–4)

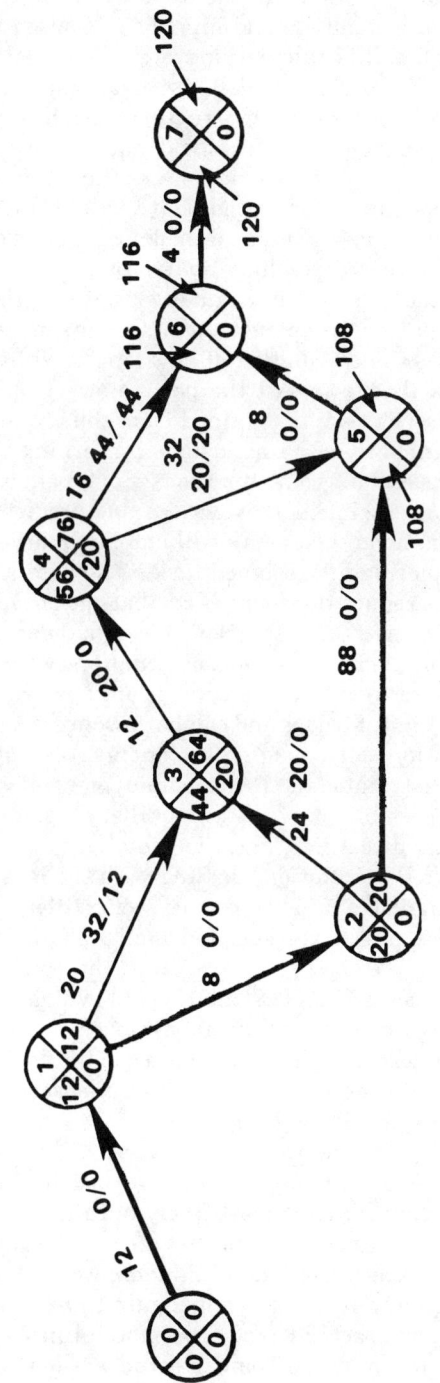

Figure 4.3b. A Calculation of the Earliest Time that an Attack Could be Launched

An important evaluation factor is enemy activities. Intelligence on the enemy is expected to be incomplete and inprecise. Consequently, the Soviet officer has to rely on probability calculations for prognostication.

Reconnaissance intelligence, as well as historical intelligence on the tactics of the enemy, his organization structure, the tactical and technical characteristics of his weapons and technical equipment, as well as other known data can be used as inputs to calculate enemy actions. In evaluating the enemy, calculations can be produced that evaluate his combat options (fire, strike, and maneuver) using same methodologies as in evaluating Soviet forces and factoring in the corresponding input data.

For example, in calculating enemy maneuver options, the Soviets use the methodology for calculating troop movements from one place to another including such things as the calculation of how long it will take the troops to regroup, how long it will take to exit the perimeter (of the assembly area), deployment times, etc. The results obtained from the calculations constitute quantitative data on which to base conclusions concerning the most probable nature of enemy actions and his combat options. Soviet officer uses these data to compare the different possible enemy actions and predict how many of his forces, resources, and actions the enemy will employ in order to prevent him from successfully completing his assigned task. The data also indicate what steps he ought to take to reduce the enemy's combat options and defeat him.

In evaluating his own troops, the Soviet commander determines what combat options he has in the most complex of situations within the framework of the assigned combat tasks. His own combat options are evaluated on the whole according to the kind of troops and combat resources he has.

To evaluate the options for engaging the enemy, the Soviet officer needs calculations that are associated with the employment of nuclear weapons, calculations for the possibility of using artillery, conducting fire upon concealed fire positions, direct fire, and the use of anti-tank guided rockets. With these are associated calculations dealing with the level of damage done to the enemy by an assigned (available) quantity of artillery pieces and shells, or calculations for the required weapons and shells to fulfill firing tasks, how long it will take to complete the firing task, what the optimal distribution of target damaging resources are, and calculations to evaluate the effectiveness of allocated resources against armored targets, etc.

In order to fully understand the place these calculations occupy in Soviet training and operations it is necessary only to examine some of the norms that have been established for the Soviet troops.

Every commander in his day-to-day activities must continuously make decisions. He must choose among possible variations in activities, and, generally speaking, decide which is most likely to fulfill his combat mission. In Soviet practice the commander first has to take into account what norms he must fulfill and what is expected of him by his commander and by his country.

Combat norms help the Soviet commander gain empirical foresight; norms are then supplemented by practical experience and intuition. They have been developed over years of simulated combat using a wide range of scientific techniques. Modern Soviet science has given Soviet officers simple instruments for practical use in quantitative methods during military studies and in the command and control of troops. These instruments have not been available for his civilian counterpart. Hand calculations are still an important tool of the commander in obtaining needed quantitative data that allow him to evaluate the effectiveness of his actions. Microcomputers are just coming into service to enable even more complex problems to be tackled, but they are not generally available Soviet society there are no "corner computer stores" and no infrastructure for producing them.

Combat activity is always carried on with a specific mission in mind. A certain combination of personnel and fire means and their proper use in relationship to the situation will ensure achieving the goal at the proper time. The commander strives to fulfill the mission assigned while inflicting optimum casualties on the enemy with the smallest number of losses for his own forces.

Great demands are made on Soviet military decision-makers. Timeliness and accuracy are the crux of their effectiveness. An expeditious decision can make the difference between success or failure on the battlefield and means life or death to many men. For this reason, the results must be obtained within a definite time period determined by external factors.[4]

Because of the requirement for rapidly implementing troop control and evaluating the situation in order to assemble and transmit combat orders, the allowable time for working out these calculations and coming to an objective decision is short. Decisions must, naturally, be as correct and accurate as possible. In the past, errors could be corrected during military operations; now the price of a mistake could be a misdirected nuclear surface-to-surface missile.

The accuracy of calculations is determined by three essentials:

(1) Selecting the correct procedures for computing the figures, which, in turn, depends on the mathematical model selected for the planned operations and the degree that the model actually corresponds to the ongoing process;
(2) The accuracy of initial data used as the basis for these calculations; and
(3) The care taken by the person performing the calculations.

The Soviets constantly strive to increase the accuracy of their calculations by improving computational procedures and increasing the reliability of initial data, in the firm belief that this will improve the efficiency of their forces. The advent of computers has greatly strengthened this belief.

The relationship between norms and situations can frequently determine their applicability. One of the factors affecting the duration of a march, for example, can be the direction and velocity of the wind at ground level. However, in practice this factor generally is not considered when working out calculations for the march because usually it is unimportant in comparison with others, such as the number of routes, the formation of the march column, and the rate of travel. The simplification in calculations does not entail serious errors in calculations for the march. But this factor would be essential, despite the complexity of calculations, in determining the direction and velocity of fallout from a nuclear explosion. Thus a norm or factor is not essential or inconsequential in itself, but rather must be judged in connection with the conditions of a particular situation.

When precisely calculated data are desired, it is necessary to work out new procedures and to perfect those already in existence, but, the most important need is to improve the accuracy and reliability of initial data. Not even the most complex procedure can yield accurate results if the initial data are not reasonably accurate.

The commander is expected to consider not only the available calculated data, but also the uncalculated variables of a situation. This can be done only by an officer who fully understands the essence, role, and significance of quantitative methods and the underlying norms, devices, and procedures. Articles appear monthly in journals such as Technology and Armament (*Tekhnika i Vooruzheniye*) raising the computer consciousness level of all servicemen, but particularly the junior officers at whom they are aimed. Until he gains personal knowledge and experience, the military commander has a great store of historical and empirical norms to provide guidance.

NORMS USED IN THE SOVIET ARMY TODAY

In the authoritative journal *Voyennaya Mysl'* (Military Thought), Major General S. Ilyin made the following statement:

> In an army where high discipline and precise action on the part of each soldier and of the entire collective is so necessary, even the slightest amount of loose talk, irresponsibility or disorganization cannot be tolerated. Here everything must be subordinate to a single goal and a single will, and the execution of regulatory norms, orders, and instructions is strict and binding upon all. In the interest of the cause, the commander must make use of his authority and if necessary, employ duress in the execution of the disciplinary requirements and of his own orders.[5]

Since norms are clearly of utmost importance, one would expect them to be published and easily available for our study, but that is not the case. Many norms are unavailable except in such documents as field service regulations which, although available to the Soviet officer corps, normally are not available to the public. Occasionally, they are found in publications generally intended for use by officers only, such as the Military Herald or Military Thought. The norms discussed in this section are the result of painstaking study of Soviet publications, many of which do not state, but merely imply, the norms. Problem statements or reports of maneuvers rarely spell out in detail the norms that apply, but in most cases these norms must be inferred from times or distances given, and carefully integrated into a consistent pattern that is confirmed by Soviet literature. A few important norms for the Soviet Ground Forces are examined in the following pages.

Movement norms are related to frontage and depth norms. These norms are set at all levels from Front down to the individual soldier and derive from firepower considerations. Figure 4.4 shows overall frontages and depths as they apply to an Army in the attack. Figure 4.5 lists the depths of the objectives and adds the factor of time in which a Soviet commander is expected to fulfill his mission, whether for Front, Army, division, regiment, or battalion.

In order to meet these norms, Soviet commanders must perform the various movement activities described in Chapter 3 (Soviet Operational Procedures). We will reexamine some of those activities in terms of the time and distance norms that Soviet commanders are expected to meet.

The first activity is the march to contact. A commander, in making his preparation for the march, selects routes, if they have not already been specified by the senior commander. The next higher commander usually also specifies start lines or start points, and lines of deployment. (See Figure 3.8.) The following norms apply:

(1) A division is assigned either a march sector or march route.
(2) As many as four routes may be designated.
(3) A regiment is assigned one or two routes.
(4) A battalion marches on one route.
(5) Distance between routes should be at least three kilometers to ensure that two units are not destroyed by one enemy nuclear weapon.

The start line designated for the beginning of the march must be far enough from the concentration area to allow columns to form and reach the required speed as they pass the start point.

Prescribed times[6] for units to pass from assembly areas to march column are:

Units	Minutes
Motorized Rifle Company	5
Motorized Rifle Battalion	10-15
Artillery Battalion	15-20
Artillery Regiment	40-50
Motorized Rifle Regiment	25
Motorized Rifle Regiment (Reinforced)	60-120

Control lines are established to ensure timely and orderly movement. The number of lines will depend on the distance to be covered, the terrain, the weather, time of day or night, and road conditions. Usually they are designated for every two to three hours of movement. Elements of the force must cross these lines at the designated time.

Movements are coordinated through march discipline, halts, and rest periods. Short halts are of 20 to 30 minutes duration every two to three hours of movement. The column formation is not disturbed during the halt and unit

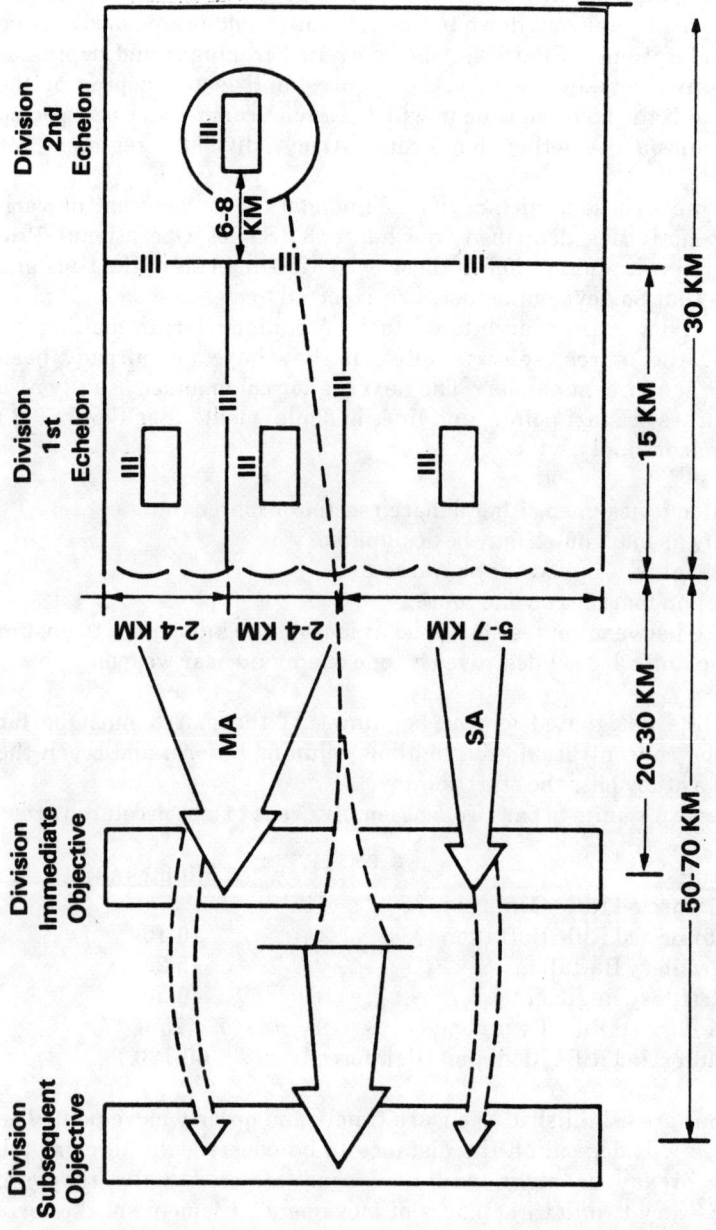

Figure 4.4. Type Army Deployment for Offensive Operation

	BN 1ST ECHELON (1ST ECH COS OF 1ST ECH BNS)	REGIMENTAL 1ST ECHELON (2ND ECH CO'S OF 1ST ECH BNS)	DIV 1ST ECHELON (2ND ECH BNS OF 1ST ECH REGTS)	ARMY 1ST ECHELON (2ND ECH REGTS OF DIVS)	FRONT 1ST ECHELON (2ND ECH DIV OF ARMIES)	FRONT 2ND ECHELON (2ND ECH ARMIES OF FRONT)
OBJECTIVE	BN IMMEDIATE	REGIMENTAL IMMEDIATE (BN SUBSEQUENT)	DIVISION IMMEDIATE (REGIMENTAL SUBSEQUENT)	ARMY IMMEDIATE (DIV SUBSEQUENT)	FRONT IMMEDIATE (ARMY SUBSEQUENT)	FRONT SUBSEQUENT
DEPTH OF OBJECTIVE FROM FEBA (KM)	2-4	8-15	20-30	50-70	150-200	300-350
EXPECTED LOCATION INTO ENEMY DEPTH WHEN COMMITTED (KM)	FEBA	2-4	8-15	20-30	50-70	150-200
EXPECTED TIME OF COMMITMENT	H HOUR	H+4	H+10	H+20	DAY 2-3	DAY 3-4
EXPECTED TIME OF ATTAINMENT OF OBJECTIVE	H+2	H+7	H+15	DAY 2-3	DAY 3-4	DAY 7+

ALL SITUATION DEPENDENT

Figure 4.5. Echelons and Objectives: Times of Commitment and Attainment

intervals are maintained. Within units, vehicles pull over to the right side of the road with spacing of not less than 10 meters between them. Refueling, minor maintenance, and, if necessary, partial decontamination are accomplished. Long halts (two to eight hours) used on marches over 24 hours' duration usually are scheduled only for daylight hours to enable maximum nighttime movement. Units are dispersed off road and camouflaged. Under nuclear conditions, the march formation must be dispersed laterally and in depth. Lateral dispersion of a division is obtained by marching in a zone some 15 to 25 kilometers wide on as many as four routes, and routes are separated by three to four kilometers. Normal intervals and some variants are shown in Figure 4.6.

In preparing for an attack from the march, or for the movements of troops from assembly areas to the line of departure, timing is critical. Usually, the next higher commander specifies the routes, start line or points, lines of deployment, and the line and time of attack. The length of the routes and distances from the initial line to each of the other lines is measured and separated into five-kilometer segments. Permissible speeds are determined for different sectors, based on the condition of the routes, the time of year and day, weather, composition of the column, and possible enemy action during movement. Based on permissible speeds, average speeds are calculated by using nomograms or charts, dividing the length of the route by the total time of the movement for all sectors of the route. From this information, schedules for troop movements are developed. Time permitting, critical path calculations will be made.

UNIT	NORMAL INTERVAL	VARIANTS
BETWEEN VEHICLES IN A COMPANY	25-50 M	INCREASED AT HIGH SPEEDS AND WHEN TRAVERSING CONTAMINATED OR RUGGED TERRAIN, OR ON ICY ROADS. CAN BE DECREASED AT NIGHT.
BETWEEN COMPANIES IN A BATTALION	25-50 M	MAY BE UP TO 300 METERS OR EVEN MORE UNDER NUCLEAR CONDITIONS
BETWEEN BATTALIONS ON THE SAME ROUTE	3-5 KM	
BETWEEN REGIMENTS ON THE SAME ROUTE	5-10 KM	CAN VARY FOR SECOND ECHELON REGIMENTS AS CONTACT BECOMES IMMINENT
BETWEEN REGIMENTAL REAR SERVICES AND MAIN FORCE	3-5 KM	
BETWEEN DIVISION REAR SERVICES AND MAIN FORCE	15-20 KM	

Figure 4.6. Normal Intervals and Variants

As a result of increased urbanization, the number of high-speed routes in most areas of Central Europe that meet Soviet norms is limited. However, Soviet doctrine calls for using secondary roads and trails if necessary, in order to provide the required lateral dispersion. Routes from assembly areas to planned deployment lines are studied. If possible, both engineer and aerial reconnaissance are used to refine results. Then the average rate of march is calculated by dividing the total distance by the time allowed for the march. Typical average march rates for mixed columns are: on roads 20 to 30 kilometers per hour by day or 15 to 20 kilometers per hour at night; crosscountry, 5 to 15 kilometers per hour. These average rates apply to tactical marches of some duration. Once contact is made, units may move at maximum permissible speeds as required. To demonstrate the effect of the intervals shown in Figure 4.6 on the depth of units in a march formation, consider a regiment marching as part of the division main force (Figure 4.7). Note that the regiment (reinforced) occupies 28 to 50 kilometers of road space. In this formation, the third motorized rifle battalion is 18 to 25 kilometers behind the head of the column. At 15 kilometers an hour, it would take more than an hour to bring it on line.

Figure 4.8 shows the normal spacing on average terrain for a lead regiment moving to probable contact with the enemy. Also shown are the expected times of employment and the frontages to be covered by each of the units. When a unit prepares to deploy for combat, as was described in Chapter 3 (Soviet Operational Procedures), it will move from regimental columns to battalion columns approximately 8 to 12 kilometers from the enemy lines; from battalion to company columns at four to six kilometers; from company to platoon columns at 1.5 to four kilometers. The infantry dismounts up to 1,000 meters from the enemy lines if it does not intend to attack mounted. Company attack formations and the distances involved are shown in Figure 4.9. Dismounted infantry will normally move as short a distance as possible behind the tank units but certainly no more than 200 meters. The BMP personnel carriers (*Bronyirovannaya Mashina Pekhoty* - Armored Car Infantry) from which they have dismounted normally will be approximately 400 meters behind them, providing cover by firing on enemy positions between the advancing units.

Reconnaissance units will be as much as 50 kilometers in front of the advancing unit. The combat organization of the advance guard, while flexible, is designed to meet the norms of staying power. The advance party of approximately a company is required to maintain its position for approximately an hour. The advance guard main force, which will normally be a battalion, is expected to delay an advancing enemy in position from two to three hours. These norms derive, in part, from ammunition expenditure rates that will be discussed later.

Whether an attack will be frontal, an envelopment, or at the flank, may be determined by the norms for maneuver space. The time available to execute a maneuver may be a major factor, but in the case of envelopment, the availability of space probably will be the controlling factor. This would be the case also in areas of small towns or where terrain barriers dominate.

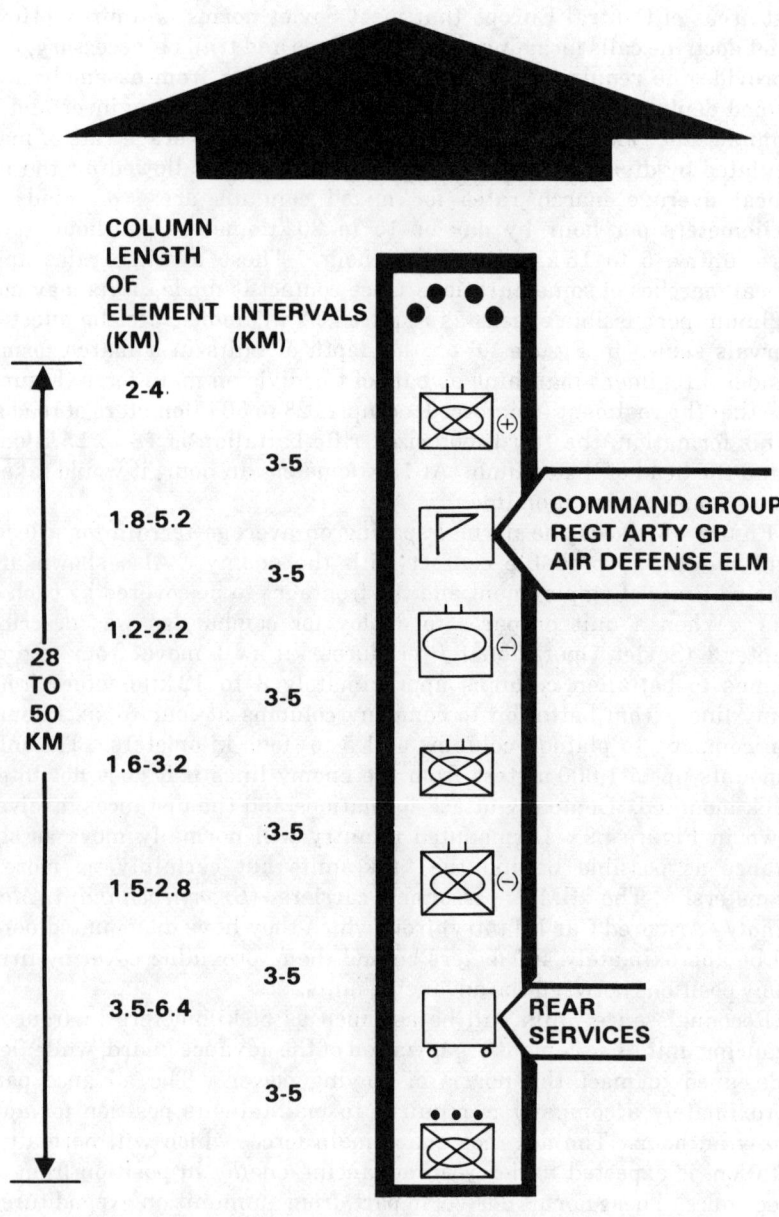

Figure 4.7. Motorized Rifle Regiment Marching as Part of a Division Main Force (A Variant)

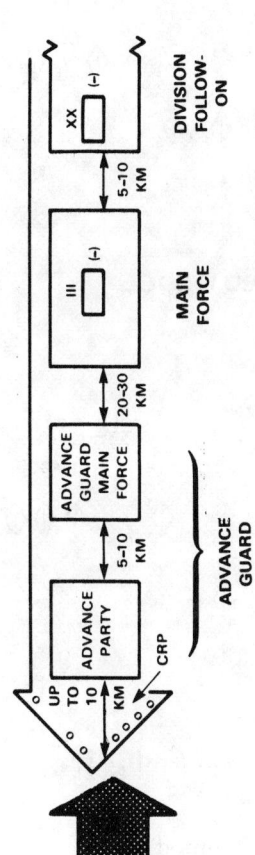

	DIVISION RECON	REGT'L RECON	COMBAT RECON PATROL (CRP)	ADVANCE PARTY	ADVANCE GUARD MAIN FORCE	DIVISION REGIMENT MAIN FORCE	FOLLOW-ON
DISTANCE FROM CONTACT	50-100 KM FORWARD	20-50 KM FORWARD	0	UP TO 10 KM	10-15 KM	35-50 KM	50-60 KM
TIME OF EMPLOYMENT	—	—	H HR	H+20-30 MIN	H+1	H+2-3	H+5-6
FORCE SIZE	DIV RECON BN. (-)	REGT RECON CO. (-)	REINF. PLAT.	REINF. CO	REINF. BN.	REINF. REGT. (-)	2-3 REGTS.
ATTACK FRONTAGES	—	—	150-200 M	500-800 M	1-2 KM	2-7 KM	4-16 KM

Figure 4.8. Meeting Engagement Lead Regiment with Division Follow-On

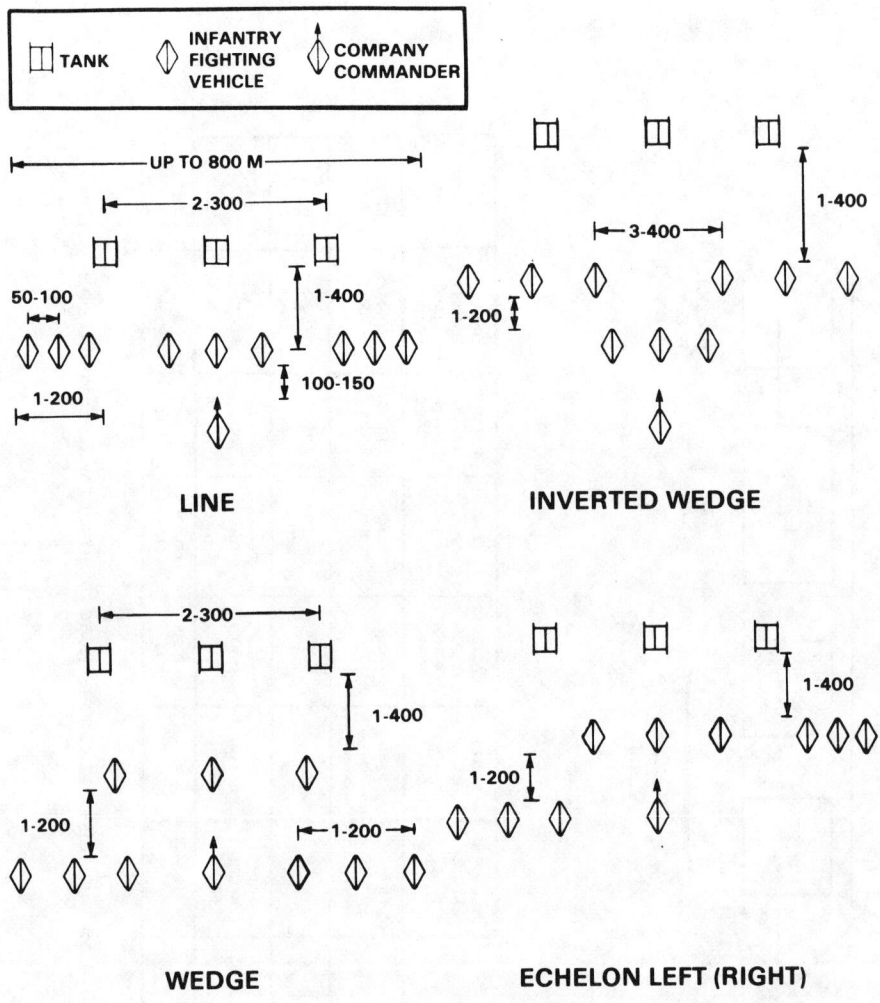

Figure 4.9. Company Attack Formations (Mounted)

Trafficable terrain must be available and must provide covered or concealed routes for the enveloping force, open ground for deployment, and good fields of fire. The area adjacent to the original route of advance must be three to five kilometers wide for the single or battalion axis. When a regiment is involved, the blocking force will be the advance guard battalion and the enveloping force will include at least one other battalion. Hence, two battalion axes with some space between them are usually needed. The same two axes might be needed where two regiments engage in mutual support operations. The width of this area is 10 to 15 kilometers, as shown in Figure 4.10. Room must be provided for the concealed movement of the enveloping force to a point about halfway along the flank of the enemy force. This is thought to be about five kilometers for a battalion and at least 10 kilometers for a regiment. In a division attack, selection of one main and one secondary axis normally is required. The entire division may be concentrated along the one main axis if that is necessary to achieve force superiority. Regiments and battalions usually attack on a single axis.

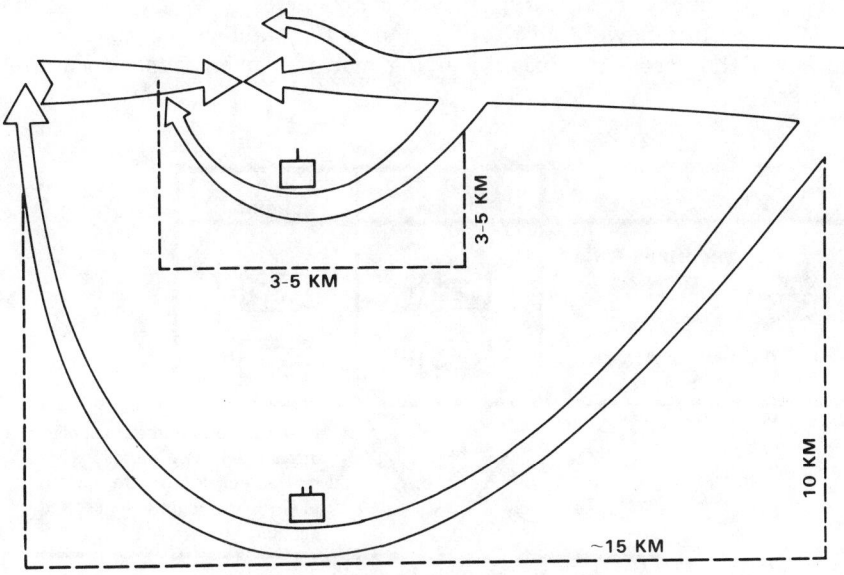

Figure 4.10. Space Norms for a Regiment Engaging the Enemy in "Average Terrain"

ECHELONMENT NORMS

As indicated in Figures 4.4 and 4.5, there also are norms for the frontages of first and second echelon units. These norms appear in detail in Figure 4.11, which shows possible variations in the echelonment and the general norms, not only for the size of echelons at the various levels, but also for the frontages they can expect to be assigned. The distances between first and second echelons in the attack, measured tail to head, will be approximately:

(1) 15 to 30 kilometers between echelons within a division;
(2) 5 to 15 kilometers between echelons within a regiment; and
(3) 1 to 3 kilometers between echelons (if any), within a battalion.

The ratio (correlation) of forces directly influences the alignment of Soviet troops for the attack. Calculation of the relative ratios of forces will be made across the entire zone of the planned action and to the full depth of the assigned mission (Figure 4.12). If nuclear weapons are employed, the commander will assess the balance of forces after expected nuclear strikes on both sides. The estimate of the size of enemy battalions and companies; the number of his tanks, artillery, mortars, and antitank weapons; and the terrain he holds, is probably the most difficult part of the decision process. The Soviets also see problems in obtaining reliable information, since what is available may be fragmentary, transitory, or even contradictory. In estimating the ratio of forces, the Soviets also must attempt to establish the quality and condition of the opposing forces, including morale, combat experience, and readiness.

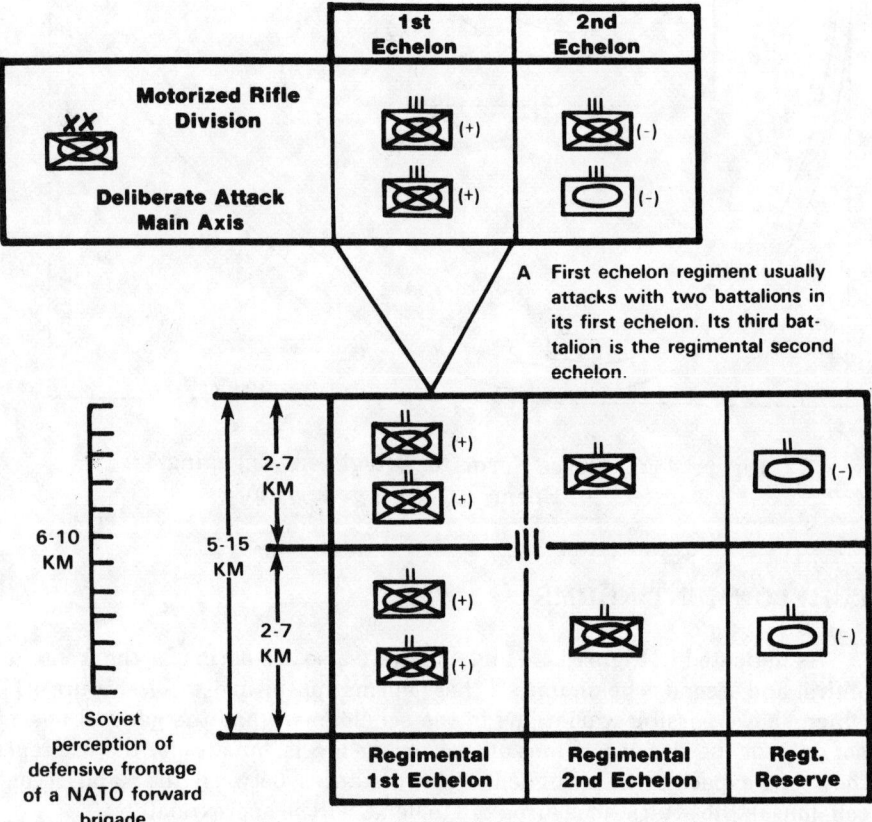

Figure 4.11. Echelonment within First Echelon Regiments

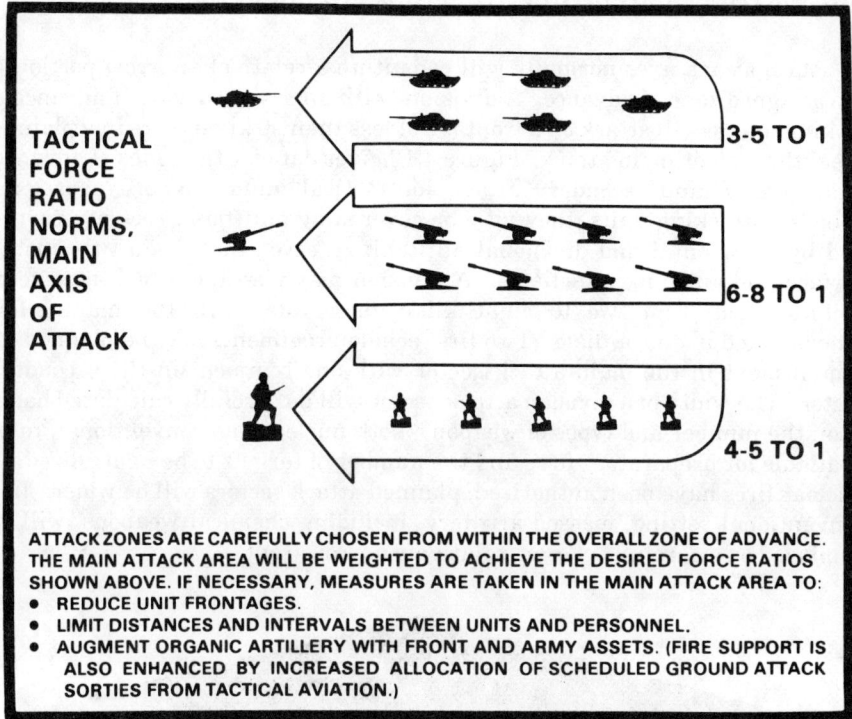

Figure 4.12. Tactical Force Ratio Norms, Main Axis of Attack

The assessment of the ratio of forces derives from intelligence estimates which give particular attention to:

(1) Grouping of forces and the structure of enemy defenses in the assigned zone of action to the depth of the attack mission;
(2) Presence and location of enemy weapons of mass destruction and their possible employment;
(3) Distribution of strong points in the defense and location of antitank weapons;
(4) Existence of gaps, breaks, and boundaries in the defense;
(5) Location of reserves, especially armor, and the possible nature of their commitment;
(6) Location and organization of enemy artillery and mortars;
(7) Positions critical to the stability of the defense;
(8) Perimeters of strong points and defensive areas in the forward area and in the depth of the defense;
(9) Defensive fire plan and plan of engineer obstacles; and
(10) Areas on the line of march where nuclear/chemical strikes are most probable.

FRONTAGES AND ZONES OF ADVANCE-ATTACK

Main attack axes normally will constitute a relatively narrow portion of the assigned zone of advance. A division, with an assigned zone of advance of 20 kilometers, will attack on a frontage of less than 10 kilometers in a planned breakthrough or main attack. Figure 4.13 gives data for the zones of advance, main attack, and secondary attack for tactical units. Where gaps exist between attacking units, they may be covered by unit flank security parties and by regimental and divisional antitank reserves that frequently install surface-laid antitank minefields. A division may plan the attack in several sectors, each from two to eight kilometers wide, with the main effort concentrated in one of them. Two first echelon regiments may be planned for commitment in the main attack sector with one regiment in the secondary sector. The width of a division attack sector will be carefully calculated based upon the number and types of weapons, both nuclear and conventional, to be available for preparatory fires and the number of targets to be neutralized. If nuclear fires have been authorized, planned attack sectors will be wider. In a conventional setting, massed artillery, including chemical weapons, will be employed on a carefully chosen, relatively narrow front.

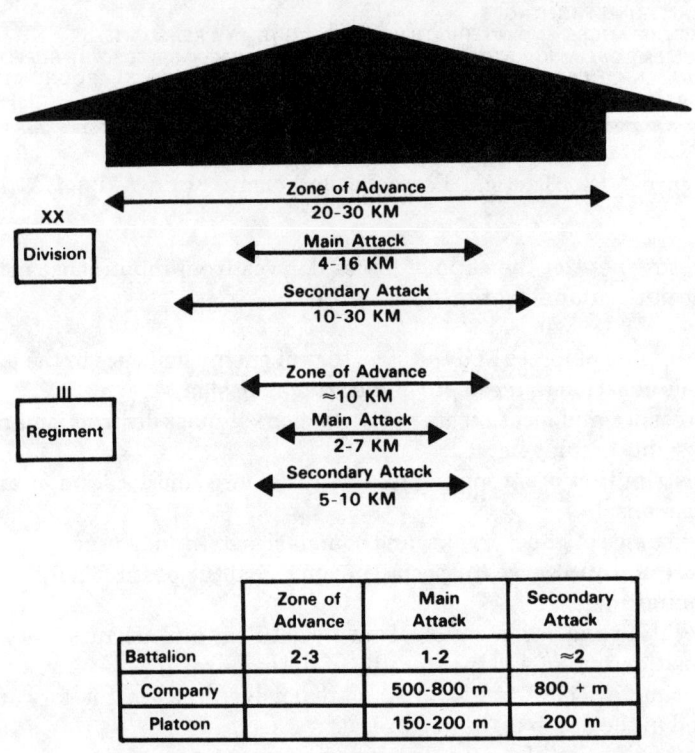

Figure 4.13. Zones of Advance and Attack Frontages

The depth of the attack objectives is determined by the depth of the defense positions, location of enemy forces, and higher headquarters objectives. Divisions and regiments are assigned an immediate and a subsequent mission or objective. First echelon battalions are assigned an immediate mission and a direction of further advance. The immediate mission of a battalion in the attack usually calls for destroying personnel and weapons in the strong points of the enemy's first echelon battalions. Subsequent objectives will then be assigned. The norms for depths of objectives are:

Depth of Objectives (Km)

Unit	Immediate	Subsequent
Division	20-30	50-70
Regiment	8-15	20-30
Battalion	2-4	8-15

The rate of advance in the initial assault will be controlled to ensure rapid attack in order to exploit preparatory suppressive fires and maintain a continuous, coordinated assault close behind supporting fires. A controlled rate of about 12 kilometers per hour (200 meters per minute) might be expected in the assault. This rate of advance permits tanks to fire "from the brief halt", 15 kilometers per hour is possible where tanks fire "from the move"; 9 to 10 kilometers per hour when tanks fire "from the halt". Attacking tanks will attempt to destroy tanks and antitank weapons in the shortest possible time and with minimum expenditure of ammunition.

Rates of advance in an attack are not governed by norms. In a fluid battle, high rates of advance can be expected. With a stable line of contact and strong defensive forces, a slower rate of advance is likely, especially from positions in contact. An attack through a covering force could approximate five to six kilometers per hour (80 to 100 meters per minute). Fighting through defensive positions may be slower, probably about two kilometers per hour (25 meters per minute).

The exploitation phases of an attack, with troops advancing in APCs and approach march formations between combat actions, may permit a rate of 5 to 10 kilometers per hour (80 to 160 meters per minute). Progress of an attack through the enemy defensive position will range from the relatively slow pace of separate attacks to a more rapid pace after defensive strong points are overrun.

Figure 4.14 depicts a division deployed for the attack. The first echelon of the division consists of three reinforced motorized rifle regiments. The second echelon, in this case a tank regiment, is located so that it can be deployed quickly in the region of the main attack. A combined arms reserve also is shown. It is an independent tank battalion with a company of motorized rifle troops from the regiment making the secondary attack. This is only one type of deployment. The division commander normally will be located at the division forward CP in close touch with the Chief of Rocket and Artillery Troops. In this case it is located near the CP of the division artillery group.

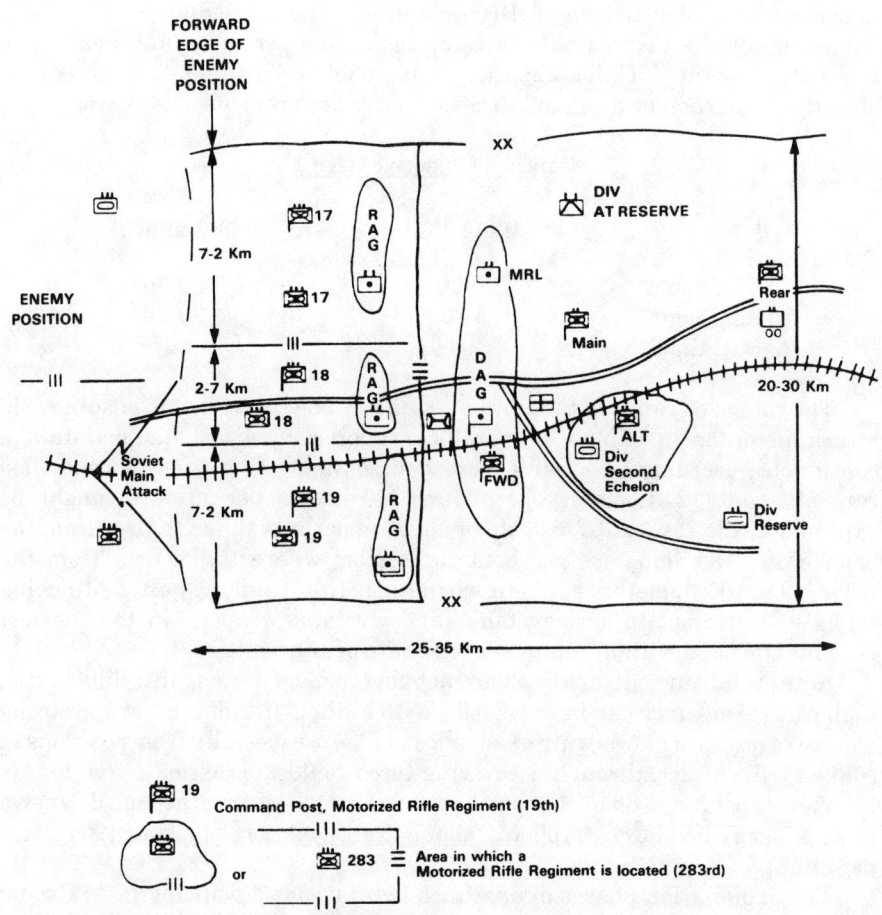

Figure 4.14. Normal Deployment of Division Elements for an Attack

AIR DEFENSE NORMS

From its World War II experience, the Soviet Ground Forces are well aware of the perils of inadequate air cover. As a result, air defense coverage provided today "by the Soviet Communist Party for the defense forces of the Soviet Union" is lavish. It is governed less by norms than by weapons capabilities and even though the two are tied together in the research and development process, the physical capabilities were designed into the system in response to initial norms. Figure 4.15 shows the coverage of selected surface-to-air missile systems. The systems usually provided at Front and Army level are SA-4 surface-to-air missile (NATO code name GANEF: the follow-on system under development is designated by NATO the SA-12), and SA-2 or 3 GUIDELINE. They normally are organized in regiments or brigades and deployed in batteries of six missiles/launchers.

Systems organic to divisions and regiments are:

(1) The SA-6 GAINFUL, five batteries of four launchers for each division;
(2) The SA-8 GECKO, five batteries of four to each division;
(3) The SA-9 GASKIN, four to each regiment, or a total of sixteen for the division;
(4) The SA-7 on an individual basis with semi-expendable launcher-missile, up to six per air defense battery and thirty-six per airborne division; (follow-on system is the SA-13)
(5) The S-60 57mm gun is available in either a single-barrel towed version or a twin-barrel self-propelled version. If neither SA-6 nor SA-8 is available, they are assigned twenty-four per division (four batteries of six) with the self-propelled gun normally provided to the tank division;
(6) The ZSU 23-4, a 23mm four-barreled, self-propelled antiaircraft gun, four to a regiment, or sixteen to a division; and,
(7) SA-11, a follow-on development for SA-6 and SA-8.

NORMS FOR THE DEFENSE

In a defensive position, a division will occupy an area approximately 15 to 20 kilometers wide and 20 to 30 kilometers deep. The echelons will be approximately five kilometers apart. A regiment will occupy a sector from 7 to 10 kilometers wide and 10 to 15 kilometers deep. Within the regiment, the echelons will be one to two kilometers apart. A battalion will occupy an area three to five kilometers deep and two to three kilometers wide. A company, the basic element, will have a frontage of approximately 1,000 to 1,500 meters and a depth of approximately 500 meters. Within the company position, tanks will be deployed 200 to 300 meters apart with APCs up to 200 meters apart. Forward of the defensive position, the security force's size and composition will vary, but the zone may extend to a depth of 30 kilometers at Front level and 16 kilometers at division level. It will be at least far enough forward to prevent aimed direct fire from reaching the main defensive area. Modern defensive doctrine at Front and Army levels continues to stress defense in depth, but rather than multiple continuous belts, the defensive area consists of clusters of strong points.

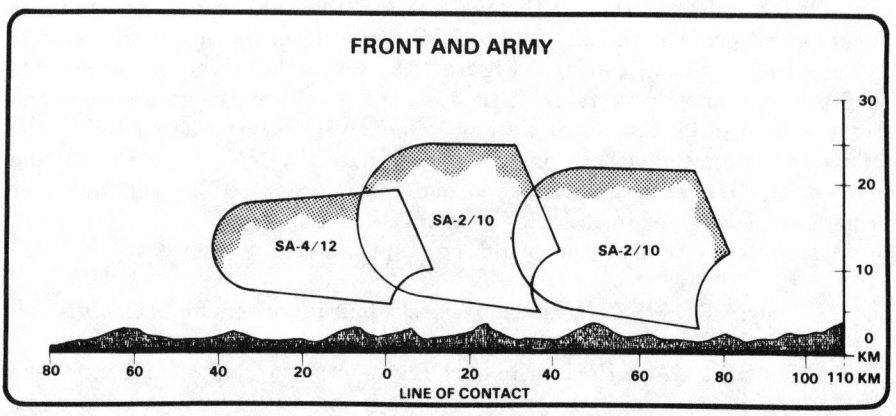

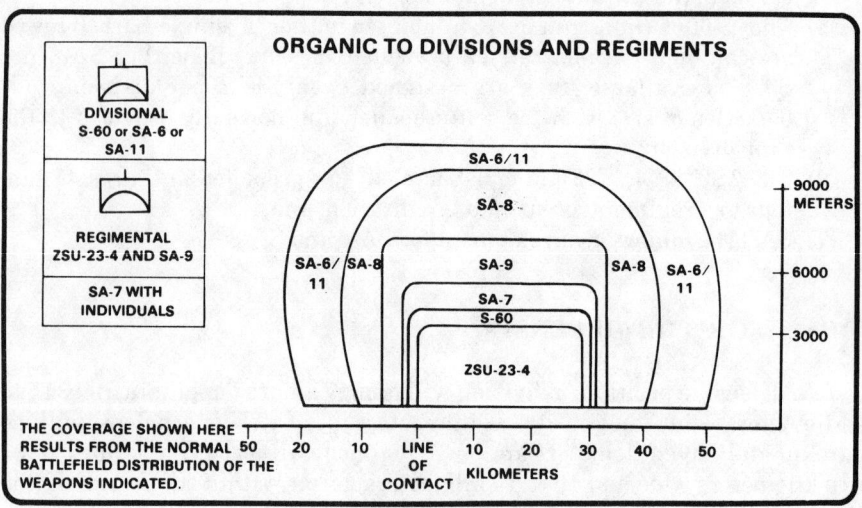

Figure 4.15. Air Defense Coverage

FIRING NORMS FOR ARTILLERY

One of the major accomplishments of the Soviet Army is the development of an array of superior artillery pieces. The 122mm howitzer, Model D-30, is considered the finest towed artillery piece in the world. The towed 130mm gun, M-46, with a range in excess of 27 kilometers, drove the United States-armed South Vietnamese out of their positions north of Hue in South Vietnam with its accuracy and range. (The United States would not field a weapon so hazardous to the hearing of its crew). The Russians believe in the use of masses of artillery in terms of both rounds and tubes. During World War II, a reporter for *Time* magazine reported that near the end of the battle for Stalingrad, one German unit came forward under a flag of surrender after a particularly heavy barrage. The German commander was quoted as saying, "Die Kanonen, die Kanonen, wir koennen nicht mehr" ("The cannons, the cannons, we can stand it no longer"). Modern Soviet practice is to establish norms for the destruction of various types of targets, norms for areas and expenditure rates, and norms for weapons and accuracy requirements. Fire coverage is calculated normally in hectares (10,000 square meters, the equivalent of 2.47 acres).

Requirements to neutralize an area, given in hectares, depend on the time allotted and the type of target. Representative coverage for a 120mm mortar battery and 122mm howitzer battalion are shown in Figure 4.16.

Neutralization is defined by the Soviets as destruction of 25 to 30 percent of the elements of the target. To achieve annihilation, 50 to 60 percent destruction of the target elements is required. For nuclear artillery targets, the criterion is annihilation rather than neutralization. When the objective is to neutralize of the target, the expenditure of rounds per hectare per minute is prescribed. Figure 4.17 gives the ammunition expenditure rate and the coverage in hectares for various weapons. Figure 4.18 expresses similar information as rounds per target for various targets.

ARTILLERY FIRE PLANNING

Artillery fire planning is determined almost entirely by norms.[7] Fragmentary orders will provide specifics concerning the missions of designated artillery units and identify the location of observation posts and unit areas for firing positions. Deadlines for units to be ready to fire will be announced. Based upon the actual requirements contained in the artillery fire plan, designated artillery will move forward in a manner and at a rate that will permit those units to occupy the new position area about an hour-and-a-half before the maneuver forces have deployed for the attack. Figure 4.19 gives the expected time for artillery units to clear one fire position, move to, and occupy a new position. Artillery units expect to draw counter-battery fire in no more than 12 to 15 minutes and therefore must plan to move quickly. Deployment-to-fire times are maintained with a land

	TANKS & APC	EXPOSED PERSONNEL & WEAPONS	PERSONNEL AND WEAPONS UNDER COVER			
	10 MIN	3-4 MIN	5 MIN	10 MIN	15 MIN	20 MIN
120MM MORTAR BATTERY	1-2	15	1	1-2	2	2-3
122MM HOWITZER BATTALION	5-6	18	3-4	5-6	7-8	9

Figure 4.16. Coverage in Hectares, Based on Type of Target and Length of Assault

	GUNS & HOWITZERS				MORTARS	
	100MM	122MM	130MM	152MM	120MM	160MM
ROUNDS/HECTARE/MIN	3	3	3	2	3	2
HECTARES/BATTERY	3	4	3	3-6	2	2-3

*POSLEDOVATEL'NOYE SOSREDOTOCHENIYE OGNYA

Figure 4.17. Ammunition Expenditure Rates, Rounds Per Hectare Per Minute, and Coverage in Hectares for *PSO* (Successive Fire Concentrations

	TARGET	MISSION	RIFLED WEAPONS CALIBER mm							MORTARS CALIBER mm				ROCKET ARTY		
			76	85	100	122	130	152	203	82	120	160	240	MEDIUM CALIBER	MEDIUM CALIBER EXTENDED RANGE	LARGE CALIBER
1	LAUNCHER	ANNIHILATION	800	720	540	300	280	200	70	--	--	140	60	510	360	200
2	BATTERY (PLATOON) SP ARMORED WPNS (MORTARS)	SUPPRESSION	1000	900	720	450	360	270	120	--	450	220	120	560	400	240
3	BATTERY SP (NOT ARMORED) ARTY OR TOWED ARTY, COVERED (MORTARS)	SUPPRESSION	540	480	360	240	220	180	100	400	240	160	100	400	320	180
4	TOWED ARTY IN OPEN (MORTARS)	SUPPRESSION	250	220	450	90	80	60	30	180	90	40	20	150	120	60
5	AD BTRY	SUPPRESSION	250	240	200	150	150	100	60	--	--	--	--	--	200	100
6	RADIO ELECTRONIC VANS IN THE OPEN	--	420	360	280	180	180	120	60	350	180	80	40	300	240	120
7	COVERED PERSONNEL AND FIRE UNITS IN A STRONG POINT WARNED	SUPPRESSION (1 Ha Tgt Area)	480	450	320	200	200	150	60	--	200	100	50	320	240	100

Figure 4.18. Norms for Expenditure of Artillery and Mortar Rounds for Destruction of Fixed, Unobserved Targets

navigation system that requires very little additional survey time prior to opening fire.

The time for any particular firing, the number of rounds, and the number of tubes are all determined using norms. A possible fire plan outlining the timing for an artillery fire preparation is shown below:

H-25 Heavy surprise concentration of nuclear strikes and conventional artillery, gas, and air (including napalm) strikes on the entire depth of the defense.

H-20 Destruction fire against strong points, command posts, observation posts, headquarters, and artillery sites. Priority fires against enemy's first echelon.

H-15 Conventional suppressive fire against enemy first echelon positions.

H-5 Heavy, surprise concentrations against enemy strong points.

H-Hour Artillery fires in support of the attack begin.

WEAPONS*	UNIT	TIME IN MINUTES REQUIRED FOR					
		EVACUATION OF FIRE POSITIONS OR ASSEMBLY AREAS		MOVEMENT (PER km)		OCCUPATION OF FIRE POSITIONS	
		BY DAY	BY NIGHT	BY DAY	BY NIGHT	BY DAY	BY NIGHT
122mm HOW, D-30	BTRY	5 - 7	9	3 (20kph)	3.5	10 - 12	18
	BN	11	14	3	3.5	23	32
152mm HOW, D-1	BTRY	5 - 7	9	3	3.5	10 - 15	15 - 20
	BN	11	14	3	3.5	23	32
152mm G/H, D20	BTRY	10	13	3	3.5	12	18
	BN	11	14	3	3.5	23	32
130mm GUN/M46	BTRY	10	13	3	3.5	12	18
	BN	11	14	3	3.5	23	32
122mm MRL, BM-21	BTRY	3 - 5	6.5	3	3.5	10 - 12	18
	BN	7	9	3	3.5	23	32
120mm MORTAR	BTRY	5.5	8	2.5	3	12	18

* Data for 122mm 1974 and 152mm 1973 SP systems are not available. Self propelled weapons provide increased mobility as well as excellent off-road and good cross-country capabilities. They can be emplaced faster than towed artillery.

Figure 4.19. Average Times for Changing Artillery Positions

The width and depth of the area for which preparatory fires will be planned depend on the strength, specific deployments, and layout of the enemy defense. When time permits, fire planning will be based on thorough, detailed reconnaissance and careful study of the attack plan. In any attack, a systematic targeting effort is basic to the fire plan at all levels.

Doctrine stresses the importance of concentrating artillery weapons and attacks. Planners will attempt to achieve certain densities of weapons for artillery in support of an attack. Relatively high numbers of artillery weapons per kilometer of attack frontage are desired. The general norms prescribed are:

(1) Breakthrough of prepared defense (main attack)--minimum 100 tubes per kilometer of front;
(2) Attack of a hasty defense (main attack)--80 tubes per Km; and,
(3) Attack on a minor axis--40 tubes per Km.

Chemical strikes probably will be used to complement the fire plan and specifically to deny enemy freedom of movement and observation. A smaller number of tubes per kilometer of front is acceptable if chemical strikes are used. If nuclear or chemical strikes are to be made, they will be planned against enemy forces on the axis of the main attack and will come at the beginning of the preparatory fires in order to achieve surprise, generally 30 minutes before H-Hour.

The duration of preparatory fires will be the time needed for maneuver battalions to deploy into combat formations. Mixed columns, deploying about 8 to 12 kilometers from the line of contact will take about 30 minutes to assume these formations, so an additional period may be needed to prepare for the assault. Preparatory fires may be, therefore, planned to last about 40 minutes. In order for the artillery to deploy and occupy firing positions in advance of the time schedule for the beginning of the preparation, it may be necessary for the artillery to deploy several hours earlier, particularly if the movement is at night.

Planning ammunition consumption for every type of operation is based on the unit of fire (*boyekomplekt*). The unit of fire is a fixed number of rounds per weapon or weapon system used for planning and accounting purposes and for distribution and stockage. It is not an authorized allowance or daily expenditure rate as prescribed in some Western armies. For example, the unit of fire for the 122mm howitzer is 80 rounds, though an attack on a prepared enemy defense might easily require an artillery battalion to expend 1.9 units of fire. Thus, the total expenditure of rounds for a battalion would be 18 guns times 1.9 units of fire times 80 rounds per unit of fire, or 2,736 rounds.

Rocket launchers, which are used only against the most important targets, fire single salvos. Multiple rocket launchers with ranges from 7 to 30 kilometers usually fire in a single ripple salvo. Single rockets, FROGs and SCUDs (NATO code names), have ranges of from 20 to 500 kilometers and normally fire individually.

TYPE WEAPON	METERS PER WEAPON	METERS PER BATTERY	METERS PER BATTALION
100 & 130MM GUNS	20-25	150	450
HOWITZER & GUN/HOWITZER	35	200	600-650

Figure 4.20. Assigned Lengths of Sectors

DISTANCES	MORTARS	GUNS & HOWITZERS	MULTIPLE ROCKET LAUNCHERS
BETWEEN WEAPONS	15-60M	20-40M	15-50M
BETWEEN BATTERIES	—	200-2000M (Normally up to 100M)	1000-2000M
FROM THE FEBA	500-1500M	3-6KM (DAG) 1-4KM (RAG)	3-6KM

Figure 4.21. Tactical Deployment Norms

Offensive rolling barrages may be fired to a depth of about four to five kilometers. Fires are delivered on main and intermediate lines in succession, using a combination of successive concentrations and barrage fires. For main lines, the fires are maintained for a minimum of five minutes, and for intermediate lines from one to two minutes. The assigned line sectors for offensive fires are as shown in Figure 4.20.

Harassment or interdiction is usually achieved by firing for short periods on preplanned lines. Coverage is assumed to be 50 meters per weapon, or 900 meters per battalion. Multiple rocket launcher fire is superimposed on other fires at important points.

Based on the fire support plan, supporting artillery for the division is deployed into positions to provide preparatory fires and the initial fire support of the attack. Figure 4.21 shows tactical deployment norms for a Soviet division's artillery.

SUPPLY NORMS

As indicated above, the Soviet Army has a unique approach to ammunition expenditure. It also uses a distinctive supply-account measuring system for quantifying requirements:

Requirement	Quantification
Ammunition	"Unit of Fire" (*BOYEKOMPLEKT*): A unit of fire is the number of rounds or metric tons of ammunition assigned to each type weapon, based on current allowance norms.
Motor Vehicle and Rocket Fuel	"Refills" (*ZAPRAVKA*): The internal and auxiliary fuel tank capacity of a tracked vehicle. For wheeled vehicles, a refill is determined using average consumption rates and established cruising range norms. Both are measured in liters.
Food	"Daily Ration" (*SUTODACHA*): The amount of food, by weight, entitled to daily mess-norms. For military units the total amount is determined by multiplying the number on the roster by the norm. In staffs and dependent family situations remote garrisons, etc., a more complex calculation is required.

Spare Parts, Accessories, and Miscellaneous	"Set" (*KOMPLEKT*): A group of specific items needed to meet a functional requirement
Special Substances	"Charge" (*ZARYADKA*): The quantity of gases fluids, and/or granular materials loaded atone time into a specialized apparatus or container, such as flame thrower or fire extinguisher.

The minimum total amount of each type of supplies to be held is specified in regulations for materiel allowance norms. For individuals and units, these norms (which will differ according to basic mission, offensive or defensive) establish consumption and reserve levels. The established norm quantities are ordered by subordinate commanders through existing supply channels.

A commander at any level may justify ordering ammunition, fuel, and rations in excess of the stated norms.

THE KEY – THE SECOND ECHELON

The norms that have been discussed generally are associated with the operations of first echelons. A critical feature of Soviet operations is the contingency commitment of the second echelon, laid out in Figure 4.22.

The Soviets will have a specific plan for the commitment of the second echelon (the follow-on force, third echelon, operational maneuver group, etc.) to seize a unit's subsequent objectives, but in the utopian case, the second echelon will not have to be used. The first echelon not only will seize the unit's immediate objectives, but also its subsequent objectives and continue moving without severe casualties. The enemy, however, will do his best to require the Soviets to commit the second echelon as early as possible, by halting or destroying the first echelon. The actual time of commitment of a second echelon will vary from the planned time to the earliest commitment time. Figure 4.22 shows the span or "window" in terms of time and distance in which the Soviet commander can commit his second echelon at each level. The earliest commitment time is, in general, based upon the distance between the line of contact and the assembly area of the particular second echelon unit when the attack commences. It is determined by the time required to exit the assembly area, road march the required distance, and deploy for combat.

For example, according to plan, the second echelon battalions of a first echelon regiment would be committed about 8 to 10 hours after the operation began, when first echelon units had reached a depth of 8 to 15 kilometers inside the enemy's position. If however, the first echelon battalions are not successful, it may be necessary to commit the second echelon battalion earlier, but it cannot be expected to reach the assault line for approximately two hours, in this situation, after the start of the attack. Figure 4.23 shows the

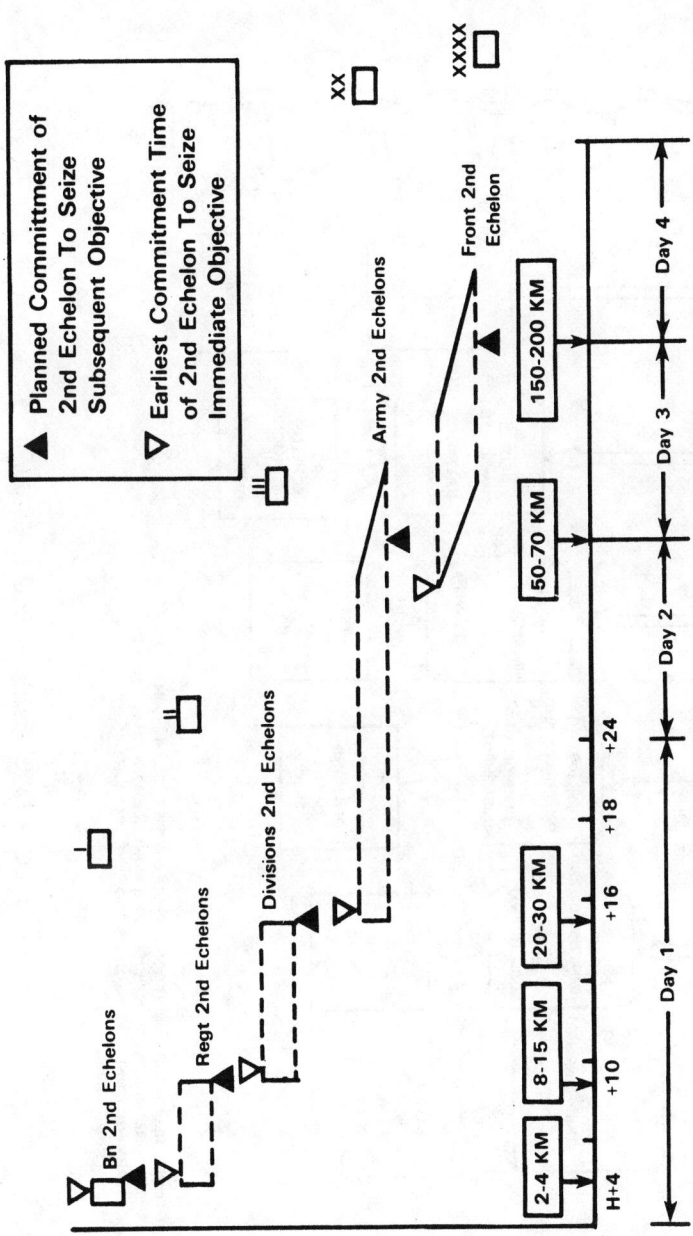

Figure 4.22. Contingency Commitment: 2nd Echelon Forces May Be Committed Earlier than Planned if Necessary to Assist in Attaining the Element's Immediate Objective

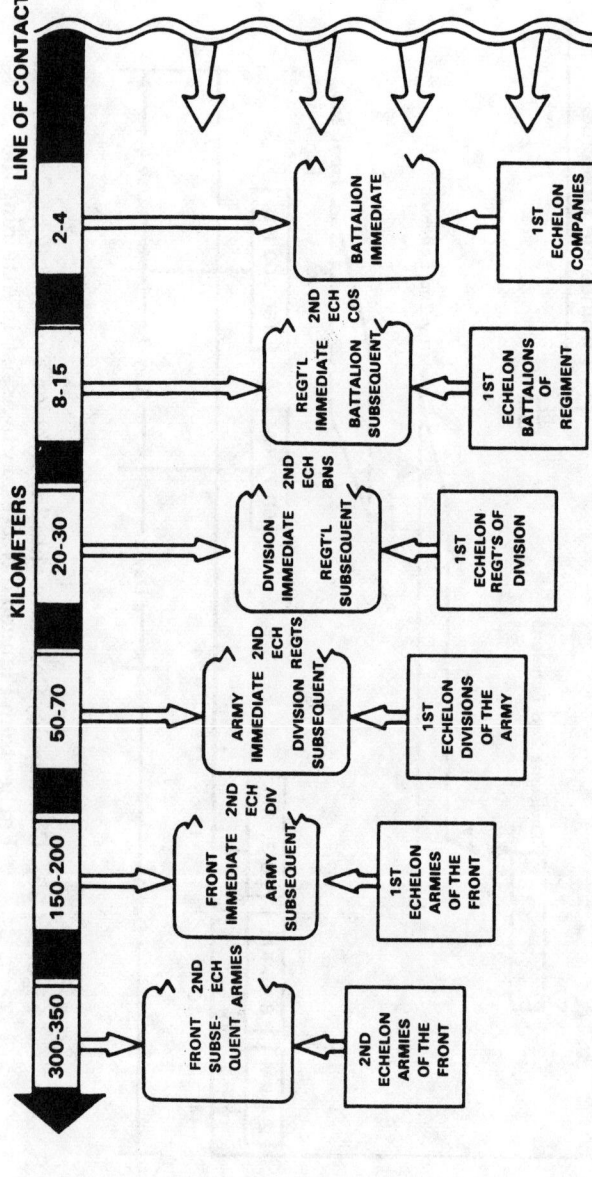

Figure 4.23. Assignment of Objectives

interrelationship of objectives and the depths of the objectives assigned at the various echelon levels.

In the event that the attack is overwhelmingly successful, forces in contact will be committed to pursuit immediately upon detection of the enemy's withdrawal. Control will be exercised by phase lines to be reached at specified times. Forward detachments of up to regimental size may seize critical objectives as much as 50 kilometers deep. Helicopter assault may be used in coordination with forward detachments. Figure 4.24 shows the formation and norms associated with the pursuit.

In an advance against an opponent in Northern Europe, the Soviets expect to make many river crossings. Their intent is to cross these rivers if possible with a hasty rather than a deliberate assault crossing. Figure 4.25 shows the norms associated with a typical hasty river crossing and some tactical variants. For example, a unit acting as the advance guard of a regiment could conduct its assault crossing alone, or a motorized rifle battalion acting as a division's forward detachment could secure undefended crossing sites, avoiding contact with defenders on the far bank. In such a case, the forward detachment might be anywhere from 20 to 70 kilometers and two to three hours ahead of the division's main body. Yet another possibility would be a battalion-size helicopter assault force employed 20 to 30 kilometers ahead of the main force to seize the far bank and establish blocking positions. It would be expected to defend from four to six hours before a linkup.

The norms, as discussed in Chapter 4, have been developed from many sources. They are not obtained directly from Soviet regulations, and could err in minor detail, but they are accurate enough to allow for a rational assessment. It must be remembered that the Soviets promulgate norms as guides, but frequently they constitute minimums that must be achieved by a commander.

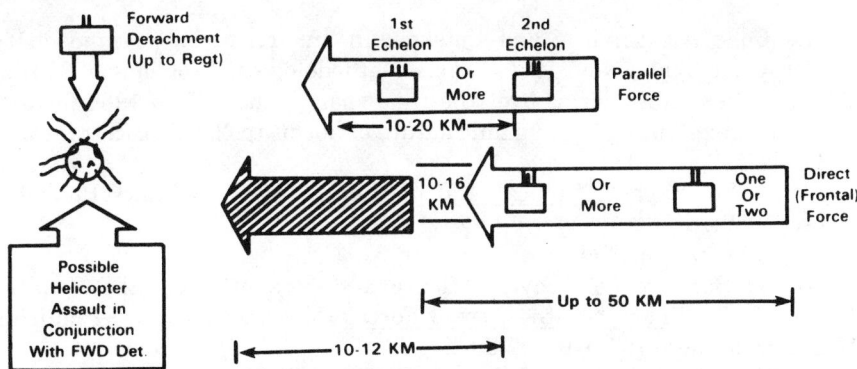

- Commitment
  Forces in contact committed to pursuit immediately upon detection of enemy withdrawal.
- Depth of Objectives
  Control exercised by phase lines to be reached by specified times. Forward detachments* of up to regimental size may seize critical objectives (choke points) up to 50 KM in depth. Helicopter assault may be used in coordination with forward detachments.

* Formed from lead units having success or from 2nd echelon forces

Figure 4.24. Pursuit – 1st Echelon Division (Not to Scale)

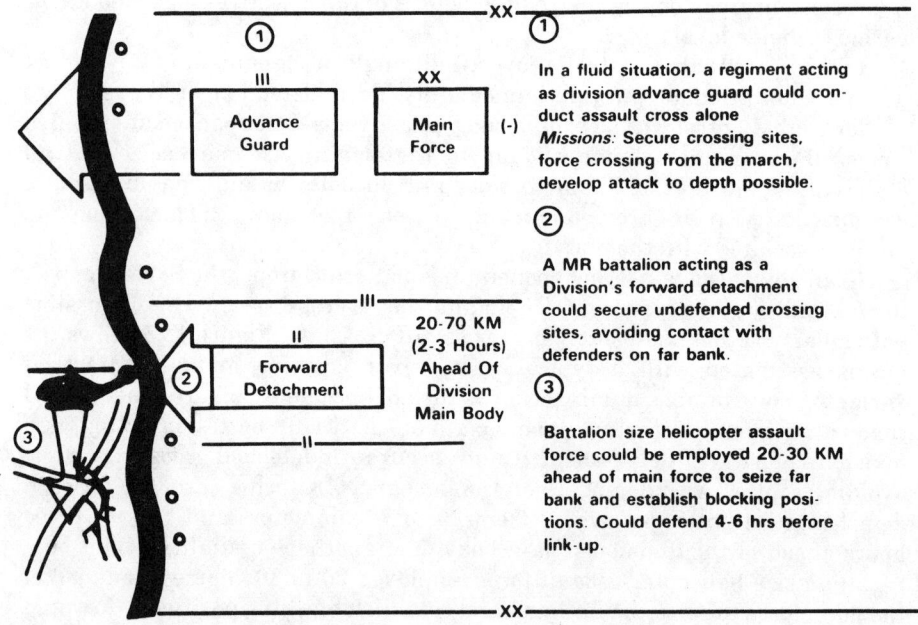

Figure 4.25. Hasty Assault River Crossing – Tactical Variants

NOTES

1. Cols. Aleksandrov and Lutskov, in an article in *Voyennaya Mysl* (Military Thought), Nov. 1966, "Some Methodological Problems of Military Teaching," examine norms over the time span from 1933 to 1960 for artillerymen in explaining the dynamic nature of norms (p. 29 of FBIS translation and p. 42, footnote 3).

2. A. Ya. Vayner, Tactical Calculation (Moscow: Military Publishing House, 1982), p. 56.

3. Ibid., pp. 163-171.

4. V. Bondarenko, "Soviet Science and Strengthening the Country's Defense," Communist of the Armed Forces (Moscow: Military Publishing House, September 1974), pp. 22-30.

5. S. Ilyin, "Methods of Educating Soviet Soldiers," *Voyennaya Mysl'* (Military Thought) (Moscow: Military Publishing House, 1973).

6. A. Radzievskiy, Tactics in Combat Example - Regiment (Moscow: Military Publishing House, 1976).

7. A. Sedykh, "Continuity of the Attack by Fire on the Enemy," *Voyenniy Vestnik* (Military Herald) (Moscow: Military Publishing House, November 1975).

Chapter 5
The Air Component

The role of the Soviet Air Forces vis-a-vis the Ground Forces tends to be clouded in Western eyes by concepts of "independent air forces" versus subordinated "army air forces." For the Soviet airman, to whom the "army" is a symbol of the nation's total military might, and the defense of the USSR is a scientific matter, there is no confusion. The Soviet Air Forces[1] is one of the five combat services. It has a separate organizational hierarchy with its own Commander in Chief who is also a Deputy Minister of Defense. The Ground Forces, Navy, Air Defense Forces, and the Strategic Missile Forces join the Air Forces in comprising the five combat services in the Soviet military establishment.

With the imprimatur of the highest levels of political and governmental leadership, Soviet military doctrine stipulates that a future war can be won only through the combined efforts of all services and arms of the Soviet Armed Forces. This principle pervades the whole of Soviet military art from strategy through operational art and tactics.

In general, combined arms involves the participation of subunits, units, and formations of all branches of troops and special troops interacting with aviation (and naval elements in coastal sectors) to achieve specific combat objectives. The combined arms army is the clearest example of this concept. It provides the mechanism for the interactive process (*vzaimodeystviye*) among the various branches of arms subordinate to the Ground Forces command. While this is most evident at the operational and tactical levels, it may also extend to the strategic level where the combined arms concept governs interaction among the five combat branches of service and other major entities of the Soviet Defense Ministry in carrying out military tasks.

The importance of strategic combined arms warfare is widely recognized in Soviet military art. Military theorists and strategists insist that strategic actions in a theater of military operations must be conducted with the efforts of all services.[2]

Here the air role is examined, not in the order of priority the Soviets attach to air operations, but according to its direct impact on the role of the Ground Forces: direct air support, reconnaissance, command and control, air accompaniment, close air support, helicopter operations, independent air operations, and air supremacy.

DIRECT SUPPORT OF THE GROUND FORCES

Providing cover for Ground Forces operations requires local or tactical air supremacy. In recent times, this has undergone a spatial expansion as modern antiair technology has appeared on the battlefield. Troop Air Defense (PVO)[3], units and subunits, are now equipped with highly mobile surface-to-air missile (SAM) and gun systems[4] intended to keep NATO aircraft off the backs of advancing Ground Forces. While the air cover mission at river crossings and other specialized operations remains essentially as before, the addition of modern PVO antiaircraft systems allows Soviet fighter-interceptors to extend the periphery of the defended area over the ground forces. Hence, current Soviet Air Forces training includes the interception of NATO aircraft before they can reach the surface-to-air missile launching zone.

The extension of the area under cover by Soviet fighters may occur under the preferred operational mode which includes strictly centralized control, with aerial encounters directed by ground intercept controllers. Front aviation pilots, however, also may function independently by identifying targets, choosing the closing direction, and selecting weapon and firing sequence.[5] In such conditions, each two-plane element or even each aircraft may maneuver independently and use different combat methods.

When flying this type of cover mission, flights and elements may be assigned particular sectors and directed to fly prescribed search patterns for the purpose of detecting low-flying, camouflaged enemy aircraft against the background of wooded terrain. A key objective is to find and hit the attacker before he can take counteraction. Thus, strict radio silence and radio discipline are practiced. This operation, with or without radar control, is essentially the responsibility of a defensive fighter patrol. It provides extended cover to the first echelon units of a Front during heavy ground fighting and leaves the air defense mission in the immediate proximity of forces in contact with PVO SAM systems.

Closely allied to the defensive fighter patrol is the "free hunt" (*svobodnaya okhota*) which allocates certain hunting areas to fighter aircraft operating in pairs, searching out targets visually or with the aid of on-board electronic equipment. This type of operation usually will involve only the most experienced, most capable pilots. In Soviet eyes, it is the ultimate in independent combat operations.

Autonomous or semi-autonomous defensive cover operations by Soviet fighters have until recently been hampered by the lack of onboard equipment for finding and attacking hostile aircraft flying at low altitude and high speed. However, the Soviets now have completed testing a lookdown, shootdown radar system for the improved FOXBAT, the MIG-31 FOXHOUND, the new MIG-29 FULCRUM, and probably the SU-27 FLANKER. When this technology, which can simultaneously track and fire at multiple targets, is fully employed in the tactical arena, it will have severe implications for NATO's ability to maintain air superiority.

Soviet exercises like NIEMAN indicate that air activity may be three tiered in some situations, such as river crossings. Assault helicopters would operate in the lower tier, with ground-attack aircraft in the middle, and fighters flying cover in the upper tier.[6]

The tiered approach also is used where ground-based PVO systems must cooperate with fighter-interceptors in providing cover. In these instances, interceptors and missile systems are assigned priorities according to zones, times, and altitudes in a manner keyed to operational contingencies. Depending on the circumstances, interceptors also may fight within the surface-to-air missile belt, continuing to harry attacking aircraft all the way to their targets. The Egyptians, for example, found that their aircraft losses from friendly missiles in the 1973 war were so small that the tactic of using both interceptors and missiles in the same airspace was operationally sound and effective against enemy formations.

Regardless of the specific conditions under which the cover mission is flown, the underlying concept is to deny the enemy's air force the possibility of interfering with the offensive actions of the Ground Forces. Thus, while it involves and is part of the struggle for air supremacy, the cover mission is successful if it disrupts the attacking aircraft and stops them from hitting their targets.

RECONNAISSANCE

The importance that Soviet military science attaches to reconnaissance cannot be overstated. In some major World War II campaigns, for example, 25 to 30 percent of all aerial sorties were for reconnaissance purposes. With the emergence of new battlefield technologies, the importance of reconnaissance to Soviet command authorities is consistently increasing.

Strategic reconnaissance is generally the province of aviation units subordinate to theater commanders and, one suspects, satellite systems. It is organized and directed by the Soviet General Staff and, where aircraft are employed, by Soviet Air Forces Commanders. Despite the national character of strategic reconnaissance, its results are usually available to the commander and staff at the operational-strategic level as well as to the aviation commander.

Operational reconnaissance is conducted for the Front command element and the air forces. Its targets are the enemy's operational reserves, rear logistics system, and airfields. Soviet aircraft such as the MIG-25, are well equipped to perform the operational reconnaissance mission at Front level. The FOXBAT-B carries five cameras in the nose section and is said to provide 70 kilometer-wide sector coverage. In the FOXBAT-D, the cameras have been replaced by a large side-looking radar (SLAR) panel that probably enhances reconnaissance capability under adverse light and weather conditions.

Approximately 70 percent of the reconnaissance missions flown by Front aviation during World War II were tactical; the remainder were operational. The enemy's defensive arrangements, command posts, artillery, force groupings, and immediate reserves were the usual targets for these sorties. The same importance would probably be given tactical reconnaissance in a future conflict. However, in World War II regular combat units flew about 80 percent of all reconnaissance sorties, while specialized reconnaissance units and subunits accounted for only 20 percent. Advances in reconnaissance technology indicate that in any future conflict this mission would be performed by specialized aircraft. At the tactical level, the FOXBAT is complemented by the MIG-21 FISHBED-H and SU-17 FITTER-H, both of which can carry a pod with cameras or other sensors, and by the YAK-28 BREWER-D and possibly the older YAK-27 MANGROVE, both with special camera mountings. Virtually all helicopters also have a reconnaissance capability but especially the smaller MI-2 HOPLITE, which has a special role as an artillery spotter.

COMMAND AND CONTROL

The success of combined arms warfare is largely dependent on the efficiency of the command and control system. This is particularly true when there is cooperation between aviation and ground troops. Firmness, continuity, flexibility, and security of the command and control mechanism are essential to success. Therefore, the commander of the supporting Air Forces unit or sub-unit (or his personal representative) works with Ground Forces staffs and bears the major responsibility for organizing cooperative methods and procedures (*vzaimodeystviye*).

Mission assignments for aviation usually come from Front or Army level with the Air Forces staff and field headquarters responsible for planning details of the supporting tactical air activities. Air Forces operations groups are present in auxiliary command posts (*vspomogatel'niye punkty upravleniya - VPU*) with ground staffs in major sectors. Such an operations group usually will consist of eight to ten air force officers representing operations, intelligence, cryptography, communications, and meteorology. Its tasks include:

(1) Controlling aircraft over the battlefield during interaction with the Ground Forces;
(2) Guiding and redirecting aircraft to priority targets;
(3) Directing Air Forces influence over the outcome of the battle by determining the most decisive use of air;
(4) Ascertaining new enemy tactics and developing countertactics; and
(5) Providing intimate contact between the Air Forces commander and the ground forces in whose interest aviation is being employed.

Within this system, the air liaison officer (*aviapredstavitel'*) plays a critical role as the bridge between ground support requirements and the air force command and control network.

Second only to the air liaison officer in the control function are forward air controllers (*aviavodchiki*) who are physically present with ground force elements. They usually are rated (flying) officers from the supporting air unit. They direct aircraft to targets on the battlefield and report changes in the battle situation to the air liaison officer. In the interests of personal safety, the forward air controller probably will follow the World War II practice of wearing a ground force uniform without proper rank insignia. His equipment will be mounted on a mobile vehicle such as an armored personnel carrier, in order to keep pace with the rapid tempo envisioned in Soviet military art.

Air warning, guidance, and communications posts (*vozdushnoye nablyudeniye, opoveshcheniye i svyaz - VNOS*) are established within a few kilometers of the line of contact with enemy troops. Headed by a pilot from a unit operating in the sector, the *VNOS* post provides a link in the command and control communications system and also serves as a navigational beacon to guide attacking aircraft and helicopters to their targets (Figure 5.1).

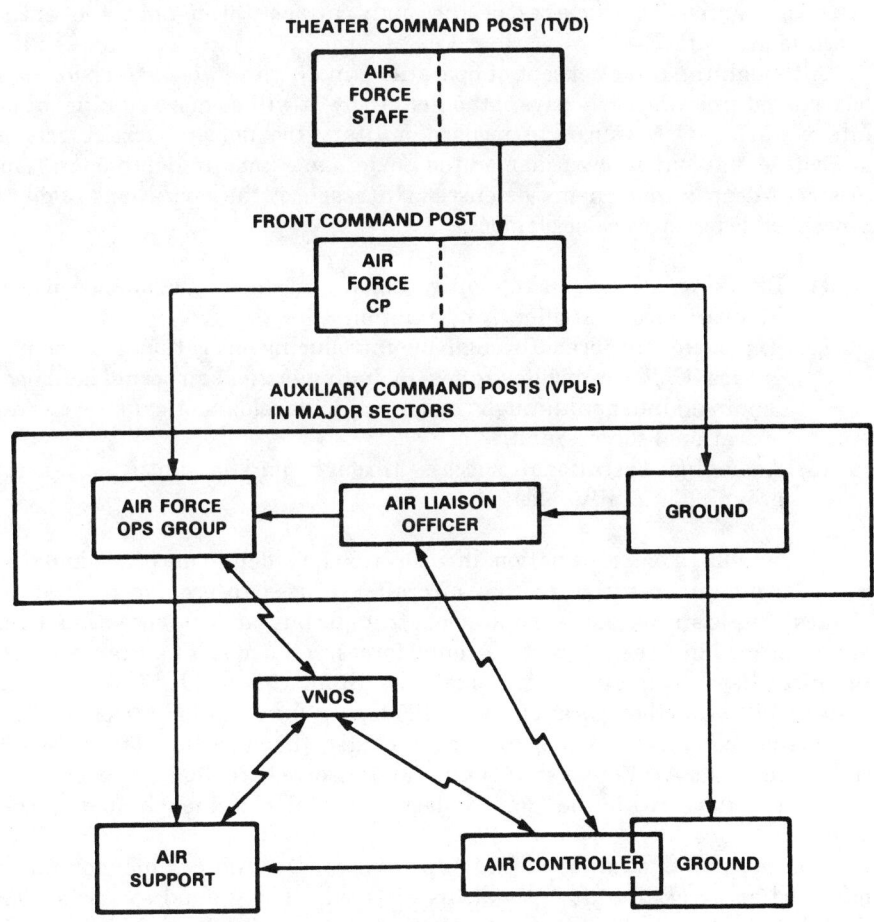

Figure 5.1. *VNOS* as Command Relay-Constructed According to Information Contained in Ye V. Koyander, *Ya - Rubin, Prikazyvayu* (Moscow: Voyenizdat, 1978)

AIR ACCOMPANIMENT

The operational art of the Soviet Air Forces does not emphasize aerial interdiction per se, but stresses air accompaniment as part of its combined arms doctrine. Interdiction, in US Air Force parlance, consists of air operations against the enemy's military potential (lines of communication, reserves, etc.) at such a distance from friendly forces that detailed integration of air interdiction missions with the fire and movement of friendly forces is not required. Air accompaniment in the Soviet view, on the other hand, involves neither interdiction nor close air support, but is the use of aviation in the offensive to complement other means of fire. According to the late head of the Frunze Academy, General A. Radzievskiy, aviation forces are massed in a decisive manner on the axes of the main attack throughout the entire operational depth.[7]

Although the basic concept of operations in depth (*glubokaya operatsiya*) has existed since the early days of the Red Army, it will be more significant for future warfare. Advances in modern military technology, particularly in aircraft and avionics, have enabled the Soviets to extend in-depth operations to strike deeper into enemy defenses. In essence, the operations-in-depth concept calls for three basic elements:

(1) Breaking through in the entire defense system by combined use of infantry, armor, artillery, and aviation;
(2) Exploiting the breakthrough by introducing operational maneuver groups (OMG) or mobile groups (including tactical airborne/ heliborne landings) into and through the breach to develop tactical success into operational success; and
(3) Achieving operational success through pursuit until an enemy grouping is totally defeated.

The employment of aviation in operations in depth may resemble an independent air operation in that aircraft are used to provide massed air strikes. These strikes, however, are not strategic but tactical- operational and are performed in direct support of ground forces in the most important sectors. Because they are tactical-operational, the Front commander bears overall responsibility for the operation, with his deputy for aviation responsible for the actual conduct of air operations. Under the direction of the Front commander, the Air Forces staff defines and resolves problems of cooperation (*vzaimodeystviye*) with the commanders and staffs of the Ground Forces armies.

For normal fixed-wing tactical air strikes, the Air commander has a balanced array of aircraft types at his disposal. The ground attack models (FLOGGER-D and FITTER-C and D) probably would fly the bulk of air accompaniment missions in support of breakthrough operations, complementing HIND and HIP assault helicopters. The optimized FENCER-A, B, C is available for deeper penetration missions in the tactical zone. However, the counterair FLOGGER and FISHBED fighters could also support the ground attack accompaniment mission by trading their air-to-air missiles for rocket pods and small bombs. The combined arms commander also can call upon assault helicopters to attack in wave-after-wave formation approaching the target from below tree top level, climbing to firing altitude, delivering their ordnance, then withdrawing at low altitude.

The stress on mobility, maneuverability, and mass in Soviet military art significantly enhances the role of the Air Forces in combined arms doctrine for a fast-moving conflict in Central Europe. As Marshal of Aviation Kutakhov said: "Aviation not only can switch attacks from one axis to another, but its mobility allows units to be shifted between theaters of military operations." Reserve formations can be flown to areas near the battlefield from military districts in the USSR as directed by the strategic leadership to achieve the mass desired at any given point or axis of operations.[8]

Maneuver can be accomplished by creating aviation formations from the strategic reserve, by moving units from their tactical operating bases to fields nearer the target sector, or simply by exploiting the increased operational radii of contemporary aircraft.[9] Moreover, FISHBED, FLOGGER, and FITTER aircraft can operate from auxiliary airfields and even from sod strips. There are also specially prepared landing strips on most major freeways (*Autobahnen*) in East Germany and Poland that could be used for dispersal and recovery bases if main operating bases were knocked out of action.

The air accompaniment mission may be divided into two phases: the preparatory attack, and strikes flown in support of advancing infantry and armor after the actual operation has commenced. The doctrine of integrated fire support requires that air strikes during the preparatory attack be closely coordinated with artillery barrages to extend the range of fire laterally or in depth. Principle targets are enemy artillery, operational reserves, and antitank weapons. Coordination is the responsibility of the air staff working closely with the Front artillery staff and ground force commanders. If artillery and air operate at the same time, aviation will strike deeper targets than will the artillery. If they operate at different times, both may be directed at the same objectives to increase fire saturation of the target area. Under some conditions, there may even be overlapping coverage, which requires closer coordination. In any case, the time, place, and targets of each air strike must be integrated with the operations of the supporting artillery.

As the operation in depth proceeds, air accompaniment changes in nature from the preparatory attack to a range of air-to-ground missions. These may be preplanned strikes in response to a combined arms commander's requirements, or free hunt search-and-destroy missions.

In the second of these options, air force units may be placed under direct operational control of a ground commander who establishes targets, objectives, and times of operations. This would be particularly likely if the supported unit is in the operational depth of the enemy defense. Under these circumstances, the air force commander would decide on tactics, weapons, and size of the air component required to carry out the mission.

In some instances, fighter-interceptors, such as FISHBED and FLOGGER B and G flying cover for advancing ground units, may be diverted from their counterair mission to attack ground targets with their cannons. As a general rule, however, tactical operations would be conducted by a strike group approximately one-third of which would be counterair fighters flying cover for ground attack aircraft.

Free hunt tactics also would be used against mobile targets. A flight of two elements, each composed of two aircraft with one element providing cover for the other, or simply a single two-aircraft sortie could be used. The free hunt mission is akin to armed reconnaissance; the objective is to search out and destroy targets that threaten the offensive action. Chief among those targets would be nuclear delivery systems. The importance of the free hunt could increase in the years ahead in light of the 1979 NATO decision to modernize its tactical nuclear weapons delivery capabilities. PERSHING II and the ground-launched cruise missile (GLCM) system now deployed are movable but difficult to conceal from penetrating hunter- killer teams.

CLOSE AIR SUPPORT

In US terms, close air support consists of air attacks against hostile targets that are in close proximity to friendly forces. Detailed integration of each aerial mission with the fire and maneuver of those forces is required.

Traditionally, Soviet ground forces have relied on tanks, artillery, and other means of direct fire to provide close support for troops in contact. Air support (*aviatsionnaya podderzhka*) has been a broader concept, defined generally as combat operations conducted for the purpose of assisting ground forces to achieve their combat objectives. While this definition included close air support, it also embraced wide-ranging forms of air attack, with less emphasis on direct support to ground forces' close contact with the enemy. Nevertheless, the Soviet Air Force does have a rich historical tradition of close support for ground operations. The IL-2 Shturmovik of World War II fame probably flew more missions in support of ground armies than any other type of aircraft. However, as the Soviet Air Force made the transition to the jet age, there were no aircraft that could continue the Shturmovik's role and tradition.

The venerable MIG-15 and its successor, the MIG-17 FRESCO, have won universal acclaim for their maneuverability in aerial combat and their longevity, but neither had the ordnance-carrying capability or range to be a true ground-attack aircraft. The SU-7 FITTER-A, the IL-28 BEAGLE, and the YAK-28 BREWER were all designed to deliver ordnance in support of ground operations but not one was an unqualified success. Technical advances in newer aircraft such as the FITTER-C, FITTER-D, FLOGGER-D, and FENCER-A, B, C certainly improved the deep strike and interdiction capabilities of the Soviet Air Forces but appear less suited to the close air support mission.

The likely heir to the legacy and, in some respects the close air support role, of the famous *Shturmovik* is the MI-24 HIND helicopter. The development of the MIG-28 HAVOC (bearing some resemblance to the US

Apache) attests to the correctness of this assumption. The HIND is considerably slower than the IL-2 but can carry a greater assortment and weight of armaments and is more responsive to a Ground Forces commander's support requirements than fixed-wing aircraft operating from fixed bases. The time from request to actual airstrike diminishes substantially if Army aviation includes helicopter gunships capable of providing air support that is limited in scope and depth. This corresponds in great degree to the most urgent demands of Ground Forces unit commanders. In fact, the requirement for an aviation force that can respond quickly to support requests has led to assault helicopter squadrons, consisting of both MI-24 HIND and MI-8 HIP-E helicopters being subordinated operationally to individual Army and division commanders for tactical purposes.

As part of a combined arms commander's operational and tactical reserves, assault helicopters could use their superior maneuver capability either to augment existing artillery or to compensate for its shortage. This would be particularly useful in a fast-moving battle where towed artillery, in particular, would be at a disadvantage. River crossings and the expansion of bridgeheads are other examples where the attack helicopters could function above operating troops at great advantage, while fixed-wing aircraft carried the attack deeper into the defensive zone.

The short turning radius of helicopters, coupled with slower airspeed and their ability to fly nap-of-the-earth mission profiles, provide substantial advantages over fixed wing aircraft in supporting troops at or near the line of contact. They can approach their targets at extremely low levels guided by forward air controllers, then "pop up" to achieve the proper attack angle, and fire from the swoop or from the hover at ranges of 1,000 to 3,000 meters. Using such tactics, exposure to enemy aircraft and anti-aircraft systems is greatly reduced and the attacking helicopters are able to turn and descend to lower levels to leave the battle area or to take up positions for a subsequent attack. The presence of a weapons system operator in addition to the pilot in the HIND and HIP also promises greater accuracy and effectiveness.

The HIND-D and E, as well as the HIP-E, appear to be especially well equipped for anti-armor warfare. With a large calibre four-barrel machine gun (or machine cannon) under its nose, in addition to its primary armament of four 32-shot rocket pods (128 unguided 57mm rockets) and four SPIRAL laser-guided antitank missiles, the HIND-E may be the world's most formidable attack helicopter. The HIP-E is less sophisticated but more heavily armed with up to 192 57 mm rockets in six pods, plus four antitank guided missiles.[10]

The deployment of the SU-25 FROGFOOT in Afghanistan suggests that the Soviets regard this new aircraft not just as a tank-buster but as a complement to the HIND in a wider range of combat support roles. In Afghanistan, FROGFOOT aircraft often operate in combat pairs with one aircraft performing the strike role while the second maintains a higher altitude dropping infra-red decoy flares to cover the attacking aircraft from missile fire by SA-2's or Stingers. The FROGFOOT carries a heavy caliber cannon, probably a 30mm gatling, and up to ten external stores capable at up to 4000 kilograms of ordnance. It seems clear that its capabilities would allow the development of special tactics involving HIND and FROGFOOT operating together to contain the anti-air mission of NATO ground forces.

EMPLOYMENT PRINCIPLES

Until May 5, 1940, the Red Army Air Force was part and parcel of the ground forces command scheme. Combined arms armies had air force directorates whose purpose was to serve the ground force commander much the same as the artillery directorates. Front aviation had 55 to 60 percent of its aircraft directly subordinated to ground force commanders in two sublevels known as Army aviation (*armeyskaya aviatsiya*) and tactical or organic aviation (*voyskovaya aviatsiya*), i.e., subordinate to the Red Army at the division level. This splitting of air power made it difficult to employ the revered principle of mass in air operations against the German invaders in World War II and eventually led to the organization of air armies, which placed command and control in the hands of air force commanders.

The relevance of this historical experience may be dubious, but the emergence of assault helicopter units in some proportion to ground force armies could lend credibility to the hypothesis that history has repeated itself. *Armeyskaya aviatsiya* is once again a reality -- certainly in terms of the missions it should accomplish. As early as 1972, Savkin[11] recognized the problems and advantages of subordination. "The effectiveness of using helicopters in combat", he wrote, "lies in the immediate dependence on their organizational subordination". He then advocated including helicopters in the table of organization and equipment of combined arms armies and combined arms commanders were exhorted to know their capabilities as well as they know the capabilities of artillery. More than any other piece of conventional military hardware, save possibly the BMP, the MI-24 assault helicopter has affected the contemporary employment of time-tested principles of Soviet military art. The air assault units that he advocated then are now part of the Ground Forces scene.

Historically, the Soviets have preferred to use artillery for fire support of troops engaged in contact with the enemy. Air support of ground forces most often occurred during the preparatory phases of an operation or for ranges exceeding those of artillery. Hence, the overly simplified idea arose that the Soviet Air Force was primarily an extension of the commander's artillery. Certainly, Soviet military science has not de-emphasized the importance of artillery. All evidence is to the contrary as illustrated by the deployment of several new self-propelled artillery systems and organizational changes involving artillery sub-units. However, a new dimension has been added by assault helicopters which, by virtue of their tactical and technical advances, now can destroy point targets close to friendly forces.

Allowing for the fact that the Soviet version of close air support may differ from traditional US understanding, the BEREZINA, NIEMAN, and ZAPAD exercises indicate that HINDs and HIPs have a fundamental close air support mission. In BEREZINA, for example:

> "Combat helicopters proved highly effective in cooperative operations with the Ground Forces. Delivering missile salvos, bomb strikes, or machine gun fire, they destroyed designated targets and met requests for air support."[12]

Air-ground cooperation (*vzaimodeystviye*) was emphasized at every level; Air Forces commanders worked closely with representatives from the Ground Forces to design different attack variants on specific targets. In the NIEMAN exercise, there again was coordination between battalion artillery and helicopters with artillery striking the center of the enemy forces and helicopters attacking the flanks.[13] In such large scale exercises as ZAPAD-81, and all subsequent ones, the attack helicopter has proven itself to be a major battlefield combat system. The limited window to Soviet exercises available to the West certainly reconfirms an old maxim in Soviet military doctrine. "Success in modern combat can be achieved only under the condition of precise cooperation between the sub-units of all branches of forces".

AIR-TO-GROUND OPERATIONS

There are three basic types of air-to-ground combat missions that can be performed by assault helicopters, preplanned strikes, strikes performed in response to a combined arms commander's call, and "free hunt" or search and destroy missions.

Although there is no reason for combat helicopters to operate in any particular combination, the Soviet basic tactical fire unit is a flight of four helicopters flying as two pairs in trail. In mid-1983, the Soviets appear to have added a third step to the basic combat pair. This third helicopter may provide defensive cover slightly rearward and higher than the attacking pair. This position provides good visual contact and possibly mutual fire support. The flight commander is probably located in this cover helicopter. In a large operation, flights will attack wave after wave, rolling in on the target to fire their ordnance, then the attacking flight will drop out of sight, using the terrain for protection against enemy fire, while four more helicopters climb to firing altitude from their ground-hugging approach. The combat pair (*boyevaya para*) also is used, particularly in the "free hunt" mode.

In many respects, assault helicopter units are used most effectively as part of the combined arms commander's reserves. Their ability to maneuver and to mass quickly is superior to artillery in a fast-moving battle and can either augment or compensate for a shortage of artillery. Moreover, helicopters add considerably to the Soviet ability to conduct aerial fire maneuver. The mobility of helicopters allows the aerial fire maneuver to be accomplished in a matter of minutes by concentrating the fire of combat helicopters with that of supporting aircraft against particular targets. The helicopters may then switch the attack to newly detected targets during the course of the battle. The Soviets view this capability as particularly important in combating nuclear weapons, artillery, tanks, and airborne landing elements.

Applying aerial fire maneuver to a fast-moving combat situation will entail significant coordination requirements. Helicopter fire will need to be integrated with that of fixed-wing ground attack aircraft, such as the SU-17 FITTER-C and the MIG-27 FLOGGER-D, while dual capable fighter-interceptors, such as the MIG-21 FISHBED-L/N and MIG-23 FLOGGER-B/G, fly overhead cover. In seizing bridgeheads, for example, aircraft may be "layered" at different altitudes. Likewise, layering occurs during breakthrough operations after Soviet mobile groups are committed. (The enemy's air defense cohesion would probably be disrupted as he is forced into a battle of maneuver.) Carefully coordinated helicopter and fixed-wing attacks also would be used to support the rapid advance envisaged for mobile groups in exploiting the success of the breakthrough. Much of the responsibility for controlling aviation in this situation would be passed to the air liaison officer traveling with tank units.

The NIEMAN exercise indicated that a primary target of combat helicopters is enemy armor. Certainly the HIND-D, E, and HIP-E are formidably armed for this task and may continue to be the primary antitank aircraft despite the operational capabilities of the SU-25 FROGFOOT. Professor of Military Tactics, Lieutenant General V. G. Reznichenko, wrote as early as 1966 that the helicopter was superior to other antitank weapons then available in terms of field of vision, maneuverability, and firepower.[14] His 1984 text, <u>Tactics</u>, emphasizes the increased capabilities and roles of the helicopter in combined arms at the tactical and operational levels.[15] The fundamental advantages of helicopters over fixed-wing aircraft in antitank operations are the helicopter's short turning radius and ability to fly nap-of-the-earth following natural contours to escape detection and hostile action. Painted to match the surrounding terrain, usually green on top and blue underneath, HIND's and HIP's could, as suggested earlier, approach their targets at below tree top level, pop up to achieve the proper attack angle, and fire from a swoop at ranges of 1,000 to 3,000 meters. This might require only 20 or 30 seconds. One military correspondent has gone so far as to say: "Let the tanks aim their machine guns at them . . . helicopters will be able to strike first from afar. The crew has everything to destroy the tanks: the most accurate sights, missiles, plus combat skills".[16,17]

Success of the mission depends to a great extent on the flight commander, who is responsible for a pre-flight preparation and the conduct of the actual mission. In training, everything is carefully calculated and practiced on the ground before the mission is flown. There is extensive use of simulation, operating models, and various displays including film projectors with tape recordings used to reproduce combat situations.

In addition to its airborne anti-armor mission, the HIND-D and E (as well as the HIP-E) can carry troops armed with antitank guided missiles into zones that have been temporarily neutralized by aerial weapons. A Soviet antitank section of eight to ten men with their weapons can easily be accommodated in the HIND's cargo area. This capability is further evidence of the flexibility afforded Soviet commanders by their assault helicopters and introduces the subject of air mobility, which will be discussed later.

It has long been Soviet practice to begin a ground offensive with a preparatory air attack that nearly always coincides with an artillery barrage. The purpose of the air attack is to suppress the enemy's artillery, weaken the main points of resistance, and disrupt command and control procedures in the tactical defense zone. The usual practice is to divide support aircraft into two echelons. One echelon will provide continuous support and escort advancing units and sub-units directly on the battlefield. The other is given the task of suppressing and destroying reserves, artillery, and other vital objectives in depth. A primary purpose is to confound and disrupt defensive artillery fire and delay the shift of artillery positions.

Assault helicopters may now be used for continuous support of advancing troops, freeing fixed-wing ground attack aircraft for missions in the depth of the enemy defense. Because the assault helicopters would operate in relative proximity to attacking sub-units, there is the usual requirement for detailed coordination and interaction. It is likely that the pilots would deploy their aircraft to an area as close as possible to the command post of the attacking Ground Forces. There they would be briefed by the forward air controller, himself an experienced pilot, who would outline the objectives, describe the expected combat situation, and work out mutual communications and recognition signals. In the breakthrough operation, the primary objective will be to suppress and destroy enemy armor and mechanized infantry units that could be used against advancing Soviet tanks and OMG's, or mobile groups seeking to exploit the success of a breakthrough on the main axis of attack. Closely allied with this objective is the task of destroying and disrupting antitank weapons.

Soviet belief in the massed use of various weapons systems, such as artillery and air power, at the decisive phases of an operation leads to the inclusion of assault helicopters in any major Soviet offensive. These helicopter armadas, composed of a mix of HIND's and HIP's, could provide a highly mobile and maneuverable means of massing fire against defensive positions. Major General Belov has noted that success of a Soviet offensive could be jeopardized unless helicopters are used in mass.[18]

Depending upon their calculations of the enemy's air defense capabilities, the Soviets also will use helicopters in the free hunt mode, aimed at locating mobile targets and delivering the first salvos against them. In conjunction with a successful breakthrough or during pursuit operations, pairs of assault helicopters looking for targets could be especially unnerving.

HELICOPTER RECONNAISSANCE

The significance of aerial reconnaissance to Soviet military theorists is demonstrated by the abundance of reconnaissance aircraft at their disposal. Reconnaissance satellites aside, there are the MIG-25 FOXBAT D and E,

MIG-21 FISHBED-H, YAK-28, BREWER-D, and SU-17 FITTER-H aircraft specifically equipped for aerial reconnaissance. To those, one must add the MI-2, MI-8, and MI-24 helicopters. One advantage of helicopters in the reconnaissance role lies in their versatility and flexibility. They can perform a number of missions in quick reaction to a Ground Forces commander without being tied to a runway. Among those missions are chemical and radiological reconnaissance of areas attacked by weapons of mass destruction before such areas are entered by advancing troops.

At the tactical and operational levels, the reconnaissance helicopter will play an increasingly important role. As noted earlier, the MI-2 HOPLITE is well suited for tactical reconnaissance in direct support of the ground unit or sub-unit commander. Its small size allows it to be based on patches of cleared land immediately accessible to the front line. In offensive operations, the information provided by reconnaissance helicopters would be useful in helping the commander determine the direction of his main strike in time to achieve the required rate of advance. World War II experience, however, indicated that most Soviet tactical battlefield reconnaissance was performed by pilots flying attack aircraft, while regular reconnaissance units filled most of the requirements at the operational level. If this experience is transferred to a future battlefield, it will be HIND's, HIP's and their follow-ons that will perform tactical reconnaissance.

In breakthrough operations, tactical aerial reconnaissance would be conducted over the battlefield and its approach routes to a depth of from 10 to 15 kilometers. For river crossings, reconnaissance helicopters are particularly important. Because of their hover and slow flight capabilities, they are able to gather information on the nature of the water obstacle such as depth, condition of banks, speed and direction of the current, etc. Other obstacles to the tempo of the offensive, such as antitank ditches, barriers, and even mines (when the helicopter is properly equipped) can be detected and described without the need to develop and interpret reconnaissance film.

In circumstances where observations must be made from friendly territory, the pilot can climb quickly to altitudes of 1,000 of 1,500 meters, make his observation and land before anti-aircraft weapons can be brought to bear. At those altitudes, good visibility conditions allow antitank ditches and trenches to be seen from a distance of six to eight kilometers and important sub-units at 15 to 20 kilometers.

AIRBORNE COMMAND POSTS

Soviet helicopters in direct support of ground operations also can serve as airborne command posts and communications relays. Specially equipped helicopters of the HIP and HOOK variety can be used to enhance significantly the transmission of reports and instructions dealing with the tactical battlefield to both operational and strategic levels. Moreover, because it does not require disassembly in order to move closer to the front, the airborne command post becomes an important adjunct to normal command arrangements in a fast-moving offensive.

HELICOPTER LANDINGS

In addition to the fire power of helicopters and fixed-wing aircraft, the Soviet Ground Forces have developed what may be called "vertical maneuver", which emphasizes the ability of rotary wing aircraft to deploy troops rapidly. According to Major General Belov, vertical maneuver involves:

> "...military transport and army aviation air-mobile troops which are organized into fundamentally new combined arms antitank and reconnaissance combined units and sections; and other air-transportable combined units and sections".[19]

Lieutenant General Reznichenko emphasizes the increased importance of this concept in the 1980s made possible by the development of army aviation.[20] Soviet interest in airborne operations has a long history and is manifested today in the existence of seven or eight airborne divisions, but that is only one aspect of vertical maneuver. In a swiftly moving combat situation, airlifting infantrymen by helicopter will be the more obscure but perhaps more threatening element of air mobility. There is no hint of special airmobile divisions in the US Army mold but rather a variety of concepts deriving from Soviet perceptions of their requirements.

The theoretical basis for vertical maneuver is the same as that of Soviet military art as a whole, although the development of tactical principles for helicopter employment was relatively slow and constrained by different and opposing concepts. Pre-World War II military science stressed mobility and maneuverability as essentials for successful combat operations. Soviet experience in the Great War and all their post-war analyses have proved the fundamental correctness and importance of pre-war theory. Speed (tempo), mass, and maneuver, all related directly to mobility, and the Soviet equipment programs of the past decade, provide ample testimony to their determination to provide the means to employ those principles. Helicopters are, then, one of the principal technological achievements that have been used to improve Ground Forces mobility.

Savkin, for example, speaks of heliborne forces being used to increase rates of advance and particularly to consolidate the results of nuclear strikes. Heliborne troops might be landed as little as 15 to 20 minutes after a nuclear strike.[21] It is worth noting that all Soviet units are outfitted with anti-radiation and decontamination gear that could allow operations in a radiologically active area. As part of the doctrine that calls for rapid rates of advance, heliborne troops used as an exploitation force after a nuclear strike could seize territory virtually unopposed.

In addition to exploiting nuclear strikes, helicopters can be used in river crossings to rapidly move a holding force to the opposite bank. Helicopters also are used to lay antitank and anti-personnel mines and to fly troops over areas mined by the enemy.

The major form of vertical maneuver involves helicopters in the airborne assault. This is particularly important in conducting operations in the tactical depth of enemy defenses as it allows tactical airborne assault and the landing of forward detachments and *spetsnaz* teams. With the appearance of the helicopter, according to Sidorenko, a major Soviet theorist for offensive combat, came the opportunity for large-scale employment of airborne assault, which ensures a more compact landing of a sub-unit sized force together with its weapons and equipment than does an air drop of paratroops.[22] In contrast to regular airborne divisions, the heliborne assault force requires very little special training and can be made up of elements of practically any regular motorized rifle sub-unit. The Soviets have nevertheless organized airborne assault brigades based on the airborne regiment reinforced by D-30 towed 122 mm howitzers, SD-44 85 mm field guns, manpack ATGM, and SPG9 73 mm recoilless AT guns.

Airborne assault (*desant*) would be used to seize and hold key positions such as road junctions, river crossings, defiles, etc. and require strict coordination with ground units and precise calculation of the time needed to carry out the entire operation, from troop loading to the actual landing.

The airborne assault force is largely responsible for organizing its own air defense even though there may be covering fighters in the area to protect the helicopters. Divided into a seizure group and a covering group, the assault force will have one sapper platoon, two platoons of manpacked antitank missiles (six launchers), two platoons of shoulder-fired SA-7 GRAIL surface-to-air missiles, jeep-mounted SA-9 GASKIN SAM's and a section (two vehicles each with four guns) of a 23 mm anti-aircraft battery. The troops in the assault force are expected to make full use of small-arms fire. In the Soviet view, every unit and sub-unit must be capable of combating hostile aircraft under all combat conditions, regardless of their location in relation to the senior commander's air defense zone. The probable absence of technical early warning support in the landing zone dictates that each sub-unit commander set up his own air observers equipped with binoculars, signal flags, and flares.

Although armed themselves, the transport helicopters may have to be accompanied to the landing zone by combat helicopters whose tasks will include destroying anti-aircraft weapons. The transport helicopter sub-unit will link up with its assault counterparts at a pre-determined aerial rendezvous point, again requiring precise timing and coordination.

A heliborne assault landing will generally not penetrate more than 80 to 100 kilometers into enemy territory. The assault unit must form up in an assembly area which theoretically may be located an additional 80 to 100 kilometers behind the front. Generally, the assembly area will be much closer in order to decrease the total time involved in the operation. Loading a battalion-sized unit with its equipment is a considerable task, involving numerous transport and logistic requirements. It has been suggested that 12 heavy lift helicopters (MI-6) and 25 smaller troop carriers could move a battalion of 430 men with trucks and 122 mm guns.

Although the success of the assault landing is largely contingent on meeting the time norms established for coordinating combat operations with other sub-units, the time spent in the landing zone may be even more critical since the helicopter's vulnerability to artillery fire would be greatest during that period. Surprise, therefore, is a critical factor. Thus, radio discipline is sure to be imposed, with the substitution of various recognition signals worked out in advance to ensure secure command and control (*skrytnoye upravleniye*), as in the case of air support operations previously described.

The most typical sub-unit for tactical heliborne assault landings is the reinforced motorized rifle battalion. With its weapons and technical equipment, it is considered capable of prolonged independent combat in the enemy rear. These operations can be sustained even in the absence of fire support from friendly forces. Such airborne assaults would be for the purpose of increasing the rate of advance. Normally helicopter or missile supporting fire would be expected, enabling the heliborne force to link up with advancing troops (for example, an OMG) before the enemy had time to destroy the landing unit. Nevertheless, a landing force may have to fight its way to a position where it can link up, or it will succumb. There appears to be no provision for extracting the assault force, should the going get tough.

Other heliborne sub-units such as *spetsnaz* may have specialized training in reconnaissance, sabotage, infiltration, and subversion. Language proficiency, probably in English, German, or Danish, would enable experts to land in the enemy rear wearing enemy uniforms, with the tasks of diversion and disruption and of winning over indigenous inhabitants.

Another specialized, usually heliborne, unit is the Special Forces Brigade (*Brigada Spetsial'novo Naznacheniya*), whose mission could be to seize airfields or landing zones ahead of advancing forces or to carry out raids and diversionary tactics in the enemy's rear. The brigade might also sabotage vital installations, paralyze communications, and link up with Communist insurgents. It is composed of 2,500 men in four battalions with four additional support detachments (medical, communications, etc.). The brigade has no armored vehicles, but is equipped with automatic rifles, light machine guns, 122 mm rockets, flamethrowers, and an assortment of demolition munitions such as satchel charges, mines, and plastic explosives.

The Soviets also write of heliborne air assaults properly classed as raids, in which infantry troops armed with light artillery penetrate the enemy's positions by air, fulfill their missions, and rapidly return to their own territory. A typical tactical airborne landing party might be composed of a reinforced motor rifle company or even a platoon. It would be landed in the enemy's rear to perform such tasks as capturing the enemy's nuclear weapons, disrupting control, and disorganizing the operation of the rear.

While most of the *desanty* described above could be performed by regular infantry troops with little specialized training, each motorized rifle division may have one company trained in special commando landings and tactics that could be used as a separate raiding party.

Soviet military theoreticians have given much consideration to using helicopters in an air-to-air role. Their experience indicates that helicopters operating in the attack mode at penetration distances of less than five kilometers are practically invulnerable to ground anti-aircraft weapons if they use nap-of-the-earth techniques. The most effective anti- helicopter weapon, they say, may be another helicopter. The development of the coaxial contra-rotating helicopter by the Kamov design bureau, designated the HOKUM, indicates Soviet belief in this principle. The adaptation of other helicopters for the air-to-air role cannot be ruled out. Moreover, the concept of aerial combat includes the possibility of combating fixed-wing aircraft. Antitank guided missiles, 20 to 30 mm automatic cannon, and even upgraded rockets have proved suitable armament for the air-to-air role. In general, the cannon appears to have been most versatile, though it is not effective against fast-moving fighters. The idea of a high-speed, maneuverable fighter helicopter, such as the HOKUM, has found substantial support in the military staffs in Moscow. Armed with cannons and the proper air-to-air missile, a fighter helicopter could attack a fixed-wing aircraft nearly head on, establishing a rapid rate of closure and forcing the aircraft to break off its attack to avoid crashing to the ground. As soon as the fixed-wing fighter overflies the fighter helicopter, the latter executes a 180 degree turn and launches its air-to-air missile.

A specifically designed fighter helicopter appears now to be a reality; but it is also assumed that general purpose assault helicopters, such as HIND and HAVOC, are capable of aerial combat with other helicopters and even fixed-wing fighters.

AIR SUPREMACY

Thorough analysis of military operations in the Great Patriotic War has convinced Soviet military theoreticians that air supremacy (*gospodstvo v vozdukhe*) is essential for victory in any future conflict. If the battle for air supremacy is won by the attacker, it is claimed, Ground Forces operations, supported by air strikes, can develop successfully at the high speeds demanded by operational norms.[23] If air supremacy is not attained, the defense will have time to organize counteraction both in the air and on the ground, and the ground offensive inevitably will fail.

Even during the war, Soviet military art maintained that air supremacy was a combined arms responsibility. In fact, however, nearly all air supremacy requirements fell to the Air Forces. It is anticipated that the air forces will bear the major responsibility in any future conflict. Nevertheless, post-war advances in technology and armaments have provided all services the means to help achieve air supremacy. Overall direction of the battle for air supremacy often will be exercised by the national strategic leadership, which determines what contributions each of the services and branches of the armed forces can make.

Consistent with the tenets of Soviet military science, air force operational art differentiates between strategic, operational, and tactical air supremacy.

The fundamental concept at all three levels is that hostile aircraft may be destroyed either on the ground (or on aircraft carriers) or in aerial combat.

TACTICAL AIR SUPREMACY

At the tactical level, interaction between air and ground forces involved in winning air supremacy is organized at Front and Army levels. Insofar as possible, an overall aerial battle plan is developed in advance and conveyed to subordinate units and sub-units. This plan may be reasonably well defined or may be the major commander's interpretation of the Soviet concept of initiative taken to conform with the combat situation. Fighter aircraft and ground antiaircraft systems are to work closely together with operations designed by zones, altitudes, and times of operations. Fighters normally operate at ranges within the maximum limits of their combat radii, along the main approaches of enemy aircraft. Zones for surface-to-air missile and antiaircraft artillery systems usually are related to the targets being defended and to the ranges and altitudes of effective fire.

Coordination at the operational/tactical level in a battle for air supremacy is not easy. One difficulty is posed by aircraft that approach at extremely low altitudes. To meet this and other problems, the Soviets have refined their methods of controlling ground-based air defense forces and frontal aviation. In addition to radar warnings, information from air observers at command posts and in all sub-units is fed into the air defense network, which uses computers to determine how much time is required to intercept the attackers with a particular type of weapon. The commander then chooses surface-to-air missiles, conventional AAA, or fighters. In the latter case, pertinent information is passed to aviation command posts that use electronic data processing to determine which aircraft are given target assignments and recovery airfields.

OPERATIONAL AIR SUPREMACY

At the operational (Front) level, aerial combat (*vozdushniy boy*) is the primary means for achieving air supremacy. Because of increased survivability of enemy aircraft provided by hardened aircraft shelters, and the difficulty of launching a surprise massed attack against enemy airfields, the importance of destroying aircraft in aerial engagements and battles (*vozdushniye bitvy*) is increasing in Soviet Air Force operational art. It is anticipated that air battles will be fought both in the course of repelling hostile strikes and in launching offensive actions. In Soviet theory, the air battle is an aggregate of air engagements unified by a common operational concept and conducted simultaneously or sequentially by main groupings of aviation, with the objective of destroying enemy aircraft in the air.

Battles for operational air supremacy usually are conducted to support ground forces of strategic or Front operations. The battle for operational air supremacy will be synchronized with the ground forces operations. During the ground forces' penetration of enemy defenses, for example, the aerial battle is expected to intensify significantly.[24]

The Air Force commander and his staff are directly responsible for conducting the air supremacy battle. In accordance with the combined arms commander's operational concept, the Air Force commander will maneuver and mass his aircraft on the axes of the main attack and ensure the availability of aircraft to support tactical as well as operational requirements. He will also coordinate with the Chief of Rocket Troops & Artillery (CRTA) for FROG and SCUD attacks (nuclear or chemical) against enemy air fields.

STRATEGIC AIR SUPREMACY

The ultimate goal is neither tactical nor operational air superiority, but strategic air supremacy within the theater (*Teatr Voyennikh Deystviy - TVD*). Soviet military theory holds that strategic air supremacy is the sum total of tactical and operational successes. But there are explicit operations aimed at achieving strategic air supremacy. These operations often include the joint efforts of all the services, but sometimes are restricted to aviation. In either case, the overall campaign for strategic air supremacy is planned and organized by the highest level of strategic leadership -- the national or *TVD* level -- with executive action by the General Staff and/or the headquarters, Soviet Air Forces.[25]

The Navy's role in the battle for strategic air supremacy is to destroy hostile naval aircraft and operating facilities within a maritime theater of operations through aerial engagements, air-to-surface attacks, surface-to-surface actions, and submarine warfare. Elements of Soviet Naval Aviation (*Aviatsiya Voyenno-Morskovo Flota*) may, however, be placed temporarily under the strategic leadership of the *TVD* air commander, and operationally subordinated to the Front Air Forces commander. Amphibious landing operations involving coordinated interaction between naval forces and ground troops to secure aviation facilities, or to eliminate enemy air defenses on coastal axes, may also become part of a combined effort to achieve strategic/operational air supremacy on a broad front.

The Strategic Rocket Forces contribute to achieving air supremacy by intermediate and medium range ballistic missile attacks to destroy enemy aircraft and facilities on the ground. Participation of the Strategic Rocket Forces in the combined arms struggle for air supremacy will depend on the nature of the conflict, particularly whether it is nuclear or non- nuclear. Because of prevailing Soviet military art, the most expedient weapons and ordnance for gaining this objective will be adopted. This stems from a basic premise in combined arms doctrine which emphasizes that the distribution of weapons among the various services and branches of the armed forces exerts a direct influence on the correlation of forces (*sootnosheniye sil*).[26] It follows that the correlation of forces after an attack (in this case, air forces) will be more advantageous to the Soviets if they use the forces with the greatest probability of overcoming enemy defenses. In addition to using nuclear weapons against airfields, chemical weapons could be used by both the Strategic Rocket Forces and by aircraft.

INDEPENDENT AIR OPERATIONS

The most massive action by the Soviet Armed Forces in pursuit of air supremacy is likely to be an independent air operation. It has often been suggested that non-nuclear hostilities in Europe would automatically commence with what has come to be called the air operation. Yet, Soviet military theory speaks only of the concept of independent air operations, implying that air operations of varying intensity may be used to achieve different objectives. This appears consistent with Soviet planning doctrine, which calls for different plans, options, and plan-variants in response to predicted politico-military situations. Launching an air operation at the outset of European hostilities would, therefore, depend to some extent on the circumstances of the conflict as perceived by the Soviets, and their calculations as to the probable outcome. It is likely that a protracted war would include several air operations, directed by central strategic authority, designed to assist in gaining strategic air supremacy.

Based on the experience of World War II, smaller air operations also could be conducted to win tactical/operational air supremacy just prior to a major offensive, such as an operation to break through or penetrate enemy defenses. Whether planned and conducted by the Front or by strategic entities, the independent air operation concept is an important element in the principles of operational art that guide the employment of Soviet aviation. In light of Soviet respect for Western air forces and the doctrinal requirement for air supremacy, one may assume that a preemptive mass airstrike against NATO air forces and other priority targets could be the preferred Soviet method of launching a full-scale war in Europe without resorting to first use of nuclear weapons.

Independent air operations conducted by the Red Army Air Force during World War II were generally considered by senior ground commanders to be ineffective because of the shortage of post-strike reconnaissance. Post-war analysis, however, has convinced the Soviets that their original operational art was correct.[27]

According to the former Commander of the Soviet Air Forces, Chief Marshal of Aviation Pavel Kutakhov, the first phase in the post-war development of their operational art lasted from the end of the war until 1953. During that period, military theoreticians grappled with the question of what kind of aircraft and armaments would be required for an evolving military doctrine. The growth of a strong US Air Force was a conditioning factor in Soviet considerations and, therefore, much attention was devoted to the problem of air supremacy. Consistent with their experience, the Soviets concluded that destroying enemy aircraft on their airfields was the most expedient method of combating American air power in Europe.[28]

The second phase in post-war development of Soviet Air Forces operational art (1953-1959) saw Front Aviation equipped with jet aircraft and nuclear weapons. MIG-15 FAGOTs and MIG-17 FRESCOs were the principal tactical fighters until early model MIG-21 FISHBEDs, YAK-25 FLASHLIGHTs, and SU-7 FITTER-As began to enter operational units in the late 1950s. Perhaps due to lack of aircraft capability at that time, the Soviets emphasized that their operational art provided new and effective methods of destroying enemy aircraft on airfields and in the air. Marshal Kutakhov pointed out that under these conditions it became even more important to solve correctly the problem of gaining air supremacy.

During the third phase, beginning in 1960, the independent air operation with operational-strategic objectives was reemphasized, to a great extent as a result of matching technology to doctrine and vice-versa. As Kutakhov pointed out, the continued development of Air Forces operational art was based primarily on the combat capabilities of aviation equipment and armament. Since the mid-1960s, the concept of independent air operations has been strengthened and today is an integral part of Soviet military art and strategy. These air operations do not represent a major change. Rather, aircraft technology and the efforts of the Kremlin's defense planners have made the implementation of long-standing operational art a contemporary reality as armament norms have been able to match doctrinal requirements.

An independent air operation consists of the aggregate of a number of offensive actions, planned and executed by the Air Forces staff and the General Staff on behalf of the Supreme High Command, in the pursuit of operational or strategic goals in specific TVs, TVDs or maritime theaters of operations. Such operations will cover the entire theater where hostile aircraft are based and usually will be timed to coincide with the start of offensive operations. The basic aim will be to destroy enemy air power along a particular strategic axis or within an entire TVD. Surprise, deception, camouflage, and secrecy will be fully implemented as part of the operation. Any surprise attack scenario should, therefore, include an initial independent air operation at the outset of hostilities. Nevertheless, independent air operations of varying size and scope would be organized periodically throughout any extended war.

Soviet military science is explicit in categorizing the types of targets that must be attacked at the outset of a war or a major campaign. The three top priorities inevitably include the enemy's means of nuclear delivery, his airfields, and his command and control systems. In 1977 Lieutenant General Gareyev, Chief of the Military Science Directorate of the Soviet General Staff, stated that the most important missions for air forces had become destruction of fixed targets, such as enemy nuclear missiles and nuclear-capable aircraft on their launching pads; airfields; and mobile targets such as aircraft in the air, missile forces on the battlefield, aircraft carriers, and guided missile warships at sea.[29]

A massive air operation to gain air supremacy probably would include medium bombers operating under the direction of strategic leadership working in close coordination with Front Aviation aircraft belonging to several air force divisions throughout the theater. If the experience of World War II is relevant, and there is no reason to assume otherwise, fighter aviation (*istrebitel'naya aviatsiya*) belonging to the Air Defense Forces, could also participate.

Such an air operation probably would be conducted around the clock and could last up to six days, although three days would appear more probable. Nevertheless, the greatest effectiveness is expected during the first massed strike. According to Air Marshal Kutakhov, the fundamental task would be to neutralize the main force of enemy aviation on the first day of hostilities.[30] This is in line with Soviet experience in conducting air operations during World War II. Post-war analysis has shown that more than 40 percent of enemy aircraft losses during air operations came during the first massed attack, 30 percent during the second, and 20 percent during the third.

Although the air operation's major contribution to the air supremacy mission is to destroy aircraft and means of nuclear attack, airstrikes also would be conducted against command and control centers, runways, fuel, ammunition, and other logistic depots. Additional targets would include reserves (especially tank reserves), radars, communications, and radio-technical means.

The operational art of the Soviet Air Forces includes the principle that neutralizing the enemy's air defense forces is a prerequisite for successful air operations; hence destroying ground-based air defense weapons would have a high priority. Many of the early sorties flown by Front Aviation fighter-bombers are likely to be for that purpose. FITTER C and D aircraft, FLOGGER-Ds, and FENCER-As, Bs, and Cs equipped with precision guided munitions would appear to be the most likely candidates for this mission.[31]

The importance of dealing with defensive systems is illustrated in the composition of a typical World War II Soviet aerial strike force in which only 35 to 40 percent were bombers and attack aircraft with the mission of hitting the primary target. Nearly two-thirds of the attacking force consisted of fighters, 30 to 38 percent of which flew cover. The remainder engaged defensive fighters. The percentages would change in later conflicts, but the principle of neutralizing the air defense systems would remain.

Penetration of the air defense system will be closely planned and tightly controlled to ensure coordinated interaction among all the forces and weapons involved.[32] This demands firmness, continuity, and security of the Soviet command and control system, which directs aircraft and other units/subunits in order to penetrate according to a specific timetable and with minimum losses. The attacking forces will have simulated every predictable aspect of the penetration in advance. As pointed out by a former commander of the 16th Air Army, Lieutenant General V. Korochkin, air force operational art includes the premise that modern combat is highly dynamic; therefore, there will be no opportunity to make new calculations or design new approaches to the target once the strike force is airborne.[33]

The attacking forces also will attempt to achieve surprise by using deception, disinformation, and general military cunning. This will include the widespread use of electronic countermeasures (ECM) which must be coordinated among attacking groups and their combat support at all phases of the mission.

A substantial number of fighter aircraft would accompany and support the attacking aircraft. In addition to close escort fighters, some special maneuver groups may be organized to engage enemy aircraft en route to intercept positions. Others, perhaps even including air defense fighters, would be held in reserve to repel enemy air attacks on friendly airfields and facilities.

The increased range and effectiveness of fighter-bombers and fighters assigned to Front Aviation enable them not only to support penetration by aircraft belonging to Long Range Aviation, but also to participate in attacks on enemy airfields in the depth of the attack zone. In East Germany the Soviets have a complete replica of the USAF base at Bitburg in the Federal Republic against which Group of Soviet Forces, Germany (GSFG), Air Forces ground attack missions are regularly flown. It should also be noted that Front Aviation aircraft are capable of delivering nuclear weapons.

A sub-category of conventional air operations probably would include small groups assigned to attack airfields deep in the enemy's rear. This mode of attack would be particularly important against aircraft dispersed to secondary or auxiliary airfields that were not under direct attack.

Despite the technological advances evident in current Soviet aircraft, it is common knowledge that they cannot match on a one-for-one basis the technical capabilities of Western aircraft such as the F-15. Thus, a prime prerequisite will be numerical superiority in air-to-air fighters. This is a doctrinal tenet that is more than a means to compensate for technological inferiority. The so-called technological gap, however, has been significantly narrowed, perhaps nearly eliminated, by the appearance of the FULCRUM and FLANKER fighters. This principle of superiority in numbers is derived from Soviet historical experience. Even during the initial period of World War II, when the Russians were being severely beaten, the Red Air Force was able to mass its aircraft to achieve quantitative local superiority of three-to-one in fighters in order to drive off the attackers. Although the ratio varied slightly during subsequent operations, no major offensives or counter-offensives were attempted by the Russians until they were assured of meeting the doctrinal requirement for numerical superiority.

The importance attached to numerical superiority is evident in Soviet aircraft production figures. The Soviet aircraft industry outproduces the United States in fighter aircraft by a factor of about two-to-one. This amounts to approximately 1,000 new fighters and fighter-bombers (not counting helicopters) each year. A typical two year production run would be equivalent to all the US tactical fighters in Europe, all US fighter replacements (including the National Guard and Reserve), plus the fighter inventory of NATO allies in the Central Region. Put another way, Soviet military aircraft production is sufficient to replace all the front line aircraft of the Royal Air Force every six months.

INTO THE 1990s

The relationship of Soviet aviation to combined arms doctrine has played, and will continue to play, a key role in Soviet operational doctrine and its relationship to strategy and comprehensive military doctrine. Developments in Soviet operational-tactical aviation during the latter half of the 1980s will reflect what the Politburo, with much advice from the General Staff, perceives as necessary to ensure that the Air Forces will be able to implement the principles of its operational art. This is, of course, a reactive process as advances in Western capabilities and their impact on Soviet military operations are evaluated. But equally important is the influence of doctrine in determining what technological capabilities and tactical innovations are needed to carry out the Politburo's politico-military strategy.

The Soviet Union's military-industrial complex has been particularly impressive in the 1970s and early 1980s in filling the norms imposed upon it by defense planners. A list of aircraft developed during the last decade, even without considering the remarkable increase in production, is testimony to the determination of the defense establishment to revitalize Front Aviation. Among these aircraft are FISHBED-K, L, N; FOXBAT-B, D; FOXHOUND; FLOGGER-B, D, G; FULCRUM; FENCER-A, B, C; FITTER-C, D; FLANKER; FROGFOOT; HIND-A, D, E; and HIP-E.

The new aircraft of the seventies probably will undergo a series of modifications during the next decade to enhance their capabilities and in some cases introduce new capabilities.[34] Look-down, shoot-down radar is just one example of technological progress in fighter-interceptors. In the ground attack field, more and better precision-guided weapons with greater stand-off range for FENCER, FITTER, and FLOGGER appear probable, with special emphasis on missiles designed to attack Western SAM systems such as ROLAND II and PATRIOT. Attack helicopters will become more plentiful and increasingly sophisticated as close air support systems and anti-armor hunter-killers. Tactical integration of HIND and FROGFOOT in combating armor and helicopters may be realized. There will be helicopters that are capable of air-to-air combat against other helicopters or even fixed-wing aircraft.

Although the Soviets conceive of innovation and initiative in terms conditioned by Marxist-Leninist theory and their own historical and social experience, it is likely that the armed forces will begin to turn away from traditional dependence on centralized control and toward greater freedom at the tactical level. As technological capabilities expand the scope of possible actions and decisions, the Soviets will have to acknowledge that tactical flexibility at the lower echelons is possible only through individual initiative. This will be particularly true for Soviet pilots who function in a fluid and nonpredictable environment. Tactical maneuver, dogfighting, and the freedom to decide the attack option, now largely confined to the pages of military journals, are expected to become realities in the early part of this decade. Free hunt operations, for example, will become a standard operational-tactical practice, especially in combating NATO's mobile missile systems.

It is certain that both fixed-wing and rotary aircraft will continue to play a vital role in Soviet combined arms theory. Developments in the 1970s and 1980s have provided balanced, technically sound offensive tactical air forces which provide a basis upon which the Soviets can build and diversify through the 1990s.

NOTES

1. *Voyenno-Vozdushnyye Sily* (VVS) denotes military air forces and includes *Dal'nyaya Aviatsiya* (Long Range Aviation) and <u>Frontovaya Aviatsiya</u> (Front Aviation).
2. Major General S. N. Kozlov (ed.), <u>The Officers Handbook</u> (Moscow: Military Publishing House, 1971).
3. *Protivo Vozdushnaya Oborona Sukhoputnikh Voysk* (anti-air defense of ground forces) was the term used until recently to designate the air defense forces whose mission was to provide close-in defense of troop units. *PVO Strany*, or Air Defense of the Nation, was the term for air defense forces whose mission was to defend the homeland. As missile ranges increased and as Soviet aviation and missiles were required to interface with other Warsaw Pact forces, the designations became clumsy and have been dropped in favor of just *PVO* air defense. At the same time (1982), some reorganization took place. Its nature is not yet fully understood.
4. Major systems include the SA-4 GANEF, SA-6 GAINFUL, and SA-8 GECKO. (See also Chapters 3 and 4.) The first two systems have one tracked vehicle outfitted with tracking and guidance radar, with other tracked vehicles serving as transporter-erector-launchers (TELs). The SA-8 is a wheeled system capable of moving at higher road speeds with vehicle columns. Since each tracked or wheeled vehicle has its own missile <u>and</u> radar, there is a decrease in launcher readying time. Other systems include the hand-held, infra-red guided SA-7 GRAIL; the SA-9 GASKIN; and the ZSU 23-4 which can fire its 23 mm anti-aircraft cannons while on the move. Follow-on systems are in the pipeline as indicated in Chapters 3 and 4.
5. The idea that Soviet pilots may exercise initiative and independence in aerial combat is not universally accepted. Nevertheless, Soviet writings about tactics emphasize the requirements for pilots to be able to fly and fight in an independent mode. Soviet experience in World War II, and that of their clients in Southeast Asia, has shown that more than 75 percent of the aircraft they shot down were hit on the first controlled pass from aft angles of approach. When given the choice, this would be their preferred tactic.
6. Colonel Yu Bondarev, "In a Complex Situation," <u>Red Star</u>, 28 July 1979, p. 1.
7. General of the Army A. A. Radzievskiy, "The Art of Gaining Victory," <u>Soviet Military Review</u>, June 1978, p. 26.

8. Marshal of Aviation Kutakhov, *Pravda*, 18 August 1974, pp. 1, 5.

9. Newer aircraft have two to three times the operational range and up to four times the payload of such predecessors as the MIG-17 FRESCO and the SU-7 FITTER-A.

10. The East German version of the HIP-E is even more heavily armed with six guided antitank missiles in addition to the six 57 mm rocket pods and an aimable machine gun.

11. V. K. Savkin, The Basic Principles of Operational Art and Tactics (Moscow: Military Publishing House, 1972), p. 241.

12. Colonel V. Izgarshev, "Helicopter Crews," Red Star, 27 August 1979, p. 2.

13. In another instance, a helicopter flight leader recounted how his sub-unit had to operate simultaneously with fighters and fighter-bombers, albeit at different altitudes, and emphasized that the exercise provided his pilots with rich experience in providing fire support for the ground force subunits while flying formation at low altitude.

14. V. G. Reznichenko, Tactics (*Taktika*) (Moscow: Military Publishing House, 1966), p. 76.

15. V. G. Reznichenko, Tactics (Moscow: Military Publishing House, 1974). This text also stresses the use of nuclear weapons far more than the 1966 version.

16. V. K. Savkin, "Characteristics of Modern Warfare," Military Herald (*Voyennyy Vestnik*), #3, March 1974, p. 25.

17. US tank gunners train to destroy Soviet helicopters with the tank main gun, and are confident that they will get first round kills. The new HAVOC helicopter is much more agile then the HIND or HIP and will be considerably harder to hit with the tank main gun.

18. Colonel M. Belov, "How to Fight Helicopters," Soviet Military Review, September 1979, pp. 18, 19.

19. Belov, ibid., p. 19.

20. Reznichenko, op. cit., p. 86.

21. Savkin, op. cit., p. 45.

22. Colonel A. A. Sidorenko, The Offensive (Moscow: Military Publishing House, 1970), p. 124.

23. Colonel I. V. Timokhovich, *Operativnoye Iskusstvo, VVS v Velikoy Otechestvennoy Voynie*, Air Forces Operational Art in WW II (Moscow: Military Publishing House, 1976), p. 16 ff.

24. The point at which tank armies take over the main thrust of the attack, assault crossings of water obstacles, and the retention of bridgeheads are other situations in which operational air supremacy operations will increase.

25. In World War II, the *STAVKA* (Headquarters, Supreme High Command).

26. Colonel L. Semeyko, *Voyennaya Mysl'*, No. 1, 1968, quoted in Leon Goure and Michael J. Dean, "The Soviet Strategic View," Strategic Review, No. 4, 1979, p. 89.

27. In late October or early November 1941, for example, the *STAVKA* ordered the Air Forces commander to conduct an air operation lasting from November 5 to 8 for the purpose of destroying German aircraft on their airfields. Three hundred Russian aircraft were to make simultaneous strikes on 19 airfields. The operation was planned by the Air Forces staff with orders written by the Air Forces headquarters and signed by the General Staff.

28. Chief Marshal of Aviation P. S. Kutakhov, "Air Forces in the Past and in the Present," *Voyennaya Mysl'*, No. 10, 1973. This short article is an excellent appraisal of aviation developments, including air doctrine and operational art, and much of the discussion concerning the phases in the development of Soviet Aviation is based on it.

29. Lt. General M. Gareyev, "*Vsegda na strazhe zavoyevaniy oktyabrya*" (Always Guarding the Gains of October), *Voyenno-istoricheskiy Zhurnal*, No. 11, 1977, pp. 19-21.

30. Marshal of Aviation P. S. Kutakhov, "The Conduct of Independent Air Operations," *Voyenno-istoricheskiy Zhurnal*, No. 6, 1972, pp. 20-28.

31. Dual capable fighter-interceptors such as FLOGGER-D and G; FISHBED-K, L, N; and future variants of these aircraft could also participate in anti-SAM activity, although their more likely mission would be counterair.

32. Combined arms doctrine provides for the possibility of other services participating in neutralizing air defenses. Heliborne raids by special subunits, such as the Brigada *spetsial'novo naznacheniya*, against specific systems are but one example of actions which might complement the air operation.

33. Lt. General V. Korochkin, "Break through to the Strike Target: New Weapons and Tactics," <u>Red Star</u>, 11 July 1979.

34. In line with a precedent established with the MIG-21 FISHBED, the modification of aircraft of the 1970s will result in a series of new letter designations for the NATO code names running through most of the alphabet. For example, FLOGGER-Bs will disappear and be replaced by Js, Ks, Ls, etc.

Chapter 6
Assessment of the Soviet Ground Forces

In assessing the capabilities of a nation's armed force, a number of questions arise. First, what are we assessing? This would seem to be rather straightforward but, for the most part, Western countries do not organize their forces as do the Soviets. The Soviet military establishment is divided into Strategic Rocket Forces, Ground Forces, Air Forces, Naval Forces, and Air Defense Forces.

The Soviet Union has several organizations that bear arms but do not come under the Ministry of Defense and usually are not considered part of the armed forces. They are the *KGB* troops, which belong to the Ministry of State Security; the *MVD* troops, which come under the Ministry of the Interior; and the paramilitary "civil police" or militia. Both the *KGB* (*Komitet Gosudarstvenniy Bezopasnost'* - Committee of State Security) and the MVD (*Ministerstvo Bnutrennikh Del* - Ministry of Internal Affairs) are organized similarly to Soviet Ground Forces units. These three organizations and units that are part of "national" air defense (formerly *PVO Strany*) will not be considered in this analysis. On the other hand, airborne forces that wear the Soviet Air Force uniform, and air defense forces of the field troops (formerly *PVO Voysk*) are included.

The Ground Forces of the Soviet Union will be assessed relative to those of NATO or of the Chinese People's Republic since they would be the two most likely foes of the USSR. The intent here is not a net assessment, but a judgment of what the Soviet Ground Forces can do. The assessment will measure, using Soviet standards, the capability to perform several tasks:

(1) Defense against US forces acting independently, NATO troops including US forces, or China.
(2) The ability to seize major areas of Western Europe or of China in a major conflict.
(3) The requirement to perform internal security in support of KGB and MVD troops which, although they cannot be forgotten, will not be addressed except in general terms.

Next the assessment assumes that the Soviet Ground Forces will be engaged principally in Central and Western Europe or on the Chinese border in the immediate future (1985-1990) before major changes are likely to be made in the organizational structure or capabilities of the Soviet armed forces.

Appraisal will be in terms of the Ground Forces' ability to carry out operations in either a nuclear war, a non-nuclear war, or a nonnuclear war that may go nuclear at any moment. Standards applied will be absolute where possible, and, if not absolute, relative to NATO or Chinese forces. The principal element in this evaluation will be an assessment of how well the Ground Forces can fulfill the norms it has set for itself.

The Soviets continually evaluate their own ability to meet norms. We must recognize that the Russians prefer empirically (scientifically) derived formulas to inexact experimental means. Lastly, many of the norms they have established are kept secret; some are not publicly revealed even after they are well known and understood in the West. A large number, however, appear in open literature.[1]

Over the years, many qualified observers have been allowed to attend Soviet exercises and maneuvers, such as: Afghans, Americans, Britains, French, East and West Germans, and a host of others including attaches, liaison officers, and trainees. Many of these observers, with good military backgrounds or experience in the area of a particular norm, have appraised the performance of Soviet units. Their reports, combined with careful analysis of published data and interviews with Soviet military personnel and emigres, have made possible what is believed to be a careful assessment.

How well do the Soviets meet the norms they have set? For the most part, the answer must be based on an analysis of observations by outsiders, that are limited in scope. The Soviet Union and the Communist Party must be very uneasy about the ability of their Ground Forces, as presently equipped, to perform assigned roles against NATO and China simultaneously. Hence, in a Soviet Union besieged by economic problems, the Communist Party continues to supply its armed forces with:

(1) New and improved equipment in quantities that are lavish by NATO standards;
(2) More and larger divisions; and
(3) More man-days for reserve and paramilitary training taken from production of civilian goods.

Obviously, the USSR believes the armed forces are not meeting equipment norms. Events in Afghanistan have given them little reason to be confident of their forces operating as aggressors in hostile territory where partisans can be expected.

There are some severe problems that the Soviets have created for themselves in their training and operational methods. Generally speaking, Soviet force ratios (page 163) require at least 3-to-1 superiority of forces for a successful offensive. This ratio is to be achieved not by massing huge formations on line, but by introducing new formations in time- phasing called echeloning. To achieve the proper time-phasing, very tight timing is required as illustrated by the contingency commitment shown in Figure 4.22. Assuming that the deployed units manage to achieve their norms for sustained combat, there is still a very narrow window for the introduction into combat of the battalion's second echelon companies. Even for Army second echelon divisions, the window is only about a day and a half--a very tight schedule. For the divisions of a Front second echelon Army, it is also about a day and a half, since these units are deployed at substantial distances to the rear for the dispersion required in case of nuclear action. As a result, extensive movements are essential prior to commitment to combat.

A measured length of time is required to get units of whatever size from road march configuration into an assembly area and from the assembly area back into the road march. During these periods, substantial bunching up of vehicles is most apt to occur, and units are vulnerable to attack by nuclear or improved conventional weapons. Units that occupy assembly areas during the daytime periods between movements also are vulnerable to such attacks. The Soviet solution to the problem of massing to achieve successful combat ratios in the face of nuclear weapons has serious difficulties. Timing is very tight, and control must be exercised by electronic means in order to ensure that units maintain their integrity during transit time. With today's radio electronic combat means and improved surveillance, it no longer is feasible for units to escape detection on the march. The range of modern surface-to-surface missiles and the penetration capability of modern aircraft and cruise missiles make units vulnerable several hundred kilometers from the forward edge of the battle area.

The effectiveness of guided munitions against bridges in North Vietnam makes it clear that the West has the capability of destroying bridges over all major European and East Asian rivers in the areas of Soviet advance. In particular, the Elbe, Oder, Weser, and Rhine could be serious obstacles to Soviet movement if bridges were destroyed in a carefully orchestrated interdiction program. The bunching up that would occur creates a vulnerable target not only for nuclear weapons, but also for conventional munitions.

The first objective of the Soviet forces is to defend the Soviet motherland and the territory of its allies against external aggression. The second basic objective derives from their view of the nature of war: only offensive action can achieve decisive results. Soviet doctrine, force structures, combat support systems, and training all indicate that the Russians would prefer a relatively short military campaign should war break out in Western Europe or in China. They would hope to seize critical territory in Western Europe or Asia in a very short campaign before defensive positions could be established or reinforcements rushed to allied areas. To achieve this objective, they need the advantage of a surprise attack, covered by deceptive actions, that will permit them to gain and keep the initiative.[2] Should it be necessary to use weapons of mass destruction, those weapons would be used in a manner that complements the conventional combat capability of Soviet forces. The Soviets deny any plan to use either nuclear or chemical weapons, and their literature imputes first use of such weapons to NATO forces. Nevertheless, the Soviets continue to make important improvements in their nuclear and chemical forces, and practice complementary military operations that include using nuclear, chemical, and biological weapons. We must expect these weapons would be used should war occur in Europe or the Far East and conventional weapons do not suffice.

Soviet capabilities are all designed to overcome an excellent defense in depth, which they may expect to encounter in Europe and China should surprise not be achieved. That is why they have given particular emphasis to techniques for creating deception and surprise. If these techniques are successful, the Soviets might occupy NATO or Chinese territory without using nuclear weapons. An analysis of Soviet military writings indicates that rates of advance of 30 to 40 kilometers a day can and must be achieved in any operation against an enemy defense. During the exploitation phase, rates of advance are expected to increase to 50 to 80 kilometers, and perhaps to 100 kilometers a day.

If deception and surprise fail, rates of advance would be forced by carefully planned conventional fires, using artillery and air. Nuclear and chemical munitions might have to be employed to augment conventional suppressive fires. Although these rates of advance are twice those used in breakthroughs and exploitation operations in World War II[3], the Soviets believe that with their modern suppression systems and improved armored fighting vehicles, the increased rates can be sustained for a few weeks.

Soviet military operations will be executed with combined-arms armies equipped to provide four important combat functions: suppression, maneuver, support, and defense. These four functions are discussed in the following paragraphs.

The success of operations is dependent on the mutually supporting activities of target acquisition systems, air forces, artillery, maneuver units, engineer and logistic support systems, and the protection provided by air defense and antitank units. The momentum of the offensive is sustained by an organization that allows division subunits to be echeloned or subordinated to another attacking regiment. The independent forces of an Army and of the Front commander also can be attached to the echeloned divisions. All aviation is controlled by the Front commander, and a Front has large quantities of artillery and armored fighting vehicles, and many transportation and engineer units in its various Army and Front units.

The means of suppression are artillery, multiple-rocket launchers, close air support, mortars, helicopter gun ships, and surface-to-surface missiles. A wide variety of conventional, nuclear, and chemical munitions is available and allows what is termed "complementary combat." Important maneuver elements are tanks of various classes and armored infantry and reconnaissance vehicles. The defense forces consist of theater and Army air defense and anti-armor systems that include wheeled or tracked units and a large number of man-portable systems. Combat support elements include trucks, railroads, helicopters, and fixed-winged aircraft. Also available is an abundance of engineering units, equipped with a wide variety of excellent bridging and river-crossing equipment.

The suppression means in Soviet Front organizations can be broken into several major groupings, one associated with supporting a breakthrough, others with exploitation. The exploitation-oriented functions are conducted by tanks supported by artillery attached to the maneuver forces, as well as the engineering, river-crossing, and logistic systems. The forces available to a Front commander are substantial and appear adequate. There is a great deal of flexibility for offensive operations.

The Soviet program for modernizing artillery has resulted in a large increase in the number of artillery tubes in motorized rifle and tank divisions. Today, the Soviet division has artillery equal or superior in both quality and quantity to that of a typical US division. The number of multiple-rocket launcher tubes, a component lacking in many Western armies, also has been increased. Many Soviet artillery pieces are now self-propelled. The range of 122mm and 152mm systems has been increased, as much as 40 percent for the 152mm. The 130mm howitzer has always had a good range (30 kilometers) and firing rate (6 rounds per minute). The increase in salvo rate since World War II is dramatic. During World War II, a division salvo was 2 tons; for artillery alone, it has been increased to more than 3 tons and, if multiple-rocket launchers are included, to almost 19 tons. The shock power of Soviet artillery is apparent. Artillery available to a Soviet division can be increased from 72 or 96 guns to more than 400 guns through reinforcements provided by a Front or Army.

The increase in numbers and quality of Soviet artillery with its high firing rates, mobility, and increased range provides much-improved suppressive firepower to the Soviets, and better survivability on a nuclear battlefield. In particular, flexibility of the Soviet organization and the large amount of artillery held by the Front commander provide superior combat potential for conventional artillery suppression.

One of the most remarkable improvements in Soviet capability for suppression has occurred in Frontal aviation. The introduction of newer aircraft during the past ten years has provided Frontal aviation with a 4-fold increase in payload and a 2.5-fold increase in range. Today, combat support aircraft compare favorably with those of the Western powers. In the early 1960's, forward deployment of Frontal aviation could provide combat support to cover only one-third of West Germany with units based in the German Democratic Republic. Today, many Frontal aircraft operating from deep bases, can cover all NATO airfields. In addition, the MIG-23 and SU-19 are capable of delivering conventional or nuclear ordnance to NATO bases, even when flying at low altitudes. The majority of Soviet Frontal aircraft are now of supersonic swept-wing design, including variable geometry. Their ground attack capability is comparable to that of NATO air forces, but the avionics of Western aircraft are probably superior. Air and antiaircraft capabilities of the Soviet forces, however, probably can guarantee air superiority over the Soviet rear areas.

Soviet surface-to-surface missiles can use both nuclear and chemical warheads, and Soviet forces are provided good chemical protective systems. Individuals have protective suits, and there is unit equipment for the detection and removal of chemical agents from troops and equipment. As a result of their operations in Afghanistan, Soviet forces have more experience with offensive use of chemical and biological weapons in actual combat than any other army.

Soviet electronic warfare ability exists at all levels, with the capability to attack key nodes, key communications, and weapons. Soviet jammers are land-, sea-, and air-based, and are being modernized. Modernization in command and control accompanying these developments has resulted in increased speed, reliability, and redundancy at all levels. In addition, there has been extensive development of hardened communications systems. There is no reason to assume that the Soviets cannot meet their command and control requirements in the environment for which engagement was designed--conventional large-scale war.

The combat potential of Soviet artillery clearly is able to meet established norms. Qualitative improvement, increased numbers, and organizational arrangements provide the ability to mass and effectively deliver large volumes of suppressive force on enemy fire weapons and antitank systems. In breakthrough operations, it is believed this suppressive fire would be quite effective. Also, roughly 80 percent of the main ground attack aircraft are now of very high quality. Soviet maneuver units equipped with armored fighting vehicles in lavish quantity and superb quality undoubtedly can meet the norms that have been set.

Because Soviet military doctrine calls for seizing the initiative early in an offensive, maneuver is one of the most important elements of Soviet tactical and operational art. Exploitation-oriented functions are assigned to tank formations. With the highest priority assigned to tanks, the Soviet Union has put vast resources into solving the problems associated with tanks and tank formations. Over the last three decades, the Soviet Ground Forces have been lavishly supplied with new tanks and tank- supporting equipment.

In World War II, the Soviet T-34 was a very fine tank, able to stand up to German Tiger and Panther tanks which, on the Western front, gave the Allies considerable difficulty. The T-34 was modernized several times during World War II to increase the bore of its main armament, ending up with an 85mm cannon. It later gave Western armies trouble right through the Korean War. The T-34 was succeeded by the T-54, which was designed around a 100mm cannon and became the mainstay for the Soviet army, and in various modernized forms, for all the satellite and surrogate forces for many years. The T-62 came into the inventory in the early 1960's with a 122mm armor-piercing discarding-sabot round. In the 1970's, this tank was superseded by a newer main battle tank, the T-72, with an improved suspension system to provide for lower ground pressure and to ensure longer time between tread failure. Several points are important here:

(1) Soviet design bureaus developed three successful main battle tanks in the same time that the US and UK each turned out one and the Germans two.
(2) Older models continue in service, even in the Soviet army.
(3) All Soviet tanks have diesel engines for long operating radii, collective protection against chemical attack and nuclear radiation, and deep

fording capability. Night vision devices, stabilized main armaments, and, recently, advanced sighting equipment and improved armor are common features.

At least as important as the constant improvement in the quality and quantity of tanks is the steady upgrading of equipment for formations in which the tanks operate. Artillery weapons that were the best in service in any modern army, have been replaced by a more mobile towed howitzer and, most recently, by a family of self-propelled howitzers. The accompanying infantry has received several new vehicles of ever-improving quality. Innovation also is apparent in the organization of these formations.

The Soviet concept of the "advanced detachment" (*peredovoy otryad*) is now easier to implement because of the presence of independent tank battalions in the tank and motor rifle divisions.[4] The very concept of tank or motor rifle units may be giving way to a truly combined-arms unit as the number and quality of tanks and accompanying armored and self-propelled vehicles in the motor rifle units rises toward the number found in tank units. In terms of strength, mobility, and staying power, there is little to choose between the two types.

Maneuver of Soviet units is made more rapid and secure by both tactics and equipment, which to the Western military observer may seem profligate in money and manpower: high-speed ditching equipment for rapidly entrenching assembly areas, multiple-rocket launchers of many sizes, truck-launched gap-spanning equipment, and automatic mine-layers, to name a few. Although automation lags everywhere else in the Soviet Union, the army has an automatic ground navigation system for its artillery and automated fire control at the battery level.

Also extremely important is the Soviet use of air power, both fixed- and rotary-wing, to enhance the maneuver potential of ground forces. Fixed-wing aviation units give the commander the ability to interdict and isolate the battlefield and to provide substantial close support at the line of contact. Rotary-wing aviation is apparent in ever-increasing numbers and quality of armament. These units are under centralized control, to prevent frittering them away as transportation for senior officers.

In summary, the Soviets clearly can meet their norms for maneuver on the modern battlefield, even if nuclear weapons are not used. The Soviet Ground Forces have the capability for extensive use of nuclear weapons, but it does not seem to be in their best interest to use them unless conventional weapons fail to maintain an advance.

In recent years, the support capability of Soviet units (i.e., their ability to sustain themselves in combat) has been scrutinized by batteries of experts, and rightly so. A nation that cannot provide gasoline for tourists to get from Leningrad to Moscow apparently has plans for moving immense military forces from its borders to the English Channel. This may seem preposterous to those not familiar with Soviet history.

It must be remembered that, within the first few months of World War II, the Germans destroyed almost the entire Red army their intelligence organization told them existed at the start of the war. The Nazi's were confident that they had won, but they found 200 new divisions in front of Moscow and the German High Command never really recovered from the shock. The Russians did not forget those early German victories. As a result, the Soviet High Command has taken elaborate precautions to train large numbers of reserves and to stockpile immense quantities of war materiel. On the strategic side of the coin, the Soviets have prepared extensively.

On the operational/tactical side, they have wrought miracles since World War II. In addition to the early post-war GAZ-51 and ZIL-150 trucks, the Soviets have built a formidable modern logistics base including pipelines and computer controls. They have all the modern accoutrements: families of trucks with considerable interchangeability of spare parts, transport aircraft, helicopters, high-speed entrenching machines, and so forth. In addition, they have done some things that have been declared impossible, like building a floating railroad bridge.

Most examinations of Soviet logistics capabilities conclude that they are adequate to do what the Soviets say they want to do in a conventional war. In a nuclear war, however, there is considerable doubt that the Soviet Ground Forces could supply its forces in the face of a determined Allied targeting program that would require frequent Soviet transloadings and reroutings and would cause massive casualties in the echeloned forces. It is doubtful that the Soviets could maintain a time schedule designed to stun the West and then take advantage of the fear, panic, and surprise with a blitzkrieg movement.

The Soviet penchant for offensive combat has not persuaded them to adopt the French attitude of World War I, "*toujour l'attaque*", which ultimately led the French nation to disaster and resulted in the Maginot mentality. This, in turn, caused them to needlessly expend thousands of lives in another disaster a generation later. While the Soviets have concentrated on the attack, they have not neglected either doctrine or equipment for defense. Defense is considered a temporary or local phenomenon but one that must be conducted successfully in order that the offense may be resumed or carried on in another sector.

The most striking evidence of Soviet attention to defense is the abundance and quality of air defense equipment available to ground forces commanders. Superb air defense missiles have been available to the ground commander for more than two decades. The ground commander also is in charge of a substantial air capability for air defense. In addition to a network of surface-to-air missiles used for area defense, the Soviet commander has more than adequate column cover provided by a variety of modern multiple-barrel automatic cannons and mobile missiles with integral radar.

While self-propelled artillery is one of the keystones of the suppression essential to successful offensive, towed artillery is the key to a good defense. Soviet towed artillery is abundant and superb. It is present in formations down to the battalion, and ammunition supply in the defense is much easier than in the offense.

Another element of a successful defense is the ability to shift reserves and employ them at the proper time and place. The Soviets have a large number of helicopters and transport aircraft that can be used for this purpose.

Forces in defensive positions are far more dependent on secrecy and deception than are those on the offensive. This is an arena in which the Soviets excel. Their capability for deception exceeds that of all of their potential opponents. They have built a wide range of equipment for jamming and exercise it frequently on their own people. Occasionally, they also use electronic deception to lure foreign aircraft into error[5] in peacetime. In wartime, one can be sure they will use the full panoply of electronic equipment observed in the forward areas. In addition, the Soviets frequently describe their radio-electronic deception devices, such as electronic dummies, corner reflectors, and phony and offset transmitters, which they will use on the battlefield. As an example, one of the sergeants in the 24th "*Zheleznaya*" division, who deployed with it into Czechoslovakia, has described the deceptive radionets that were kept operating for more than a week at their old location just to confuse Western intercept units.

It is clear from the foregoing that the Soviet Union has an unparalleled and virtually invincible capability for defense in a conventional combat environment. There is no nation today that has the ability to penetrate Soviet antitank defenses, especially when backed up by the density of Soviet tanks on the battlefield, unless extensive use is made of nuclear weapons or improved conventional munitions. On the other hand, against an armed force equipped with a moderate number of nuclear weapons of all sizes or a large inventory of improved conventional munitions (ICM), the Soviet Union probably would be unable to maintain the norms it has set for the ratios of forces necessary to achieve victory.

TOWARD 2000

For several hundred years, the Russians believed that artillery and infantry vied for primacy on the battlefield. During the Soviet period, armor has held center stage briefly, as did the Strategic Rocket Forces during the Khrushchev regime, but both gave way to the present combined arms concept based on infantry.

Wars are initiated to achieve victory. Certainly, if the next war were nuclear, the Strategic Rocket Forces would be the most prominent arm, at least initially, but still within a combined arms concept. Victory in either a nuclear, or a more likely conventional, war can be won only by seizing and holding the enemy's territory with men on the ground; hence, the infantry is likely to remain the nucleus of the combined arms concept, although its traditional identity may be clouded by a fusion of forces.

The Soviet Union has come closer to creating a combined arms outlook among its forces than any other country. Starting from the level of the squad, the armored infantry (fighting) machine (BMP) comes close to uniting artillery, armor, and infantry.

The Soviets have so blurred the difference between "artillery" and mortars at the appropriate levels that artillery truly can be said to be integrated with infantry in the Soviet Ground Forces. Similarly, the Soviets have blurred the distinction between armor and infantry by emphasizing combined arms at the expense of tanks.[6] Not only does the BMP provide an armored fighting vehicle (AFV) at the lowest organizational levels but tanks are being integrated into the infantry at lower and lower levels.

Just as the French, British, and Americans learned in the jungles of Southeast Asia that tanks cannot do everything, so is the USSR learning the same painful lesson in Afghanistan. A determined infantryman with modern antitank weapons can be effective in any terrain where he can find concealment and cover, including the central European jungle of urban sprawl.

By no means do the Soviets consider the tank outmoded or ineffective. They do consider that it must be supported by infantry and artillery at the closest possible level. There is nothing in sight to indicate that they intend to alter that concept in the next fifteen years. Combined arms is the king of the battlefield. Firmly wedded to the primacy of combined arms branch, *obshevoyskoy rod voysk*, is the tactical/operational concept which we shall call the "daring thrust" because it most aptly describes it. When Phil Karber (former Congressional staffer, now with The BDM Corporation) used the term a few years ago, he was laughed off the platform by Soviet experts who had not yet seen the coming modernization of the Soviet force.

From the days of Tukhachevskiy, the Soviets have felt instinctively that the war of position was a "loser." As Fred Turner points out in his foreword, there is continuity right through to the operational maneuver group (OMG).

Daring is the right word to describe such a concept. If the commander does not have courage to expose his flanks and abandon his lines of communication, he cannot expect success on a fluid battlefield. He will be unable, almost by definition, to thrust through weak points in the enemy's defenses and seize critical nodes that can cause the enemy's rapid collapse. This assumes that the enemy has critical nodes; a possible defense against such a strategy by a powerful opponent is to not have critical nodes. Another defense against the daring thrust is a well organized defense in depth. If the thrusting force is quickly subjected to attrition on flanks and rear and its line of communications is nonexistent, its life will be short and the cost to the commander high. Clearly, the Soviets do not expect to meet such a resistance in the early hours of World War III.

Examples of "daring thrusts" are everywhere in Soviet literature from the *peredovoy otryad*, advance detachment, to the mobile group, to the OMG. The idea is the same in all. At the earliest possible moment, force a highly mobile combined arms team through the enemy's position as far as possible to seize the most vital objective it can. The size of the team can be a reinforced motorized rifle company, when it is called an advanced detachment, or a two division tank corps, when it is called an operational mobile group. The depth of objective is limited only by the skill and daring of the commanders, the one who sends and the one who goes. New historical examples are created every day as Soviet authors edit history to suit the need.

What kind of organization can best accomplish the daring thrust? It must have:

- Artillery to suppress antitank weapons;
- Tanks to kill tanks and the lightly armored vehicles;
- Helicopters to destroy self-propelled artillery and tanks;
- Infantry to solve the difficult problems;
- Engineers to solve the impossible problems; and
- Communications to keep the act together.

It must have a flexible command structure so that daring thrusts can be organized at any level without difficulty. The brigade concept with many independent battalions would do such a job, and is being tried in the Air Assault Brigade. Another likely solution is to add more regimental headquarters to provide the division commander with flexibility.

A tank force tailored to the daring thrust role might typically be comprised of:

- One tank regiment;
- One artillery regiment;
- One MR battalion (this battalion will undoubtedly be a mix of tank and BMPs);
- One helicopter battalion including one antitank company;
- One artillery company and one utility company;
- One signal company; and
- One engineer company.

This would lead to a tank division of:

- Three tank regiments;
- One MR regiment;
- Two self-propelled artillery regiments;
- Two towed artillery regiments;
- One helicopter regiment; and
- One signal regiment, including a tactical battalion and one operational strategic battalion.

That organizational scheme would give a division a total of 16,500 troops. This force would include two "new" elements: a large helicopter addition and a large signal increment, both required for the new deep strike or daring thrust concept.

In recent years the Soviets have introduced new types of helicopters in ever increasing numbers. They have written extensively on the use of helicopters in the fire support and antitank/anti-helicopter roles (e.g., <u>Red Star</u>, August 5, 1981, LTG V. Kostyler/June 21, 1983, Central Asia M.D.). They also have increased their deployments of helicopter units in the forward areas. Air assault brigades have appeared in all the Front sized forces, and helicopter squadrons in each division, intended to fill antitank, anti-helicopter, and especially anti-antitank roles as well as all the usual utility roles.

The MRD would be the inverse of this division for use in jungles or urban warfare. The Soviets will preserve their tradition of tank and motorized rifle just as they have for nearly a century.

NOTES

1. Some believe these are part of a hoax designed to mislead the enemies of the Soviet state. However, the open publications are, in general, the only training publications available. The effort required to promulgate two different standards and be sure that all the troops in more than 175 divisions, spread over one-sixth of the earth's land surface, learned only the correct norms would be immense, even for the Soviet Army.

2. The Soviet Union's Manchurian campaign against the Japanese Army is an historical example of a successful campaign that receives great emphasis in Soviet professional literature. It is claimed that Soviet forces achieved both strategic and tactical surprise. An examination of Soviet writings on this campaign indicates that multiple-phased axes of advance would be established, and a necessary rate of advance would be forced by applying massed conventional suppressive fires.

3. At that time, Soviet tank forces were able to move at about 45 to 50 kilometers a day in the exploitation phase, while combined armed forces advanced roughly 25 to 35 kilometers per day.

4. The concept has been extended to larger formations in the Operational Maneuver Group which is easier to implement because of the presence of self-propelled artillery and helicopters.

5. In January 1962, a T-39 was decoyed into East Germany and shot down over Erfurt; a month later, an RB66 was similarly lured into East Germany and shot down over Gardelegen. In 1984, a Korean Air Lines jet was probably lured into Soviet air space and shot down.

6. One of the few changes which Chernenko signed into law (26 April 1984) in his brief term as head of the USSR was the elimination of senior positions for Tank officers while retaining the position of Chief Marshal of Artillery. The net result is a strong push for the concept of combined arms while reaffirming the relative importance of the Strategic Rocket forces.

Glossary

ACTIVE RADIO JAMMING *(AKTIVNYYE RADIOELEKTRONNYYE POMEKHI)* - Jamming can be either electromagnetic, acoustic or optical and can be effected by signals generated locally or by retransmitting signals from other sources. Jamming can be of several forms, such as: IMITATIVE - placing false information on display screens; *MASKING* - generating background noise to interfere with displays; or RESPONSIVE - triggered by an external source. (p. 616)*

ADVANCE TO CONTRACT *(CBLIZHENIYE)* - A march in anticipation of a meeting engagement in which a unit moves from one location to another while maintaining unit integrity and in which the march organization establishes the organization for combat. (p. 657)

ADVANCE GUARD *(AVANGARD)* - A detachment proceeding ahead or behind the main body of a marching unit in order to protect the troops manning the march, to safeguard them from surprise attack by hostile ground forces, and to ensure suitable conditions for the main body to deploy and enter the battle. (p. 9)

AERIAL RECONNAISSANCE *(VOZDUSHNAYA RAZVEDKA)* - One of the main types of reconnaissance which obtains information concerning enemy targets of the ground, in the air, or at sea. Air reconnaissance is done by reconnaissance aviation units, by reconnaissance subunits of aviation units, and by all air crews carrying out combat missions. Air reconnaissance is accomplished both by piloted aircraft and by unmanned means in support of the combined operations of major units of all services of the armed forces. Among the principal methods of air reconnaissance are visual observation, aerial photography, and the use of radio-technical facilities. (p. 148)

AIR DEFENSE *(PROTIVOVOZDUSHNAYA OBORONA (PVO))* - Defense against the air enemy. Air defense is the complex of combat operations of the various air defense forces and weapons at the disposal of strategic or major field forces of ground troops, conducted for the purpose of repulsing strikes by enemy aviation and missile units against troops and their rear installations, in coordination with national air defense forces. (p. 597)

---

* Numbers at the end of definitions indicate the page in the Soviet Military Encyclopedic Dictionary, Military Publishing House, Moscow, 1983, on which the definition can be found.

AIR DEFENSE ARTILLERY *(ZENITNAYA ARTILLERIYA)* - A type of artillery intended for engaging air targets. It is a part of ground and naval forces' air defense. It includes towed, self-propelled, and stationary weapons of small (20-60mm), medium (60-100mm), and large (over 100mm) caliber, radar stations, and fire control systems. The 57-, 100-, and 130mm guns are the main types in the Soviet army. They can be used against surface (ground or water) targets. (p. 275)

AIR DEFENSE MISSILE UNITS *(ZENITNYYE RAKETNYYE VOYSKA)* - Units armed with air defense missiles. Organizationally, they are part of the air defense troops. (p. 276)

AIR OBSERVERS *(VOZDUSHNIYE NABLYUDATELY)* - A function of air defense reconnaissance, observers who are posted in all units when operating close to enemy forces or in areas where enemy attack is considered likely.

AIR PREPARATION (PHASE) *(AVIATSIONNAYA PODGOTOVKA)* - Air strikes which take place before an attack by ground forces for the purpose of defeating the enemy. They are usually carried out simultaneously and in conjunction with artillery strikes. Air preparation is carried out by Frontal (Tactical), Army, and sometimes Long-Range Aviation. Air preparation is subdivided into preliminary (begins 1-3 days before the offensive) and direct (continues from 10-15 minutes up to 1.5-2 hours). Priority of targets is: nuclear strike capability, command posts, tank and artillery concentrations, centers of resistance, strong points, aircraft, and nearby airports and crossings. (p. 12)

AIR SURVEILLANCE POST *(PUNKT NABLYUDENIYA ZA VOZDUKHOM)* - A function of air defense reconnaissance established in defensive operations, usually on terrain offering good visibility, near command posts, and/or close to air defense units in firing positions.

AIRBORNE ASSAULT FORCES *(VOZDUSHNO-DESANTNIYE VOISKA)* - A service branch intended for combat operations in the enemy's rear. Organic to these forces are air-droppable tanks, self-propelled artillery, and other units and detachments of the special forces and the rear services. (pp. 148-149)

AIRBORNE ASSAULT *(VOZDUSHNYY DESANT)* - Troops airlifted to the enemy rear to conduct activities there. According to its scale, an airborne assault may be tactical, operational, or strategic. The assault may be effected either by parachute, from landed aircraft, or by a combination of both. (p. 229)

AIRBORNE COMMAND POST *(VOZDUSHNYY PUNKT UPRAVLENIYA)* - Aircraft or helicopters equipped for controlling troops (forces) during combat operations. It is a command post element and can be used as a secondary command post. Usually manned by the commander or his deputy and a group of officers. (p. 150)

AIRBORNE DIVISION *(VOZDUSHNO-DESANTNAYA DIVIZIYA)* - The basic combined arms operational-tactical formation of airborne troops. It consists of several regiments, artillery battalions, subunits of the various services, and special troops. An airborne division is intended to carry out missions in the enemy's deep rear, in coordination with ground troop and missile force formations, and also with the air force and navy.

AIRBORNE OPERATION *(VOZDUSHNO-DESANTNAYA OPERATSIYA)* - Actions coordinated and interrelated by a single concept and plan, involving airborne troops, the air force, missile forces, and air defense forces in connection with the transfer, landing and support of large airborne assault forces in the enemy rear, to obtain operational and strategic objectives. (p. 148)

ALTERNATE COMMAND POST *(ZAPASNYY KOMANDNYY PUNKT (ZKP))* - A control post deployed at the same time as the command post and intended for immediate assumption of control in the event that the command post is put out of action, threatened with destruction, or becomes difficult or impossible to use. Personnel in an alternate command post must know the situation and must be well informed concerning orders and instructions being issued for the troops. Radio facilities of an alternate command post maintain uninterrupted communications with the command post and forces being controlled. An alternate command post is usually organized in a defensive situation. (p. 266)

AMBUSH *(ZASADA)* - A type of combat operation used by troop subunits in reconnaissance for the purpose of capturing prisoners, documents, and samples of the enemy's weapons and combat material. (p. 269)

AMPHIBIOUS TANK *(PLAVAYUSHCHIY TANK)* - A light tank capable of negotiating water obstacles.

ANTITANK ARTILLERY *(PROTIVOTANKOVAYA ARTILLERIYA)* - Artillery intended for use against enemy tanks, self-propelled artillery mounts, and armored personnel carriers. Usually, they deliver direct fire from open firing positions. (p. 600)

ANTITANK GUIDED MISSILE *(PROTIVOTANKOVAYA UPRAVLYAEMAYA RAKETA (PTUR))* - A weapon designed to engage tanks and other armored targets. It usually has a hollow warhead, solid-fuel engine, on-board guidance, and the means for receiving and deciphering command signals. (p. 600)

APPROACH MARCH FORMATION *(PREDBOYEVOY PORYADOK)* - A troop grouping, differentiated frontally and in-depth to ensure less vulnerability to weapons of mass destruction, artillery fire, and air strikes, rapid maneuvering of troops on the field of battle, rapid deployment of troops into battle formation and rapid reversion to the march formation, and high speeds of movement and rapid negotiation of zones of contamination and devastation. (p. 585)

ARMY ARTILLERY GROUP *(ARMEYSKAYA ARTILLERISKAYA GRUPPA (AAG))* - An artillery group intended for missions in support of a main army group combatting enemy tactical nuclear assault and artillery, destroying reserves, command posts, and other important targets, and reinforcing 1st echelon division artillery fire on the main axis of advance. (p. 48)

ARTILLERY *(ARTILLERIYA)* - One of the service branches possessing great fire power. Also a type of weapon, or the aggregate of armament items, including the entire complex of a firearm and all the equipment needed for its effective utilization in combat. (pp. 49-50)

ARTILLERY COUNTERPREPARATION *(ARTILLERIYSKAYA KONTRPODGOTOVKA)* - Massed artillery fire by a defender against an enemy who is preparing or deploying for an attack. Artillery counterpreparation is done in conjunction with nuclear strikes and, in combination with air counterpreparation, for the purpose of breaking up an attack or weakening the enemy's initial thrust. (Soviet Military Encyclopedia, Vol I, pp. 265-266)

ASSAULT DETACHMENT *(SHTURMOVOY OTRYAD)* - A battalion augmented with regimental and division artillery, air defense, tanks, and engineer assets. (p. 822)

ASSAULT GROUP *(GRUPPA PRORYVA)* - An augmented company-size group under an assault detachment. This unit is the predominant tactical formation in military operations in urban terrain.

ASSAULT LINE *(ISKHODNYY RUBEZH)* - A prearrranged line from which a unit proceeds to fulfill a combat mission (a march, an attack, etc.). An assault line or line of departure is defined by clearly visible landmarks on terrain or on a map. (p. 303)

ASSAULT WATER CROSSING *(DESANTNAYA PEREPRAVA)* - An operation whereby troops cross a water barrier which is either held by the enemy or under enemy observation, using assault crossing equipment. (p. 549)

AUDIBLE SIGNALS - The use of signals such as sirens, whistles, and horns to communicate orders.

AVIATION STRIKE GROUPS - Groups of two to three air divisions capable of conducting independent operations against key targets at operational and strategic depths. They could also support ground maneuver formations at operational and tactical depths. (p. 762)

BACTERIOLOGICAL WEAPONS *(BAKTERIOLOGICHESKYYE ORUZHIYA)* - (A foreign term) Missiles, artillery shells, and mines consisting of microbes and the toxins caused by micro-organisms, both of which are intended for the mass destruction or incapacitation of people or animals, and destroy plants or food supplies. (pp. 80-81)

BARRIER CROSSING *(PEREPRAVA PREGRADY)* - The crossing of a water barrier (river, canal, lake, bay, reservoir, etc.). Can be: by a landing operation, by a temporary bridge, fording, on ice, with underwater tanks, by ferry, or a deceptive crossing. (p. 549)

BRIDGE CROSSING *(MOSTOVAYA PEREPRAVA)* - One of the methods whereby troops may cross a water obstacle. Also, a bridge, together with the adjoining sectors of terrain, equipped for the passage of troops. A bridge crossing permits continuous movement by troops, and possesses the capacity for a high rate of traffic, and is therefore the best method of troop transit when negotiating water obstacles. (p. 549)

BRIDGE EQUIPMENT *(PONTONNYY PARK)* - Authorized items issued to engineer troops and intended for erecting pontoon bridges and arranging ferry crossings. Bridge equipment is made up of various materials and is of diverse design and load-carrying capacity (up to 40 tons). Bridge equipment is transported on motor vehicles. When afloat, it may move under its own power or be towed. (p. 539)

BRIGADE *(BRIGADA)* - A formation of troops from different service branches and special troops from the various services, consisting of several battalions (artillery battalions) and special subunits. There are motorized rifle brigades, motor transport brigades, railroad brigades, etc. (p. 101)

CHEMICAL RECONNAISSANCE (PATROL) *(KHIMICHESKIY RAZVEDYVATEL'NIY DOZOR) (KhPD)* - A patrol sent out to gather information concerning the character and extent of radioactive, chemical or biological (bacteriological) contamination. The patrol is usually made up from the radiation or chemical intelligence services or from detachments of the chemical troops or motorized rifle (tank) forces. The patrol can operate independently or in company with tactical reconnaissance units, etc. (p. 618)

CHEMICAL WEAPONS *(KHIMICHESKOYE ORUZHIYE)* - (A foreign term) Artillery and mortar shells, missiles, mines, and aircraft sprayers which disseminate chemical agents as either a liquid or a vapor. The major types of chemical agents are nerve, blood, blister, choking, psychochemical, and irritant. (p. 794)

COMBAT RECONNAISSANCE PATROL *(BOEVOY RAZVEDYVATEL'-NIY DOZOR) (BRD)* - A patrol sent out in the course of a battle and in the absence of direct contact with the enemy from a motorized rifle (tank, airborne or marine, *(morskoy pekhoti)*) battalion, but sometimes from a regiment. It operates in advance of or on the flank of the combat formation of its own detachment. (p. 618)

COMBAT SERVICE SUPPORT *(OBESPECHENIYE VOENNYKH DEYSTVIY)* - Complex measures directed toward the support of forces at high combat readiness, the preservation of their combat effectiveness, the creation of favorable conditions for organized and timely entrance into battle and the successful execution of all assigned missions and also toward preventing enemy surprise attacks and the lessening of the effectiveness of his attacks. (p. 496)

COMBINED ARMS ARMY *(OBSCHEVOYSKOVAYA ARMIYA)* - A major field force which usually consists of 3-4 and up to 10-13 infantry divisions and 1-2 detached air assault brigades and other formations and units. The numbers and types of combat support and combat service support elements vary from one Army to another. Armies are capable of independent operations, but are normally committed as part of a front. (p. 47)

COMMAND/CONTROL/COMMUNICATIONS-C^3 - The system which details the responsibilities of a unit commander and his subordinate commanders, to include the establishment of a series of command posts for the exercise of control over a combat operation, and the establishment of the communications network necessary for effective control. (Western term)

COMMAND AND OBSERVATION POST *(KOMANDNO-NABLYUDATEL'NYY PUNKT) (KNP)* - A control post from which subunits receive direction in combat. A command and observation post in accommodated in an armored personnel carrier, tank or shelter and, during combat operations, it is a part of the combat formation of the subunit, located in a place from where it may best observe the enemy, the operations of its own and neighboring subunits, and from where it may exercise continuous control. (p. 343)

COMMAND POST *(KOMANDNYY PUNKT) (KP)* - The main post for the control of troops in units and major field forces, from which constant direction of the troops is accomplished, as well as various measures directed toward ensuring successful activities when fulfilling assigned missions. The site of a command post is decided by the commanding officer and is usually at such a distance and in such a direction from the troops that convenient and continuous command and control of the troops in the operation will be assured. In particular cases, the site of a command post will be decided by the superior command. A command post must be mobile and highly maneuverable, thus permitting command and control of troops under conditions of rapid and abrupt changes in the situation. Command posts must be deployed covertly and dispersed, taking account of all measures of support. (p. 343)

CONTAMINATED AREA *(ZONA ZARAZHENIYA)* also *(ZARAZHENIYE MESTNOSTI)* - An area contaminated by chemical or bacterial agents or radioactive substances. (p. 268)

CONTROL LINES *(RUBEZH REGULIROVANIYA)* - Terrain lines, designated in advance by the senior commander, which the troops must reach or go through at a certain time and in a certain formation. (p. 641)

COUNTERATTACK *(KONTRATAKA)* - An attack undertaken by defending troops against an attacking enemy for the purpose of putting him to rout or destroying him and achieving complete or partial restoration of the position lost by the defending troops. A counterattack consists of defeating the enemy troops which have made the breakthrough by air strikes, missiles, artillery and mortars with subsequent attacks by 2nd echelon forces in coordination with 1st echelon forces. Counterattacks are carried out, as a rule, at the moment when the enemy is wedged in and has stopped but has still not had time to consolidate his position or, his advance has slowed and it is impossible to use reserves or to introduce them into the battle quickly. A counterattack is concluded by the capture and holding of designated boundaries. (p. 352)

DECONTAMINATION *(SANITARNAYA OBRABOTKA)* - The removal of radioactive substances from personnel, and rendering harmless and eliminating toxic and bacterial agents. Decontamination may be partial of complete. (p. 655)

DEFENSIVE BELT *(OBORONITEL'NYY RUBEZH)* - A section of the terrain occupied or prepared by engineers for occupation by troops for conducting defensive operations. Defensive belts are laid out as 1st belt, a space, and then the 2nd belt or an army belt or a front belt. In deep defense, isolated defensive belts may be created. (p. 499)

DEFENSIVE OPERATION *(OBORONITEL'NAYA OPERATSIYA)* - The aggregate of battles fought in individual sectors for the purpose of disrupting an enemy offensive still in preparation or already begun, and also for the purpose of gaining time and creating favorable conditions for going over to the attack. A modern defensive operation is based on the use of nuclear strikes and strikes with all other types of weapons, on the extensive use of maneuver with fire, forces, and weapons, and on counterattacks, imparting an aggressive and decisive character to the defense. (p. 498)

DELIBERATE ATTACK *(ZABLAGOVREMENNO PODGOTOVLEN-NOYE NASTUPLENIYE)* - A planned and coordinated mounted or dismounted attack from forces in contact. The attack is heavily supported by artillery and is organized in echelons.

DEPLOYMENT LINE *(RUBEZH RAZVERTYVANIYA)* - The sector of terrain on which troops deploy from march formation or approach march formation into combat formation. (p. 641)

DIRECT FIRE *(PRYAMAYA NAVODKA)* - A type of gun-laying performed by direct visual at the target. Direct fire is delivered from open firing positions and from tanks, against stationary or moving targets. Direct fire is delivered at short range and is distinguished by the high accuracy and speed with which the assigned fire mission can be accomplished. (p. 602)

DISMOUNTED FORMATIONS - Combat formations in which the infantry deploy from their APC/IFVs to engage the enemy on foot.

DIVISION ARTILLERY GROUP *(DIVIZIONNAYA ARTILLERYSKAYA GRUPPA) (DAG)* - An artillery group intended for fighting an enemy's tactical nuclear weapons and artillery, destroying his reserves, radio electronic equipment and control points, and for reinforcing regimental artillery fire on the main axis. The DAG includes artillery weapons of one or several calibers. (p. 48)

ECHELONMENT, TROOP (FORCES & RESOURCES) *(ESHELON-IROVANIYE VOISK (SIL I SREDSTV))* - Deployment of units and major field forces or strategic formations in depth (in the case of aviation, also by altitude), in accordance with the concept of the plan for impending combat operations or maneuver.

EFFECTIVE RATE OF FIRE *(BOYEVAYA SKOROSTREL'NOST') (ORUZHIYA)* - The greatest number of rounds which may be fired in a unit of time (usually one minute) from a given weapon without damaging it, taking into account the time needed for reloading, changing aim, etc. (p. 677)

ENCIRCLEMENT *(OKRUZHENIYE)* - Isolation of an enemy grouping from the rest of his troops. Encirclement is most often achieved by troops advancing in convergent directions. Under modern conditions, the encirclement and destruction of the enemy are simultaneous, ensured by effective use of nuclear weapons and by the great mobility of troops. (p. 512)

ENGINEER RECONNAISSANCE *(INZHENERNAYA RAZVEDKA)* - Obtaining and assembling information on the following: defensive works, obstacles, and nature and degree of engineer preparation on the terrain at the disposal of the enemy; the state of the roads, bridges, river crossings, and hydrotechnical works, possibility of the terrain, and its protective and camouflaging qualities in the area of impending action; water sources; and the presence of local facilities and materials needed to support combat operations of the troops. (p. 290)

ENGINEER SUPPORT *(INZHENERNOYE OBESPECHENIYE)* - Assistance provided to combined arms operations for maintaining a high rate of advance in the offensive and for preparing positions in the defense. Some engineer responsibilities might include: constructing, repairing, and developing roads, bridges, river crossing equipment; operating water purification systems; constructing barriers; detecting and laying mines; providing fire protection and cleaning damage; and camouflaging defensive positions. (p. 290)

ENVELOPMENT, CLOSE *(OKHVAT)* - A troop maneuver accomplished in tactical and fire coordination with the troops acting from the front. Close envelopment is used for the purpose of inflicting decisive and sudden strikes on enemy flanks and rear. (p. 531)

ENVELOPMENT, DEEP *(OBKHOD)* - A troop maneuver in depth which is performed in tactical or operational coordinated action with troops advancing from the front. Deep envelopment is used for the purpose of inflicting decisive, surprise strikes on enemy flanks and rear. (p. 500)

FERRY CROSSING *(PAROMNAYA PEREPRAVA)* - A method whereby troops are transported across a water obstacle by ferries. Also a water obstacle of limited extent, both sides of which are provided with landing stages and approach roads. Depending on the width of the water obstacle, from one to three ferries shuttle between the landing stages. The ferries are assembled from authorized bridge trains, or from among locally-available craft (small vessels, barges, boats, etc.). A ferry crossing is intended to carry tanks, artillery with tractors, and other combat material which cannot be transported in assault landing craft. (p. 549)

FIRE CONTROL *(UPRAVLENIYE OGNEM)* - The aggregate of organizational measures and activities performed by commanders and staffs for the purpose of effective use of fire to destroy the enemy under specific conditions of the situation. Fire control includes: use of target reconnaissance data; transmission of target designations; assignments of fire missions; determination of initial settings for conducting fire; call for fire (or "cease fire"); adjustment of fire; maneuver with fire; and checking the results of firing. (p. 766)

FIRE SACK *(OGNEVOY MESHOK)* - Preplanned fires of artillery and other weapons in specific areas such as in conjunction with minefields or obstacles, against an attacking enemy in order to inflict maximum losses. (p. 508)

FIRE SUPPORT *(OGNEVAYA PODDERZHKA)* - Successive neutralization and destruction of the enemy by concentrated artillery fire and air strikes in the course of an offensive, for the purpose of ensuring a rapid advance by attacking troops. Fire support is conducted by various means, and to the entire depth of the troops' combat mission. (p. 507)

FIRST ECHELON *(PERVYY ESHELON)* - That part of an operational order of battle or combat order of troops which is in the first line or in close contact with the enemy and is used to carry out specific missions. (p. 547)

FLANK ATTACK *(FLANGOVYY UDAR)* - An attack directed at the flank of an operational, combat or march formation of troops with disengagement at the rear of the enemy's main forces. A flank attack is one of the types or methods of maneuver. (p. 780)

FLANK SECURITY *(OBESPECHENIYE FLANGOVI STYKOV)* - Arrangement and operations of forces directed at excluding surprise and repulsing enemy strikes along formation and unit flanks and the intervals between them *(STYK*-COORDINATING POINT). Reciprocal action is organized between adjacent formations and units to carry out continuous reconnaissance, maneuvers on the flanks are carried out by the 2nd echelon and reserves, plans are made for strikes by missile forces, aviation, artillery and other means, and engineer obstacles are built. (p. 497)

FORWARD COMMAND POST *(PEREDOVOY KOMANDNYY PUNKT)* - A major field force command post, deployed near the troops on the 1st echelon, from which the commander controls the troops in action in the main sector, when control of them from the main command post becomes difficult. A forward command post is also used for troop control purposes when the main command post is being moved or has been put out of action. (p. 548)

FORWARD DETACHMENT *(PEREDOVOY OTRYAD)* also **ADVANCED DETACHMENT** - A detachment of troops consisting of a tank or motorized infantry unit or subunit reinforced by subunits of special troops. In offensive combat, a forward detachment is put out ahead of a combined arms unit to seize and hold important lines and objectives, major road junctions, mountain passes, or bridgeheads on the opposite bank of a river, pending arrival of the main body. In defensive combat, a forward detachment is sent out to conduct defensive actions in the security zone. (p. 548)

FRONT *(FRONT)* - The highest strategic formation of armed forces. It may include units, formations, and major field forces or strategic formations of ground forces, air forces, and sometimes even naval forces. Also, a term used to designate the forward zone of a country at war where armed conflict is taking place. Under modern conditions of nuclear missile warfare, the distinction between front and rear has virtually disappeared. (p. 787)

FRONTAGE *(SHIRINA FRONTA)* - The width of a unit's area of responsibility.

FRONTAL ATTACK *(FRONTAL'NYY UDAR)* - An attack which is directed at the strength of the enemy and is sometimes employed because of the failure or inability to attack on the flanks. When possible, it will be conducted in coordination with flank attacks. (p. 787)

HASTY ATTACK - A rapid mounted attack off the march against a stationary defender. Forward deployed artillery is used in the attack.

HASTY DEFENSE *(POSPESHNO ZANYATAYA OBORONA)* - A defense created by troops in the course of combat operations. At the beginning of its organization, such a defense is characterized by the following: an insufficient developed and organized fire plan; hurriedly organized coordination; insufficient development of the system of engineer structures; weak exploitation of the terrain; and insufficiently stable control. A hasty transition to defense, under modern conditions, may stem from the following: the need to repulse counterstrikes by superior enemy forces in the course of offensive operations as a result of an unsuccessful meeting engagement; the efforts of a defender to halt, with his reserves, further advance of enemy troops which have broken through on some intermediate line; and also, in a withdrawal, when the retreating side, defended by rear-guard elements on an intermediate line, tries to extricate the main body under attack.

HELIBORNE OPERATIONS *(VERTOLETNYY DESANT)* - Operations which are limited in size, scope, depth and frequency to tactical operations by availability and capability of helicopters. They afford rapid maneuver, and require less training than airborne operations.

ILLUMINATION FIRE *(STREL'BA OSVETITEL'NYMI SNARYADAMI)* - Lighting support for night defense for the purpose of illuminating the ground area or blinding the enemy. Illumination is carried out by artillery and mortar elements.

INTELLIGENCE *(RAZVEDKA)* - The means through which the enemy is identified as to location and disposition and target options assessed. Also identifies terrain features, weather conditions, and radiological/ chemical conditions. (The Soviets do not differentiate between Intelligence and Reconnaissance and use only one word to name both but distinguish many kinds of razvedka.) (p. 616)

LINE COMMUNICATIONS *(PROVODNAYA SVYAZ')* - Communications accomplished by field and permanent cable and overhead lines. With the aid of line communication facilities and the corresponding station equipment, several types of communications may be effected, such as telephone, telegraph, photo-telegraph, and television communications. Line communication facilities ensure high-quality telephone, telegraph and phototelegraph communications regardless of the time of day or year and atmospheric interference, and also ensure convenience in operation, relative security of conversations and transmissions, and the possibility of multiplexing to obtain several channels on one circuit. (p. 593)

LOGISTICS *(MATERIAL'NOYE OBESPECHENIYE)* - Satisfying force requirements for weapons and military equipment, ammunition, POL, provisions, clothing, medical technical stores and other material resources. (p. 431)

LONG-RANGE RECONNAISSANCE *(DAL'NYAYA RAZVEDKA)* - Reconnaissance conducted by platoon-size detachments 50 to 100 kilometers in front of the main body.

MAIN BODY/MAIN FORCE *(GLAVNYYE SILY)* - The principal part of forces and equipment designated for the execution of the primary mission. The main force includes the staff, attached and support forces and equipment of all branches of troops and special forces. (p. 195)

MANEUVER *(MANEVR)* - An organized transfer of troops or naval forces, a redirection of weapons, or a redistribution of material and technical facilities, for the purpose of gaining an advantage over the enemy under conditions for conducting military operations. As a result of a maneuver, a favorable grouping of men and equipment is created in a given sector or theater of operations. According to its scale, a maneuver may be strategic, operational or tactical. (p. 421)

MARCH *(MARSH)* - An organized movement of troops in column by road and/or crosscountry route for the purpose of arriving at a designated region. A march may be made to the front, from the front to the rear, or along the front. The distance covered in a day will depend on the degree of troops effort and the degree to which motor transport is used. The goal of forthcoming combat operations, and the probability of an encounter with the enemy enroute are considered when setting up a march formation. (pp. 428-429)

MARCH FORMATION *(POKHODNYY PORYADOK)* - A troop formation, consisting of columns, for use on a march. It must ensure the following: high speed of advance and maneuver; rapid deployment for combat; conservation of strength of personnel and vehicles; and ease of troop control. (p. 583)

MARCH SECURITY *(POKHODNOYE OKHRANENIYE)* - The safeguarding of troops on the march by advance guards, rear guards, detachments, outposts, and patrols. (p. 583)

MARCH SECURITY DETACHMENT *(POKHODNAYA ZASTAVA)* - An element of march security. The march security detachment is detailed from the advance guard, or directly from subunits or units for which security is provided. A march security detachment may be in the forward, rear or flank category. (p. 583)

MEETING ENGAGEMENT *(VSTRECHNYY BOY)* - Actions of detachments, units or formations in which both sides are attempting to carry out an assigned offensive mission. It can occur: during a meeting with the enemy on the march; in an offensive while repulsing counterattacks or counterstrikes; during a skirmish with enemy forces sent out to close a breach in the defenses or to occupy important boundaries; on the defense during the conduct of counterattacks and counterstrikes and during operations against air or sea landing forces. A meeting engagement is characterized by: rapid approach of the sides and an entrance into battle from the march; a tense struggle for seizing and maintaining the initiative; development of combat operations on a wide front; insufficient clarity of the situation, its frequent and sharp changes; the limitations of time for the organization of combat operations. The most important conditions for success in a meeting engagement are: continuous reconnaissance, timely making of decisions and rapid sending of missions to the forces; the creation, ahead of time, of the necessary groups of forces and equipment, forestalling the enemy by conducting fire strikes, by deploying and moving groups of forces to the attack and conducting with them strikes on the flanks and in the rear of the enemy main forces. (p. 168)

MILITARY OPERATIONS IN URBAN TERRAIN (MOUT) (US term) - Offensive or defensive missions conducted in heavily populated cities and towns. Urban combat is characterized by increased difficulties in command and control (and therefore, a need for greater independence by subordinate commanders), restrictions on maneuver, observation and fields of fire, and fragmentation of a battle into numerous actions fought by combined arms teams.

MINE-CLEARING PLOW *(NOZHEVOY TRAL)* - Equipment attached to a tank which is designed to uncover or push aside mines which cannot be cleared using a mine roller attachment. (p. 749)

MINE ROLLER *(KATKOVYY TRAL)* - An accessory that can be mounted on the front of a tank, or special engineering vehicle for making safe passages through antitank mine fields. A roller attachment makes a two-rut channel, leaving an uncleared median strip, which is cleared by a second pass, by detonation, or by other means. (p. 749)

MINEFIELD-BREACHING TANK *(TANK-TRAL'SHCHIK)* - A tank equipped with a mine roller, a mine plow, or a mine roller/plow combination. (p. 749)

MINELAYER *(ZAGRADITEL')* - An engineering vehicle intended for rapid laying of antitank mines in the ground or by distributing them on the surface of the earth. (p. 260)

MOBILE OBSTACLE DETACHMENT *(PODVIZHNYY OTRYAD ZAG-RAZHDENIY) (POZ)* - A detachment made up of engineer subunits (or units) with the means of constructing obstacles in sectors which show promise for enemy tank counterattacks, and of covering troops and limiting points. A mobile obstacle detachment carries out its mission in close cooperation with the antitank reserves, with the subunits (or units) in action in the given sector or, independently. (p. 564)

MOBILE SUPPLY BASES - At division level, supplies which are generally maintained aboard vehicles. These bases are approximately 25-40 kilometers behind the FEBA.

MOTORIZED RIFLE BATTALION *(MOTOSTRELKOVVY BATAL'ON)* - A combat organization which consists of a staff, three motorized rifle companies plus combat support and combat service support units. (p. 69)

MOTORIZED RIFLE COMPANY *(MOTOSTRELKOVAYA ROTA)* - A combat organization which consists of three motorized rifle platoons, one antiaircraft missile squad, one weapons squad, and a company headquarters. (p. 640)

MOTORIZED RIFLE DIVISION *(MOTOSTRELKOVAYA DIVIZIYA)* - A combined arms formation which consists of six or more regiments: three motorized rifle regiments, one tank regiment, one artillery regiments, and one surface-to-air missile regiment. In addition, various combat support and combat service support units are included in a motorized rifle division. (p. 233)

MOTORIZED RIFLE PLATOON *(MOTOSTRELKOVYY VZVOD)* - A combat unit consisting of three motorized rifle squads and one headquarters section. (p. 128)

MOTORIZED RIFLE REGIMENT *(MOTOSTRELKOVYY POLK)* - A basic combined arms organization and most common maneuver element of the Soviet ground forces which consists of three motorized rifle battalions, one tank battalion, and one artillery battalion plus combat support and combat service support units. The regiment usually operates as part of a division but is capable of short-term independent operations. (p. 572)

MOTORIZED RIFLE SQUAD - A combat unit consisting of one infantry fighting vehicle or one armored personnel carrier with a two-man operating crew and a seven-man fighting squad.

MOVEMENT SUPPORT DETACHMENT *(OTRYAD OBESPECHENIYA DVIZHENIYA) (OOD)* - A temporarily-created group of engineer subunits (mostly road engineer subunits), together with chemical and radiological reconnaissance subunits, assigned by a combined arms unit to support the movement of troops. A movement support detachment carries out reconnaissance, removes obstacles from the route to be used, organizes by-passes around debris and obstacles, marks the route, and also does a limited amount of road repair work. (p. 530)

NEGOTIATING WATER OBSTACLES *(PREODELENIYE VODNYKH PREGRAD)* - The crossing of water obstacles by troops, accomplished either with combat (i.e., and assault crossing), or without combat activities. (p. 519)

NON-NUCLEAR WARFARE ENVIRONMENT (US term) - Combat conditions that might involve conventional, chemical, or biological warfare operations but not operations involving nuclear weapons.

NUCLEAR WARFARE ENVIRONMENT *(YADERNAYA VOYNA)* - An environment in which nuclear weapons are the principal means of destruction. (p. 842)

NUCLEAR WEAPONS *(YADERNOYE ORUZHIYE)* - The general term for weapons whose action is based on the utilization of intranuclear energy liberated as a result of nuclear reactions, namely fission, fusion, or both simultaneously. Nuclear weapons include missiles and aerial bombs having a nuclear charge. (p. 842)

OBSERVATION POST *(NABLYUDATEL'NYY PUNKT) (NP)* - A specially equipped place from which the activities of friendly and enemy units are observed on the battlefield. (p. 468)

OBSTACLES *(YESTESTVENNYYE PREPYATSTVIYA)* - Local features and elements in the relief of the terrain, a sector, or separate region which slow down or stop movement, thus hampering troop combat actions, especially the use of combat vehicles. Also natural obstacles, such as rivers, canals, marshes, high ground with steep slopes, ravines, cliffs, and dense forests, which can facilitate the strengthening of a defense. Obstacles can change depending upon the time of year and the weather. (p. 254)

OFFENSIVE OPERATION *(NASTUPATEL'NAYA OPERATSIYA)* - The aggregate of nuclear strikes, coordinated and interrelated with regard to target, time, and place, and the vigorous, offensive actions of the troops of a Front or an Army, accomplished in accordance with a unified concept for the attainment of operational or strategic goals. The general purpose of an offensive operation is to destroy enemy means of nuclear attack, break up enemy main groupings, and seize regions of operational or strategic importance. According to its scale and the forces and weapons involved, an offensive operation may be an Army or a Front operation, but in either case, it will be conducted by ground troops in coordination with the other services. (p. 476)

OPERATIONAL ART *(OBSCHEVOYSKOVOYE OPERATIVNOYE IS-KUSSTVO)* - Combat activity conducted by operating formations of Fronts (the basic formation) and Armies (the basic combined arms formation). In a campaign, operational art, the basis of military art, governs the preparation and conduct of operations at the level of Fronts and Armies within a Theater of Military Operations. The operational art is the connecting link between strategy and tactics. Operating within the requirements of strategy, it determines the means of preparation and conduct of operations for the achievement of strategic aims, and it provides the initial data for tactics, organizing for the preparation and conduct of battle. (p. 515)

OPERATIONAL MANEUVER GROUP (OMG) - An operational level (i.e., Army, division) detachment which is inserted through the enemy line to carry out an independent large scale mission.

OPERATIONAL RECONNAISSANCE *(OPERATIVNAYA RAZVED-KA)* - A most important type of support for the combat operations of troops, being the aggregate of measures adopted by commanding officers and staffs of units and major field forces of all services of the armed forces, branches, and special services for the purpose of obtaining intelligence concerning the enemy, the terrain, and the radiation and chemical situations in the region of the forthcoming actions. Operational reconnaissance is conducted by reconnaissance subunits and by troops directly engaged in combat operations. (p. 617)

OUTPOST *(ZASTAVA)* - The means of guarding troops on the march (march security detachment) and in static deployment (guard outpost). (p. 269)

PERIMETER (ALL-ROUND) DEFENSE *(KRUGOVAYA OBORONA)* - A defense without an exposed flank, consisting of forces deployed along the perimeter of the defended area. (p. 377)

PERSISTENT CHEMICAL AGENTS *(STOYKIYE OTRAVLYAYU-SHCHIYE VESHCHESTVA)* - Agents which can retain their disabling or lethal characteristics, depending on their physical-chemical properties, the method of use, meteorological conditions, and the nature of the terrain, for several hours, days, or even weeks. (p. 529)

POL - Petroleum, oil, and lubricants. (US term)

POLITICAL INDOCTRINATION *(POLITICHESKAYA RABOTA V BOYEVOY OBSTANOVKE)* - The system of measures in propaganda, agitation, and political education, implemented by political organs, Party, and Komsomol organizations, commanders, and political workers, among servicemen and the civilian population in the zone of combat operations, and also among enemy armed forces personnel and population.

PREPARATORY FIRE *(OGNEVAYA PODGOTOVKA ATAKI)* - Powerful prepared strikes with artillery, missile and aviation delivered prior to the start of an attack, for the purpose of neutralizing and destroying the most important enemy installations which are not to be destroyed by nuclear weapons, and for the purpose of rendering the enemy incapable of offering organized resistance to the advancing troops. (p. 507)

PREPARED DEFENSE *(ZARANYEYE PODGOTOVLENNAYA OBORONA)* - A type of combat operation conducted for the purpose of repulsing an attack mounted by superior enemy forces, causing many casualties, retaining important regions of terrain, and creating favorable conditions for going over to a decisive offensive. Prepared defense is based on the following: strikes by nuclear and all other types of weapons; on extensive maneuver with firepower forces, and weapons; on counterattacks with simultaneous stubborn retention of important regions which intercept the enemy direction of advance; and also on the extensive use of various obstacles. Prepared defense makes it possible to gain time and to effect an economy in force and weapons in some sectors, thereby creating conditions for an offensive in others.

PROTECTIVE FIRE - In defensive situations, final protective fires which are planned within 100 meters of the FEBA to halt the advance of enemy forces that may break through the defenses. (p. 508)

PURSUIT *(PRESLEDOVANIYE)* - An attack on a withdrawing enemy, undertaken in the course of an operation for the purpose of finally destroying or capturing his forces. Destruction of a withdrawing enemy is achieved by hitting his main body with strikes from missile units and aircraft, by artillery fire, by relentless and energetic parallel or frontal pursuit, by straddling his withdrawal route, and by the pursuing troops attacking his flank and rear. Pursuit is conducted in march, approach march, or combat formation. For deep penetration into the enemy's withdrawal route, tank troops are used in the first instance, but airborne assault forces may also be employed. (p. 587)

RADIO ELECTRONIC COMBAT *(RADIOELEKTRONNAYA BOR'BA)* *(REB)* - The use of radio jamming equipment to effect deleterious results on enemy C^3 and to intercept enemy radio transmissions. (The US terms are Electronic Warfare (EW) and SIGINT, frequently REC is used to refer to this Soviet activity.) (p. 615)

RAID *(REYD)* - Offensive action on a separate axis from the main attack(s). The raiding force may be as small as a battalion or as large as an Army, depending upon the depth and size of the objective. The mission of a raid is to destroy enemy rear area installations, to delay enemy reserves, to create disruption in the rear, to hold key areas or terrain features. Raids are normally carried out by tank units augmented by other assets. Air assault units may support or carry out raids. (p. 631)

REAR GUARD *(AR'ERGARD)* - March protection element, intended to safeguard troops moving from the front to the rear. Strength, composition, missions, and distance of a rear guard from the main body will depend on the size of the main body column being guarded and on the situation. (p. 51)

REAR SERVICES SUPPORT *(TYLOVOYE OBESPECHENIYE)* - The complex of measures related to the organization of rear services, to the preparation and utilization of all types of transportation routes and transport, to material, technical, medical, airfield engineering, airfield- technical, and other types of support and servicing. (p. 759)

RECONNAISSANCE IN FORCE *(RAZVEDKA BOYEM)* - One of the methods of reconnaissance, in which data on the enemy are obtained by the combat operations of subunits especially detailed for this purpose. Reconnaissance in force is done only in those cases where the necessary information about the enemy cannot be obtained by other means (for example, during military operations in urban terrain). (p. 617)

RECONNAISSANCE GROUP *(REKOGNOSTSIROVOCHNAYA GRUPPA)* - A party detailed by the commander or staff to reconnoitre an area of impending combat operations, or to the disposition of troops, combat material, control posts, etc. (p. 632)

RECOVERY DETACHMENT *(EVAKUATSIONNAYA GRUPPA)* - Units formed after CBR attack from organic subunits or from higher headquarters to conduct recovery operations, and which include chemical reconnaissance, motorized rifle, engineer, medical, and vehicle repair personnel.

RECOVERY OPERATIONS *(EVAKUATSIONNO - SPASATEL'NAYA SLUZHBA)* - In the event of CBR attacks, operations which entail restoring control, monitoring the area of destruction, conducting rescue work to include repair of vehicles and evacuation of wounded, extinguishing fires, performing decontamination of personnel and equipment, and forming new combat units from surviving ones and reinforcements.

REGIMENTAL ARTILLERY GROUP-RAG *(POLKOVAYA ARTIL-LERIYSKAYA GRUPPA-PAG)* - Artillery consisting of more than one artillery division, at the direct disposal of a regimental commander, assigned at the time of a battle to carry out missions on behalf of the regiment, and unified by a common command. It would normally be augmented by assets organic to the division. (p. 48)

REPAIR AND EVACUATION GROUP *(REMONTNO-EVAKUATSIONNAYA GRUPPA) - (REG)* - An organization formed at various echelons and consisting of a tracked recovery vehicle, a tank repair workshop van, and a parts truck. Vehicles or equipment damaged beyond the repair capability or capacity of the regiment will be evacuated to the division level and higher, if necessary. Evacuation is accomplished by the higher level assets. (p. 633)

RESERVES *(REZERVY)* - Part of the operational structure of a major field force or strategic formation, or part of the combat order of a unit. Also, the human and material resources which may be used in a war as a whole or in an operation. (p. 630)

REVERSE SLOPE DEFENSE *(OBORONA OBRATNOGO* (pronounced *OBRATNOVO) SKATA)* - A defense technique in which forces will be left in contact with the enemy on the forward slope of a hill, while the remainder of the force prepares the position on the reverse slope.

RIBBON BRIDGE *(MOST-LENTA)* - A truck transported bridge which has accordion-folded pontoons launched when the trucks are braked at the water's edge. They are automatically opened by a torsion-bar gravity, rotated manually 90 degrees, and quickly joined to form a continuous strip of floating roadway. Soviet motorized rifle and tank divisions have a half-set of 16 center pontoons and two end (ramp) sections in their engineer battalion. (p. 465)

ROUTE OPENING DETACHMENT - See Movement Support Detachment.

ROUTE RECONNAISSANCE *(RAZVEDKA MESTNOSTI)* - Measures taken to study the roads or cross country routes in a zone of impending action, and to determine their state, traffic capacity, vulnerable sectors, camouflage conditions, degree of demolition and contamination, and the availability of materials for road and bridge repair, so as to ensure the movement of troops, combat, and other materiel. (p. 617)

SECOND ECHELON *(VTOROY ESHELON)* - The part of an operational or combat formation of troops which is not directly participating in an engagement at a given moment, but which is intended to be used to build up the force of a strike during an offensive, to increase the stability and aggressiveness of defense, and to replace troops of the first echelon in the event that the latter sustains heavy losses. The existence of a second echelon creates favorable conditions for building up strength, carrying out a maneuver, or rapidly transferring effort from one sector to another during an operation. In contrast to a combined arms reserve, combat missions for a second echelon are assigned at the same time as those for the first echelon. (p. 376)

SECURITY FORCE *(OKHRANENIYA)* - A defensive screening force usually consisting of mobile units which seek to delay attacking forces before the attacker reaches the main defensive line. (pp. 531-2)

SECURITY ZONE *(POLOSA OBESPECHENIYA)* - A zone created ahead of the forward edge of defending troops. A security zone is created when there is no close contact with the enemy and usually consists of several positions, covered by obstacles and defended by the troops in action in the security zone. The depth of a security zone depends on the concept of the defense, the nature of the terrain, and the availability of time for its preparation. (p. 573)

SPETSNAZ - The Soviet special forces which are an integral part of the GRU, the Soviet military intelligence service. SPETSNAZ units are deployed with every Soviet Army, Front, and Fleet. Individual raiders (*reydoviki*) often serve abroad in civilian capacities such as truck driver etc to learn the language and terrain where they expect to be employed.

STRATEGIC OPERATIONS *(STRATEGICHESKAYA OPERATSIYA)* - Combat at a global, national, or theater level which is manifested in campaigns phased by objectives and time. The objectives of each phase are met by simultaneous and successive operations. The general groupings of operational formations. (p. 716)

STREAM CROSSING - See WATER CROSSING.

STRONG POINT *(OPORNYY PUNKT)* - That part of a defensive position which is most fortified, contains the most weapons, is most reinforced with obstacles, and which is equipped for all-round defense, primarily against tanks. A strong point is the main defensive position and is organized in the most probable sector of enemy attack. Strong points are equipped with trenches, communication trenches, shelters, and other defensive structures. They must be well camouflaged and connected to each other frontally and in depth by a unified fire and obstacle plan. (p. 517)

SUPPLY AND EVACUATION ROUTES *(PUTI MANEVRA PODVOZA I EVAKUATSII)* - Roads especially established in the operational rear and troop service areas, suitable for maneuvering the second echelon and for motor vehicles and other forms of transport used for supplying troop units with material and for evacuating wounded, sick, and equipment that is not needed. Supply and evacuation routes are subdivided into main, controlled, and reserve categories. The number of them depends on the situation, the state of the road network in the rear area, the possibility of maintaining them, and the demand for them. (p. 607)

SUPPLY STOCKPILES *(ZAPASY MATERIAL'NYKH SREDSTV)* - The quantity of the various types of materiel in regular supply which is to be maintained in troop units and in various rear services elements. According to their purpose, place of storage, and the unit responsible for them, stockpiles of supplies may be in the following categories: emergency, minimum level, mobile, center, front, naval, or army. Mobile supplies are sometimes grouped under the general classification "unit". (p. 266)

SURFACE TO AIR MISSILE-SAM *(ZENITNAYA UPRAVLYAYEMAYA RAKETA) (ZUR)* - A type of missile of the ground-to-air class, intended for antiaircraft or antimissile defense. The flight of a ground-to-air guided missile is controlled from the ground from the moment of launching until it approaches the zone of the target. The charge is detonated with the aid of a radio detonator installed at the missile itself. Such guided missile may be armed with a conventional or a nuclear charge. SAMs have a range of 0.5 to 700 km, target altitude 15 m to more than 30 km, weight of charge 8 kg to 7.3 tons, and speed of flight 270 to 1,700 m/sec. (p. 275)

TACTICAL AIR SUPPORT *(AVIATSIONNAYA PODDERZHKA)* - Air force combat operations conducted for the purpose of helping ground forces to achieve success in an operation. Air support is provided by the centralized forces and facilities of fighter-bombers, bombers, and winged missiles with a view to annihilating the enemy's nuclear attack facilities, his nearest reserve and command posts detected by reconnaissance, as well as important objectives on the field of battle which for some reason cannot be destroyed by unit weapons on the ground. In an attack, air support begins when friendly troops go over to the attack, and in defense, when the enemy troops begin their attack, and it continues throughout the entire period of combat operations. (p. 12)

TACTICAL LEVEL OPERATIONS - Combat activity conducted by large tactical units below the Army level such as divisions (*soyedineniye*), regiments (*chast'*), and battalion or smaller units (*podrazdeleniye*). Military tactics govern the conduct of combat action within any operation at the division level and below.

TANK ARMY *(TANKOVAYA ARMIYA)* - A major field force or strategic formation of ground troops which usually consists of two to four tank divisions and one or two motorized rifle divisions. The numbers and types of combat support and combat service support elements will vary from one Army to another. Armies are capable of independent operations, but are normally committed as part of a Front. (p. 47)

TANK BATTALION *(TANKOVYY BATAL'ON)* - A combat organization which consists of three tank companies plus combat service support.

TANK COMPANY *(TANKOVAYA ROTA)* - A combat organization which consists of three tank platoons and a company headquarters.

TANK CREW *(TANKOVYY EKIPAZH)* - One tank with a tank commander, driver/mechanic, and gunner.

TANK DIVISION *(TANKOVAYA DIVIZIYA)* - A combined arms formation which consists of six or more regiments: three tank regiments, one motorized rifle regiment, one artillery regiment, and one antiaircraft regiment. Other elements of the tank division are virtually identical to those of the motorized rifle division, except there is no antitank battalion or independent tank battalion.

TANK FORDING - Crossing technique for shallow water obstacles.

TANK PLATOON - A combat unit consisting of two tank sections and one headquarters sections.

TANK REGIMENT *(TANKOVYY POLK)* - A combined arms organization which consists of three tank battalions, one motorized rifle, and one artillery battalion plus combat support and combat service subunits but no antitank missile battery.

TANK SNORKELING - Technique by which specially equipped tanks can cross a water obstacle which is up to 5.5 meters deep.

TECHNICAL OBSERVATION POINT - Observation point formed in the forward area of each combat battalion to ensure prompt recovery and equipment repair during battle by monitoring the battlefield for damage, giving help to crews, and calling repair or recovery teams.

THEATER OF MILITARY OPERATIONS *(TEATR VOYENNYKH DEYSTVIY) (TVD)* - A particular territory, together with the associated air space and sea areas, including islands, within whose limits a known part of the armed forces of the country or coalition operates in wartime, engaged in strategic missions which ensue from the war plan. A theater of military operations may be ground, maritime, or intercontinental. According to their military-political and economic importance, theaters of military operations are classified as main or secondary. (p. 732)

TRAFFIC CONTROL *(REGULIROVANIYE DVIZHENIYA)* - A system of measures adopted to control troop and supply movements, regulate traffic, protect highway objectives, maintain order, and organize service points. Tropps of traffic regulator units are posed along routes of march of their parent unit (regiment or division) with special uniforms and equipment to guide vehicles of their parent unit. (p. 629)

VISUAL COMMUNICATIONS *(ZRITEL'NAYA SVYAZ')* - The use of signals such as flags, flares and pyrotechnics to communicate orders. (p. 280)

WATER STREAM CROSSING EQUIPMENT *(PEREPRAVOCHNYYE SREDSTVA)* - Floating equipment (organic, local, and improvised) and bridging structures, used by troops when negotiating water obstacles. Organic water crossing equipment is subdivided into individual, crossing and assault, pontoon bridge, treadway bridge, and sectional bridge categories. Individual water crossing facilities, i.e., flotation suits, pneumatic vests, etc., are used by individual soldiers to negotiate water obstacles, for work in water, and as lifesaving equipment. Local water crossing facilities include ships, barges, constrained ferries, and boats of various types. Improvised water crossing facilities include barrels, logs, planks, and other materials which may be used to build rafts or to provide extra buoyancy to individual soldiers swimming across a water obstacle with their weapons. (p. 549)

WATER STREAM CROSSING FROM THE MARCH - An operation whereby troops cross a water barrier against nonexistent or weak defenses and when the current and condition of the banks on both sides of the obstacle are favorable, using water crossing equipment.

A Few Words About Sources

Much of the material presented has come from personal contacts of the authors with Soviets over the "90 years," but by and large it has come from what is called "open source literature." It is called that because the Soviet society itself is closed, and one can neither talk with Soviet persons nor go to Soviet places nor read Soviet sources in the same sense that one can do in any other country in the western world. However, the Soviets publish an immense volume of literature in the military field which anyone can buy; by contrast this is "open" literature. There is also available to most researchers "classified"--not open--material. By and large there is little startling information in the "classified" arena but it has the advantage that in most cases the Soviets believe it to be true.

For one who has not spent time in the Soviet Union, it is extremely difficult to accept and understand the level of control exerted by the Soviet leadership over every aspect of Soviet life. This is coupled by an intense drive to maintain security over every aspect of defense information. Some examples will give a flavor of the situation. It is against the law for a Soviet citizen to speak to any foreigner except on official business, as tourist guides, etc. It is against the law to take a photograph from any moving vehicle. It is against the law to photograph any military object--a soldier is a military object. Obviously, the laws are frequently, innocently broken, but the sanction is available if the government should want to apply it.

The government prints truth and fiction side by side with the intent of preventing foreign researchers from learning which is which. The authors have spent most of their "90 years" learning to reach and judge which is truth but we can only hope that the information you read here is correct.

The Soviet armed forces do not publish field manuals as do most other countries which conveniently categorize all types of military knowledge. Soviet military schools do not publish texts such as those published by the United States Army Infantry School or other such institutions. Instead, the Soviet soldier and officer rely on journals and periodicals published by the Ministry of Defense for the various military services and levels of development. For the department of defense, there is *Krasnaya Zvezda*, Red Star, a "news" paper which contains world "news," communist exhortations, and a few professional articles.

For example, in a five-year period from 1979 to 1984, there were 35 articles on artillery. A more useful source is *Voyenno-Istoricheskiy Zhurnal* (*VIZ*), the Military Historical Journal. Even more useful is *Voyenniy Vestnik*, the Military Herald, which is designed to provide battalion level officers with a guide to conduct. It was the principal source of the data which filled the tables in Chapters 3 and 4. Some Soviet units keep the Military Herald in a safe, mistakenly considering it "classified." Included in the bibliography is a listing of useful articles from *Voyenniy Vestnik* referring only to "weapons of mass destruction" and their effects on combat operations for the period 1965-1975. This gives the idea of the kinds of detail which were available for synthesis into the norms and operational methods portrayed in Chapters 3 and 4.

More justifiably kept in the safe, if available at the unit level, is *Voyennaya Misl'*, Military Thought. This is a journal intended for field grade officers which is very tightly held because it covers operational level and some strategic matters.

The ministry of defense has recently published a military encyclopedia in an eight volume edition and a one volume encyclopedic dictionary, both of which are extremely useful. Where Soviet society infringes on military life, the Great Soviet Encyclopedia (*Bolshaya Sovetskaya Entsiklopediya*) is useful.

Some individual reminiscences or historical analyses are useful. An example is *Tankoviy Udar*, Tank Strike by General Radzievskiy, written when he was head of the Frunze Academy. Such books purport to be reminiscences with commentary or sometimes analyses; but, because they are written by authoritative sources as in *VIZ*, they carry considerably more value.

Just as figures/statistics can be used to prove and support any case, so military history can be used to support a great variety of tactical and operational concepts.

As an official organ of the ministry of defense, *VIZ* carries articles by the experienced leaders of the Soviet army. While the major part of each article ostensibly deals with history, in general, the conclusion specifically and directly relates the essential thrust of the article to the validity of current doctrine or a need for change. Although occasionally articles are framed in Marxist-Leninist jargon, frequently they are developed along the lines of historical perspective which promotes a new approach based on a rediscovered old truth. A series of retrospective articles on a subject, such as corps and mobile group operations in the 1977 to 1979 period, perhaps heralded the OMG (Operational/Independent Maneuver Group). As such, they help to illuminate the independent army corps development. Likewise, an emphasis on night operations in the early 1980s (together with the subject being one of the principal objectives of the training year in 1982 and 1983) may augur some changes in doctrine with respect to the principle of continuity and tempo/pace of operations. These articles may also give added emphasis to a continued current Soviet emphasis on a "full court press" in combat operations by night as well as by day.

The authors of the *VIZ* articles are nearly all authoritative and well-known spokesmen (unlike many *Krasnaya Zvezda* and *Voyenniy Vestnik* authors). They all support the unchanging themes of mass, mobility, continuity of advance, and cooperation with other branches (now including, specifically, aviation). Emphasis on multiple rocket launchers (MRLs) and aviation on the part of artillery officers seems to have increased substantially over the period. Organizational-tactical questions discussed and generally agreed to in VIZ indicate a need/trend to centralize/combine artillery units (particularly for counterfire) at army level and to decentralize artillery (generally self-propelled (SP)) allocated for fire support at division and regimental levels. Reference is made rather frequently to unspecified reconnaissance means and tactical airborne landings and river crossings from the march in support of rapidly moving mobile formations.

Unfortunately, few of these works are available in translation and sometimes the translations are done by machines or by shoemakers. In either case, there are some serious flaws. The end notes have made reference where possible to sources in English. In recent years, a number of books have been made available on the Soviet armed forces: Scott, Erickson, Donnelly, and Isby to name but a few of the most well-known authors. In general, the western reading public can be much better informed about the Soviet armed forces than can the Soviet reading public. During the SALT negotiations, General Ogarkov requested that the US team not tell the Soviet negotiators the numbers of Soviet missiles saying, "We don't inform our civilians on these matters."

The bibliography which follows can only be exemplar in nature since the sources consulted by the research team were so numerous. The range and depth are both obvious. All members of the team were experienced in the field of Soviet open source literature interpretation and were/are widely read in all possible sources and have personal experience in the Soviet Union or Soviet Occupied Germany.

Members included:
(1) Colonel Rolfe L. Hillman Jr., USA (Ret.)
(2) Colonel William P. Schneider, USA (Ret.)
(3) Colonel Martin Sullivan, USA (Ret.)
(4) Lieutenant Colonel William R. Bell, USA (Ret.)
(5) Colonel Gerhard L. (Jake) Jacobsen, USA (Ret.)

Many of the graphics were provided by Robert Mitchell.

Selected Bibliography

HANDBOOKS

East German Field Artillery Commander's Handbook.

Czech Manual for Military Chemical Corps.

The Officers Handbook. Edited by Major General S. N. Koslov. Moscow: Military Publishing House, 1971.

Polish Manual for Platoon Leaders.

DICTIONARIES AND ENCYCLOPEDIAS

Large Soviet Encyclopedia, Volume 5, "War." Moscow: Soviet Encyclopedia Publishing House, 1971, p. 282.

Military Encyclopedic Dictionary. Moscow: Military Publishing House, 1983.

Soviet Military Encyclopedia, Volume I. Moscow: Military Publishing House, 1976.

    Army Offensive Operations, p. 239 ff.

    Army Defensive Operations, p. 242 ff.

    Army, p. 248 ff.

Soviet Military Encyclopedia, Volume II. Moscow: Military Publishing House, 1976.

    Military Power, p. 183

    Military Science, p. 185 ff.

    Military Preparation of the Population, p. 190

    Military Policy of the Communist Party, p. 191

    Soviet Air Force, p. 201 ff.

    Military Affairs, p. 210

    Military Art, p. 211 ff.

    Military Consumption, p. 218

    Military Structure of the State, p. 219

    Naval Art, p. 213 ff.

The Fleet, p. 235 ff.

Military Patriotic Education, p. 245

Military Industrial Complex, p. 270

Military Representatives, p. 271

Military Director, p. 272

Military Counsel, p. 272

Military Specialist, p. 274

Air War, p. 280

Airborne Operations, p. 284

Airborne Forces, p. 286

Military Service Obligations, p. 302

War, p. 305 ff.

Air Defense Forces, p. 317

Armed Forces of the Soviet Union, p. 345 ff.

Meeting Engagement, p. 406 ff.

Main Political Directorate, p. 562 ff.

Main Military Counsel, p. 566 ff.

Deep Operations, p. 574 ff.

Soviet Military Encyclopedia, Volumes III-VIII. Moscow: Military Publishing House, 1977-80.

BOOKS AND JOURNALS

Astashevkov, P. T. Soviet Rocket Forces. Moscow, 1967.

Chernenko, K. Decree of the Presidium of the Supreme Soviet, No. 318, on Ranks of Officer Personnel in the Armed Forces of the USSR. Moscow: Kremlin, 1984.

Donnelly, Christopher. Protection of the Sub-Units in an Encountering Battle. 1977.

Fendrikov, N. M., et al. Methods for Calculating Combat Effectiveness of Armament. Moscow, 1972.

Glasstone, S. The Effects of Nuclear Weapons. 1962.

Goure, Harvey and Prokofieff. Science & Technical Technology as an Instrument of Soviet Policy. Miami: University of Miami Center For International Studies, 1972.

Holfer and Nerlick. Beyond Nuclear Deterrence. 1976.

Kohler, Harvey Goure, and Soll. Soviet Strategy for the Seventies. Miami: University of Miami Center For International Studies, 1973.

Kukhtevich, V. I. Protection from Penetrating Radiation of a Nuclear Explosion. Moscow, 1970.

Marshal of the Soviet Union, Grechko. Armed Forces of the Soviet States. Moscow: Military Publishing House, 1975.

Martin, Laurence W. "Tactical Nuclear Weapons & Europe." Survival (Nov./Dec. 1974).

Martin, Lawrence W. Arms and Strategy. 1973.

Marxism-Leninism on War and Army (USAF translation). Moscow: Progress Publishers, 1972.

MSU, Bagramyan, etc. History of War & the Military Art (in Russian). Moscow: Military Publishing House, 1970.

Radzievskiy, A. Tactics in Battle Examples - Division (in Russian). Moscow: Military Publishing House, (1976).

Savkin, Colonel V. Ye. (Candidate Military Science). Basic Principles Of Military Art and Tactics. Moscow: Military Publishing House, 1972.

Sidorenko, A.A., The Offensive. Moscow: Military Publishing House.

Sokolovsky and Harriet Scott, Soviet Military Strategy, 3rd ed. New York: Crane Russak, 1975.

The following articles, which appeared in the Soviet Army Journal Military Herald between January 1965 and September 1976, deal with a single topic, chemical and nuclear activities. The list provides an example of the volume of material researched for each topic covered in this publication. Due to the amount of material reviewed in preparation of this text, a comprehensive bibliography will not be attempted.

Chief Direction (Jan. 1965)

Special Processing (Jan. 1965)

Training Communications Personnel to Use Protective Means (Jan. 1965)

For Combat Skill (Feb. 1965)

Preparation Leads to Success (Feb. 1965)

Use of Chemistry in Military Affairs (Mar. 1965)

A Training Calibration (Apr. 1965)

Innovations (Apr. 1965)

Outstanding Experience in Training Chemical Defense Units (July 1965)

Fighting Every Second (Aug. 1965)

Dependable Sources of Water Supply (Sept. 1965)

A Training Device for "Predicting" the Radiation and Chemical Situation (Oct. 1965)

Accelerated Preparation of the DDA53 (Nov. 1965)

Basis of Success (Nov. 1965)

The Skillful Use of Individual Protective Equipment in a Contaminated Area (Nov. 1965)

Actions Taken in Centers of Destruction (Mar. 1966)

Answer to Technical Problems (Mar. 1966)

How to Form a Battalion Column (Mar. 1966)

Instructions of a Commander Concerning *ZOMP* (Mar. 1966)

Together with Tactics (May 1966)

Defense Against Weapons of Mass Destruction (Mar. 1967)

Protection of *Podrazdeleniye* at Night (Mar. 1967)

Reconnaissance Training of the Troops (Apr. 1967)

When Initiative is Displayed (May 1967)

Firing in Protective Equipment (June 1967)

Partial Special Processing in an Anti-Aircraft Battery (June 1967)

With a Chemical Defense Company (June 1967)

Working Out the Norms in Defense Against Weapons of Mass Destruction (June 1967)

Minimizing the Effects of Chemical Contamination (Aug. 1967)

A Good Physical Plant - The Guarantee of Success (Sept. 1967)

Students in Training (Sept. 1967)

Against Simplifications and Arbitrary Approaches (Nov. 1967)

The Chemical Service and Chemical Troops (Feb. 1968)

The Company in Reconnaissance (Feb. 1968)

In the Interest of Psychological Training (Mar. 1968)

The Company in March Security (Mar. 1968)

The Unified Process of Training and Indoctrination (Mar. 1968)

The Decontamination of a Tank by Its Crew (Apr. 1968)

Trainer for Estimate of Radiation and Chemical Situation (July 1968)

Drills in Defense Against Weapons of Mass Destruction (Aug. 1968)

Special Features of Protection in the Desert (Aug. 1968)

Wide Envelopment Detachment (Oct. 1968)

Field Maneuvers (Dec. 1968)

Special Decontamination Techniques (Jan. 1969)

Gas Masks Sight Correction (Jan. 1969)

Solve This Problem (Mar. 1969)

Engineer Reconnaissance of a Site to Construct a Bridge (Apr. 1969)

To Teach Radiation Reconnaissance (Apr. 1969)

Instilling Moral - Psychological Qualities in Classes on Protection (Sept. 1969)

Detection of Toxins (Oct. 1969)

Operational and Tactical Training Exercise in Evaluating the Radiological and Chemical Situation (Nov. 1969)

Protection Training (Jan. 1970)

Problems of Protection on a Winter Tactical Exercise (Feb. 1970)

Signal Troops Learn Protection Techniques (Feb. 1970)

Psychological Seasoning - A Field Training Element (Mar. 1970)

Methods Class with Officers (June 1970)

Competition Between Chemical Defense Companies (July 1970)

In Order to Maintain Combat Efficiency (July 1970)

Measures for Defense Against Mass Destruction Weapons in the Motorized Battalion (Aug. 1970)

Modifying the ARS-12U Decontamination Vehicle (Aug. 1970)

When the "Enemy" Employs Chemical Weapons (A Training Methodology) (Sept. 1970)

Marking Limits of Contaminated Sectors (Sept. 1970)

Evaluating Radiation and Chemical Situations (Oct. 1970)

On Contaminated Terrain (Oct. 1970)

Operations of a Chemical Observation Post (Dec. 1970)

Operations of Special Processing *Podrazdeleniye* in Winter (Experience of DVINA Combined Arms Maneuvers) (Nov. 1970)

Tank Bn in Tactical Drill Involving Simulated Gas Strike. Tank Drills on Foot (Jan. 1971)

Organization of Communications for Troop Management (Apr. 1971)

Protection of a Motorized Rifle Battalion in Defense (Apr. 1971)

Radiological and Chemical Reconnaissance in *Podrazdeleniye* (May 1971)

Eliminating the Aftereffects of Enemy Nuclear and Chemical Strikes (July 1971)

Engineer Measures for Troop Protection (July 1971)

Restoring the Combat Efficiency of a Battery (July 1971)

Tanks Close the Breach (July 1971)

The Nuclear, Biological and Chemical Warfare Specialist (Aug. 1971)

For Control of Vehicles (Sept. 1971)

Special Processing at Night (Sept. 1971)

Prior to a Special-Tactical Training Exercise (Oct. 1971)

A Method: Group Control (Oct. 1971)

Combatting Airborne Landings (Oct. 1971)

Improving Methodological Expertise of Commanders (Oct. 1971)

Local Protection and Self Defense (Oct. 1971)

Route Reconnaissance Party of an Anti-Aircraft Battery (Oct. 1971)

Route Training (Oct. 1971)

Secret Arsenal of the Pentagon (Oct. 1971)

After Chemical Contamination (Nov. 1971)

Partial Decontamination (Nov. 1971)

Solvent Filling Point for Vehicles (Nov. 1971)

An Exercise With a Special Treatment Platoon (Dec. 1971)

Artillery Reconnaissance in a Division (Dec. 1971)

Troop Radiation Control Training Ground (Dec. 1971)

Actions of a Chemical Defense Company in the Attack (Jan. 1972)

Podrazdeleniye Competition in Defense Against Weapons of Mass Destruction (Jan. 1972)

Peculiarities of Protection at Night (Feb. 1972)

Defense of Sub-Units During the Winter (May 1972)

Chemical Contamination Simulator (Mar. 1972)

Evaluating a Chemical Situation (Mar. 1972)

Actions of a Chemical Reconnaissance Patrol When Reconnoitering a Route of March (Apr. 1972)

Posters on Protection of Troops (Apr. 1972)

Exercise: After a Nuclear Strike a Tank Company is Withdrawn into the Reserve to Recover Its Combat Fitness, 1 Diagram, p. 90-91 (Excerpt) (May 1972)

Restoring the Efficiency of Tank Companies After Nuclear or Chemical Attacks (May 1972)

Technical Training of Chemical Corps Cadets (May 1972)

Improving Protection of Personnel (July 1972)

Tank Personnel Restore Fighting Efficiency (Aug. 1972)

Training in Overcoming Zones of Destruction and Contamination (Aug. 1972)

Commander Organizes *Podrazdeleniye* Defense (Sept. 1972)

Personnel Trained to Wear Gas Masks for 6 Hours or More (Oct. 1972)

Protection of the Tank Battalion on the Defensive (Oct. 1972)

The Psychological Makeup of a Soldier is Developed in the Field (Oct. 1972)

The Path to Success is Difficult (Nov. 1972)

Blowing Out of ARS-12 Liquid Systems (Jan. 1973)

Decontamination Company on the March (Jan. 1973)

Rescue Operations in Areas Hit by Mass Destruction Weapons (Feb. 1973)

We Harden Soldiers Psychologically (Apr. 1973)

Elimination of the Aftereffects of Nuclear and Chemical Strikes (May 1973)

Characteristics of Action with Radioactive Contamination (Aug. 1973)

Training of Tank Crews in Field Conditions, Simulating Enemy Use of Nuclear Explosion and Gases (Excerpt) (Aug. 1973)

By Their Own Forces and Resources (Sept. 1973)

A War Gas Simulator (Sept. 1973)

Drawing Showing Device for Special Treatment of a Tank With Use of Exhaust Gases (Sept. 1973)

Picture: Tank Crew Preparing to Carry Out Radioactive Decontamination of a Tank (Sept. 1973)

Tank Troops Cope with Aftereffects of Chemical Contamination Using Own Resources (Excerpt) (Sept. 1973)

We Increase the Effectiveness of Radiation and Chemical Reconnaissance (Dec. 1973)

Special Processing During an Offensive in the Mountains (Jan. 1974)

We Eliminate the Shortcomings in the Training of Defense (Jan. 1974)

The Specifics of Decontamination at Night (Feb. 1974)

An Exercise in Defense (Apr. 1974)

Our Consultations (Apr. 1974)

We Are Improving the Methodological Training of Officers (May 1974)

In the Region of a Nuclear Burst (July 1974)

Technical Servicing of Specialized Vehicles (July 1974)

Protecting a Battalion During a March and a Meeting Engagement (Aug. 1974)

Defending *Podrazdeleniye* in Mountanious Desert Terrain (Oct. 1974)

A Training Practice Route (Nov. 1974)

Aerial Radiation Reconnaissance (Jan. 1975)

Not a Stereotype (Feb. 1975)

Field Expertise of Chemical Troops (Mar. 1975)

In an Atmosphere of Fire and Death (Mar. 1975)

Chemical Reconnaissance of the Enemy (Apr. 1975)

The Set-Up of a Sanitation (Decontamination) Platoon (June 1975)

New Training Aids (July 1975)

Creativity of Innovators (July 1975)

The DDA-53 Training Stand (July 1975)

With Consideration for the Theater of Military Operations (Aug. 1975)

Control Exercise with a Company (Sept. 1975)

Eliminating the Aftereffects of Chemical Contamination at a River Crossing (Sept. 1975)

Command Classes in Protection (Nov. 1975)

Use of Instruments in Winter (Dec. 1975)

Performing Podrazdeleniye for the March (Jan. 1976)

Radiation and Chemical Reconnaissance at Night (Jan. 1976)

Trainer Exercise (Feb. 1976)

To Fulfill Norms More Quickly (Mar. 1976)

From Experience of Training Heat Engine Operators (Apr. 1976)

Complex Problems (May 1976)

Special Tactical Training (from the Experience of the Training of the Chemical Protection Company) (June 1976)

Training in the Evaluation of the Radiation Situation (June 1976)

Decontaminating Individual Weapons and Clothing (June 1976)

People and Equipment (June 1976)

Protecting an Artillery Battalion in Defense (July 1976)

Training Chemical Observers (July 1976)

Group Exercise with Officers (Aug. 1976)

In Field Practice (Aug. 1976)

Initial Factors of Predicting the Chemical Situation (Aug. 1976)

In an AMilitary Publishing Houseibious Assault (Sept. 1976)

Nuclear Burst Simulators (Sept. 1976)

Index

Academic Approach to Strategy, The, xv
Active defense theory, 37
Active protection concept, 66
Advanced detachment, 25, 27–28, 64, 86, 119, 157, 160, 215, 218
   attack operations, 93–94
   march to contact, 74–75
   meeting engagement, 72, 75–77
   pursuit and, 102
Advance rates, 165, 212, 220(n3)
Aerial combat, 198, 199–200
Afghanistan, 36, 37, 49(n22), 55, 109, 111, 114, 143, 189, 210, 213, 218
Air accompaniment, 186–188
Air army, 15. *See also* Army aviation
Air Assault Brigade, 219
Airborne assault, 120–121, 195–198
Air defense, 1–2
   norms, 166–167, 168(fig.)
   of pursuit forces, 102
   systems, 31, 44, 83–84
   tactical, 3
Air Defense Force, 1, 2, 3, 21, 22, 26, 49(n26), 181, 199, 203, 209, 216, 220(n5)
Air Defense of Nation, 206(n3), 209
Air Forces, 1, 3, 47(n1), 181–208, 209, 215
Air preparation, 15
Air support, 15–16, 66, 91–92, 181–183
   of breakthrough operations, 86–87
   close, 188–190
   of pursuit, 102
Air supremacy, 198–199, 202
   numerical superiority, 204
   operational, 199–200
   strategic, 200–201
   tactical, 199
Air-to-ground operations, 191–193. *See also* Vertical maneuver
Air units, 7
Air warning, guidance, and communications posts (*VNOS*), 185
AK 47/74 weapon, 3

Aktivnaya oborona. See Active defense theory
"Always Ready to Defend the Homeland," xviii, 129
Ammunition consumption, 170(fig.), 171(fig.), 173
Amphibious landings, 200
Andropov, Yuri, 36
Angola, 143
Annihilation, 169
Anti-aircraft guns, 108. *See also* Air defense
Anti-air defense of ground forces, 206(n3)
"Anti-nuclear defense," 28
Anti-tank guided missiles (ATGMs), 105, 106
Anti-tank warfare, 66, 105–106, 192–193, 207(n24)
Antitank Warfare, 105
APCs. *See* Armored personnel carriers
Arab-Israeli conflicts, 138, 183
Armament norms, 32, 35
Armed Forces Depots, 126(fig.)
Armed Forces Ministry, 48(n10)
Armeyskaya aviatsiya. See Army aviation
Armored infantry machine (*BMP*), 31, 217–218
Armored offensive, 12
Armored personnel carriers (APCs), 7
Army. *See* Soviet Army; Workers-Peasants Red Army
Army Advanced Supply Bases, 126(fig.)
Army aviation, 190, 195
Artillery, 57, 190
   as anti-tank defense, 106
   attack operations, 15–16, 92, 94–95
   breakthrough operations and, 89–90
   combat potential, 214
   defense and, 108, 216
   engagement support, 72, 79
   fire planning, 92–93, 169, 172–175
   firing norms, 169, 170(figs.), 171(fig.)
   integration of, 218
   modernization, 213

mountain operations support, 112–113
post-Khrushchev buildup, 3, 21, 22, 31–32, 35
pursuit and, 102
range, 213
withdrawal support, 110–111
in World War II, 10, 15, 16–19
See also Fire
"Artillery offensive" concept, 15–16
Assault river crossings, 119–120, 179, 180(fig.), 182, 194
ATGMs. See Anti-tank guided missiles
Attack operations. See Offensive operations
Austria, 26, 37, 49(n29)
Aviatsionnaya podderzhka. See Air support
Aviatsionnaya podgotovka. See Air preparation
Aviatsiya Voyenno-Morskovo Flota. See Naval Aviation

Balance of forces, 56, 162–163, 210
Barriers, 108, 109–110
BDM International Corporation, 7(n2)
Belov, M., 193, 195
BEREZINA exercise, 190–191
Berlin crisis, 40
Biological weapons, 55, 66, 211–212, 213–214
Biryukov, G., 105
BMP. See Armored infantry machine
Breakthrough operations, 193, 214
 combat formations, 88
 operational, 83–93
 reconnaissance, 194
 tactical, 98–99
Brezhnev, Leonid, 30–31, 36, 55
Brigada Spetsial'novo Naznacheniya. See Special Forces Brigade
Bulgaria, 44

Casualties, 128–129, 130(fig.)
Cavalry divisions, 22
Centers of resistance, 97
Central Committee of the Communist Party, 131
Central Group of Forces, 6, 40, 42
Centralization, 19, 129, 131
Central Military Medical Directorate, 122
Central Motor Vehicle–Tractor Directorate, 122
Chemical Troops, 122
Chemical weapons, 55, 66, 109, 173, 211–212, 213–214

Chernenko, Konstantin, 36, 220(n6)
Chief Marshal of Artillery, 220(n6)
Chief of Rear Services, 123, 124, 125, 128
Chief of Rocket Troops and Artillery (CRTA), 92, 200
Chief of Staff, 131
Chief of Veterinary Services, 122
Civil defense, 35
"Civil police," 209
Close air support. See Air support, close
Clothing Directorate, 122
Cohesion, 20
Column cover, 66
Combat activeness, 53
Combat effectiveness, 53–54, 56
Combat support, 212. See also Air support; Artillery; Fire
Combat tasks, 146–147
Combined arms concept, 16–19, 21, 25, 27, 36, 181, 186, 190, 191, 198, 200, 208(n32), 212, 217–218
COMECON. See Council for Mutual Economic Assistance
Command
 calculations and, 151
 posts (CPs), 67, 131–132, 166, 194–195
 unity, 129, 131
 See also Command and control; Command, control, and communications
Command and control, 70, 109, 214
 in airborne assault operations, 182, 197, 206(n5)
 in Air Forces, 184–185
 in mountain operations, 112
 in World War II, 19–20
Command, control, and communications (C^3), 129, 131–134
Communications, 2, 129–139, 214
 in airborne assault operations, 197
 equipment, 134–135
 nets, 135–136, 137(fig.)
 organization, 134
 See also Command, control, and communications
Communist Party, 1, 131, 210
"Complementary warfare," 55
Computers, 151
Concentration of Efforts principle, 53, 56
Conformity to the Goal principle, 54
Control, 129, 131–134, 151. See also Command and control; Command, control, and communications

Cooperation, 186, 191. *See also* Combined arms concept
Coordination, 54–55
Correlation of forces, 200
Council for Mutual Economic Assistance (COMECON), 44
Counterattack, 79, 95–96, 107
Covering forces, 93
CPs. *See* Command, posts
Critical path, 147, 148(fig.), 149(fig.)
CRTA. *See* Chief of Rocket Troops and Artillery
C³. *See* Command, control, and communications
Czechoslovakia, 6, 37, 39(fig.), 40, 41, 44, 45, 46, 217

DAGs. *See* Division artillery groups
Dal'nyaya Aviatsiya. See Long Range Aviation
"Daring thrust," 218–219
DDR. *See* East Germany
Deception, 108–109, 110, 115, 212, 217
"Deep Operation, The," xv–xvi
Deep operation concept, xv–xviii, 186–187
Deep tactics, xv, xvi
Defense forces, 212, 216–217
Defense in depth concept, 212, 218
Defensive operations, 103–111, 114–115, 211
　active theory, 37, 66
　deliberate, 106–108
　in the desert, 115
　hasty, 109
　in mountains, 113
　night combat, 107
　norms, 166–167, 168(fig.)
　support, 108–110
　urban, 107
Deliberate attacks, 81, 82(fig.)
Demobilization, 21
Deployment, 36–37, 40–43, 45–46
　against defending enemy, 96(fig.), 96–97
　for attack from march, 67, 68(fig.), 69
　forward, 40
　linear, 37
　tactical, 174(figs.)
"Depths," 58, 59(fig.), 157, 186–187
　defense, 212, 218
　norms, 153, 154(fig.), 155(fig.)
　of objectives, 165
　See also Deep operation concept; Deep tactics
Deputy Commander of the Rear, 123

Deputy for Technical Affairs, 123
Desant. See Airborne assault
"De-Stalinization," 29
Deterrence, 36
Dictionary of Basic Military Terms, A Soviet View, 99
Direction finding, 138
Directorate of Medical Support, 128
Directorate of Rear Services, 128
Discipline, 152
Disengagement, 110
Dispersion, 73, 90, 156, 157, 158(fig.)
Division artillery groups (DAGs), 90. *See also* Artillery
Doctrine, 51–56, 195
　of attack, 81
　defensive, 103–104, 107
　for meeting engagement, 78
　nuclear weapons, 87
　principles, 52–56

East Germany (*DDR*), 37, 44, 45–46, 48–49(n20), 187, 213, 220(n5)
ECCM. *See* Electronic counter-countermeasures
Echelonment, 58, 60(fig.), 61, 64, 83–86, 87, 88, 95–97
　of Air Forces, 193
　interval norms, 161–163
ECM. *See* Electronic countermeasures
Edinonachaliye. See Command, unity
Egypt, 183. *See also* Arab-Israeli conflicts
Electronic counter-countermeasures (ECCM), 136, 138–139
Electronic countermeasures (ECM), 136, 139, 203–204
Electronic warfare (EW), 136, 138, 214
Encirclement operations, 24–25. *See also* Envelopment
Engineers
　defensive operations, 107, 108
　mountain operations, 112
　support, 66
Engineer Troops, 122
Envelopment, 78, 157, 160. *See also* Encirclement operations
Equipment
　holdings, 124
　recovery and maintenance, 127–128
Ernest, N., xvi
Europe
　objective against, 35
　targets in, 2
　U.S. presence, 37
　vulnerability, 24

See also North Atlantic Treaty Organization
EW. See Electronic warfare
Exercise DNIEPR, 30
Exploitation, 212–213, 214

Field Service Regulations, xvii, 16
Fighter aircraft, 182, 202, 205, 208(n31), 208(n34), 213
  air accompaniment operations, 186–187
  capabilities, 207(n9)
  close-air support operations, 188–190
  combat deployment, 192
  objectives, 203
  offensive operations, 203–204
  reconnaissance, 193–194
Finland, 31
Fire, 16, 212
  column cover, 66
  defensive operations, 104–105, 108
  meeting engagement and, 72, 73
  norms, 169, 170(figs.), 171(fig.)
  nuclear, 92. See also Nuclear weapons
  "on call," 95
  planning, 92–93, 169, 172–175
  preparatory, 173
  suppressive, 80, 81, 83, 92–93
First strike, 35
Flank attack. See Envelopment
Flexible response, 31
Follow-on forces, xvi, 78–79, 176, 177(fig.). See also Echelonment
Food Directorate, 122
Force assessment, 209–220
Force balances, 56, 162–163, 210
Force strength
  in World War II, 16, 17(fig.), 19
Forest combat, 116, 118
Forward detachment. See Advanced detachment
France, 216, 218
"Free hunt," 182, 188, 191, 205–206
Frontages, 164–166
Frontal aviation, 15, 199, 206(n1), 213
Front commands (WWII), 19. See also Command, posts
Frontovaya Aviatsiya. See Frontal Aviation
Fronts, 52, 212
  echelonment of, 58, 60(fig.), 61, 64, 83–86, 87, 88, 95–97
  plans, 57
  See also Theater of Military Operations
Frunze Military Academy, xv, xvi

Fuel and Lubricant Supply Directorate, 122
Fuller, J.F.C., xvi, xvii

Gareyev, M., 202
General Headquarters (WWII), 19
General Staff, 19, 56
German Democratic Republic. See East Germany
Germany, 9–20, 37, 43, 215–216. See also East Germany; West Germany; World War II
Gibkoe Reagirovaniye. See Flexible response
Glavkoms. See High Command
Glubokaya Operatsiya. See "Deep Operation, The"
Glubokiy boy. See Deep tactics
Gorbachev, Mikhail, 36
Gospodstvo v vozdukhe. See Air supremacy
Great Britain, 218
"Great Patriotic War of the Soviet Union." See World War II
Great Soviet Encyclopedia, xvii
Grechko, A. A., 30, 40, 44
Group of Soviet Forces, Germany (GSFG), 31, 39(fig.), 204
  deployment, 41, 42
  order of battle, 37, 38(fig.)
  structure of, 40
Gruppa artillerii razrusheniya. See Heavy bombardment/demolition artillery group
GSFG. See Group of Soviet Forces, Germany
Guided munitions, 2, 105, 106, 108, 167, 168(fig.), 182, 211, 213, 216
Gun systems, 182, 206(n4)

HAWK air defense missiles, 2
Heavy bombardment/demolition artillery group, 15
Helicopters, 112, 120, 182, 186, 205, 206, 207(n10), 215, 217, 219–220
  close air support, 188–190
  combat deployment, 191–193, 207(n13), 207(n17), 208(n32)
  as command posts, 194
  employment principles, 190
  landings, 195–198
  reconnaissance, 193–194
High Command (WWII), 19
High Tempo, 53, 97, 99. See also Advance rates; Speed
Hitler, Adolf, 9

Hungary, 26, 29, 37, 39(fig.), 41, 44, 49(n29)

Ilyin, S., 152
Independent air operations, 201–204
Infantry. *See* Motorized rifle division; Naval Infantry
Intelligence, 66, 150. *See also* Reconnaissance
Interdiction, 186
Intervals. *See* Dispersion
Israel. *See* Arab-Israeli conflicts
Isserson, G. S., xv

Jamming, 109, 136, 138, 139, 214
Japan, 9, 220(n2)

Kalinovskiy, K. B., xv
"Kaplan papers," 37, 48(n13)
Karber, Phil, 218
KGB. See Komitet Gosudarstvenniy Bezopasnost'
Khrushchev, Nikita, 217
  alliances and, 44
  Berlin crisis and, 40
  force reductions under, xv, 26
  strategic "new look," 28–30, 37, 55
Komitet Gosudarstvenniy Bezopasnost' (KGB), 131, 209
Kompaktnost. See Cohesion
Koniev, 26, 29, 40, 44
Korean War, 26, 214
Kulikov, 44, 46
Kutakhov, Pavel, 187, 201, 202, 203

Large Soviet Encyclopedia, 141
Law on Military Service, 30, 40
Logistics, 43, 109, 121–129, 216
  in desert operations, 114
  of march to contact, 66–67, 156
  organization, 125–127
  pursuit and, 103
  recovery and maintenance, 127–128
  supply-account measuring system, 124–125, 175–176
  in World War II, 12, 122, 216
Long Range Aviation, 56, 204, 206(n1)

Main Missile and Artillery Directorate, 122
Main Tank Directorate, 122
Malinovskiy, 28, 30
Maneuver, 27, 52, 57, 212, 214, 215
  Air Forces and, 187
  anti-nuclear, 48(n16)
  in attack operations, 95

Maneuver units, 84
Manpower, 41, 47–48(n9), 48(n15)
March to contact, 61–69, 73–74, 153, 156–157
  command posts, 67
  formations, 69, 75
  through nuclear battlefield, 67
Marines. *See* Naval Infantry
Mass, 195
Massing, 211
Mechanized corps (WWII), 10–15, 19(fig.), 47(n3)
Mechanized forces
  nuclear arms and, 27
  offensive employment, xvi–xvii
  postwar strength, 21, 22, 24, 25
Medical support, 128–129, 130(fig.)
Meeting engagement, 28, 63–80, 159(fig.)
  conduct of, 75–80
  initiation phase, 75–76
  in nuclear battlefield, 27–28, 73
  targeting situations, 72, 73
Mekhanizirovanniye armii. See Mechanized forces
Melnikov, G., 105
Military art, 51–56, 198, 200
Military Herald, 152
Military Thought, 152
Military Transport Service, 122
Minefields, 105, 110
Ministerstvo Bnutrennikh Del (MVD), 209
Ministry of Defense, 209
Ministry of State Security, 209
Ministry of the Interior, 209
Mirovozrenie, xv, xviii
Mobile obstacle detachments (*POZs*), 66, 67
  defense operations and, 105, 106, 110
  pursuit and, 102–103
Mobile Rocket Technical Base (*PRTB*), 140(n23)
Mobility, 53, 56, 70, 73, 81, 187, 195
MOBs. *See* North Atlantic Treaty Organization, main operating bases
Modern Art of Operations, The, xv
Modernization, 3, 21, 26, 29–30, 36, 37, 40, 44, 55, 218
Motorized rifle division (MRD), 7(n1), 27, 43, 213, 215, 217, 220
  breakthrough operations, 88–89
  buildup of, 31–32, 33(fig.), 35
  combat capability, 35–36
  force strength, 7
  logistics, 124

march to contact, 64, 65(fig.), 67
meeting engagement, 75–78
structure, 3, 4(fig.), 5(fig.), 6
Motor-Rifle Regiments (MRRs), 7
Motostrelkovaya diviziya. See
   Motorized rifle division
Mountain operations, 111–113
Movement support detachments
   (*OOD*s), 66, 67
   defensive operations, 106
   pursuit and, 102–103
MRD. *See* Motorized rifle division
MRLs. *See* Multiple rocket launchers
MRRs. *See* Motor-Rifle Regiments
Multilateralism, 43
Multiple rocket launchers (MRLs), 31
*MVD. See Ministerstvo Bnutrennikh
   Del*

NATO. *See* North Atlantic Treaty
   Organization
Naval Aviation, 200
Naval Infantry, 2
Navigation systems, 114–115
Navy, 1, 2, 3, 28, 47(n1), 181, 200, 209
Nedelin, M. I., 48(n12)
Neutralization, 95, 169
NIEMAN exercise, 182, 190–191, 192
Night operations, 107, 118–119
Nomograms, 143, 145(fig.), 146
Norms, 122, 141–180, 210
   calculations with, 143–152
   defense, 166–167, 168(fig.)
   defined, 141, 142–143
   depths, 153, 154(fig.), 155(fig.)
   frontage, 153, 154(fig.)
   movement, 153–161
   in Soviet life, 141
North Atlantic Treaty Organization
   (NATO)
   air defenses, 2
   air forces, 213
   communications, 136, 138
   fighter inventory, 204
   ground forces, 209
   main operating bases (MOBs), 2
   missile systems, 188
   no-first-strike policy, 2
   nuclear capabilities, 2
   objective against, 35
   vulnerability, 2, 3
Nuclear battlefield, 27–28, 67, 73
Nuclearization, 26–27, 36, 40, 202
Nuclear weapons, 70, 200–201, 211
   advent of, 26–27, 36, 40, 202
   breakthrough operations and, 87–88

conventional strike against, 57
doctrine and, 55, 104
echelonment and, 162
first strike, 57
in forested battleground, 118
mountain operations and, 113
offensive operations and, 61, 92
planning, 173
tactical deployment of, 27
theater applications, 32
vulnerability to, 81

Objectives, 90–91
   assignment of, 178(fig.)
   designation of, 58, 59(fig.)
   Europe, 35
Observers, 210
Obshchevoyskovaya armiya. See
   Combined arms concept
Obstacles, 194. *See also* River crossings
Offensive operations, xv, 24–26,
   48(n17), 80–81, 82(fig.), 211–212
   against defending enemy, 80–81,
   82(fig.)
   airborne, 195–198, 202–204
   attack initiation, 61–62
   breakthrough, 83–93, 98–99, 193–194,
   214
   calculations for, 147–152
   combat instructions, 90
   conduct of, 56–61, 93–97
   depth of objectives, 165
   in the desert, 115
   formations, 88, 90, 157, 160(fig.),
   160–161
   at night, 118–119
   norms, 164–166
   in nuclear environment, 27–28
   objectives, 90–91, 165
   preparatory attack, 187, 193
   procedures, 56–61, 93–97
   progress, 78–79. *See also* Advance
   rates
   urban, 116, 117(fig.)
Ogarkov, Nikolai, xvii–xviii, 47, 129,
   134
Ogon. See Fire
OMG. *See* Operational manuever group
OODs. See Movement support
   detachments
Operational defense, xvi
Operational maneuver group (OMG),
   xv, xviii, 42, 186, 218, 220(n4)
   breakthrough operations, 86–87
   meeting engagement and, 79
Operational procedures, 51–140

norms, 153–161
Operational progress, 58. *See also*
   Advance rates
Operation Barbarossa, 9
Operation in depth concept, xv–xviii, 186–187
Order of battle, 37, 38(fig.), 41–43, 44
Otryad Obyespecheniya Dvizheniya. See
   Movement support detachments

Parachute assault forces, 121
Paramilitary forces, 209
Parity, 30, 32
Passive protection concept, 66
PATRIOT air defense missiles, 2
People's Republic of China, 6, 35, 40–42, 209
Peredoviye otryady. See Advanced detachment
Personnel replacements, 89, 129. *See also* Manpower
Planning
   fire, 92–93, 169, 172–175
   nuclear, 173
   operational level, 81
   pursuit, 99–100
Podvizhnaya Raketnaya Tekhnicheskaya Baza. See Mobile Rocket Technical Base
Podvizhniy otryad zagryazhdeniya (POZ). See Mobile obstacle detachments
Poland, 36, 37, 41, 44, 45, 46, 49(n27), 49(n28), 93(fig.), 187
Political Directorate, 131
Political officers, 131
Positions in contact, 61, 63(fig.), 80–81, 82(fig.)
POZs. *See* Mobile obstacle detachments
"Prague Spring." *See* Czechoslovakia
Predstaviteli, 19
Protivo Vozdushnaya Oborona Sukhoputnikh Voysk. See Anti-air defense of ground forces
PRTB. *See* Mobile Rocket Technical Base
Pursuit, 99–103, 179, 186
   control and, 101
   planning, 99–100
PVO. *See* Soviet Air Defense
PVO Strany. See Air Defense of Nation
PVO Voysk, 209

Quick attacks, 81, 82(fig.)

Radar systems, 182, 183

Radiation environment, 27. *See also* Nuclear battlefield
Radioelectronic combat (REC), 109, 136
Radioelectronicheskaya bor'ba (REB), 136
Radios. *See* Communications, equipment
Radzievskiy, A. A., 70, 186
RAGs. *See* Regiment artillery groups
Rates of advance, 165, 212, 220(n3)
Rationalizers, 146
Rear services. *See* Logistics
REB. See Radioelectronicheskaya bor'ba
REC. *See* Radioelectronic combat
Reconnaissance, 64, 66, 91, 157, 183–184
   chemical, 109, 194
   evaluation and, 150
   in forest operations, 118
   helicopter, 193–194
   for march to contact, 74–75
   meeting engagement, 73
   operational, 183
   pursuit, 101–102
   radiological, 194
   tactical, 183–184, 194
   in World War II, 183, 194, 201
Red Army. *See* Workers-Peasants Red Army
Regiment artillery groups (RAGs), 90. *See also* Artillery
Reinforcements, 89, 129. *See also* Manpower
Reserves, 21, 217
Reznichenko, V. G., 52, 192, 195
Rifle division
   postwar strength, 21, 22, 23(fig.), 24, 25
   in World War II, 12, 14, 16, 17(fig.), 19
   See also Motorized rifle division
Rifle regiments, 48(n11)
River crossings, 119–120, 179, 180(fig.), 182, 194
RKKA. *See* Workers-Peasants Red Army
Rocket launchers, 31, 173
Rocket troop units, 24
Rokossovskiy, 43
Rumania, 44
RVGK. See Supreme Command

SA. *See* Soviet Army
SALT. *See* Strategic Arms Limitation Talks
SAMs. *See* Surface-to-air missiles
Savkin, V. (colonel), 55, 190, 195

Secrecy, 110, 217
Security, 64, 66
Security forces, 104, 106
Security zones, 104, 108
Selective integration, 45–46
Shock Army Offensive Operations, xv
Shock power, 213
"Short war/long war" controversy, 28–29
Shtemenko, 48(n13)
Side-looking radar (SLAR), 183. *See also* Radar systems
Sidorenko, A. A., 196
Signal Troops, 122
Signal units, 136. *See also* Communications
Situation evaluation, 147, 150
SLAR. *See* Side-looking radar
Snorkeling, 119, 120
Sokolov, Sergei, 46–47
Sokolovskiy, V. D., 51
Sootnosheniye sil. See Correlation of forces
Soprovozhdeniye. See Air support
Soviet Air Defense (*PVO*), 46, 182
Soviet Army (SA), 47(n1)
Soviet Army Medical Service, 128
Soviet Army Operations, 7(n2)
Sovietization, 43
Soviet Military Dictionary, 55
Soviet Military Encyclopedia, 142
Spanish Civil War, xvii
Spearhead unit, 64
"Special conditions," 111–121
Special Forces Brigade, 197, 208(n32)
Speed, 195. *See also* High Tempo
Spetsnaz teams, 196, 197
Sputnik, 29
Spy operations, 197
SRF. *See* Strategic Rocket Forces
Stalin, Joseph, xvii, 10, 19, 20, 21, 26, 36, 37, 55
Standardization, 124
State Treaty with Austria, 26
Stavka. See General Headquarters
Stavka reserves, 21
Strategic Arms Limitation Talks (SALT), 32
Strategic Missile Forces, 36, 181
Strategic Rocket Forces (SRF), 1, 2, 3, 56, 200–201, 209, 217, 220(n6)
Supply. *See* Logistics
Supply directorates, 122
Support. *See* Air support; Artillery; Combat support; Defensive operations, support; Fire; Medical Support
Suppression, 80, 81, 83, 92–93, 95, 212–213. *See also* Fire
Supreme Command (*RVGK*), 15, 16
Surface-to-air missiles (SAMs), 2, 108, 167, 168(fig.), 182, 213, 216
Surprise, 53, 95, 202, 212
Surprise and security principle, 53
Sustained combat viability, 35–36
Sverdlov, 52
Svobodnaya okhota. See "Free hunt"

Tactical aircraft, 7. *See also* Fighter aircraft
Tactical air units, 28
Tactical aviation, 91–92. *See also* Fighter aircraft
Tactical densities, 16, 17(fig.), 19, 20, 25
Tactical doctrine, 52, 55
Tank armies, 47(n2)
Tank division (TKD), 213, 215
  breakthrough operations, 88–89
  force strength, 7
  logistics, 124
  march to contact, 64, 67
  meeting engagement, 78
  offensive operations, 97–98
  organizational form, 3, 4(fig.), 5(fig.), 6
  post-Khrushchev buildup, 31, 34(fig.)
  post-Stalin, 21, 22, 25, 27
Tankoviy udar, 12
Tanks, 31
  modernization, 214–215
  in mountain operations, 112
  in World War II, 10, 11(fig.), 12–15, 16–19, 214
  See also Mechanized forces; Tank division
Targets, 202–203. *See also* Objectives
Teatr Voyennikh Deystviy. See Theater of Military Operations
Technical Observation Point (*TNP*), 128
Technicheskiy-Nablyudatel'niy Punkt. See Technical Observation Point
Technological gap, 204
Technology and Armament (journal), 152
Tekhnika i Vooruzheniye, 152
Telecommunications, 2. *See also* Communications
Tempo. *See* High Tempo; Speed
Theater of Military Operations (*TVD*), xviii, 45, 47, 52, 56, 200, 202
Third Guards Tank Army, 40

Timing, 210-211
TKD. *See* Tank division
TNP. *See* Technical Observation Point
Traffic control units, 67, 114
Triandafillov, Vladimir K., xv
Troop Air Defense (*PVO*), 182
Troop control. *See* Control
Tukhachevskiy, Mikhail N., xv, 1, 142, 218
Turner, Fred, 218
TVD. *See* Theater of Military Operations
20th Guards, 40

United States, 6, 37, 47(n5), 169, 201, 204, 218
Upravleniye voyskami. *See* Command and control; Control
Urban combat, 107, 115-116, 117(fig.)

van Cleave, William, 32
Varfolomeyev, xv-xvi
Vasilevskiy, 19
Vertical maneuver, 195-198
"Viability doctrine," 35
Vietnam, 169, 211
VNOS. *See* Air warning, guidance, and communications posts
Vorobyov, xvii
Voronov, 19
Voyennaya Mysl', 152
Voyenno-Vozdushnyye Sily (*VVS*), 206(n1)
Vozdushnaya armiya. *See* Air army
Vozdushnoye nablyudeniye opoveshcheniye i svyaz. *See* Air warning, guidance, and communications posts
Vulnerability, 81, 211
VVS. *See Voyenno-Vozdushnyye Sily*
Vzaimodeystviye. *See* Combined arms concept

Warsaw Pact, 40
  air defense systems, 2
  military establishments, 45
  military integration, 43-47
Warsaw Treaty, 29
Weather, 113-114
West Germany, 213
Withdrawal
  by enemy forces, 100
  in defense, 110-111
Workers-Peasants Red Army (*RKKA*), 9, 47(n1), 186
  Air Forces, 190, 201
  establishing of, 20
  organization of, xvii
  in World War II, 10-20, 40, 122, 215-216
World War II, 1, 9-20, 215-216, 220(n2)
  Air Forces, 190
  air operations, 201, 203, 208(n27)
  casualties, 10
  deep operation in, xvii
  logistics, 12, 122, 216
  mechanized corps, 10-15, 19(fig.), 47(n3)
  reconnaissance, 183, 194, 201
  rifle division, 21, 22, 23(fig.), 24, 25
  tanks, 10, 11(fig.), 12-15, 16-19, 214
  Workers-Peasants Red Army, 10-20, 40, 122, 215-216

Yom Kippur War, 138

Zakharov, M. V., 40, 42
ZAPAD exercise, 190
Zhivuchest'. *See* Sustained combat viability
Zhukov, Georgiy, xvii, 19, 26, 27, 28, 29-30, 40, 55
Zones of advance, 164